# THE UNITED STATES OF AMERICA v. ONE BOOK ENTITLED ULYSSES BY JAMES JOYCE

Documents and Commentary —
A 50-Year Retrospective

yce 6.
[?] 1937  7 rue Edmond Valentin
Paris 7e

Dear Mr Ernst : By a post boat
a few days ago I sent you a copy
of the (still highly-priced) first
edition of *Ulysses* with a few words
inscribed which are a very meagre
return for the great service you
have done to me and it. The reason
I did not send you a copy before
is that, until I had the pleasure
of meeting Mrs Ernst and yourself
here and of talking with you,
I had no idea that you were
my 'lawyer', that is, enlisted
almost voluntarily and from
conviction for the general cause

[A typeset version of this letter appears as Document 290, on page 481.—ED.]

particular causes you sustained so brilliantly: Evidently I was in error: and I hastled to try to repair my blame.

Thank you for the copy of the book about the censorship law. I shall send this on to my London lawyers when I have read it.

Please tell Miss Ernst I have ordered her book through Brentano's here and if she has not already succeeded in getting a copy of Charlotte Zomp's book in the U.S. I believe I can find one for her over here.

With kind regards to you both from us sincerely yours

James Joyce

# THE UNITED STATES OF AMERICA v. ONE BOOK ENTITLED ULYSSES BY JAMES JOYCE

Documents and Commentary —
A 50-Year Retrospective

INTRODUCTION BY
Richard Ellman

EDITED BY
Michael Moscato
Leslie Le Blanc

UNIVERSITY PUBLICATIONS OF AMERICA, INC.

University Publications of America
44 North Market Street, Frederick, MD 21701

Because of the number of separate copyright notices, please see page xxv for copyrights and acknowledgments.

Library of Congress Cataloging in Publication Data
Main entry under title:

The United States of America v. one book entitled
    Ulysses by James Joyce.

    1. Random House (Firm)—Trials, litigations, etc.
2. Trials (Obscenity)—New York (N.Y.)   3. Joyce, James,
1882–1941. Ulysses.   I. Moscato, Michael.   II. LeBlanc,
Leslie.
KF224.R33U53   1984   345.73'0274   83-25929
ISBN 0-89093-590-4   347.305274

# CONTENTS

## Documents

# INTRODUCTION

The trial of James Joyce's *Ulysses* in 1933 was decisive. But *Ulysses* was first brought to court thirteen years earlier, even before it had been published as a book. Margaret Anderson and Jean Heap serialized half of it in their *Little Review* in New York beginning in April 1918. The United States Post Office confiscated and burned three issues of the magazine because of Joyce's text. The first time was in January 1919 (the *Lestrygonians* episode), the second in May (*Scylla and Charybdis*), the third in January 1920 (*Cyclops*). But it was the July-August 1920 issue, containing the *Nausicaa* episode, that proved to be crucial. John S. Sumner, the mild-mannered secretary of the New York Society for the Prevention of Vice, lodged an official complaint against it in September 1920.

Joyce had been warned by his friends, notably by Ezra Pound and the New York lawyer and collector John Quinn, that *Ulysses* would probably run afoul of the law. They urged him to withdraw the book from the *Little Review* because the defense of *Ulysses* was the complete text, while individual sections might well be found judicially obscene. Joyce did not follow their advice. When Margaret Anderson and Jane Heap were summoned to police court, on the grounds of having published indecent material, John Quinn loyally agreed to serve as their attorney without fee. On October 22, 1920, the police magistrate bound the two women over for trial in the Court of Special Sessions. Proceedings began on February 14, 1921. Quinn made various legal maneuvers, the first to delay the trial, the second to contest the competence of this particular court to try such a case. Neither worked. He then summoned his witnesses, who were Scofield Thayer, the editor of the *Dial*, Philip Moeller of the Theatre Guild, and the novelist John Cowper Powys.

Powys declared unequivocally that *Ulysses* was 'a beautiful piece of work in no way capable of corrupting the minds of young girls.' Moeller tortuously tried to justify *Ulysses* in terms of Freud, a name as new to the judges, and therefore as suspect, as that of Joyce. Thayer praised the book but conceded that he would probably not have published the *Nausicaa* episode in the *Dial*.

It was now time to read the obscene passages, which Sumner had meticulously culled. One judge urged that they not be read in the presence of Miss Anderson. 'But she is the publisher,' said Quinn. 'I am sure she didn't know the significance of what she was publishing,' the judge gallantly replied. The passages were read. Two of the judges found them incomprehensible. Quinn was glad to agree, since what could not be understood could not be corrupting. He rather lamely attributed the difficulty to the lack of punctuation, which, lamely again, he attributed to the failure of Joyce's eyesight. It was decided to adjourn the trial for a week to give the judges time to read the entire *Nausicaa* installment.

On February 21, 1921, trial was resumed, and Quinn made a final argument. He drew an analogy between Joyce's work and cubist painting. As for the morality of the *Nausicaa* episode, he contended that it was disgusting rather than indecent. (However serviceable, this line of defense was one that Joyce might have scorned.) As for Gerty MacDowell's exhibition of her drawers, Quinn said that the mannikins of Fifth Avenue were much more revealing. The prosecuting attorney rejected these points loudly and apoplectically. Quinn took advantage of his opponent's choler to point to his face and say, 'There is my best exhibit. There is proof that *Ulysses* does not corrupt or fill people full of lascivious thoughts. Look at him! He is mad all over. He wants to hit somebody. He doesn't want to love anybody . . . That's what *Ulysses* does. It makes people angry . . . But it doesn't tend to drive them to the arms of some siren.'

The judges laughed and Quinn thought he had won. But they recovered sobriety and convicted the two editors of publishing obscenity. They were each sentenced to pay a $50 fine. It was understood also that they must discontinue the publication of *Ulysses*. To save his clients from being sent to prison, Quinn had to certify that the *Nausicaa* episode was the worst in the book. When they had left the courtroom, Quinn said to them, 'And now for God's sake don't publish any more obscene literature.' 'How am I to know when it's obscene?' asked Margaret Anderson. He replied, 'I'm sure I don't know, but don't do it.'

Not to receive a jail sentence was a small disappointment, both for the editors and their friends. Joyce, too, had hoped for a much greater furore, and for a court case like that of *Madame Bovary* in 1857, which had made Flaubert's novel famous. There was some feeling that Quinn's defense had been equivocal and concessive, so that the issue had not been fully joined. Quinn wrote to Joyce to explain that a loftier defense would have been of no use with these judges. The trial did at least serve the useful purpose of stirring the principal New York newspapers to editorial comment. The *New York Times* thought the book was incomprehensible and dull but not immoral, though it allowed that the use of certain 'realistic' words was deplorable and deserved punishment. The *New York Tribune*, under the heading of 'Mr.

Sumner's Glorious Victory,' more tolerantly agreed with Quinn that the book was disgusting rather than indecent; it pointed out that the sentences objected to were not nearly so broad as the Porter's speech in *Macbeth*, then being produced on Broadway. This argument, with some flattering allusions to his earlier work, pleased Joyce, and he copied it out for future dissemination.

The effect of the *Little Review* decision was to bear out Quinn's fear that the publication of *Ulysses* as a book was no longer feasible. B.W. Huebsch at the Viking Press, who had published Joyce's earlier books, reluctantly informed Quinn on March 24 that he could not bring out *Ulysses* unless Joyce consented to some alterations in the text. Quinn, on Joyce's behalf, refused all changes. On April 5 Huebsch formally declined the manuscript. Joyce cabled huffily to withdraw it. Quinn tried another publisher, Boni and Liveright, but their interest had also abated. The news filled Joyce with misgivings close to despair. It was now that he went round to Shakespeare and Company in Paris, the bookstore run by Sylvia Beach, to tell her of the unhappy development. 'My book will never come out now,' he said. A thought struck her. 'Would you let Shakespeare and Company have the honor of bringing out your *Ulysses*?' she asked. Joyce was as startled to hear this proposal as she was to make it. He advised her mournfully that no one would buy the book, but at the same time he unhesitatingly accepted.

So *Ulysses* was published in 1922, behind the bushes in Paris, rather than in New York or London. Tourists soon began to bulge at bodice or waist as they smuggled it past the British and American Customs officials, who relieved them of it when they noticed it. After some years they paid less attention. The book won a considerable clandestine reputation. But not everyone could travel to Paris for reading matter. There was also another complication. Because it could not be published in the English-speaking world, *Ulysses* could not be copyrighted. In New York Samuel Roth seized the opportunity to pirate the book serially in a magazine he started chiefly for that purpose, the *Two Worlds Monthly*. Joyce was furious. Since he could not claim violation of copyright, he instituted legal proceedings based on the exploitation without consent of his name. He also had friends draw up and secure signatories for an 'International Protest,' which was given to the world on his birthday, February 2, 1927. This contained 167 prominent names, including Einstein, Croce, Gentile, Maeterlinck, Unamuno, Hofmannsthal, Valéry, Virginia Woolf, Yeats, and T.S. Eliot. But Roth relentlessly continued to pirate *Ulysses* through October 1927. On December 27 of the following year, Joyce's lawyers at last won an injunction from the Supreme Court of the State of New York, enjoining Roth from using Joyce's name in any way. Roth consented to the decree, perhaps feeling that he had already made as much money as he could from Joyce's work.

At the Customs, *Ulysses* continued to be forbidden as obscene, under the

Customs Act of 1922. On August 1, 1928, the United States Customs Court, Second Division, affirmed its exclusion in a list of obscene books. None the less, the possibility of publishing *Ulysses* straightforwardly in London and New York, rather than just in Paris, began to be reconsidered. T.S. Eliot discussed it at his publishing firm, Faber & Faber, in London, but the probability of all the directors of the firm having to go to jail discouraged him. B.W. Huebsch took up the matter again, and on October 20, 1931, conferred with the principal American lawyer in obscenity cases, Morris L. Ernst. Huebsch might have gone ahead had it not been for the opposition of his partner, Harold Guinzburg.

It was now that Bennett Cerf and his firm Random House decided to risk all the perils of publishing *Ulysses* in New York. He engaged Ernst to defend the book. Since legal fees were likely to be high, they agreed that, apart from day-to-day expenses, Ernst's fee would be contingent upon his winning the case. If publication could be managed, Ernst would receive a 5 percent royalty on the first 10,000 copies and 2 percent for life on subsequent reprintings.

The detailed records which this volume gathers together indicate how intelligently and cautiously Morris Ernst and his associate Alexander Lindey shepherded their case. First a copy of *Ulysses* had to be officially imported and officially confiscated, under Section 305 of the Tariff Act of June 17, 1930. Unfortunately the copy slipped through, so Ernst had to prompt the customs officials to call it back. They officially confiscated the copy on 8 May 1932, and another copy (for Ernst tested the judicial waters again) on 10 May 1933. This second copy the Customs decided to relinquish on 5 July 1933 on the grounds that the book was a classic—a testimonial that Ernst was to make much of in the eventual trial. As the case moved towards court, Ernst and the prosecution agreed to have a judge rather than a jury decide the matter. But in the United States District Court, several of the judges were known to be strait-laced. Ernst therefore prudently postponed the case so that it might be tried before a judge in whose fair-mindedness he felt confidence, John M. Woolsey. Woolsey, fifty-six years old, was a man of cultivation, fond of old furniture and of old books. Dr. Johnson was a particular favorite of his, and Woolsey's decisions often showed a stylistic elegance remotely derived from this master.

In preparing for trial, Ernst and Lindey had Random House send out about 500 letters to educators, writers, clergymen, businessmen, and librarians. A fair number replied, many as well known as John Dewey, William Rose Benét, John Dos Passos, Louis Untermeyer, F. Scott Fitzgerald, Theodore Dreiser, and James Branch Cabell. Many librarians indicated that they had or wanted to have copies of *Ulysses* in their institutions. Reviews and articles, by such writers as Stuart Gilbert, Rebecca West, Shane Leslie, Arnold Bennett, Gilbert Seldes, Ernest Boyd, and Edmund Wilson, were also collected. The powerful brief submitted by Ernst and Lindey contended that standards of obscenity change, and that *Ulysses* was not obscene by the standards of 1933.

It was, instead, a classic, as the customs had conceded. As such, it was far too complicated to challenge the curiosity of the lascivious, and it was written on the whole for 'edification and delight.' Whatever might be said of isolated passages, the context was fully justifying.

Justice Woolsey delayed hearing oral arguments until November 25, 1933, because he needed more time to read *Ulysses* through. He also wanted to read some of the books about it, such as Stuart Gilbert's and Paul Jordan Smith's. At the hearing Ernst defended the use of ancient and direct words, such as fuck, which he said was more expressive than 'sleep together.' Woolsey remarked that it was usually more accurate as well. Ernst also insisted upon the actuality of Joyce's stream of consciousness technique, pointing out how varied some of his own thoughts were, even when talking to the judge in the attentive atmosphere of a trial. Woolsey said that his thoughts wandered also. Moreover, he did not like censorship, though he added that he had not yet made up his mind about Molly Bloom's soliloquy.

On December 6, 1933, he announced his decision so eloquently and emphatically that Joyce achieved his old ambition of obtaining a famous verdict. Woolsey's decision said much more than it had to. It pointed out that Joyce was seeking to represent the screen of consciousness, by means of a clear foreground and a background visible but somewhat blurred and out of focus in varying degrees. The intention and the method required frankness, and without frankness would have been dishonest. 'In respect of the recurrent emergence of the theme of sex in the minds of his characters, it must always be remembered that his locale was Celtic and his season Spring.' He nowhere found 'the leer of the sensualist' but an 'honest,' 'sincere,' 'somewhat tragic but very powerful commentary on the inner lives of men and women.' Woolsey's final sentences put his view with a pungency that Dr. Johnson would not have scorned:

> I am quite aware that owing to some of its scenes 'Ulysses' is a rather strong draught to ask some sensitive, though normal, persons to take. But my considered opinion, after long reflection, is that whilst in many places the effect of 'Ulysses' on the reader undoubtedly is somewhat emetic, nowhere does it tend to be an aphrodisiac.
>
> 'Ulysses' may, therefore, be admitted into the United States.

The triumphant verdict was at once telephoned to Bennett Cerf at Random house. Within ten minutes he had the typesetters at work on the book. There was some fear of another piracy, so the first one hundred copies were published to secure copyright in January 1934, and the rest followed in February. By coincidence, as Morris L. Ernst noted in a statement for the press, the prohibition law was repealed during the same week that *Ulysses* was released from interdict. The simultaneity of the two events appeared to give warrant to a feeling that moral standards had shifted.

But all was not to proceed smoothly. Although the government attorneys involved in the case did not wish to appeal it, the United States Attorney for the Southern District of New York, Martin Conboy, whose moral standards had not shifted, decided to take it to the Circuit Court of Appeals. Ernst prepared a new brief, even more persuasive than the old one. The case was heard on August 8, 1934, with Justice Martin T. Manton presiding, and Justices Learned Hand and Augustus N. Hand completing the court. The majority decision, by the Hands, followed Woolsey in finding the book 'pitiful and tragic, rather than lustful.' They argued that 'Art certainly cannot advance under compulsion to traditional forms.' Justice Manton dissented on moral grounds. The passages quoted could not be regarded, he said, as anything but obscene. (He would later be convicted and imprisoned for corruption in office.) For a time the prosecution considered an appeal to the United States Supreme Court, but finally gave it up.

Although *Ulysses* quickly took its place in the American literary scene, it had to undergo further delays in England. The publisher there, John Lane, had planned to bring it out in the summer of 1934, but the printer protested against certain passages. It did not appear until October 3, 1936. In Joyce's Ireland, the book had to be sold by booksellers clandestinely for almost a decade more. His own countrymen were the last to lift the ban on *Ulysses*.

To read the long record of the *Ulysses* case in the United States is to recognize afresh how defiant Joyce's book was. Something of that defiance persists when it is read even in our more permissive day. The defense that the able lawyers used, and that the able judges espoused, was that *Ulysses* was somewhat tragic. It was only by seeing Molly Bloom and her husband as thwarted and frustrated that the book's respectability could be assured. Neither the attorneys nor the judges acknowledged another quality, its humor. The comic spirit in the book is maintained in spite of difficulties, but it is maintained. *Ulysses* is much more funny than sad. The courts demanded high seriousness, however, and found enough to satisfy them. Fortunately, we need no longer be so glum.

Richard Ellmann
Goldsmiths' Professor of
English Literature at Oxford University,
Woodruff Professor at Emory University

# EDITORS' NOTE

The commentaries and documents in this volume are arranged in chronological order in their respective sections, with several exceptions occurring because of the nature of particular documents. For example, a sworn statement dated December 7, 1932 (Doc. 92) follows the libel filed against *Ulysses* by the United States (Doc. 91), which is dated December 9, 1932, because the sworn statement refers to "the foregoing libel." In cases where the articles are undated, efforts were made to determine as accurately as possible their approximate dates, allowing us to insert them into this volume with little or no disruption of the chronological sequence of events.

Many of the letters in this book were taken from carbon copies and photostats made at the same time as the originals, and a number of these copies are unsigned. Their specific authors are usually identifiable, however, by noting the identification initials at the end of each letter (for example, AL:JF denotes Alexander Lindey as the author).

We have tried to present all of the major original documents relating to the *Ulysses* trial. Only the transcript of Morris Ernst's oral argument before Judge John Woolsey is missing, apparently lost.

Bracketed editors' notes occasionally appear within the text to clarify that which may be unclear. Also, we corrected spelling errors that appear in the original documents, as well as grammatical and any other errors that may have caused confusion and possible misunderstanding during the reading of this volume.

# ACKNOWLEDGMENTS

The following documents from the Morris Ernst Papers, collected at The Humanities Research Center, The University of Texas at Austin, are used with the kind permission of Constance Ernst Bessie: 1–10, 12, 14–19, 21–22, 24–33, 35–36, 38–60, 62–72, 74–81, 84–100, 102–37, 139–48, 150–62, 165–68, 170, 172–73, 175, 177, 179–87, 189, 191–92, 196–201, 203–17, 222–23, 225–28, 230–34, 236–37, 239–40, 243–82, 284–88, 290; the frontispiece; commentaries 1–11. These documents are from boxes 93, 126–27, 160–62, 238, 243, 269–70, 600, 610, 639. Copyright 1984, © Constance Ernst Bessie.

The following documents are used with the kind permission of Phyllis Cerf Wagner: 7, 9, 11, 13, 16–17, 21, 23, 25, 34, 40–41, 46–49, 55, 61, 63–64, 71, 73, 77, 83, 85, 89, 96, 149, 159, 169, 171, 176, 186, 188, 194, 202, 217, 219–21, 235, 240, 242, 283, 289. Copyright 1984, © Phyllis Cerf Wagner.

The following documents are from the Bennett Cerf/Random House Papers, Rare Book and Manuscript Library, Columbia University: 11, 13, 20, 23, 34, 37, 61, 82–83, 101, 138, 149, 169, 170–71, 174, 176, 178, 188, 190, 193–95, 202, 218–21, 224, 229, 238, 241–42, 283, 289. All rights reserved.

The following documents are used with the kind permission of Alexis Léon: 32–33, 37, 82, 101, 138, 170, 174, 190, 195, 218, 224, 238. Copyright 1984, © Alexis Léon.

The following documents are reprinted from the *New York Herald-Tribune*: 179, 204, 211, 248, 255, 261, 266, 269, 275, 280; commentaries 3, 5. Copyright 1933, 1934, © I.H. Corporation, reprinted with permission.

The following documents are used with the kind permission of the Society of Authors on behalf of the James Joyce Estate: 20, 164, 193, 290; the frontispiece. Copyright 1983 © James Joyce text.

The following documents are reprinted from the *New York Times*: 127, 205, 276. Copyright 1933, 1934, © *New York Times*, used with permission.

# COMMENTARY

# The First Reader
## by Harry Hansen

That monumental one-man study of one day in Dublin called *Ulysses*, which has been responsible for many a headache in a humanist and lots of sore eyes in the rest of us, is free at last to enter the domain of the United States openly, instead of coming in between the covers of a mail-order catalogue. And what a lot of ironies are bound up with that!

For eleven years *Ulysses* has been outlawed. In the course of that time I have had it offered to me five times at prices varying from $10 to $35. Something like 30,000 copies of it were printed in Paris and sold to American tourists during the lush years. A whole generation has grown up with the idea that it is a literary Bible, and thousands have gone haywire trying to find any risqué passages that they could really enjoy.

It is now fifteen years since the first extract from *Ulysses* appeared in the most famous of the advance guard magazines, the *Little Review*, edited by Margaret Anderson and Jane Heap. In 1920 a copy fell into the hands of the Comstockians, who turned purple. Action was brought against the *Little Review*, and Margaret Anderson was haled into Police Headquarters and finger-printed. She was just beginning to feel pepped up by the suit, but the finger-printing humiliated her. When she wrote *My Thirty Years War* she was still worried about the police records. Maybe now the police will give them back.

---

### *Ulysses* Becomes a Paris Publication.

John Quinn defended *Ulysses*, but the best he could do was to get the editor released on her promise to stop printing. Margaret Anderson then shook the dust of this uncultured land from her shoes and joined the literary expatriates in Paris. There Sylvia Beach published the complete *Ulysses* in 1922 under the name of Shakespeare & Co.

By that time Joyce's one day had become so full that the book exceeded the size of *Anthony Adverse* by several tons. Joyce had done his best to condense it, even telescoping his words. His influence was so effective that a number of young writers began dropping syllables—so that their copy looked as if the typewriter had jammed.

When Judge Woolsey decided that the book was a serious literary work and that he did not detect "the leer of the sensualist" he made literary history. He definitely cleared up the contention whether or not a book shall be condemned because it contains frank passages. Judge Woolsey definitely said "No!" He might have added Laurence Sterne's admonition that there are no obscene books, only obscene readers.

You might say that the presses began running the moment Judge Woolsey's decision was announced, but that would be an exaggeration. Everything was ready for the presses to run, however—and Bennett Cerf immediately announced the book for January 25. It will be a Random House publication and will cost $3.50. What with repeal and Judge Woolsey's decision and President Roosevelt's protest against lynching—a protest sought by New York's writers—the literary world considers this a week of wonders.

---

First appeared in the *New York World-Telegram*, December 7, 1933.

---

[Commentary 2]

# *Ulysses*
## by Forrest Davis

The eminently intelligent, scholarly and likewise courageous Federal Judge John M. Woolsey has lighted another lamp of literary freedom.

"If one does not wish to associate with such folks as Joyce describes, that is one's own choice," Judge Woolsey said in admitting the heretofore proscribed novel *Ulysses* to the United States for publication.

In a civilization which hopes to be adult and to grow that is an indispensable license for the writer. There must be other ways than the policeman's club and the fine collector's warrant to stay the blush from the maiden's cheek when she deliberately pries into books not intended for her.

But this is not the full test of Judge Woolsey's dictum. He does not uphold salaciousness, pornography and other salty or obscene writings when such are cooked up and vended as a commercialized "come-on" unconnected with genuine literary intentions.

Judge Woolsey, who found the book to be "brilliant" and at the same time "dull" and "a rather strong draught to ask some sensitive, though normal persons to take," held it also to be "a sincere and serious attempt to devise a new literary method for the observation and description of mankind."

Half the value of the notable opinion lies in this judicious definition. Judge Woolsey does not sail in and make the sky the limit for unbridled writing. It must be serious and sincere in intent and execution. That is the test, and an eminently just and necessary one.

No limit is out on the frankness of writing done for experts in medicine, biology, physiology, and other intimate sciences. Non-professional members of the general public can have as legitimate an interest in explorations into frank domains such as that treated in *Ulysses*.

Judge Woolsey's opinion is an emancipation of the knowledge-seeking laymen in fields too long closed with the sign "Verboten."

---

First appeared in the *New York World-Telegram*, December 7, 1933.

---

[Commentary 3]

# The "Repeal of Squeamishness"

"*Ulysses* may, therefore, be admitted into the United States." The opinion wherewith Judge Woolsey sustains this historic decision is studded with important contributions to the tangled and unsatisfactory law of literary suppression. It is true that the effect may be limited, for the customs law, as Judge Woolsey points out, required him to decide only whether *Ulysses* was "obscene" and not whether it might fit any others in the "spectrum of condemnatory adjectives" commonly used by similar statutes. To take some examples of these spectra, the Criminal Code bars from the mails not only obsene books but those which are "lewd or lascivious" or "filthy" or of "an indecent character." New York law widens this list, so far as publications are concerned, by the addition of "disgusting," and in respect to theatrical productions bars those which are "immoral or impure" as well as those fitting the other categories. James Joyce's celebrated (and singularly unreadable) literary monument, cleared after a decade of the charge of obscenity, may thus still fall into some other part of the far-flung and lamentably loose-woven nets spread by the legislators for the protection of our morals. Yet if Judge Woolsey has shed light upon the definition of "obscenity" alone, his sane conclusions are bound to have an effect upon the interpretations of the other mysteries involved in the application of these laws.

Judge Woolsey clearly declares the principle that the book must be considered "in its entirety." He rejects that narrow scrutiny of selected passages upon which censors have so often relied (to the vulgar edification of courts and jurors) and refuses to be swayed by a "dirty" word if the general character of the work demonstrates that in purpose and probable effect it is not pornographic. To the distinguished company of the "reasonable man" and the "man learned in the art"—fictitious personages who have long been pillars of other branches of legal interpretation—he adds the "person with average sex instincts" as the testing standard by which the general effect of a book is to be determined. And finally, in applying that test, he introduces canons of intelligent literary criticism. "If Joyce did not attempt to be honest in developing the technique which he has adopted in *Ulysses* the result would be psychologically misleading" and "artistically inexcusable." This alone is not enough to free any consequence of an honest technique from the charge of obscenity; it is, however, only sensible to extend the legal purview to such considerations in passing upon the question of general purpose and effect.

The public has learned illegally to take its *Ulysses* or leave it through the last ten years or so, and it is scarcely to be expected that the sudden stamp of legality will lead to any greater abuses of Irish literature than have developed with Irish whisky. In view, moreover, of the great burden of personal judgment which the principles of the Woolsey opinion would still impose upon the individual jurist, Mr. Morris Ernst may be too quick in proclaiming that "squeamishness in literature" has been repealed as completely as prohibition. Yet that the opinion does represent a substantial victory for proportion, common sense and legal flexibility in the difficult areas of literary censorship, few will doubt.

---

First appeared in the *New York Herald-Tribune*, December 8, 1933.

---

[Commentary 4]

# Another Repeal

James Joyce's *Ulysses*, for eleven years the most famous of our bootleg classics, is legal at last—at least in so far as the government of these United States is concerned. Prohibition, to be sure, did not prevent the literati from being as familiar with the book as they were with cocktails, and copies of *Ulysses* carried on the hip gave young collegians a kind of prestige comparable to that achieved by a pocket flask. Perhaps, indeed, some of them scanned its difficult pages for the same reason that they scorched their tender palates with white mule, and we should not be surprised if a certain decline in reckless *Ulysses* reading took place among the young. In any event, however, Random House, its only licensed publisher, did not prepare for repeal with as much foresight as the distillers did, and the public will have to wait until sometime in January for its first legal copies. When the great day comes, we hope that it will be celebrated with as much restraint as was December 5. All lovers of law and order, all upholders of true temperance, will pray that there be no orgies. Youth must show that it knows how to use its liberties, and it will be an ill augury if the streets are filled with young men and maidens drunk upon immoderate drafts of Mrs. Bloom's meditation.

Federal Judge Woolsey says that the court is bound to consider both the work as a whole and the intention of the author; and perhaps more important, that one must consider only its effect upon a person "with average sex instincts." Holding that *Ulysses* is a "sincere and honest book" not written with pornographic intent but constituting a "serious experiment" carried out with "astonishing success," he cites the legal definition of "obscene" as "tending to stir the sex impulses," and declares Joyce's work innocent in this respect. Commenting further on the contention that sex plays a disproportionately large part in the thoughts of the characters, he adds a sly sentence which should go down in the annals of judicial humor: "It must be remembered that his locale was Celtic and his season Spring."

We cannot, however, help noting that we wish it had been possible— though we know it was not—to add a paragraph something like this: "Only a legal fiction makes it necessary to pretend that the real question at issue is whether or not *Ulysses* is likely to 'stir the sex impulses.' At least half the recognized diversions of civilized mankind are intended to do that to a greater or less extent, and society recognizes the process as not only permissible but necessary to its welfare. Only hypocrisy could insist that the law makes any pretense of interfering with such diversions, for if it did, then it would be necessary not only to proceed against almost every love story, but to raid the very dances sponsored by the Young Women's Christian Association. The real question is whether or not Joyce's rare use of four Anglo-Saxon monosyllables constitutes a threat to society sufficiently great to engage the attention of the law. Since the prominence of these same four words in the epigraphy of the public-school outhouse makes them familiar to every literate person long before he is acquainted with the meaning of most of the other words in *Ulysses*, I hold that the police and the courts have more important business to attend to."

---

First appeared in *The Nation*, December 20, 1933.

[Commentary 5]

# Books and Things
## by Lewis Gannett

James Joyce's *Ulysses* appears legally in the United States for the first time today (Random House, $3.50), buttressed with what the publishers call "the monumental decision of the United States District Court, rendered December 6, 1933, by the Hon. John M. Woolsey"; a foreword by their attorney, Morris Ernst, who sees in that decision a repeal of hypocrisy comparable to the end of prohibition, and a letter from Joyce himself, reciting the history of *Ulysses'* suppression.

### *Ulysses*, the Youngest Classic

*Ulysses* was suppressed in this country almost fourteen years ago, when Margaret Anderson and Jane Heap were fingerprinted as common criminals for daring to print parts of it in their *Little Review*. Copies of the Paris edition were bootlegged into the United States; a pirate edition was printed here, and when 167 writers of distinction protested against that bit of cheapness a photographic forgery of the Paris edition replaced it and continued to circulate surreptitiously and at a fantastic price. More important, professors and literati talked about *Ulysses*; books were written about it; its mannerism and method were imitated. Within fifteen years of its appearance it has already taken its place as an almost undisputed classic.

### "Worthless," Said Gosse

Only a few critics dissented. Some thought Joyce obscene, others called him pernicious; but of his influence on a whole generation of young writers there was no doubt. Only a few old fogies like Sir Edmund Gosse denied his importance. Edwin J. Barrett tells me that when the *Revue des Deux Mondes* observed its centenary, in 1929, he strolled through its Exposition of One Hundred Years of French Life. There, under glass, he saw copied Gosse's letter to Louis Gillet, written in June, 1924:

"I should very much reject your paying M. James Joyce the compliment," Gosse wrote, "of an article in the *Revue des Deux Mondes*. You could only expose the worthlessness and impudence of his writings, and surely it would be a mistake to give him this prominence. I have a difficulty in describing to you in writing the character of M. Joyce's notoriety. It is partly political; it is partly a perfectly cynical appeal to sheer indecency. He is, of course, not entirely without talent but he is a literary" . . .

At that point the letter turned the page, and the rest was hidden. Today the letter characterizes not Joyce but Gosse. Gosse was blinded by Victorian morality; Joyce had used bad words which Gosse understood but could not bear to see in print. Arnold Bennett, also in some ways a Victorian, had a broader mind. When he was reading D. H. Lawrence's *Lady Chatterley's Lover* (not yet printed in its integrity in this country) he jotted down in his journal that Lawrence was "the most original novelist now writing, except James Joyce."

### Interpretation by a Judge

Judge Woolsey agreed, and his opinion is an amazingly able piece of literary criticism. He summarized, polysyllabically but accurately: "Joyce has attempted—it seems to me, with astonishing success—to show how the screen of consciousness, with its ever-shifting kaleidoscopic impressions carries, as it were on a plastic palimpsest, not only what is in the focus of each man's observation of the actual things about him but also in a penumbral zone, residua of past impressions, some recent and some drawn up by association from the domain of the subconscious. He shows how each of these impressions affects the life and behavior of the character which he is describing. . . . His attempt sincerely and honestly to realize his objective has required him incidentally to use certain words which are generally considered dirty words and has led at times to what many think is a too poignant preoccupation with sex in the thoughts of his characters . . . such words as would be naturally and habitually used, I believe, by the types of folk whose life, physical and mental, Joyce is seeking to describe. . . . If one does not wish to associate with such folk as Joyce describes, that is one's own choice. But when a real artist in words, as Joyce undoubtedly is, seeks to draw a true picture of the lower middle class in a European city, ought it to be impossible for the American public legally to see that picture?"

### Hard Reading

This new edition of *Ulysses* has had an advance sale of 25,000 copies; most of these would-be readers, one may guess, will be most grievously disappointed. *Ulysses* is not an easy book to read; it is obscure and often dull. Fully to understand all that Joyce has packed into these 768 pages one should have an understanding of a half dozen foreign languages, of Catholic theology and metaphysics, and of Freudian psychology, an intimate knowledge of the *Odyssey*, and some familiarity with Irish politics and literature in 1904, in which year the book is set. Young hunters for the pornographic will have to work hard to locate, or to comprehend, Joyce's sexual passages; and they will find them discouragingly intellectual when they are not dully matter-of-fact. Which is not to say that *Ulysses* will not shock most readers who have the energy to plow through it. Nothing so distastefully honest has before appeared in legal print.

Those who really want to devote themselves seriously to the study of *Ulysses* will do well to begin with Joyce's earlier, shorter and simpler books, *Dubliners* and *The Portrait of the Artist as a Young Man,* both of which may be obtained in the Modern Library. They may find a help in Paul Jordan Smith's *A Key to the Ulysses of James Joyce,* first published in 1927 and today reissued by Covici-Friede at $1. If they want to go farther, they will find Herbert Gorman's *James Joyce, His First Forty Years;* Edmund Wilson's interpretation in *Axel's Castle* and Stuart Gilbert's formidable *Joyce's Ulysses: A Study,* enlightening; next month Cape & Smith will publish Frank Budgen's comprehensive *James Joyce and the Making of Ulysses.*

### Joyce . . . Monologist?

Many of the ablest young writers of today hail Joyce as their supreme master. I have never felt the magic of his genius in ecstatic terms. Genius he is; but a curious poseurishness, an affectation has grown through all his work; it is sadly apparent in the title of his forthcoming *Our Exagmination Round his Factification for Incamination of Work in Progress,* Joyce more and more seems to prefer to address a monologue to his disciples rather than to communicate openly with a public. Yet it is of little use to lament what he might have been; his influence is apparent in virtually every serious novel published today. No man in our generation, unless it be Proust, has so profoundly influenced other writers; and that is enough to say of any man. I suspect that in years to come Joyce will be read by students rather than by readers; he will take a place akin to that of Samuel Richardson, whom every one reads in college as an influence on the Novel, and almost no one rereads for pleasure.

I may be wrong. When I rewaded through *Ulysses* yesterday, twelve years after my first venture, it seemed to me more intelligible than it had been in 1921. Possibly the world will catch up with Joyce instead of sliding past him.

---

First appeared in the *New York Herald-Tribune,* January 25, 1934.

---

[Commentary 6]

# The First Reader

## by Harry Hansen

If you see three lean men standing in front of a bookstore window today and joyfully hammering one another on the back you may be sure that they are Bennett Cerf and Donald Klopfer, the publishers, and Morris Ernst, the barrister. The object that draws them to one bookstore window after another is the first printing of *Ulysses*, by James Joyce, which they have just released from the chain gang.

And I'll bet they feel very much as George Washington, Ben Franklin and John Adams felt when the Revolution was won. They are hoping that the American people will agree—at $3.50 a head—that it was worth fighting for.

As one who has been against the censorship and on side of free printing I suffer from something of an embarrassment. I have been reading the book again in my spare time, and I hope my grandchildren won't embarrass me by asking how I ever came to think of this as literature.

Judge Woolsey who gained high literary praise for the opinion which released *Ulysses* from the floating hulks, says that the question of obscenity is easily disposed of. Does the book tend to stir the sex impulses or lead to sexually impure and lustful thoughts? Does it affect the average normal man evilly? He says, "No!"

I'm glad he didn't ask: Does it tend to suggest the need of an emetic? I certainly wanted to get out and inhale some fresh air.

### How *Ulysses* Was Planned.

As a piece of printing *Ulysses* is remarkable. Anyone who has wearied his eyes poring over the cumbersome bootleg edition which came from Paris must consider the present work nothing short of a typographical miracle. Ernest Reichl designed it.

Since nearly every chapter has a different form, the book was full of typographical problems. After a number of experiments Mr. Reichl decided on the Baskerville font of the Mergenthaler Linotype Co., with about 800 pages to the book; fewer would have crowded the book, and more would have made it too heavy.

As the book was likely to be read and consulted during a period of years, heavy boards were provided, and in order to make them easy to handle the edges were bevelled. For this purpose a new attachment to a cutting machine was developed. Ornamentation was not used in the book, chapters carry neither number nor title, but the break in the different parts is indicated by a huge initial letter in black which fills a whole page.

Mr. Reichl has given me the following account of the great days in the printshop when *Ulysses* became an American book:—

"What with repeal and a number of wine books going to print in a hurry, what with 6,000 copies of *Anthony Adverse* having to be delivered every day, two months had about gone when the dummy of *Ulysses* was finally done. Judge Woolsey's decision was expected shortly, and everything had to be co-ordinated in such a manner that the book could be set, proofread, paged, read again, plated, read for a third time, printed, bound and delivered within five weeks. All materials were selected and work scheduled in such a way that it would proceed in relays; while the last part was still being set preceding chapters were to be made into pages, the middle of the book being plated and the beginning actually on the presses. The initials were drawn, the wrapper marked up for type. To prevent any mistakes it was decided to set from the French edition, published by Shakespeare & Co., in Paris, and to read against the German edition of the Odyssey Press in Hamburg.

"On December 7, 1933, at 10:15, Mr. Klopfer called me up at the H. Wolff Estate and said, 'Go ahead.' Five minutes later, after a wait of fourteen years, the first American edition of *Ulysses* was on its way."

First appeared in the *New York World-Telegram*, January 25, 1934.

[Commentary 7]

# Let *Ulysses* Alone

Martin Conboy, the able United States Attorney, will be wise, we believe, to reconsider his announced intention to appeal from Judge John M. Woolsey's decision which permitted the importation of James Joyce's novel, *Ulysses*.

The object of such an appeal is censorship. The American people in theory are opposed to censorship, and there was seldom a time when its actual practice seemed to find less support than at present.

Judge Woolsey's decision refusing to censor *Ulysses* was one of the most widely praised opinions of recent years, particularly supported by two classes who might be considered experts in the case. These were lawyers, who indorsed its legal reasoning, and literary persons of eminence, who praised its critical judgment.

Mr. Conboy, furthermore, would approach his appeal under the disadvantage, although not a disqualification, of possible partisan interest. That is his former close association with the New York Society for the Suppression of Vice and his service as personal attorney for John S. Sumner, superintendent of the society.

Appealing *Ulysses* would be, we believe, an unprofitable distraction from the important work of the United States Attorney's office.

First appeared in the *New York World-Telegram*, March 14, 1934.

[Commentary 8]

# Too Busy Snooping

United States Attorney Martin Conboy is a very busy man these days. He has just read James Joyce's *Ulysses*, probably the greatest book to come out of modern Ireland, and Mr. Conboy is all hot and bothered.

Mr. Conboy, who was long associated with the professional snoopers of the New York Society for the Suppression of Vice, announces that he will appeal Judge John M. Woolsey's decision holding that this great Irish classic is not obscene.

It so happens that Judge Woolsey's decision is one of the most civilized opinions to be handed down from our bench in a good many years. It also happens that Mr. Conboy will be spending the taxpayers' money in riding his little purity hobby.

Maybe when he gets through with this more important matter he will find time to look into the narcotic traffic uncovered on Welfare Island and into the political protection that made it possible.

---

First appeared in the *New York Evening Post*, March 15, 1934.

---

[Commentary 9]

# Padlocking Minds

United States Attorney Conboy, we believe, can expend his fine talents and his own time and his staff's to better advantage upon the urgent problems of law enforcement than upon a crusade against a book—James Joyce's *Ulysses*.

We believe there is a serious issue of intellectual and even moral freedom in America involved in this appeal from Judge John M. Woolsey's opinion admitting the book to this country.

It is a highly significant fact, we think, that the able Mr. Conboy does not found his pleading upon the premise that the book is untruthful as to fact or psychology or that the author had evil intent. He only argues that there is a statute against obscenity in books and that the court decisions provide a test showing *Ulysses* to be obscene. "It is settled that the object or motive in publishing a questioned book is immaterial," he declares.

Then it is high time that object or motive be admitted as material.

Mr. Conboy admits that medical books dealing with psychological and biological facts are not bannable under this statute. But he neglects the great growth in general interest in psychological, literary and other explorations once regarded as limited to physicians and scholars.

If every aspect of man, however brutal or sordid, is a proper study for professional men, it is nonetheless a proper and useful study for enlightened intellects generally. Human progress will come best when the greatest possible number of intellects are active in the unrestricted search for means of understanding and ameliorating human life and adding to its creativeness and interest.

What Mr. Conboy seeks to do is to place a censor over the minds of the American people which the government would never dare place over physicians and scientists, enforcing a literary "Volsteadism" as backward as the legalistic reasoning he is compelled to resort to to make out any case at all.

We think that Mr. Conboy should drop this attempt to put padlocks on the intellect of the American people and get on to the important legitimate questions demanding action in his office.

---

First appeared in the *New York World-Telegram*, April 23, 1934.

---

[Commentary 10]

# Ulysses the Dirty
## by Francis Talbot, S.J.

A great pother has been bubbling up for the past twelve years about James Joyce's writings. He tells forlornly in a letter to Dear Mr. Cerf, of Random House, who made a scoop on the sale of American copies of *Ulysses*, how he could never get Dublin publishers "to publish anything of mine as I wrote it." No less than twenty-two publishers and printers read the manuscript of *Dubliners*, but not one wished to be entangled in the muck. The twenty-second printed it; one "kind" person bought out the entire edition; and, since it was highly inflammable, the whole edition became burned up. Mr. Joyce arrived in Paris, in 1920, in the summer, with the voluminous manuscript of *Ulysses* and his umbrella. Miss Sylvia Beach, energetic, ran a small English bookshop and lending library, and called herself Shakespeare and Co. Brave, she was braver than professional publishers. Mr. Joyce says, "She took the manuscript and handed it to the printers." The author's eyesight, those eyes which had evidently seen so many sights, permitted him to read the proofs himself. He approved of his work when the first printed copy was presented to him on February 2, in the year 40, James Joyce, otherwise 1922.

The book was written in a new technique, in a pseudo-English, of words that were sometimes normal, sometimes foreign, sometimes archaic, sometimes merely a succession of letters, meaningless and inane. Many of the words were scummy, scrofulous, putrid, like excrement of the mind. The words are listed in the dictionary, but never in the writings or on the tongue of anyone except the insane, or the lowest human dregs. The critics said how brave. The sexual neurotics said how lovely. The normal person said I'm sick.

Mr. Joyce used his words to tell what flowed through the minds of three people, Stephen Dedalus, a Dublin man in shabby black and cast-off shoes, Leopold Bloom, a Dublin Jew, and Marion, who was as the reader suspects she was. The flow through their minds continued for twenty-four hours, according to the Joyce recording; though the events, it may be concluded, summarized twenty-four years. What they and the other characters thought and imagined, what trivialities, what nonsense, what drunken dreams, hallucinations, eroticisms, vulgarities, blasphemies, silliness, malice, and the like streamed through their consciousness and unconsciousness is what James Joyce labored for seven years to transmit to 768 closely printed pages. The poor man, with his own distorted twist of mind, was unable, or did not choose, to express this stream of thought intelligibly. Because of this, the esoteric critics exclaimed what incomparable art. Because of the filthiness that whirled in the stream, those seeking to be pornographicized exclaimed what excitement. And the man with a sound brain and a sound heart exclaimed what twaddle and what rot.

The book sold in Paris, I am told, for forty dollars. And so everybody wished to read it, and a lot of literary fustians wished to write of it. *Ulysses* became internationally famous. It was barred entry into the United States, and that captivated the American imagination and aroused the American curiosity, which curiosity is unequalled the world over. The professional defenders of literary vice exploiters labored indefatigably to spread the mess made by James Joyce before the eyes of all Americans. They arranged a test case which was duly brought before John M. Woolsey, United States District Judge. His decision that "*Ulysses* may, therefore, be admitted into the United States," rendered December 6, 1933, was hailed ecstatically by Morris L. Ernst, the legal protagonist of literary sexuality, as "the New Deal in the law of letters," as "a major event in the history of the struggle for free expression," as raising Judge Woolsey "to the level of former Supreme Court Justice Oliver Wendell Holmes as a master of juridical prose," and other Oriental exaggerations.

In his Foreword to the American edition of *Ulysses*, as in his numerous pleas for unrestricted sexual expression, Mr. Ernst is quite distempered. We who disagree with him have no desire "to emasculate literature." We have not tried "to set up the sensibilities of the prudery ridden as a criterion for society." It is not our aim "to reduce the reading matter of adults to the level of adolescents and subnormal persons," and we have not, at all, "nurtured evasions and sanctimonies." We desire that Mr. Ernst and his authors should not seek "to phallicize literature." We have objected to those who "set up the eroticism of the sex ridden as a criterion for society." It is our aim to withstand those who would wish "to reduce the reading matter of adults to the level of pornographers and neurotic persons." We are opposed to those "nurturing vilenesses and corruptions." Then again, Mr. Ernst devotes a paragraph to a parallel, that "the first week of December, 1933, will go down in history for two repeals, that of Prohibition and that of the legal compulsion for squeamishness in literature." Mr. Ernst's preoccupations would not allow him to see that the Prohibition repeal brought, or was intended to bring back, the pure in alcohol, not the poisonous stuffs. We have never had a Prohibition law against the pure and wholesome in literature. His success through Judge Woolsey has opened the way for the poisonous and the soul killing in literature.

But it is not Mr. Ernst, though he is a prime mover in this immoral crusade against decency, that I would discuss. It is Judge Woolsey. In the first place, *Ulysses* was not judged by a jury, but by the Judge alone. His decision is worth what he is worth, only less, under the circumstances. He read the entire book once, and the passages complained of several times; he read its "satellite" books; he gave all his spare time, through several weeks to reading, and thinking. It was a "heavy task." He was thus equipped by study. Was he equipped in fundamental moralities, was he equipped in psychological perceptiveness, was he equipped with the firm conviction of philosophical thought? He was not guided infallibly; he judged as his personal determinants led him.

The Federal law governing the exclusion of books from this country uses but one word, *obscene*; State laws employ as many as seven words in their definitions of objectionable books. The word obscene, in Judge Woolsey's determination, which he bases on other decisions, is synonymous with "pornographic, that is, written for the purpose of exploiting obscenity." And that definition, to my mind, is woefully loose; but on it, the Judge rendered his verdict. He strives to analyze the intent of Joyce in writing *Ulysses* as an entirety, and states:

> Joyce has attempted—it seems to me with astonishing success—to show how the screen of consciousness with its ever-shifting kaleidoscopic impressions carries, as it were on a plastic palimpsest, not only what is in the focus of each man's observation of actual things about him, but also in a penumbral zone residua of past impressions, some recent and some drawn up by association from the domain of the subconscious.

Joyce truly attempted this, and, due to the abysmally degraded characters whose consciousness he explored, attempted as an essential part to show how obsessed they were with certain organic functions, with erotic impulses of the lowest nature, with lewd and vulgar stories and incidents, with blasphemies that curdle the blood. These references and sections are the point of issue. These, Judge Woolsey admits are in the book but excuses as part of the entirety of the recital. I wonder that the loyal Irish have not risen up in violent protest at his summarizing excuse of Joyce: "In respect of the current emergence of the theme of sex in the minds of his characters, it must always be remembered that his *locale was Celtic* and his season Spring." As if to say, the sex theme is inherent in a Celtic locale.

Judge Woolsey dove into the labyrinthine mind of Joyce, into a crawling diseased mire, as it were, without aid of bathysphere, and rose to the surface with the declaration that Joyce did not intend to exploit obscenity as his primary purpose in his entire 768 pages. Was he intentionally obscene in 100 pages, or fifty pages? If not intentionally, was he actually detailing obscenity in very many specified passages? These, the Judge expurgated from his mind. Yet these, I repeat, are the passages at issue.

"The Monumental Decision" of Judge Woolsey goes on to state that "the meaning of the word *obscene* as legally defined by the Courts is: tending to stir the sex impulses or to lead to sexually impure and lustful thoughts." He passes, then, from the subjective standard, that of the author's intent, to what he calls a "more objective standard," that is, the result on the minds of readers. He used as a test for this two friends with average sex instincts, "what the French would call *l'homme moyen sensuel.*" They reported that the book, in its entirety, did not tend to excite their sexual impulses or lustful thoughts. I can well understand that. But I would like to understand more about these two "assessors." And I would like to have assurance that the thousands who have read and will read *Ulysses* are gauged as they are.

Martin Conboy, United States Attorney, carried the case of *Ulysses* to the United States Court of Appeals. Judges Learned Hand and Augustus N. Hand upheld Judge Woolsey in his opinion. Judge Martin Manton dissented, and declared: "Who can doubt the obscenity of this book after a reading of the passages referred to, which are too indecent to add as a footnote to this account? Its characterization as obscene should be quite unanimous."

Mr. Ernst and Judge Woolsey have had their way. Most surprisingly, a Catholic critic of standing, most inexplicably, pronounces that "we must recognize that Judge Woolsey is right." He states that the Judge "won the approval of authorities both literary and legal." He instances that "the ruling is in harmony with that sound principle of Canon Law, namely, that when the hearing of the law is adverse it is to be given the narrowest possible interpretation." These are three whoopingly misleading statements. I counter them with the simple statement made by one who, in my opinion, is most competent to judge the book: "*Ulysses* is against the natural law."

As far as Catholics are concerned, the case of *Ulysses* is quite clear. Judge Woolsey states that the effect of the book is "emetic;" he does not find it to be "aphrodisiac." It is truly emetic. Our most emetic reactions would be caused not so much by its vulgarity, nor by its indecency, but by its rampant blasphemy. Only a person who had been a Catholic, only one with an incurably diseased mind, could be so diabolically venomous toward God, toward the Blessed Sacrament, toward the Virgin Mary. But the case of *Ulysses* is closed. All the curiosity caused by the extraneous circumstances of

18

its being banned is over. It has now subsided into just a book. It will be discussed, undoubtedly, in the little literary pools of amateurs and young Catholic radicals. But for the most part it is in the grave, odorously.

First appeared in *America*, September 1, 1934.

[Commentary 11]

# *Ulysses* by James Joyce
## Summary of Facts

1. The book first came up for consideration in the Federal Courts in an action entitled *A. Heymoolen* v. *United States*, in the Customs Court. The case was tried on August 1, 1928 before Justices Fischer, Weller & Tilson. Judge Weller did not participate. The book was among a lot of 43 separate items of merchandise, representing 11 different titles. It was held to be obscene under the Tariff Act of 1922, and was denied admission into this country (Treasury Decision, #42907). Greenbaum, Wolff & Ernst did not appear in this case.

2. We subsequently succeeded in getting the book into the United States as a classic, and later securing its admission generally. In both instances we acted as attorneys for Random House, Inc.

3. We were retained by Random House on March 23, 1932. Upon our instructions a copy of *Ulysses*, addressed to Random House, Inc. was sent into this country. It was seized at the Customs and forwarded to the United States Attorney for libel proceedings. Proceedings were instituted December 9, 1932.

4. The Government delayed prosecuting the case. In order to force matters we gave instructions that another copy of the book be sent into this country consigned to Alexander Lindey. This copy slipped through the Customs, and on May 5, 1933 we apprised the Collector of Customs of this fact. At his suggestion the copy in question was surrendered to the Law Division of the Customs Service, and the Collector was notified that we proposed to make formal application to the Secretary of the Treasury for the admission of *Ulysses* under that portion of Section 305 of the Tariff Act which permits the Secretary in his discretion to release the so-called classics or books of recognized scientific or literary merit.

5. On June 1, 1933 a petition for the admission of the book as a classic was forwarded to the Collector.

6. On July 5, 1933 we were advised by the Collector that "authority was given for the release of the book . . . on the ground that it is a classic, and

therefore comes within the purview of the Secretary's discretionary authority granted in Section 305 of the Tariff Act of 1930."

7. In the meantime we had been pressing the libel proceedings. On May 15, 1933 we had stipulated with the United States Attorney to adjudicate the libel by motion in lieu of trial. On May 15, 1933 the Government moved for judgment on the pleadings, and two days later we made a cross-motion for the same relief.

8. The motions were argued before Judge John M. Woolsey on November 23, 1933. Mr. Coleman argued for the Government; Mr. Ernst for the claimant.

9. On December 6, 1933 Judge Woolsey dismissed the libel with opinion. A decree of dismissal was entered on December 15, 1933.

10. On March 16, 1934 the Government took an appeal to the Circuit Court of Appeals. The appeal was argued before Justices Manton, Learned Hand and Augustus N. Hand on May 16 and 17, 1934. Mr. Conboy argued the case for the Government, and Mr. Ernst for the claimant. On August 7, 1934 the Circuit Court affirmed the lower court, rendering an opinion. Judge Manton dissented, with opinion.

11. On October 1934 we were advised by the United States Attorney that no appeal would be taken to the United States Supreme Court; and on November 1, 1934 the libeled copy of *Ulysses* was delivered to Random House, Inc. Shortly thereafter it was presented to the Columbia Library.

---

From the files of Greenbaum, Wolff & Ernst.

---

[Commentary 12]

# The Censor Marches On

## by Morris L. Ernst

In 1870 a pitiful dirty-minded man—Anthony Comstock—backed by J.P. Morgan shifted the course of our national pattern on censorship. A decade previously, England had for the first time started to define obscenity. Comstock engineered through Congress with less than ten minutes of debate our first censorship on the grounds of sex. All states except New Mexico followed suit. And then until 1915 publishers were enslaved, often sending manuscripts before publication to Comstock's Society for the Suppression of Vice for approval or editing.

In 1915 the tide turned when Mitchell Kennerly contested the ban on *Hagar Revelly*. It has been one of the profoundly satisfactory portions of my life as a lawyer to be called upon to represent dozens of authors and publishers against the censors, private or public. I happened to hit a tide, a stream which made it easy to win all the cases save only two: one an early volume, Donald Henderson Clark's *Female*, temporarily banned only in Queens County, New York; the other, John Herrmann's *What Happens*, published in France. Both would be approved by the courts if retested now.

It has been a useful crusade—much of it without financial compensation. It has involved classics such as the *Decameron*, brave new themes like *The Well of Loneliness*, historic writing such as Joyce's *Ulysses*, sex educational writings such as Mary Ware Dennett's pamphlet "The Sex Side of Life," and "The Birth of a Baby" article in *Life* magazine. Magazines, novels, fiction, history, etchings, radio programs, theatrical productions, art exhibits—a gamut of human expression.

Each case raised a different aspect of the censors' fears—Anglo-Saxon words, glorification of adultery, pioneer treatment of the theme of homosexuality. Obscenity is still a vague concept. Censors shout that all impure ideas of sex which are capable of corrupting the readers should be banned. We asked: Corrupt whom? Children? If so, is adult reading to be reduced to the level of youth or of the feeble-minded? What kind of ideas are impure sexually? To the pure all things are pure. And what does corrupt mankind? For years I made inquiries in the professions to find evidence that reading had any objective traceable effect—corrupting or otherwise. I followed tests showing the reading of prisoners arrested for crimes of passion. If we used their testimony as a guide, then the daily papers and all movies would be the first to be blue-penciled. Even the Vice Society has no worthy testimony bearing on the relation of books and antisocial deeds.

We know little about our sexual folkways. Soon it will be proved that homosexuality, masturbation, and petting are more prevalent among the sophisticated, or what is called the upper stratum of society, than among other people, who show a higher percentage of premarital sexual relationship. The figures on sexual relations with girls under eighteen years of age—which acts, no doubt, run into millions of incidents a year—may cause a reappraisal of headlines concerned with juvenile delinquency. But the law in the main and particularly in the police courts is administered by judges stemming from one stratum of life, unconsciously applying their codes vis-à-vis the other stratum. All of which not yet reduced to scientific terms is nevertheless the ever-changing basis of the law of changing obscenity.

We had fun educating juries and judges. We never argued a case without trying to bring home the fluidity of sexual standards and the constant shift in man's fears of ideas. Originally censorship was applied to protect the church—blasphemy was the charge. As the church's power dwindled, man feared any attack on the king, the state, and the crime shifted from blasphemy to sedition. And now, in the main, the current insecurity in our society is in sexual matters.

After twenty or more years of such cases before courts or government agencies I am convinced that there is no book openly published, reviewed by reputable publications, which will be banned by our courts. I am disturbed, however, at the new rampages in Boston and at the Post Office Department. All these cases can be won only if the publishers and authors believe in their product, stand up and fight unafraid. It is also important that the publishers' advocates never apologize, never blush, never feel ashamed. They need not identify their own taste with the manuscript they defend. But stoutly they must believe in the right of the public to hear and see all.

Once more the censor marches on. In Boston, *Strange Fruit* was withdrawn by agreement of booksellers on a mere unofficial threat by a police official. What timidity on the part of these merchants of our most precious commodity; even though it's unfair to ask a retailer to stand the brunt and expense of a test case! His financial stake in the sale of any single title is negligible. The book doesn't carry his imprint. It is not of his making. Freedom of thought would be better served if retailers in peril, rather than submit to a cop's appraisal of literary crime, called on the publisher and author to stand up openly in support of what carries their names. Certainly, agreements between merchants to withdraw an article from sale seem to be clearly in contravention of our state and federal antitrust laws. Recently I wrote Attorney General Francis Biddle and suggested that conspiracy to withdraw a book—in this case, *Strange Fruit*—seemed to me to be a more antisocial restraint of trade than an agreement not to sell wall or toilet paper. Words on paper should not deteriorate the value of pulp in the eyes of the law.

A test case was brought by vigilant Bernard De Voto. His attorney, acting for the Civil Liberties Union, has been in our office to look over all our briefs and records in other cases. The surest way to lose that case—involving, as it does, a single word—is to be apologetic for the use of any word or concept in a book of such dignity and distinction. Dozens of recent books have used the same Anglo-Saxon word which the Boston authorities object to in Lillian Smith's great volume.

The most amusing legal instance on this score that I know of occurred during the defense of James Joyce's *Ulysses*. In 1925, dealers had gone to jail for selling it in sophisticated New York. In 1933, Random House had courage enough to decide to publish an American edition. We advised that obscenity, a vague concept at best, is always subject to reinterpretation against the changing mores at the day of trial, and that we thought we could clear Joyce's much-discussed opus.

As in all these cases, hundreds of people turned out and went to the courtroom. This figurative burning of books under modern juridical blessing can well be compared to the burning of heretics at the stake four hundred or so years ago. One of the government prosecuting attorneys, intelligent, generous and capable, came up to me before the hearing. "The government can't win the case," he said. I asked why this defeatism. He said, "The only way to win the case is to refer to the great number of vulgar four-letter words used by Joyce. This will shock the judge and he will suppress the book. But I can't do it." "Why?" I queried. Prudishly he replied, "Because there is a lady in the courtroom." Sure enough, when I looked around, there was Maggie, taking a day off from school to hear the argument.

"But," I said, "that's my wife. She's a former newspapergal and a present schoolteacher. She's seen all these words on toilet walls or scribbled on sidewalks by kids who enjoy them because of their being taboo."

Well, the government didn't pick up the "word" argument. The second day of the trial gave me an opportunity. I told Judge Woolsey about all these words unused by the polite. I tried, after going over the etymology of each word with Margaret, to trace the convention in words. Tastes change, taboos vary, but man has always found a new combination of letters to convey a concept if the old word was deemed disgusting. No better series in our own generation can be found than in the travelogue of bathroom, toilet, water closet, W. C., gentleman's room, john, can, and now "I'm going to telephone." No one is ever really deceived.

When I got to the word "fuck," I explained how one of the possible derivations was "to plant," an Anglo-Saxon agricultural usage. The farmer used to fuck the seed into the soil. I told the Judge I liked the word. I didn't use it in parlors because it made me unpopular, but the word had strength and integrity.

"In fact, your Honor, it's got more honesty than phrases that modern authors use to connote the same experience."

"For example, Mr. Ernst?" asked the Court.

"Oh—'they slept together.' It means the same thing."

The Judge smiled. "That isn't even usually the truth."

At that moment I knew that the case was half won.

The other half of the battle gave rise to one of those rare experiences which make court work involving ideas such a joy.

Many times Judge Woolsey, a man of great culture and wisdom, asked whether I had really read through the entire volume. I feared he might tend to condemn on the theory that it would do society no harm to suppress a book so long, so dull and so dreary. I had to answer this potential state of mind.

I decided to wade in on a personal note.

"Yes, Judge—ten years ago I tried to get through *Ulysses* but couldn't. This year in preparation for the trial, I *had* to read it. And while reading it I was invited, in August, to speak at the Unitarian Church in Nantucket on the New Banking Act and the reopening of the banks after the Holiday."

"What's that got to do with my question?" said Judge Woolsey.

"Well, I addressed about four hundred people. I was intent on what I was saying. And still, when I finished, I realized that while I was talking about banking, I was also thinking at the same time about the long ceiling-high windows on the sides, the clock and eagle in the rear, the painted dome above, the gray old lady in the front row, the baby in the sixth row, and innumerable other tidbits.

"Judge," I said, "that's *Ulysses*. I went back to my reading with a new appreciation of Joyce's technique, the stream of consciousness put into words. And now, your Honor, while arguing to win this case I thought I was intent only on this book, but frankly, while pleading before you, I've also been thinking about that ring around your tie, how your gown does not fit too well on your shoulders, and the picture of George Washington back of your bench."

The Judge smiled. "I've been worried about the last part of the book but now I understand many parts about which I've been in doubt. I have listened as intently as I know how but I must confess that while listening to you I've also been thinking about the Heppelwhite chair behind you."

"Judge," I said, "that's the book."

The next summer Margaret and I were in Paris and picked up Joyce— nearly blind—for dinner at Fouquet's. Joyce was interested in the trial. I told him how Martin Conboy, the Federal District Attorney in New York, had opened the argument by describing this book as one day in the life of a Hungarian Jew. One would have imagined that the scene was not Ireland and that the trial was for blasphemy instead of obscenity. Conboy had been counsel for the Vice Society for many years and it had done something to his attitude toward writing. He had looked too long and too often for dirt.

I paused to ask Joyce just when he had left the Catholic Church. He said, "That's for the Church to say." Which to me meant that inside himself he had never left the Church, try as he might have.

This tale I related to Judge Woolsey at a later date when we both spoke at the opening of an exhibit of Banned Books of the World, a great exhibit put on by the New York Junior League under the direction of Mrs. Tex Moore, oddly enough Harry Luce's sister. Judge Woolsey then made what seemed to me to be a profound observation, not picked up, so far as I knew, by any of the Joyce students. "Maybe Joyce's inner conflict as to Catholicism explains why the secondary streams of the non-Catholics in the book are penciled with more clarity than are the inner thinkings of the Catholics."

Judge Woolsey's decision legalizing *Ulysses* spelled out a new approach to the appraisal of works published in the open by established publishers. For years judges of all courts have in their written opinions on censorship cases referred to authorities for support of suppression or clearance. Although Sainte-Beuve and the Encyclopaedia Britannica, among others, were cited in the *Mlle. de Maupin* case, the same court suggested that defendants might not call living authorities to the witness stand to testify to the literary, educational or psychological impact of an attacked volume. Judge Woolsey broke through this monopoly of jurists. The jury henceforth may gain wisdom also from experts. His decision, wise and epoch-making in this field of law, was enjoyed by many who never read *Ulysses*. It will no doubt be quoted for years, at least for two brilliant sentences:

> The words which are criticized as dirty are old Saxon words known to almost all men and, I venture, to many women, and are such words as would be naturally and habitually used, I believe, by the types of folk whose life, physical and mental, Joyce is seeking to describe. In respect of the recurrent emergence of the theme of sex in the minds of his characters, it must always be remembered that his locale was Celtic and his season Spring.

---

First appeared as Chapter 8 of *The Best Is Yet*, 1945.

---

[Commentary 13]

# Obscenity, the Law, and the Courts
## by Terrence J. Murphy

The modern period of governmental control of obscenity began with the celebrated court case over the importation of James Joyce's *Ulysses*. How *Ulysses* came to America is an interesting commentary on its obscene passages, its literary merits and especially on American obscenity laws. In the fall of 1922, five hundred copies of this book were stopped at the port of New York by the United States Customs Office and banned on the grounds that the book was obscene. Then, Samuel Roth, seemingly the same Samuel Roth who was to figure so prominently in later court cases over obscene publications, saw the financial gain that could be gleaned from readers who enjoy "leaping from obscenity to obscenity."[1] In July 1926, he began publishing a magazine entitled *Two Worlds Monthly*. This literary gem was "Devoted to the Increase of the Gaiety of Nations." In it he serialized *Ulysses*. It was a bowdlerized edition. Apparently Mr. Joyce had not authorized the publication and received no royalties. He was unable to protect his literary property because the ban on his book precluded a copyright.

This victimization of Mr. Joyce became something of an international incident. A protest was published bearing one hundred and sixty-seven names including those of such illustrious men of letters as T. S. Eliot, John Galsworthy, Ernest Hemingway, D. H. Lawrence, H. G. Wells, Virginia Woolf, and W. B. Yeats. Emboldened by this support, Joyce tried through an American law firm to get the courts to stretch a legal point and grant an injunction restraining Roth. In this he succeeded. But to no avail. Another unauthorized version of *Ulysses* appeared in New York.

The next chapter in *Ulysses'* American odyssey began when Bennett Cerf of Random House decided to make a court test of its prohibition. He arranged for a copy to be sent to the United States in such an open manner that it would be sure to be seized.[2] The result was the precedent-making decision of Judge John M. Woolsey of the Federal District Court who ruled that *Ulysses* was not obscene and consequently should be admitted to American shores.[3]

*Ulysses* had long been a subject of controversy in many parts of the world. Its English reviews are illustrative of the comments it evoked. To cite only a few reviews, Mr. Arnold Bennett in the course of a very laudatory review in the *Outlook* called it a "very astonishing phenomenon in letters" and then added: "the book is not pornographic, but it is more indecent, obscene, scatological, and licentious than the majority of professedly pornographic books. . . ."[4] Alfred Noyes was unreserved in his condemnation: "It is simply the foulest book that has ever found its way into print . . . there is no foulness conceivable to the mind of man that has not been poured forth into its imbecile pages."[5] James Douglas was equally condemnatory: "It is the most infamously obscene book in ancient or modern literature." Obscenity reaches its highest point in the last forty pages of the book. They contain the revery of the wife of Leopold Bloom as she drops off to sleep. In her fantasy she relives her long list of illicit loves. A great admirer of Joyce, S. Foster Damon, has written that Marian Bloom's monologue "outdoes Swift's Lady's Dressing Room."[6] He describes Mrs. Bloom as "carnality triumphant." Speaking of the entire book the same critic writes, "Most people manage to scramble through *Ulysses* for the first time by leaping from obscenity to obscenity!"[7]

But it would be a great error to characterize Joyce's masterpiece as simply a controversial book containing obscene passages. For *Ulysses* has considerable literary merit. It reveals keen and deeply moving insights into the soul of modern man. Its technique has opened up new approaches to literary expressions of reality. *Ulysses'* influence in literary circles has grown with the years. Some literary critics regard it as among the top half dozen books of the twentieth century.

Judge Woolsey acknowledged that "many" think that James Joyce has a "too poignant preoccupation with sex in the thoughts of his characters." However, he found *Ulysses* "a sincere and honest book" and concluded that the "criticisms of it are entirely disposed of by its rationale."[8] But realizing that the "meaning of the word 'obscene' as legally defined by the Courts is: tending to stir the sex impulses or to lead to sexually impure and lustful thoughts," he could not dispose of the issue that simply. He had to find "that reading *Ulysses* in its entirety, as a book must be read on such a test as this, did not tend to excite sexual impulses or lustful thoughts. . . ."[9] He was happy to learn that two of his cherished friends, "literary assessors," agreed with his opinion.

In the *Ulysses* decision exciting sexual impulses is the subject matter of obscenity. But it is not enough that a book merely contain obscene passages to be banned. The obscene sections must be weighed against the non-obscene. In affirming the *Ulysses* decision Judge Augustus Hand of the Court of Appeals picked up this element, *inter alia*, in his opinion. In judging obscenity he thought it necessary to weigh the "relevancy of the objectionable parts to the theme. . . ."[10] Thus the core element of obscenity, i.e., lustful sex, must be judged by its relevancy to the theme.

Judge Augustus Hand in affirming the lower court held that a book could not be declared obscene because it contained some obscene passages. For the obscene section could be overshadowed by the rest of the book. "No work may be judged from a selection of such paragraphs alone. Printed by themselves they might, as a matter of law, come within the prohibition of the statute. . . . We believe that the proper test of whether a book is obscene is its dominant effect." The court must grant the same latitude to literary products as it does to scientific, medical, and sex-instruction books.

The prelude to the *Ulysses* era began with the case of *United States* v. *Dennett*.[11] Mrs. Mary W. Dennett[12] had long been dissatisfied with the available sex information. As Director of the Voluntary Parenthood League she spearheaded an effort to persuade Congress to change the law prohibiting the sending of birth control information through the mails. The Postmaster General was a special object of her importuning. But what brought her into conflict with the Post Office was another matter.

She wanted to instruct her two sons, ages fourteen and eleven, on the sex side of life. In her opinion none of the publications on this subject was adequate. She wanted more emphasis on the emotional element of sex. To provide just such information for youngsters she wrote a pamphlet entitled the "Sex Side of Life." Twenty-five thousand copies were sold before the Post Office Department declared the pamphlet non-mailable. A jury found her guilty of mailing obscene matter and she was fined three hundred dollars.

Judge Augustus N. Hand speaking for a three judge circuit court reversed Mary Dennett's conviction. After pointing out that the pamphlet was intended to be given by parents to their children and thus not distributed to children indiscriminately he came to the heart of the matter, namely, the scope and meaning of prohibited obscenity. He expressed the opinion that any article dealing with sex may arouse lust under some circumstances. But the law did not prohibit everything that "might stimulate sex impulses."

> We hold that an accurate exposition of the relevant facts of the sex side of life . . . cannot ordinarily be regarded as obscene. Any incidental tendency to arouse sex impulses which such a pamphlet may perhaps have is apart from and subordinate to its main effect. The tendency can

only exist in so far as it is inherent in sex instructions, and it would seem
to be outweighed by the elimination of ignorance, curiosity, and morbid
fear.[13]

In the following year it was found lawful to import a book written,
seriously and decently, to give information to the medical profession on the
operation of birth control clinics and the instructions to be given in such
clinics.[14] Sex instructions to married persons were also found to be
importable.[15]

The medical-sex and sex-information cases represent a clarification or
qualification of sex as the core idea of obscenity. Sex serving a medical or
social purpose, at first under rigid conditions and then more freely, was
distinguished from sex tending toward moral depravity.

Long before the *Dennett* case Judge Learned Hand had indicated a similar
line of thinking that was eventually to influence judicial thinking in regard to
literary works. While feeling obliged to follow in his decision the traditional
strict interpretation, he nevertheless pleaded for a more liberal view in the
*United States* v. *Kennerley*.[16] The book under fire was Daniel Carson
Goodman's *Hagar Revelly*. Undoubtedly "such parts of this book as pages
169-170 might be found obscene, because they certainly might tend to corrupt
the morals of those into whose hands it might come."[17] But these obscene
passages were auxiliary to innocent ideas and therefore the book as a whole
was really not obscene. Here in germinal form was the distinction, later to
assume major influence, between a book that contained obscene matter and
one that is shot through with obscenities. Judge Hand questioned "whether in
the end men will regard that as obscene which is honestly relevant to the
adequate expression of innocent ideas" and he looked forward to the time
when "men [would] think innocent all that which is honestly germane to a
pure subject, however little it may mince words. . . ." This concept of
obscenity being cleansed by its relevancy to wholesome ideas is similar to the
view that the emotional excitement inherent in sex information is outweighed by the "elimination of ignorance, curiosity, and morbid fear."

This narrower concept of what constitutes a restrainable obscene publication, first proposed but not allowed in *Kennerley*, edged closer to in *Dennett*,
became controlling doctrine in *Ulysses*. This new view is a long step away
from the earlier court doctrine. The *Ulysses* decision is a landmark in the
federal government's policy of controlling obscenity. It is important,
however, to realize that the way was prepared for the *Ulysses* decision (1933)
by the *dicta* of Judge Learned Hand in the *Kennerley* case (1913) and by the
court's holding in *Dennett* (1930).

The federal courts' swing in the 1930s toward less restraint was also
prepared for by a liberalizing trend in the New York courts which had begun
approximately fifteen years earlier. The New York shift was due, in
considerable measure, to the tireless efforts of a handful of lawyers. It is

noteworthy that the names of the same attorneys consistently reappear in behalf of defendants in obscenity cases. The name of Morris L. Ernst, for example, recurs from *Ulysses* (1933) to *Roth* (1957).[18]

*Ulysses* marks a turning point toward less control in the long history of government prohibition of obscenity. That history has deep roots in Anglo-Saxon traditions. Laws forbidding obscene publications are at least as old as printing. The invention of the printing press was soon followed by licensing laws. The first such law was promulgated in England in 1538. The Stationers' Company became the effective instrument of implementing royal decrees in regard to the press. While the British government was mainly concerned with heresy and sedition, the records of the Stationers' Company contain instances of the censorship of obscenity. The Licensing Law expired in 1695.

English Common Law soon filled the legal vacuum. In 1727 an English court sentenced Edward Curl to the pillory for publishing an obscene book. But even before that, as early as 1712, Massachusetts had a criminal statute pertaining to obscenity.[19] After the War for Independence the newly formed states generally regarded obscenity as a common law offense.[20] The earliest court case on record in the United States seems to be that of *Commonwealth* v. *Sharpless* in 1815.[21] Jesse Sharpless was convicted in Philadelphia of displaying an obscene picture which depicted "a man in an obscene, impudent, and indecent posture with a woman." The defense claimed the court lacked jurisdiction because the offense was one of private morals and in England would have been dealt with in an ecclesiastical court. Chief Justice Tilghman held the offense was criminally punishable. For more than a half century after *Sharpless* the issue arose seldom but when it did the courts generally followed the *Sharpless* precedent.

The United States Federal Government first concerned itself with obscene materials as an incident of its customs powers. It outlawed the importation of obscene materials as early as 1842[22] and again in 1857. The use of the United States mail service for conveying obscene material was denied in 1865.[23] The period following the Civil War saw an aroused public concerned with indecent literature. This sentiment was both reflected in and stimulated by Anthony Comstock who for forty years crusaded against lascivious literature under the banner "Morals, Not Art or Literature."[24] His greatest legislative triumph was the Act of June 8, 1873, in which Congress declared "that no obscene, lewd, or lascivious book, pamphlet, picture, paper . . . shall be carried in the mail. . . ."[25] All together there have been at least twenty federal enactments dealing with obscenity.

The last quarter of the nineteenth century and the first quarter of the twentieth witnessed a number of legal contests involving obscenity. In 1879 a federal court dealt at length with the issue of obscenity in *United States* v. *Bennett*[26]. The constitutionality of obscenity laws was not directly at stake. However a unanimous court in speaking of the exclusion of obscene matter from the mail service said: "Nobody can question the justice, the wisdom, the necessity of such a statute." The court reviewed at length the trial court's instructions to the jury. In approving it the court said: "The matter must be regarded as obscene, if it would have a tendency to suggest impure and libidinous thoughts . . . and *thus* deprave and corrupt their morals. . . ." [Emphasis added.] Thus, a federal court early implied the constitutionality of obscenity laws and found that obscenity pertains to sex. In view of later discussions it is informative that impure thoughts were said to corrupt morals.

A decade later in the *United States* v. *Clarke* Federal Judge Thayer expressed his opinion that the obscenity mail law is a "wholesome statute."[27] He noted that the law was intended to protect the "young and immature, the ignorant, and those who are sensually inclined." In applying the law it would be wrong to use as a standard the effect of a publication upon those "steeled against such influences." He reiterated the opinion of the *Bennett* case that obscene literature is that "the reading whereof, by reason of its contents, is calculated to excite lustful and sensual desires (that is to say, a desire for the gratification of the animal passions). . . ."[28]

During this period the United States Supreme Court performed the useful function of gradually clarifying the legal meaning of obscenity and of determining some of the ramifications of the laws on obscenity. The Court interpreted obscenity statutes to mean that the term "writing" did not involve a letter;[29] that a letter not obscene in itself but containing information on where obscene pictures can be obtained is illegal;[30] that it is not necessary to incorporate obscene matter into the court record.[31] It distinguished obscene from coarse, vulgar, and libelous language.[32] In making the distinction between the obscene and the vulgar in this case, it found that obscene words "signify that form of immorality which has relation to sexual impurity, and have the same meaning as is given them at common law in prosecutions for obscene libel." Obscene literature is that which is "calculated with the ordinary reader to deprave him, deprave his morals, or lead to impure purposes. . . ."[33] It found in the case of *Lew Rosen* v. *United States* that the words obscene, lewd and lascivious are antonyms of "decency, purity, chastity."[34]

Years later Judge Learned Hand[35] argued that the question of the constitutionality of obscenity laws had been ruled out in the *Rosen* case. It is certainly safe to say that the dicta in the *Rosen* case are indicative of a firmly settled conviction of the court in 1896 on the question of constitutionality. The validity of obscenity laws seemed so clear and universally agreed upon that the courts even pointed to them as evidence of the federal government's power to regulate restrictively in areas that seemed to involve collisions with the guarantees of the Bill of Rights. Thus, the early development does not bear directly on the constitutional validity *per se* of obscenity laws. They were simply assumed to be constitutional. The courts marched against obscenity in unison with the legislative branch and the people.

The much publicized case of *Ulysses* began a decided change in the obscenity policies of this country. From Joyce's *Ulysses* to Henry Miller's *Tropic of Cancer* the obscenity laws were rendered increasingly less prohibitive. The agent of the new trend was the judiciary aided and even guided by vocal libertarians. The courts had started down a new path and the farther they journeyed in this new direction the more removed they became from the legislatures and the voters who put the legislators in office. Eventually this separation would turn into hostility and then into a struggle for power. State and federal legislators and their constituents would see the United States Supreme Court take from them a power they had traditionally exercised in the conduct of public affairs.

---

First appeared as Chapter 1 of *Censorship: Government and Obscenity*, 1963.

# *Notes*

1. The phrase is from Foster Damon, "The Odyssey in Dublin" in Sean Given (ed.), *James Joyce: Two Decades of Criticism* (New York: Vanguard Press, 1948), p. 235.

2. For a more detailed account of the early history of *Ulysses* in the United States, see Herbert Gorman, *James Joyce* (New York: Rinehart and Co., 1948), pp. 306-317.

3. *United States* v. *One Book Called ULYSSES*, 5 F. Supp. 182 (1933), aff'd 72 F 2d 705 (1934).

4. Arnold Bennett, *The Outlook,* April 29, 1922, quoted by Gordon, *op. cit.*, p. 294.

5. Quoted by Gorman, *ibid.*, p. 295. For J. Douglas, *loc. cit.*

6. *Op. cit.*, p. 235.

7. *Ibid.*, p. 208.

8. *United States* v. *One Book Called ULYSSES*, 5 F. Supp. 182 (1933), 184.

9. *Ibid.*, 185.

10. *Ibid.*, 72 F 2d 705 (1934), 708.

11. *United States* v. *Dennett*, 39 F 2d 564 (1930). The appeals case and not the original trial is cited because only the opinion of the circuit court is significant for present purposes.

12. For further details on her activities see Mary Ware Dennett, *Who's Obscene?* (New York: Vanguard Press, 1930).

13. *United States* v. *Dennett*, 39 F 2d 564 (1930), 569.

14. *United States* v. *One Book Entitled "Contraception,"* 51 F 2d 525 (1931). Similarly, see a recent ruling of the Post Office Department, *Minneapolis Star*, Dec. 13, 1961.

15. *United States* v. *One Obscene Book Entitled "Married Love,"* 48 F (2d) 821 (1931).

16. *United States* v. *Kennerley*, 209 F. 119 (1913).

17. *Ibid.*, 120.

18. Morris L. Ernst, *The First Freedom* (New York: The Macmillan Co., 1946), pp. 18-20; Huntington Cairns, "Freedom of Expression in Literature," *Annals of the American Academy of Political and Social Sciences*, CC (1938), pp. 82-83.

19. Acts and Laws of the Providence of Massachusetts Bay, c. CV, 8 (1712), cited in *Samuel Roth* v. *United States*, 354 U.S. 476 (1957), 582.

20. See *Commonwealth* v. *Holmes*, 17 Mass 336 (1821).

21. *Commonwealth* v. *Sharpless*, 2 Sergeant and Rawle 91 (1815).

22. U.S. Tariff Act, Act of August 30, 1842, Sec. 28, 5 Stat. 548, 566.

23. Chap. 89, Sec. 16, 13 Stat. 501.

24. Heywood Broun and Margaret Leech, *Anthony Comstock: Roundsman of the Lord* (New York: Boni Co., 1927); Trumbull, Charles G. *Anthony Comstock, Fighter* (New York: Fleming H. Revell Co., 1913).

25. 17 Stat. at L., 598.

26. 16 Blatchf. 338 (1879), Fed. Cas. No. 14, 571. Bennett was indicted for mailing a pamphlet called *Cupid's Yokes or The Binding Forces of Conjugal Life.* A jury found the pamphlet to be obscene and Bennett in violation of Section 3893 of Revised Statutes as amended by Sec. 1 of Act of July 12, 1876 (19 Stat. 90).

27. *United States* v. *Clarke*, 38 Fed. 732 (1889), 734. Clarke was charged with mailing an obscene pamphlet entitled *Dr. Clarke's Treatise on Venereal, Sexual, Nervous, and Special Diseases* and two obscene circulars. Judge Thayer in instructing the jury said the only question to be decided was whether the material was obscene. The jury found Clarke guilty.

28. *Ibid.*, 733.

29. *United States* v. *Leslie G. Chase*, 135 U.S. 255 (1890), 261. Chase was charged with mailing an obscene letter in violation of Sec. 1 of the Act of Congress, July 12, 1876, 19 Stat. 90. The Court interpreted the word "writing" in the statute to refer to a publication and not to a letter. Congress responded to this decision by passing an amendment which expressly included obscene letters in the category of the non-mailable. See 25 Stat. 496. Similarly see the recent decision, *Ackerman* v. *U.S.*, 293 F. 2d 449 (1961).

30. *Grimm* v. *United States*, 156 U.S. 604 (1895). To the same effect see *DeGignac* v. *United States*, 113 Fed. 197 (1902).

31. *Grimm* v. *United States*, 156 U.S. 604 (1895); *Joseph R. Dunlop* v. *United States*, 165 U.S. 486 (1897); *Warren E. Price* v. *United States*, 165 U.S. 311 (1897); *Lew Rosen* v. *United States*, 161 U.S. 29 (1896); *Lester P. Bartell* v. *United States*, 227 U.S. 427 (1913).

32. *Dan K. Swearingen* v. *United States*, 161 U.S. 446 (1896). See also *United States* v. *Males*, 51 F. 41 (1892).

33. *Joseph R. Dunlop* v. *United States*, 165 U.S. 486 (1897), 500.

34. *Rosen* v. *United States*, 161 U.S. 29 (1896). Rosen was convicted of mailing an obscene paper. He denied the matter was obscene. Before the U.S. Supreme Court he argued that his conviction was based on a defective indictment because it did not give in detail the contents of the paper. The Court found the indictment to be sufficiently definite.

35. *United States* v. *Samuel Roth*, 237 F. 2d 796 (1956).

[Commentary 14]

# Four-Letter Words and the Unconscious
## by Morris L. Ernst
## and
## Alan U. Schwartz

Law has its own unique small secrets. One of the most imponderable and attractive is the mystery of how—as often happens—a case that seems unimportant at the time is appraised at a later date as having vast significance. Such a case was the legal battle against suppression in this country of James Joyce's novel *Ulysses*.

From the date of its original publication in Paris in 1922, the book had been in endless legal troubles, but we shall consider here only those it encountered in the United States. Here it was a prime target of the censorious. But the more our postal and customs officials burned copies, the greater the inducement for smuggling and bootlegging. It became a vogue to own one of those blue-paper-jacketed copies of *Ulysses* from Paris—a vogue that soon led to prices in the hundreds of dollars for one such copy. Men went to jail for publishing or vending the book in the United States of America.

Even then some eminent critics thought the book was an important literary experiment. Nevertheless when, after twelve years of suppression, *Ulysses* faced once more the test of the obscenity law, as Random House prepared to challenge the official ruling that it was not importable, the entire court proceeding was viewed more as a stunt than as an opportunity to lay down new rules of law. Within a few years the opinion of Judge John M. Woolsey was hailed as a landmark in the battle of freedom for books. And yet, after more than a quarter of a century, it is difficult even today to find any new principle laid down by the Court on the *Ulysses* case. As we have indicated, general rules come hard in this field of law, mainly because the standards remain essentially subjective. If anything, the *Ulysses* case set a precedent not so much because of any rule it enunciated as because it represented a psychological breakthrough in the censorship field. After the *Ulysses* case the general community notion of what was dirty became just a little more sophisticated—a process that, despite recidivism here and there, has thankfully continued.

The case opened in the Federal Court in New York City under the Tariff Law of 1930 that allowed the authorities to proceed against a book itself instead of against the person who published, bought, or sold it. It was tried before Judge John M. Woolsey. A copy of *Ulysses* had been ordered for import. In fact, it slipped through Customs by oversight and had to be returned to them in order to have the case tested in court.

There were two grounds for opposition to the importation of *Ulysses*. First, the use of four-letter Anglo-Saxon words. This is not the first or the last case to involve the use of suspect words. A few years before *Ulysses*, a book entitled *What Happens* was convicted because, as the jurors later said, the word used was *masturbation* instead of a term acceptable to them—such as *self-abuse*. The counsel for *Ulysses* took the offensive on this score, explaining in court the sad hypocrisy and lack of reality displayed by people in our culture, and indeed in all cultures, where certain functional and historical words are concerned.

Counsel for the book gave an exposition on the words used by Joyce. Each four-letter word was explained in historic terms. It has been said by some that the turning point in the battle came when shame was removed from the mind of the judge in respect to these words in the book. This was accented in a dialogue between Judge Woolsey and Joyce's lawyer, which went something like this:

COUNSEL: Judge, as to the word *fuck*, one etymological dictionary gives its derivation as from *facere*—to make—the farmer fucked the seed into the soil. This, your honor, has more integrity than a euphemism used every day in every modern novel to describe precisely the same event.
JUDGE WOOLSEY: For example . . .
COUNSEL: Oh—"They slept together." It means the same thing.
JUDGE WOOLSEY (smiling): But, Counselor, that isn't even usually the truth!

Some believe the case was determined at that precise moment. Who knows?

In this connection, the fate of *Strange Fruit* (a novel by Lillian Smith) in Massachusetts provides a relevant sidelight. The book, a highly praised best seller, was denied circulation in Massachusetts in 1945 by the highest court of that Commonwealth. The story is told that one of the judges of that great bench felt he had to vote for suppression because the defense attorney said he could not mention in court or print in his brief an Anglo-Saxon word used in the novel several times by one of the characters. The jurist explained:

"He wanted us to legalize for general circulation the word *fucking*, a word he was ashamed to print in a brief for our eyes alone."

Although this is less than sound law, we understand the judge to mean that freedom is for the brave; those who run deserve to be chased. The lawyer's prudish shame had contributed to the ban on his client's book.

The other ground of opposition to *Ulysses* concerned the frankness of the unconscious stream of thought depicted by Joyce in the dreams of important characters in the volume such as Molly Bloom. Here again there was a colloquy between lawyer and judge that may have had significance in the case:

JUDGE WOOLSEY: Did you really read this entire book? It's tough going, isn't it?

COUNSEL (fearing the judge might suppress on the theory that nothing much will be lost if an unreadable volume is prevented entrance to our shores): I tried to read it in 1923 when it had just come out but could not get far into it. Last summer, however, I had to read it—in preparation for this trial. And while lecturing in the Unitarian Church in Nantucket on the bank holiday . . .

JUDGE WOOLSEY: What has that to do with my question—have you read it?

COUNSEL: Will your honor let me explain how I was able to plough through it? While talking in that Church I recalled after my lecture was finished that while I was thinking only about the banks and the banking laws I was in fact, at that same time, musing about the clock at the back of the Church, the old woman in the front row, the tall shutters at the sides. Just as now, Judge, I have thought I was involved only in the defense of the book, this one cause—I must admit at the same time I was thinking of the gold ring around your tie, the picture of George Washington behind your bench and the fact that your black judicial robe is slipping off your shoulder. This double stream of the mind is the contribution of *Ulysses*.

JUDGE WOOLSEY (rapping on the bench): Now for the first time I appreciate the significance of this book. I have listened to you as intently as I know how. I am disturbed by the dream scenes at the end of the book, and still I must confess, that while listening to you I have been thinking at the same time about the Hepplewhite furniture behind you.

The judge, it appeared, was a collector of antique furniture and for quite a while the audience in the court was entertained by a discourse on furniture manufacture in colonial times.

Seldom is a case capable of being acted out in this fashion. But the double stream of consciousness was acted in the courtroom on that occasion.

These two episodes may have helped make the law in the case. But surely the opinion of Judge Woolsey made history in the sense that it was read by a multitude of people, as incorporated as a Foreword in *Ulysses* editions that have sold close to a half-million copies. Perhaps the clarity of the judicial pen made *Ulysses* a pivotal case. We should like to think that gracious writing made the contribution:

UNITED STATES V. ONE BOOK CALLED *ULYSSES*

District Court, New York
1933

WOOLSEY, District Judge.

I have read *Ulysses* once in its entirety and I have read those passages of which the Government particularly complains several times. In fact, for many weeks, my spare time has been devoted to the consideration of the decision which my duty would require me to make in this matter.

*Ulysses* is not an easy book to read or to understand. But there has been much written about it, and in order properly to approach the consideration of it, it is advisable to read a number of other books which have now become its satellites. The study of *Ulysses* is, therefore, a heavy task.

The reputation of *Ulysses* in the literary world, however, warranted my taking such time as was necessary to enable me to satisfy myself as to the intent with which the book was written, for, of course, in any case where a book is claimed to be obscene it must first be determined whether the intent with which it was written was what is called, according to the usual phrase, pornographic,—that is, written for the purpose of exploiting obscenity.

If the conclusion is that the book is pornographic that is the end of the inquiry and forfeiture must follow.

But in *Ulysses*, in spite of its unusual frankness, I do not detect anywhere the leer of the sensualist. I hold, therefore, that it is not pornographic.

In writing *Ulysses,* Joyce sought to make a serious experiment in a new, if not wholly novel, literary genre. He takes persons of the lower middle class living in Dublin in 1904 and seeks, not only to describe what they did on a certain day early in June of that year as they went about the City bent on their usual occupations, but also to tell what many of them thought about the while.

Joyce has attempted—it seems to me, with astonishing success—to show how the stream of consciousness with its ever-shifting kaleidoscopic impressions carries, as it were on a plastic palimpsest, not only what is in the focus of each man's observation of the actual things about him, but also in a penumbral zone residua of past impressions, some recent and some drawn up by association from the domain of the subconscious. He shows how each of these impressions affects the life and behavior of the character which he is describing.

What he seeks to get is not unlike the result of a double or, if that is possible, a multiple exposure on a cinema film which would give a clear foreground with a background visible but somewhat blurred and out of focus in varying degrees.

To convey by words an effect which obviously lends itself more appropriately to a graphic technique, accounts, it seems to me, for much of the obscurity which meets a reader of *Ulysses*. And it also explains another aspect of the book, which I have further to consider, namely, Joyce's sincerity and his honest effort to show exactly how the minds of his characters operate.

If Joyce did not attempt to be honest in developing the technique which he has adopted in *Ulysses*, the result would be psychologically misleading and thus unfaithful to his chosen technique. Such an attitude would be artistically inexcusable.

It is because Joyce has been loyal to his technique and has not funked its necessary implications, but has honestly attempted to tell fully what his characters think about, that he has been the subject of so many attacks and that his purpose has been so often misunderstood and misrepresented. For his attempt sincerely and honestly to realize his objective has required him incidentally to use certain words which are generally considered dirty words and has led at times to what many think is a too poignant preoccupation with sex in the thoughts of his characters.

The words which are criticized as dirty are old Saxon words known to almost all men, and, I venture, to many women, and are such words as would be naturally and habitually used, I believe, by the types of folk whose life, physical and mental, Joyce is seeking to describe. In respect of the recurrent emergence of the theme of sex in the minds of his characters, it must always be remembered that his locale was Celtic and his season Spring.

Whether or not one enjoys such a technique as Joyce uses is a matter of taste on which disagreement is futile, but to subject that technique to the standards of some other technique seems to me to be little short of absurd.

Accordingly, I hold that *Ulysses* is a sincere and honest book and I think that the criticisms of it are entirely disposed by its rationale.

Furthermore, *Ulysses* is an amazing tour de force when one considers the success which has been in the main achieved with such a difficult objective as Joyce set for himself. As I have stated, *Ulysses* is not an easy book to read. It is brilliant and dull, intelligible and obscure by turns. In many places it seems to be disgusting, but although it contains, as I have mentioned above, many words usually considered dirty, I have not found anything that I consider to be dirt for dirt's sake. Each word of the book contributes like a bit of mosaic to the detail of the picture which Joyce is seeking to construct for his readers.

If one does not wish to associate with such folk as Joyce describes, that is one's own choice. In order to avoid indirect contact with them one may not wish to read *Ulysses*; that is quite understandable. But when such a great artist in words, as Joyce undoubtedly is, seeks to draw a true picture of the lower middle class in a European city, ought it to be impossible for the American public legally to see that picture?

To answer this question it is not sufficient merely to find, as I have found above, that Joyce did not write *Ulysses* with what is commonly called pornographic intent, I must endeavor to apply a more objective standard to his book in order to determine its effect in the result, irrespective of the intent with which it was written.

The statute under which the book is attacked only denounces, in so far as we are here concerned, the importation into the United States from any foreign country of "any obscene book." It does not marshal against books the spectrum of condemnatory adjectives found, commonly, in laws dealing with matters of this kind. I am, therefore, only required to determine whether *Ulysses* is obscene within the legal definition of that word.

The meaning of the word *obscene* as legally defined by the courts is: tending to stir the sex impulses or to lead to sexually impure and lustful thoughts.

Whether a particular book would tend to excite such impulses and thoughts must be tested by the Court's opinion as to its effect on a person with average sex instincts—what the French would call *l'homme moyen sensuel*—who plays, in this branch of legal inquiry, the same role of hypothetical reagent as does the "reasonable man" in the law of torts and "the man learned in the art" on questions of invention in patent law.

The risk involved in the use of such a reagent arises from the inherent tendency of the trier of the facts, however fair he may intend to be, to make his reagent too much subservient to his own idiosyncrasies. Here, I have attempted to avoid this, if possible, and to make my reagent herein more objective than he might otherwise be, by adopting the following course:

After I had made my decision in regard to the aspect of *Ulysses*, now under consideration, I checked my impressions with two friends of mine who in my opinion answered to the above-stated requirement for my reagent.

These literary assessors—as I might properly describe them—were called on separately, and neither knew that I was consulting the other. They are men whose opinion on literature and on life I value most highly. They had both read *Ulysses*, and, of course, were wholly unconnected with this cause.

Without letting either of my assessors know what my decision was, I gave to each of them the legal definition of obscene and asked each whether in his opinion *Ulysses* was obscene within that definition.

I was interested to find that they both agreed with my opinion: that reading *Ulysses* in its entirety, as a book must be read on such a test as this, did not tend to excite sexual impulses or lustful thoughts but that its net effect on them was only that of a somewhat tragic and very powerful commentary on the inner lives of men and women.

It is only with the normal person that the law is concerned. Such a test as I have described, therefore, is the only proper test of obscenity in the case of a book like *Ulysses* which is a sincere and serious attempt to devise a new literary method for the observation and description of mankind.

I am quite aware that owing to some of its scenes *Ulysses* is a rather strong draught to ask some sensitive, though normal, persons to take. But my considered opinion, after long reflection, is that whilst in many places the effect of *Ulysses* on the reader undoubtedly is somewhat emetic, nowhere does it tend to be an aphrodisiac.

*Ulysses* may, therefore, be admitted into the United States.

Judge Woolsey's erudite and beautifully written opinion has been often read and well remembered—and with reason. If judges are, in the nature of the judicial process, to be the final censors, we are relieved when we find one who attempts, and with success, to understand what the artist is doing and saying. Because Woolsey knew how to read he realized, as he says, that for Joyce to abandon his "stream of consciousness" technique from time to time in order to satisfy the more Victorian among us would be dishonest and "artistically inexcusable."

In addition to his firm understanding of the book, Woolsey quietly takes a large step in the direction of freedom to read. He states clearly and unequivocally that a book must be judged not by its effect on the abnormal or the young but rather on the average man, his *"l'homme moyen sensuel."* This view is a far cry from that of Judge Wagner in the *Seltzer* case. Rather it stands with Judge Hand's opinion in the *Dennett* case as the "modern view" of obscenity law.

The government appealed Judge Woolsey's decision in the *Ulysses* case to the next highest court, the Circuit Court of Appeals, only to come face to face with Judge Augustus Hand! We print here excerpts from Hand's opinion as well as others from the dissenting opinion of Judge Manton. Incidentally, you will note that there were two "Hands" ruling for the book, Augustus and Learned. They were cousins—and two of the most brilliant jurists and lucid writers ever to sit in judgment in the United States. Here now are parts of the appellate decisions:

L. HAND, and AUGUSTUS N. HAND, Circuit Judges:

## The Author and the Book

James Joyce, the author of *Ulysses*, may be regarded as a pioneer among those writers who have adopted the stream of consciousness method of presenting fiction, which has attracted considerable attention in academic circles. In this field *Ulysses* is rated as a book of considerable power by persons whose opinions are entitled to weight. Indeed it has become a sort of contemporary classic, dealing with a new subject-matter. It attempts to depict the thoughts and lay bare the souls of a number of people, some of them intellectuals and some social outcasts and nothing more, with a literalism that leaves nothing unsaid. Certain of its passages are of beauty and undoubted distinction, while others are of a vulgarity that is extreme and the book as a whole has a realism characteristic of the present age. It is supposed to portray the thoughts of the principal characters during a period of about eighteen hours.

We may discount the laudation of *Ulysses* by some of its admirers and reject the view that it will permanently stand among the great works of literature, but it is fair to say that it is a sincere portrayal with skillful artistry of the stream of consciousness of its character. Though the depiction happily is not of the stream of consciousness of all men and perhaps of only those of a morbid type, it seems to be sincere, truthful, relevant to the subject, and executed with real art. Joyce, in the words of *Paradise Lost*, has dealt with "things unattempted yet in prose or rime"—with things that very likely might better have remained "unattempted"—but his book shows originality and is a work of symmetry and excellent craftsmanship of a sort. The question before us is whether such a book of artistic merit and scientific insight should be regarded as "obscene."

That numerous long passages in *Ulysses* contain matter that is obscene under any fair definition of the word cannot be gainsaid; yet they are relevant to the purpose of depicting the thoughts of the characters and are introduced to give meaning to the whole, rather than to promote lust or portray filth for its own sake. The net effect even of portions most open to attack, such as the closing monologue of the wife of Leopold Bloom, is pitiful and tragic, rather than lustful. The book depicts the souls of men and women that are by turns bewildered and keenly apprehensive, sordid and aspiring, ugly and beautiful, hateful and loving. In the end one feels, more than anything else, pity and sorrow for the confusion, misery, and degradation of humanity. Page after page of the book is, or seems to be, incomprehensible. But many passages show the trained hand of an artist, who can at one moment adapt to perfection the style of an ancient chronicler, and at another become a veritable personification of Thomas Carlyle. In numerous places there are found originality, beauty, and distinction. The book as a whole is not pornographic, and, while in not a few spots it is coarse, blasphemous, and obscene, it does not, in our opinion, tend to promote lust. The erotic passages are submerged in the book as a whole and have little resultant effect. If these are to make the book subject to confiscation, by the same test *Venus and Adonis, Hamlet, Romeo and Juliet,* and the story told in the Eighth Book of the *Odyssey* by the bard Demodoeus of how Ares and Aphrodite were entrapped in a net spread by the outraged Hephaestus amid the laughter of the immortal gods, as well as many other classics, would have to be suppressed. Indeed, it may be questioned whether the obscene passages in *Romeo and Juliet* were as necessary to the development of the play as those in the monologue of Mrs. Bloom are to the depiction of the latter's tortured soul.

## Read a Book as a Whole

It is unnecessary to add illustrations to show that, in the administration of statutes aimed at the suppression of immoral books, standard works of literature have not been barred merely because they contain some obscene passages, and that confiscation for such a reason would destroy much that is precious in order to benefit a few.

It is settled, at least so far as this court is concerned, that works of physiology, science, and sex instruction are not within the statute, though to some extent and among some persons they may tend to promote lustful thoughts. We think the same immunity should apply to literature as to science, where the presentation, when viewed objectively, is sincere, and the erotic matter is not introduced to promote lust and does not furnish the dominant note of the publication. The question in each case is whether a publication taken as a whole has a libidinous effect.

The book before us has such portentous length, is written with such evident truthfulness in its depiction of certain types of humanity, and is so little erotic in its result, that it does not fall within the forbidden class.

We do not think that *Ulysses*, taken as a whole, tends to promote lust and its critcized passages do this no more than scores of standard books that are constantly bought and sold. Indeed a book of physiology in the hands of adolescents may be more objectionable on this ground than almost anything else.

## Dominant Effect

We believe that the proper test of whether a given book is obscene is its dominant effect. In applying this test, relevancy of the objectionable parts to the theme, the established reputation of the work in the estimation of approved critics, if the book is modern, and the verdict of the past, if it is ancient, are persuasive pieces of evidence; for works of art are not likely to sustain a high position with no better warrant for their existence than their obscene content.

## Offensive to Many but Not Obscene

It may be that *Ulysses* will not last as a substantial contribution to literature, and it is certainly easy to believe that, in spite of the opinion of Joyce's laudators, the immortals will still reign, but the same thing may be said of current works of art and music and of many other efforts of the mind. Art certainly cannot advance under compulsion to traditional forms, and nothing in such a field is more stifling to progress than limitation of the right to experiment with a new technique. The foolish judgments of Lord Eldon about one hundred years ago, proscribing the works of Byron and Southey, and the finding by the jury under a charge by Lord Denman that the publication of Shelley's "Queen Mab" was an indictable offense are a warning to all who have to determine the limits of the field within which authors may exercise themselves. We think that *Ulysses* is a book or originality and sincerity of treatment, and that it has not the effect of promoting lust. Accordingly it does not fall within the statute, even though it justly may offend many.

Decree affirmed.

MANTON, Circuit Judge, dissents.

I dissent.

Who can doubt the obscenity of this book after a reading of the pages referred to, which are too indecent to add as a footnote to this opinion? Its characterization as obscene should be quite unanimous by all who read it.

In the year 1868 Regina v. Hicklin stated that "the test of obscenity is this, whether the tendency of the matter charged as obscenity is to deprave and corrupt those whose minds are open to such immoral influences, and into whose hands a publication of this sort may fall."

Judge Manton goes on to cite a number of Supreme Court cases, dating from 1879, which, to his mind at least, show that the Supreme Court had consistently followed the Hicklin rule. Since most judicial opinions are a mixture of the *decision* in the case (that is, "Mr. X is right and the case should be affirmed") and a variety of comment on the decisions (that is, "Mr. X wins because of *a, b* and *c* . . . and also, it is worth noting that . . . ") not all of which are necessary to reach the *decision*, it is not always easy to agree on what a Court is saying in a particular case. Whether the cases and theory used by Judge Manton actually support the rule he says they do is open to question. But his interpretation is certainly not an unsupportable one. Nor, in this field of relativity, would a contrary interpretation be wholly right or wholly wrong.

Manton now turns his guns on *Ulysses*, and opens fire:

> Thus the court sustained a charge having a test as to whether or not the publications depraved the morals of the ordinary reader or tended to lower the standards of civilization. The tendency of the matter to deprave and corrupt the morals of those whose minds are open to such influence and into whose hands the publication of this sort may fall, has become the test thoroughly entrenched in the federal courts.
>
> *Ulysses* is a work of fiction. It may not be compared with books involving medical subjects or description of certain physical or biological facts. It is written for alleged amusement of the reader only. The characters described in the thoughts of the author may in some instances be true, but, be it truthful or otherwise, a book that is obscene is not rendered less so by the statement of truthful fact. It cannot be said that the test above has been rejected by *United States* v. *Dennett*, nor can that case be taken to mean that the book is to be judged as a whole. If anything, the case clearly recognizes that the book may be obscene because portions thereof are so, for pains are taken to justify and show not to be obscene portions to which objection is made. The gist of the holding is that a book is not to be declared obscene if it is an "accurate exposition of the relevant facts of the sex side of life in decent language and in manifestly serious and disinterested spirit." A work of obvious benefit to the community was never intended to be within the purview of the statute. No matter what may be said on the side of letters, the effect on the community can and must be the sole determining factor. "Laws of this character are made for society in the aggregate, and not in particular. So, while there may be individuals and societies of men and women of peculiar notions or idiosyncrasies, whose moral sense would neither be depraved nor offended, . . . yet the exceptional sensibility, or want of sensibility, of such cannot be allowed as a standard." *United States* v. *Harman*, supra.
>
> And are we to refuse to enforce the statute Congress has enacted because of the argument that "obscenity is only the superstition of the day—the modern counterpart of ancient witchcraft?" Are we to be persuaded by the statement, set forth in the brief, made by the judge below in an interview with the press, "Education, not law, must solve

problems of taste and choice (of books)," when the statute is clear and our duty plain?

The prevailing opinion states that classics would be excluded if the application of the statute here argued for prevailed. But the statute, Tariff Act 1930, section 305, provides as to classics that they may be introduced into the commerce of the United States provided "that the Secretary of the Treasury . . . in his discretion, admit the so-called classics or books of recognized and established literary or scientific merit, but may, in his discretion, admit such classics or books only when imported for non-commercial purposes." The right to admission under this proviso was not sought nor is it justified by reason thereof in the prevailing opinion.

Congress passed this statute against obscenity for the protection of the great mass of our people; the unusual literator can, or thinks he can, protect himself. The people do not exist for the sake of literature, to give the author fame, the publisher wealth, and the book a market. On the contrary, literature exists for the sake of the people, to refresh the weary, to console the sad, to hearten the dull and downcast, to increase man's interest in the world, his joy of living, and his sympathy in all sorts and conditions of men. Art for art's sake is heartless and soon grows artless; art for the public market is not art at all, but commerce; art for the people's service is a noble, vital, and permanent element of human life.

The public is content with the standard of salability; the prigs with the standard of preciosity. The people need and deserve a moral standard; it should be a point of honor with men of letters to maintain it. Masterpieces have never been produced by men given to obscenity or lustful thoughts—men who have no Master. Reverence for good work is the foundation of literary character. A refusal to imitate obscenity or to load a book with it is an author's professional chastity.

Good work in literature has its permanent mark; it is like all good work, noble and lasting. It requires a human aim—to cheer, console, purify, or ennoble the life of people. With this aim, literature has never sent an arrow close to the mark. It is by good work only that men of letters can justify their right to a place in the world.

Under the authoritative decisions and considering the substance involved in this appeal, it is my opinion that the decree should be reversed.

The excerpts we have run from the Circuit Court of Appeals decision are significant in comparison to the dissent of Judge Manton, who ends his opinion by reverting to the "noble and lasting." His plea for professional chastity did little to lead the law to a more precise standard for burning books or sending authors or purchasers to jail.

And still, after all, the historic impress of the *Ulysses* case may be only: (*a*) if literary persons of repute value a writing it shall be allowed to circulate. This rule of law is not far from the anti-law concept of counting noses or bowing to pressure of a picket line or being swayed by people in a sit-in or sit-down—scarcely the reaching for truth by reason or logic; and (*b*) ideas may be expressed in combination of letters—that is, words—which at any one moment of history are not considered agreeable for parlor use. Scarcely an adult legal test for more than "taste." Certainly the "less coarse" or the "more polite" may have a more potent influence on the mind and glands of a man or woman in the direction of romance and lovemaking, or—if you please— "sleeping together."

You will note that Judge Woolsey was sustained on appeal by a vote of 2 to 1—and the Government of the United States did not choose to appeal to the Supreme Court of the United States to see if that final censor power would pass on the obscenity of *Ulysses* by James Joyce.

Judge Hand may confuse you—he weighs, as you have noted, pity as an antidote to obscenity and portentous length as an antidote to the libidinous, and asks: Is a book in effect only a little erotic—as if man, or at least this great judge had, as we suspect every human has, his own private erotica meter. Fortunately, this same court had held, as you have read in the *Dennett* case, that works under attack must be read as a whole.

Perhaps it would be unfair for us to chuckle at the majority's statement, "It may be that *Ulysses* will not last as a substantial contribution to literature." Hindsight is a terribly unfair weapon. Nevertheless, the obvious incorrectness of that statement does point up that even the best of judges do not necessarily make good literary critics—and if we put criticism in their hands, or in the hands of a jury, we are risking unjust results.

First appeared as Chapter 14 of *Censorship: The Search for the Obscene*, 1964.

[Commentary 15]

# Reflections on the *Ulysses* Trial and Censorship[1]
## by Morris L. Ernst

A surprise came my way recently. I had forgotten that it is now a quarter of a century since the highest law officials of our Republic sought to suppress James Joyce's *Ulysses*. Thoughtful writers, critics, scholars and believers in the quaint custom of celebrating anniversaries took their pens in hand and wrote me pleasant notes of congratulations. I was prodded into writing the story of the trial by Professor Silverman of the University of Buffalo, which has one of the great Joyce collections in its library.

I must confess that at the time of the trial I had not appraised the case as being as significant as many others carried through the courts in that dark period from 1915 to 1935. Mary Ware Dennett's sex instruction pamphlet helped open the way for something better than sex instruction in the gutter or on toilet walls. Radclyffe Hall's *Well of Loneliness* was the first defeat of the censorious in the area of writings on lesbianism. Then there was that quaint law title—*United States of America* v. *Married Love*, and the more improbable title to go down into law history as *United States* vs. *Enduring Passion*, both by Marie Stopes. Only one case title has amused me more. It involved a movie during World War I—*United States* vs. *The Spirit of 1776*.

But I seem to have been in error as to the importance of the *Ulysses* case. *Ulysses* did in fact open the minds of writers and readers to seemingly new skills, weaving in one novel several streams of thought by various characters. All of which must be added to our great debt to Sigmund Freud.

It is not irrelevant to note that those who read without concern for their own corruption should be expected to have a deep protective concern for you and me, particularly when authors dare dig into those secondary streams of thought—those more important and less obvious mental operations of man which so seldom can get past the blockades set up by our own internal censors.

The trial came up before Judge Woolsey—one of those rare jurists who was a rounded, physically as well as spiritually, human being who, unlike many members of the bench and bar, read widely in fields remote from his professional interests.

The court room was crowded, as was usual in censorship cases of that era. The Vice Society represented by John S. Sumner, successor to the psychotic masturbator-with-guilt Anthony Comstock, had popularized suppression so as to titillate the prurient—although that word was not yet in that era used as a synonym for the lewd, lascivious and obscene. Not until the U.S. Supreme Court in 1957 entered the game of synonym chasing was prurient used as a symbol of avoidance for the courts' inability to evolve an objective standard for testing what until 1870 was unnecessary to label and from 1870 on was called obscenity.

The prosecutor was a highly skilled and honorable lawyer, now an esteemed judge. Sam Coleman carried with vigor his duty of searching for truth by adversary relationships and, unlike other or most prosecutors, was not interested in producing convictions. He was probably unwittingly in the British tradition of prosecutors—"The Crown can't win, the Crown can't lose—the Crown seeks only justice."

As usual between adversaries of good will—and much to the disgust of the vice-hunting type of lawyer—Sam and I chatted before the opening of the argument. In wise and friendly fashion he indicated that the way to produce "shame"—one of the odd tests for a basis for suppression—would be to mention in court the many four-letter Anglo-Saxon words used in the volume. I assumed this would be the thrust of his argument. But he demurred in this tactic and said he could not so proceed because there was a lady in the court room. I turned around. Then I suggested he should have no reluctance, for the lady was my wife—former reporter and now a school teacher who had seen all the four-letter words on the walls of public and children's toilets. At that time I may even have suggested that such words were written in women's toilets, but of course this is far from the truth. Later studies show that there is little if any of the obscene in women's toilets and at most the scribblings in such places are of the romantic school—hearts, valentines, "John loves Mary," etc., written in lipstick. This is consistent with the now proven fact that women are unaffected by sexual writing or pictures; pornography, so-called, is bought only by men or by women to read to men, and the obscene nudges women not one inch nearer to bed, even though romantic kisses of a glamor boy of Hollywood may have some slight effect on women—something in the nature of a spring breeze or a new full moon.

But Sam, in spite of my assurances, simply could not utter those horrid or torrid words out loud in a court room. This hesitance is interesting since it lost the case of Lillian Smith's *Strange Fruit* in the Massachusetts courts. The publisher, the author, and the lawyer for the defense, under the odd quixotic prudery of Bernard de Voto, apologized for the word *fuck*, used a few times and in keeping with plot and character—but apologized to such an extent and with such confession of shame that, as one of the high judges told me, the court was led to suppress the book because the lawyer wanted public dissemination of material which he was ashamed to voice in a court, or even mention in his printed brief. Maybe it is good, in historic terms, that the cowards shall be chased, and that the timid, in the realm of ideas, shall not inherit the market place of thought.

As the *Ulysses* case proceeded, the government of our Republic made evident three separate and distinct objections. The sexual titillation of episodes, more particularly the dreams at the end of the book, and the use of unparlorish words was the publicly avowed basis of attack. The second mainspring for action was close to the outworn penal sanction of blasphemy. This was made apparent when Martin Conboy, the top legal prosecutor of our nation in this circuit—and a recognized Roman Catholic layman—opened his argument on appeal by stating in effect: This book is one day in the life of a Hungarian anti-Christ Jew. I did not take this crack to be evidence of anti-Semitism but as being consistent with the attitudes of those who looked on Joyce as a Catholic renegade. This line of attack was not disturbing to me even though Judge Manton, the chief justice of the Circuit Court of Appeals, was the lone dissent and, without carrying the inference to an extreme, it must be noted that Manton was a Roman Catholic. The religious attack was, if anything, helpful to the defense—it was so sadly ignorant of the wide latitudes of the Catholic Church with respect to adult reading. My friends are still aghast when I explain that not a single book from the United States has been put on the Roman Catholic index in the past half century and only two

English author novels are thereon. Joyce's *Ulysses* has never been on the Index of Rome. Maybe our cultural confusion derives from the bigots who paint the Catholic Church as monolithic in the area of reading habits—not realizing the wide gap between Irish-overlaid-on-Puritanism as compared to the gay sexy Catholic mores of the Latin world, the absence of any obscenity statute in Spanish-speaking New Mexico, the election of a divorced Catholic Communicant as Governor of Puerto Rico, or the spread of contraceptives through government agencies in Catholic Puerto Rico.

Some years later the absurdity of the Conboy position was made clear to me. While dining with Joyce in Paris at Fouquet's, I think, I told him in detail of this anti-Christ attack on his book and then asked: "When did you leave the Catholic Church?" To which he replied: "That's for the Church to say"— interpreted by me to mean that he had never really left the Church.

The third basis of attack was probably the most significant because it was never fully articulated in any brief or argument. As I mentioned before— there was danger to conscious Man. James Joyce put down in words, not the sleeping nightmares of men and women, not the idle musing while relaxed— such had been often written before Joyce—but here was a dramatic incisive attempt to record those thoughts and desires which all mortals carry within themselves and which are seldom allowed to come near the surface. Few of us can stand the bite and scars of the ideas which our own stern built-in censors push back into our minds and bodies to deform much of the lives of most people. On this level a frank discussion of the relation of the Freudian theory of the subconscious and the extrovert process of confessional might have had illuminating values.

The trial was conducted without disputes as to matters of fact. The volume had been sent to the United States to Random House which intended to publish it if it was cleared. In 1930 I had counseled with Senator Bronson Cutting on a revision of the Customs Law dealing with obscenity. I had persuaded the Senator to make the action one of *In Rem* type: that is, a case of the United States against a book rather than against the importer or addressee. The copy of *Ulysses* came in on the SS *Majestic* or *Olympic*, I forget which, and although I had written to the Custom authorities that the book was being imported as a test volume, the book came through and I had to redeliver the copy to the Custom official in charge. Since 1922 our government had hounded this book first published in Paris. In fact this is part of our intellectual isolationism. French postal cards are deemed ipso facto more corrupting than those on our shores. Sylvia Beach printed an edition in 1922, another edition of 1923 was seized by our Post Office and 1000 (?) copies were burned. Men had been convicted for selling copies of *Ulysses*.

Our hearing was not in an ordinary court room but in one of those pleasant and unfrightening chambers that seated only 40 or 50 people. The argument was unhurried and the questions from the bench were to seek knowledge and by no means to play for headlines in our daily press.

I recall that during the argument I traced some of the ring-around-a-rosies of vocabulary. In my youth the sign read Water Closet—not quite accurate, but when our society knew what was behind the door, the sign was changed to W. C. As soon as this was recognized for its real connotation, we changed to Toilet, then to Gents, then to Men's Lounge (which it isn't), then for the girls to Powder Room, or anything but what it really is. From here I shifted from values of gracious living to make clear that I possess a large amount of squeamishness about the excretionary, scatalogical areas of life and language. But popular books deal with all such outhouse humor, and naturally our courts have long said that toilet concepts are not within the ban of sexual titillation—the target of so-called obscenity. "Wipe your dirty ass" has been judicially determined by the courts of our land not to be obscene.

But surely I had no way of knowing if the pleasant cultured judge used the four-letter Anglo-Saxon words at his club, among men, at college reunions or even when exasperated, as was the case with Holmes and at least one other famed federal jurist at judicial conferences. There is no way to help evaporate invalid fears except by open dignified disclosure. I took up the four-letter words one by one for exposition etymologically. When it became apparent that I had to address myself to the use of the Anglo-Saxon words, I took some query of Judge Woolsey's head-on. Surely man always is worried about arrangements of letters to spell a word rather than about the meaning of the words, and with Margaret's assistance I dug up the derivatives of each one I could locate in the writings of great etymologists. When I got to the word *fuck* I explained to the court that this is a word of strength in integrity. One of the possible derivations was that the farmer fucked the seed into the soil. A slight friendly but admonishing glance from the Prosecutor. From the Judge no comment in speech or of the eye or eyebrow.

I carried on to indicate that I used the phrase, but not in parlors for it made me unpopular. I played it straight and said I used the word in private situations and that it meant the same as a euphemism to be found in every novel, a phrase of cowardice and circumlocution. The judge asked: "For example?" I replied "They slept together." At this point Judge Woolsey rapped again and said "Mr. Ernst, that isn't even usually the truth."

And so I crossed one hurdle, and rested content that the book would not be suppressed because of letters arranged in certain orders.

I had one greater hurdle. On several occasions the Judge implied that it was a tough book to read through, ending with "Counselor, did you really read it from cover to cover?"

Back of the query I felt lay a line of thought—If it's this tough reading what great harm will there be if the public is denied the strain of going through it?

I had to give answer. As I recall it I spoke for quite a time to this point. In effect:

"Yes Judge. I tried to read *Ulysses* in 1923 or 1924 but could not get through it. This was before glossaries and instructional aids had been published. But in preparation for this trial I was trying again when an odd event made the reading easy. I was invited to speak at the Unitarian Church in Nantucket last summer (that is the summer of 1934) on the bank holiday, the Federal Reserve System and the function of the New York State Banking Board of which I was a member."

I sensed I was losing the Judge's interest and recall feeling delighted when he said: "What's this got to do with *Ulysses?*"

I was unhurried because this little episode is one of those rare occurrences in a court room when a member of the bar makes a point by acting out the subject of the litigation.

I continued, "I talked with true concern about our banking system and when I sat down I remembered, Judge, that while I was talking about banks I was at the same time thinking about the long windows on the sides, the clock in the rear, the old gray woman in the front row, the baby in the rear and a myriad of items unrelated to banks or my conscious mind." I said when I finished, "this is *Ulysses*, and now in court while I thought I was thinking only about Joyce and *Ulysses* and my argument in defense of the book, I must tell you that I have also been thinking—if that's the word for it—about the gold ring around your tie, how your gown is slipping off your left shoulder, and about the picture of George Washington hanging up behind the bench. That, Judge, is the essence of *Ulysses.*"

I wasn't quite happy. I was uncertain if I had made the point of two streams in one mind at the same time. But Judge Woolsey turned and said in effect: "I understand your argument on this level. In fact, I have been much worried about the last 50 pages or so of the volume. But now although I have listened as intently as I know how to the argument I must confess that all the time you were discussing the book I was also thinking about the Hepplewhite chair in back of you."

I was relieved. This *was* the book. This *was* my case. And for the next ten or fifteen minutes we discussed antique furniture of which the Judge was an authority and a collector.

The trial ended on this note—a colloquy of exploration—an inquiry insofar as our egos would permit into that secondary stream of thought which every human conducts through shoals, storms, locks and on occasion comfortable harbors. Few dare go into gunk holes.

The case was appealed by the government to the Circuit Court of Appeals—sitting, Judges Manton, Learned Hand and Augustus Hand. Judge Manton was silent, Augustus Hand was acute in his questions and Learned Hand as usual was crabbed to the point where, with his basically considerate personality, he apologized to me long afterwards.

The test for obscenity is still at the subjective stage. This is natural since this basis for censorship is a new dread of man. Originally the fear was of blasphemy but when the temporal power of the clergy—that tight little early trade union of the only men who could read and write—dwindled, the courts went after sedition. Kings and Queens lived in terror of ideas. And later when democracy started on its arduous path man needed a new ideational worry, and came up with obscenity. In Anglo-Saxon terms it began in earnest in England around the middle of the 19th century, and hopped the Atlantic pond in 1870 when the fever of the hypocrites caught on, and all states but one went into the chase after all sexual ideas in print—ideas which might corrupt those into whose hands the material might fall.

Not stopping to discern the substantive evil which bothered society, the judicial standards included the quixotic such as: expensive books were allowed circulation on the theory that the rich were incorruptible or already corrupted; the motive of the author was at times looked into, overlooking the historic fact that an author with the motive of corruption might fail where one with a so-called clean motive might unintentionally corrupt; then the problem of the classics reared its disturbing head—how long must an author be dead to immunize his obscene writings; must the book be read as an entirety or could the vice hunter successfully attack because of one chapter, one page or one word? The intellectual rat race hunt went on from 1870 to 1915 when Mitchell Kennerly fought back over—of all books—*Hagar Revelly*. Up to 1915 respectable publishers slunk into the offices of Comstock and Summer to ask approval and editing. This was the dark ages for creative writers. This naturally encouraged—as all unacceptable taboos and prohibitions always do—the development of secrecy and stealth.

Publishers fought with courage from 1915 until about 1950 and then a dire trend developed. The attacks were increased against newsdealers and book store clerks, and publishers compromised their significant prestige as men of imprints. They salved their consciences or toadied to their retail book store customers by paying fines, supplying counsel, paying in money—in fact doing everything except standing in a commons to sell a book, or in a court room and with dignity defending *in personam* their choice of a volume and their imprint.

Hence the rampage against books is now at its height, conducted by little groups of vigilantes in hundreds of towns and villages, threatening book vendors and pressuring police and other officials.

Those who rightly hold that groups in a democracy should exercise their responsibility by recommending for or against the reading material of our culture are unable to control the excesses visible in the town operations many steps removed from headquarters. The Legion of Decency in the film industry has little trouble in conducting maneuvers and compromises with the movie industry, intellectually more pliable under Eric Johnston than even under Will Hays. Television is oddly enough unaffected by outside controls and obviously will be immune since the network owners contend that they give the people what they want. Do they? How do they know what the people want? And is it the function of this potent mass media to give the people what they want? If three great citizens—Goldenson, Sarnoff and Paley—give the public what each of *them* wants the television diet would be quite different than at present when the highest prestige lies in breasts and guns.

The newspapers are protected not only because the founding fathers had not imagined movies or television but because papers, drifting fast to monopolistic status in most cities, wield supposed political power, or at the least the weapons of blackmail or even libel. Yet libel is a useless weapon in a culture where papers have a virtual cartel never to report libel suits no matter how gay and provocative.

Thus the press goes deep into the gutters of life. *The New York Post*, our main editorially liberal daily in New York, satisfies its pocketbook and conscience by a justification of sorts—we need the orgy, crime, and lust readers in order to make enough dollars to support liberal columns and editorials. Such a pretentious position scarcely justifies a paper which if read by any young lad may lead him to believe that it is normal for a boy to cut a girl's throat.

And so books continue to be the main target for attack. And will be until publishers believe in freedom of the press not for dollars but as a way of life. Then we will ask: What are the evils that bother the censorious—adultery, fornication, masturbation, homosexuality, extramatrimonial sexual affairs, etc.? What proof is there of any possible causal relationship between reading and behavior? Do we need further proof that women are unaffected by the salacious? That children treat fiction quite differently than they do nonfiction? Is there a distinction in social scientific terms between impact of the sexually exciting and the sadistic on adolescents or adults? Does the specific create an additional effect in the field of sadistic pictures or words? What does society do if it desires to reduce the sexual excitements of men and women with the pictures of nudes in art galleries, in advertisements of bras and black stockings (which incidentally as with all advertising is aimed only at the male gonads), and above all what happens to men and women when the sap runs in the trees, when a spring breeze inkles its way to our cheeks, and a full moon comes out of a calm sea?

*Ulysses* seems to have been a judicial landmark in the history of legal censorship. But landmarks are only as enduring and firm as the will of the people. A look at banned books through history—from the Tyndale Bible, to Galileo, to Shelley's *Cenci*, to Havelock Ellis, to the more recent attacks on *Huckleberry Finn* must make man less than confident that cases end trends.

After the Woolsey decision had been affirmed Mrs. Maurice Moore arranged an exhibit of banned books at the Junior League of New York. The Judge made an address, and I was asked to say a few words. The exhibit was illuminating in showing the invalidity of man's fears of ideas and the changing mores in accepted concepts. I recall referring to an unproven hunch which the exhibition, including tables of books banned in Russia and in Hitler's

Germany seemed to indicate. It seemed to me natural that man must always be interested in the beginning and end of all living matter. This is the price we pay for mortality. And it may be true that since the beginning is birth or sex, and the end is death or sadism, that the more we suppress consideration of the one the more we accent the other.

But long after *Ulysses*, its publisher Random House and Judge Woolsey have been put in their proper places in history—man will still have to consider aspects of culture that fall outside of *judicial* controls. I refer to Taste. Our mass media, within the law, is producing a tawdry, vulgar and tasteless people. No school system can give decency in human relationship high prestige in the face of much of the daily press and television.

In a world of newspapers and TV when only bad news is news, the people of our Republic must lower their visions, and lose insight into the mysteries, joys and gaieties of the loveliness of life, and the gaiety of sexual relationship turns into a bit of vulgar gymnastics.

June, 1959
New York, N.Y.

First appeared in *The James Joyce Quarterly*, Fall, 1965.

# *Note*

1. In June 1959 I was asked to put on a record some of the stories of the trial of James Joyce's *Ulysses*. I never made the record. This is the transcript. When requested by this Quarterly to write my reminiscence, knowing that memory plays tricks, I chose to send for publication my memory of a quarter century after the trial rather than today in 1965.

Since 1959 I have reached many new conclusions relevant to forces other than the sovereign's power of censorship to reduce the tawdriness of our market place of thought. Some of my revised thinking—and it is constantly being reappraised—is incorporated in *Censorship—The Search For the Obscene*—a volume I wrote this year for non-lawyers with my partner at the Bar, Alan U. Schwartz.

All professions unwittingly make a mystery of their skills and all too often invent new gobbledegooks to confound the public. Law is a romantic profession for inventors—so that jurisprudence may open new legal paths to accommodate to new pressures of life itself. This recent book updates some of the following philosophies of the market place of thought.

[Commentary 16]

# From *At Random*
## by Bennett Cerf

Our great *Ulysses* adventure, which culminated in 1934, had really begun in 1932, when James Joyce's *Ulysses* was contraband in the United States, absolutely forbidden. The only way you could buy it was under-the-counter in an edition published by Miss Sylvia Beach in Paris under the colophon of Shakespeare and Company, the name of her very famous little bookstore on the Left Bank, where many American tourists found their way. Everybody would buy copies of *Ulysses* bound in paper: a light-blue—Columbia-blue—cover. You couldn't come home from Europe without a copy of *Ulysses*, which Sylvia Beach sold for ten dollars. I think Shakespeare and Company really lived on *Ulysses*. The *Little Review* had done some of it in successive issues, but it had even less money than Joyce. A man had pirated some of it and gone to jail, and not only for *Ulysses*; he was also publishing alleged "pornography" of a less literary nature.

I had heard Morris Ernst, the great lawyer, say one night that the banning of *Ulysses* was a disgrace and that he'd like to wage a fight to legalize it. So in March, 1932, I had lunch with Ernst and said, "If I can get Joyce signed up to do an American edition of *Ulysses*, will you fight the case for us in court?" I added, "We haven't got the money to pay your fancy prices"—he was a very high-powered lawyer—"but I'd like to make you a proposition. We'll pay all the court expenses, and if you win the case, you'll get a royalty on *Ulysses* for the rest of your life."

Ernst said, "Great, great." He loves publicity just as much as I do!

So I wrote to Joyce in care of Shakespeare and Company, where I knew he made his headquarters. I said I was coming to Europe and that I'd love to meet him in Paris to see if we could work out a way of publishing *Ulysses* officially in America. I received a letter saying that he'd be delighted to meet me. Why not? He'd never gotten a penny out of America on *Ulysses*. Maybe this was opening a door for him!

On the morning agreed upon I walked into Sylvia Beach's, and there was James Joyce sitting with a bandage around his head, a patch over his eye, his arm in a sling and his foot all bound up and stretched out on a chair. He looked like one of those characters in "The Spirit of '76." I retreated a pace, and Miss Beach, a very lovely gray-haired lady, said, "Oh, Mr. Cerf, don't think he always looks that way. He was so excited about meeting you, on his way here he was run over by a taxicab. But he insisted on seeing you today, because he needs money and he thinks maybe you're going to get some for him."

I said, "Well, I'm certainly ready to give him some."

The eye-patch, I learned later, he always wore, but the other damages were temporary.

I said, "I don't know whether we can win this case or not, but I do think the climate is changing in America, and I'm willing to gamble on it. I'll give you fifteen hundred dollars, with the understanding that if we legalize the book, this is an advance against regular royalties of fifteen percent. If we lose our case, you keep the fifteen hundred."

He was delighted with that; it was a lot more money then than it would be today. He said, "I don't think you'll manage it. And you're not going to get the fifteen hundred back."

I said, "Of course not. That's to make the deal binding." I wanted ours to be the official *Ulysses*—with his full authorization. (Viking Press had published his other books but were afraid to do this one.)

When I met him, Joyce was just over fifty. After he removed those bandages he looked like quite a vigorous fellow. His wife, Nora, was a typical Irish lady—garrulous and friendly. We spent several evenings together, and the last one was the funniest, because this time Joyce, who always had quite a lot to drink, got really potted. Back in his apartment after dinner, he decided he was going to sing me some Irish ballads, but Mrs. Joyce decided he was *not* going to sing me some Irish ballads. And so a great fight started when Joyce went over to the piano. There was a long bench in front of it, and Nora grabbed one end and Joyce the other—both pulling in opposite directions. Suddenly she deliberately let go, and Joyce went staggering back and landed on his behind on the floor against the wall with the piano bench on top of him. Nora said, "Maybe this will teach you a lesson, you drunken . . . " I thought the time had come to retreat, and so she and I left Joyce still sitting on the floor, quite happy and in no pain. Nora took me downstairs and put me in a taxicab and apologized for the vulgar display, but of course we were both laughing—it was so ridiculous. The last thing I heard from her as I got in the cab was, "Someday *I'm* going to write a book for you, Bennett, and I'm going to call it *My Twenty Years with a Genius—So-Called*."

I came home and told Mr. Ernst that I had a signed agreement, for whatever it was worth—Joyce's approval that ours was to be the official edition of *Ulysses*. Now several problems had to be solved. We hoped to get a judge who we thought would be favorably disposed to our cause. This was where Ernst's experience was invaluable. He knew that John M. Woolsey was a man of erudition who had already established a reputation for liberal literary opinions, so he timed our case to come up when Woolsey was sitting in New York.

The next big problem was: How were we to get into the court records the pieces that had been written about *Ulysses* by men like Arnold Bennett, Ford Madox Ford, Edmund Wilson, Ezra Pound and other great men of the times. All of these great people and others had written about *Ulysses*, proclaiming it a landmark in literature. We couldn't enter their opinions because the court would not allow outside criticisms to be read in a case of this kind—why, I don't know, but the United States had established that rule. The only way we could do it was to make them part of the book, since anything that was in the book could be used as evidence. So we took one of the Paris paperbound editions of *Ulysses* and pasted in it every opinion we wanted to use—dozens of them in several languages. By the time we finished, the covers were bulging. Since that copy had to be the one that would be used as evidence, we got somebody to take it over to Europe and bring it back on the *Aquitania*, and had our agent down at the dock when it landed. It was one of the hottest days in the history of New York. The temperature on that dock must have been a hundred and twenty degrees, and the customs people wanted only one thing: to get returning passengers off and get the hell out themselves. They were stamping everything without opening it, saying, "Get out; go on out." When our man arrived, the customs inspector started to stamp his suitcase without even looking at it. Our agent, frantic, said, "I insist that you open that bag and search it." The inspector looked at him as though he were an absolute lunatic, and said, "It's too hot."

"I think there's something in there that's contraband," our agent said, "and I insist that it be searched."

So, furiously, the fellow had to open the suitcase. And the agent said "Aha!" as he produced our copy of *Ulysses*. The customs man said, "Oh, for God's sake, everybody brings that in. We don't pay any attention to it." But the agent persisted, "I demand that you seize this book."

After a short argument the customs inspector called over his chief and said, "This fellow wants me to seize this book." Then the chief started to argue; he said that was ridiculous. But our agent had his way. He was right legally, and *made* them seize the book. So when the case came up, that was the copy in evidence.

Morris Ernst made a brilliant defense of *Ulysses* before Judge Woolsey, who fully understood the points being made. The trial, in which there was no jury, was over in two days, and though we had to wait quite a while for a ruling, the judge's attitude made us feel confident that we had won. Woolsey's famous decision, which took him some time to write, concluded that *Ulysses* "is a sincere and serious attempt to devise a new literary method for the observation and description of mankind." He ruled that it was not obscene and could be admitted to the United States.

The case was appealed once, before Judges Augustus and Learned Hand and Judge Martin Manton. The appeal was denied irrevocably, and that was the end of it. We published *Ulysses* in January, 1934, with Woolsey's landmark decision in it—and it is still included in our edition. The book has had an enormous sale; it is one of the leading Modern Library and Vintage Giants and sells thousands of copies every year. Morris Ernst has been getting royalties on *Ulysses* ever since, but he richly deserved them. We never begrudged him this. He's made a lot of money out of it but so did we, and of course Joyce made a fortune too. So everybody was very happy—except the bluenoses, the self-appointed censors.

The year after publication I presented our special copy of *Ulysses* to the Columbia University Library and wrote a letter explaining some of our strategy in the famous case:

May 21, 1935

Dr. Hellmut Lehmann-Haupt,
Columbia University,
The Library,
New York City.

Dear Dr. Lehmann-Haupt:

Various accounts of the *Ulysses* case have appeared in newspapers and magazines, but I think I can give you all the facts that you want most succinctly in this letter.

The reason that we chose to fight our case against the government through the expedient of importing a copy and having it seized by the Customs was for the purpose of economy. Had the government refused entry of the volume and had its claim been sustained by the courts, we would have been out only the cost of this single copy plus, of course, the advance that we had paid Mr. Joyce and legal fees. The other alternative was to set up the book in America and publish it and then wait for our tilt with the government. This, of course, would have been a very expensive way of doing things.

Once we had decided to import a copy and have it seized, it became essential that the book actually be apprehended and not slipped through in one way or another. We therefore were forced to the somewhat ludicrous procedure of having our own agent at the steamer to make sure that our property was seized by the government. The copy itself was a rather special one, since inside its blue paper cover (Columbia blue, by the way) were pasted critical essays on the book by leading authors and critics of both England and France. Only by having these reviews pasted inside the copy were we able to quote from them when the case actually came before the court.

In due course Judge Woolsey tried the *Ulysses* case, with the results that you know. It was only in the courtroom that we got a second look at our copy of *Ulysses*. The impeccable copy that we had imported was already in the tattered, dog-eared condition in which you now find it. Obviously, everybody in the Customs department spent some time on this erudite volume. The district attorney had also gone to the trouble of marking with a heavy cross every line of the book that he considered pornographic. This marking will undoubtedly be of great help to Columbia students who, I hope, will have a chance to examine this volume in the years to come.

Cordially yours,
Bennett A. Cerf

*Ulysses* was our first really important trade publication. We had already added O'Neill and Jeffers to our list, and we had done *Moby Dick*, which was an enormous success but was, after all, a standard classic. But here was a big commercial book—with front-page stories to help launch it—and it did a lot for Random House.

There's a very amusing story connected with this. We had never been able to do much business with the American News Company. Macy's was our big customer for Modern Library, but for new books at that time the American News Company, with branches all over the country, was *the* big customer. They distributed all the magazines, and they also distributed books, not only to the bookstores but to stationery stores and all the little miscellaneous outfits. The buyer for the American News Company was a very tough, very efficient fellow named Harold Williams. Donald and I knew Harold and liked him, and we played golf together occasionally. He was a great kidder, with a dry kind of wit. We had done only a little business with him—he had ordered about a thousand copies of *Moby Dick*—but here at last was a book that we thought was going to be a big national best seller. So I went to see Harold Williams down on Varick Street, where the American News Company had a whole building. I told him I thought we had a big book for him, one he could really sell in quantity.

He said, "Oh, I suppose it's that dirty book *Ulysses*. I don't think it's for us."

I said, "What do you mean, dirty? It's all been cleared by the court."

"Well, it's not really our kind of thing," he insisted. "But you're nice fellows, we'll help you a little bit. We'll take two hundred and fifty copies." This was for the whole country, of course! So I started screaming. I got him up from two fifty to five hundred; then, after some more screaming, he made it a thousand. Then, after considerably more battling, I pushed him up to twenty-five hundred, and finally, wringing wet with perspiration, I got him up through several stages to five thousand. He had started at two hundred fifty! Williams said, "Well, are you satisfied?"

I felt very proud of myself, and said, "Yes, at last you've given me the right order."

He opened a drawer and handed me a typewritten order, made out before I came, for five thousand copies! He said, "I thought I'd make you work for it."

It really was a masterly performance. Of course they sold them all, and thousands besides. *Ulysses* was a great best seller, partly because, I think, it was one of those books that are considered smart to own and which many people buy but don't read. Perhaps many did read the last part to see the dirty words; in 1934 that sort of thing was shocking to the general public. But *Ulysses* for a long time now has been an established classic, an important part of the curriculum in literature courses.

We almost lured Joyce to America once, but he was afraid of boats. At the last minute he welshed. By this time he had moved to Switzerland, and had received quite a lot of money from us. His *Portrait of the Artist as a Young Man* and *Dubliners* were also selling well for Viking Press. Harold Guinzburg, the founder of Viking, was one of my best friends, and I didn't want to harm that relationship. There are some publishers who respect the rights of others. Viking and Random House would never dream of doing anything to hurt each other. But some of the best-known publishers in America are veritable pirates. They'll have dinner with you one night and steal an author from you the next day, and if that's their game, we'll play it. But there are certain publishers we feel very close to, Viking and Knopf in particular. That's why we were able to get together years later with Alfred Knopf, because there was that bond of friendship and trust. I only wish we could have Viking with us, too. Phyllis and I love Harold's son Tom. We've watched him grow up. He's one of my favorite people, Tom.

---

First appeared in *At Random*, 1977.

---

[Commentary 17]

# *Ulysses* on Trial
## by Kenneth R. Stevens

Bennett Cerf called it "our great *Ulysses* adventure," and it began in 1932 when he heard New York attorney Morris L. Ernst say that he would like to defend James Joyce's novel against the charge that it was obscene. Although *Ulysses* had been available in Europe for years, United States customs regulations against admission of obscenity prohibited its importation into this country. True, Americans returning from travels in Europe had brought copies surreptitiously from time to time—a practice which customs officials largely ignored—but there was always the possibility of seizure. Joyce's novel needed legality before it could be published and distributed in the United

States, and accomplishing that task would require the combined efforts of Ernst, a leading censorship lawyer, and Cerf, the president of Random House. The Morris L. Ernst Papers at the Humanities Research Center make it possible to follow the defense of this influential literary masterpiece.[1]

Ernst was just the person for the defense and Cerf just the publisher for the book. Beneath his jovial and friendly manner, Cerf was a creative and ambitious businessman. After graduating from Columbia University in 1919, he worked on Wall Street, then joined the Boni and Liveright publishing firm. In 1925 he purchased the Modern Library series from Horace Liveright and established Random House. When he became the firm's president three years later at the age of thirty, Cerf had emerged as a major figure in the world of books.[2] For his part, Ernst was one of the premier censorship lawyers in America. The son of a Czech emigrant, Ernst was born in Alabama in 1888 but raised in New York from the age of two. At sixteen he entered Williams College and after graduation attended law school at night while selling shirts and furniture during the day.[3]

As an attorney, Ernst soon made a name for himself in obscenity law. In collaboration with William Seagle, a free-lance writer, he coauthored *To the Pure* (1928), a flamboyant attack on literary censorship. The book attracted attention, and a number of important cases came his way following its publication. In 1929 Ernst defended Radclyffe Hall's novel about female homosexuality, *The Well of Loneliness*. Subsequently, he successfully represented sex educator Mary W. Dennett, who had been indicted for distributing her pamphlet *The Sex Side of Life*, and defended the publishing firm of G. P. Putnam's Sons, which had sought to import a book entitled *Married Love* for publication in the United States.[4] As early as 1931 Ernst and his law partner, Alexander Lindey, had in mind the possibility of instigating a case on behalf of *Ulysses*. In a memorandum to Ernst, Lindey wrote that he felt "very keenly that this would be the grandest obscenity case in the history of law and literature, and I am ready to do anything in the world to get it started."[5] Lindey was already in touch with a relative of Joyce's European publisher, Sylvia Beach, about the possibility of arranging for an American edition of *Ulysses*.

From the beginning, when Joyce was writing *Ulysses*, the novel experienced a history of legal problems. Excerpts had been published in the literary magazine *The Little Review*, and its editors, Margaret Anderson and Jane Heap, soon found themselves in trouble on several fronts. Many of their readers complained about Joyce's work, one denouncing it as "damnable, hellish filth from the gutter of a human mind." More seriously, the Post Office blocked mailing of the *Review*, and eventually Anderson and Heap were indicted through the efforts of the New York Society for the Suppression of Vice. At their trial in February 1921, the editors were convicted and each fined fifty dollars.[6]

Another controversy occurred in 1926 when Samuel Roth, a literary pirate, began publishing, without Joyce's permission, portions of *Ulysses* in Roth's quarterly, *Two Worlds*. Unlike *The Little Review* editors, Roth avoided difficulties with the censors by bowdlerizing Joyce's text. When news of his audacity reached Paris, 167 of Joyce's friends and admirers—including T.S. Eliot, D.H. Lawrence, and Thomas Mann—protested the "appropriation and mutilation" of the writer's work. Such complaints, however, had little effect on Roth, who continued to trade on Joyce's name. At length the author filed for an injunction in the United States, but that accomplished little, since *Ulysses* had no American copyright. In December 1928, Roth agreed to stop publishing Joyce's work, but it was a hollow victory, for *Two Worlds* had folded in July.[7]

The experience with Roth convinced Joyce that he needed a legitimate American publisher. In 1932, shortly after talking with Ernst, Cerf visited the author in Paris. Gambling that the New York attorney could win legality for *Ulysses*, Cerf acquired publishing rights to the novel for a $1,500 retainer and a promise of fifteen percent royalties on the book's future profits. Back in New York, Cerf completed arrangements with Ernst. The lawyer agreed to a small fee for such an important case—$500—but if he won, he would receive a five percent royalty from the first edition of *Ulysses* and a lifetime royalty of two percent from all subsequent editions.[8]

The legal struggle remained. The stumbling block to publishing *Ulysses* in the United States was the tariff act of 1930. Section 305 of the act prohibited the importation of obscene material, but it gave the Secretary of the Treasury discretion to admit "the so-called classics or books of recognized and established literary or scientific merit" for noncommercial purposes. Ernst's job would be to convince the Treasury Department, or a federal court, that the novel was not obscene.[9]

As a first step, Ernst directed Cerf to order a copy of *Ulysses* from Paris, making sure that the novel did not slip through New York Customs without scrutiny. As a possible aid for the defense they pasted laudatory reviews of the novel inside the book's covers. If the case went to trial, they reasoned, the copy in evidence before the court would contain testimony of the work's merits. The book arrived on a hot day in early May 1932 that found officials in no mood for careful inspections. A customs man started to clear the suitcase containing *Ulysses*, but Random House's agent pointed out the illegal volume. "Oh, for God's sake," the exasperated inspector cried, "everybody brings that in. We don't pay any attention to it." Cerf's representative persisted, and the book, which became the copy used in the test case, was duly seized.[10]

Once the government had the book, it seemed uncertain what to do with it. Not until May 13 did the government advise Lindey officially that *Ulysses* had been seized for violation of the tariff act. The district attorney's office was also reluctant to take action. A month after the book had been sent to their office, Lindey talked with prosecutor Samuel Coleman, who said that he was reading it to form an opinion but "having a difficult time." Coleman finished the novel in July and reported to Lindey that, while he agreed that *Ulysses* was a "literary masterpiece," it was nonetheless obscene. Still, he did not want final responsibility in the case and had decided to turn it over to his superior, District Attorney George Medalie.[11]

Meanwhile, the lawyers went ahead with plans for the book's defense. Ernst asked Cerf to inform various editors, authors, and literary critics that Random House had acquired the American rights to *Ulysses* and intended to defend the book. Denouncing prohibition of the novel as "unconscionable and vicious," the letter asked for an appraisal of the book's value, especially as a social document, to provide evidence for the defense. Cerf also contacted a number of college and public librarians across the country. In a questionnaire he asked whether their libraries had acquired *Ulysses*, which patrons asked about the book's availability, whether publication of an American edition would be worthwhile, and what the librarian thought of the novel's literary and psychological importance.[12]

By the end of May, Cerf had received favorable responses from many important literary figures, including George Jean Nathan (cofounder of the *American Mercury* with H.L. Mencken), Robert M. Coates (author of the surrealist novel *Eater of Darkness*), and Theodore Dreiser, who had himself suffered from bouts with censors. A consternating reply arrived from John Dos Passos, who praised Joyce's art, while expressing his opinion that "even the dumbest judge" ought to know better than to ban *Ulysses*. At Lindey's request, Cerf asked Dos Passos for a less inflammatory statement.[13]

While mostly favorable, the replies from librarians demonstrated that acceptance of *Ulysses* was significantly more subdued outside literary circles. A librarian and professor of English at Hunter College called the novel a "decidedly overrated . . . psychological extravaganza rather than a work of fictional art." From Johns Hopkins came the opinion that the book was interesting but not a classic, while a Jesuit priest from St. Louis University denounced *Ulysses* as literary jazz for "sophisticated half-morons." A public librarian in Riverside, California, reported that queries about the availability of *Ulysses* came mostly from "army officers and men of leisure."[14] Generally, however, the library responses were what the lawyers wanted. The questionnaires revealed that patrons who most often asked about the book were college students and faculty, a social group which a judge might be less likely to consider smut-seekers. Most of the librarians felt that American publication of *Ulysses* would be worthwhile and that the novel had literary and psychological importance.

The letters and questionnaires made an impressive collection of evidence. Ernst and Lindey could show that the body of literary opinion represented by authors and critics regarded *Ulysses* as a sophisticated and complex work of art rather than pornography. Indeed, Cerf wrote, some of the letters showed that "even many intelligent people can't make head or tail out of *Ulysses*," a point which he believed confirmed the view that "dumbbells in search of smut will certainly throw down the book in hopeless disgust after trying to wade through the first two chapters."[15] The cumulative responses indicated that *Ulysses* had gained broad acceptance in the genteel community.

Two months after prosecutor Samuel Coleman said he intended to turn the book over to George Medalie, the government still had reached no decision about *Ulysses*. Medalie had read the book and was dubious about its legality, "particularly as to the musing of the wife," but he wanted to see the results of the questionnaires before he made a decision. It would be best, Ernst felt, not to rush him, in the hope that the government might admit the book without a court battle.[16] By November, however, it seemed likely that the district attorney's office would proceed against the book. Hope that *Ulysses* would be admitted without a court appearance finally collapsed on December 9, when the government filed a libel against the novel, declaring that Random House had imported it in violation of section 305 of the tariff act of 1930. In reply, Cerf's lawyers admitted importing the book, but denied the government's right to condemn it.[17]

Of all the judges in the Southern District of New York Court, Ernst felt that John M. Woolsey was the most likely to rule in favor of *Ulysses*. A successful admiralty lawyer before his appointment to the district court in 1929, Woolsey was known as a liberal and literate judge. In previous cases he had shown himself unsympathetic toward censorship. Like prohibition, he reasoned, repression increased interest in the forbidden while driving it underground. Society could control indecent publications only by "the development of educated taste in the individual."[18] By background and philosophy, Woolsey was the ideal person, from the defense's perspective, to hear the case.

Manipulating the court's calendar in order to bring *Ulysses* before Woolsey would not be easy. Late in May the case came before a judge whom Ernst and Lindey had hoped to avoid, but fortunately he declined to hear it for unspecified technical reasons. He adjourned the proceedings until June 16, but early in the month Lindey learned from the court clerk that the "worst man on the bench for us" would preside that day, while Woolsey might be available later. With the consent of the district attorney, Lindey and Ernst asked for and received a postponement. Finally, after a series of delays, the court scheduled the case for August, before Judge Woolsey.[19]

The lawyers for *Ulysses* and the government already had agreed that a jury trial, which probably would involve reading the entirety of Joyce's novel in court, would take too long. Instead, the case would be heard before a judge. District Attorney Coleman proposed that the defense lawyers ask the judge for a ruling on a motion to dismiss the libel against the book, and the government would then present a cross-motion upholding the charges.[20] In their first appearance before Woolsey on August 30, the two sides presented their motions, which the judge took under advisement. By October 16 the defense lawyers had completed a fifty-six page brief in favor of the motion to dismiss the libel. Opening with a claim that *Ulysses* had become a *"cause célebre"* in the literary world, the brief asserted that the court now had an opportunity to "thrust back the narrow frontiers fixed by prudery."[21] James Joyce, they continued, was the most important literary figure alive, a "Colossus of creative writing," comparable to Shakespeare. It was "monstrous to suppose that a man of the stature of Joyce would or could produce a work of obscenity."

The attorneys presented six arguments in support of their motion for dismissing the libel charge. First, they held that *Ulysses* should be judged according to the contemporary mores of the community rather than the standards of an earlier day. Quoting from Judge Learned Hand's opinion in *U.S.* v. *Kennerley*, they maintained that in the absence of any precise definition of obscenity, acceptable literature could be separated from the unacceptable only by locating the "present critical point in the compromise between candor and shame at which the community may have arrived here and now."[22] To prove their thesis the lawyers presented a history of fashion in women's swimsuits. In 1900 the law required long skirts and sleeves, but by the next decade bare knees and stockings were permissible. The one-piece suit followed, and as for the 1930s, declared the brief, "so-called sunsuits leave very little of the human form concealed." The same principle of evolution could be seen in literature. Works now calmly accepted, such as *Jane Eyre* and *The Scarlet Letter*, once had been denounced virulently. Moral standards of the present were "sturdier" than those of the past. Tabloids were filled with graphic accounts of crime, perversion, and lust. Motion pictures were becoming ever bolder with sexual themes, "culminating in Mae West's frank and unashamed *She Done Him Wrong*." In theatres, one could see presentations such as *Mourning Becomes Electra*. Even if *Ulysses* had been obscene by the standards of the previous decade, changing social values had shifted moral standards to a more permissive plane. Ernst and Lindey were asking the federal court to acknowledge the change.

Their second contention was related to the first: according to legal definitions of obscenity laid down by various courts, *Ulysses* was not an obscene book. For years obscenity had been defined by the rule set down in a nineteenth-century English case, *Regina* v. *Hicklin*, as anything that might "deprave and corrupt those whose minds are open to such immoral influences."[23] Strictly adhered to, the *Hicklin* standard reduced all literature to a level suitable for children.

The third point contained perhaps the strongest argument. The tariff act of 1930 allowed the Secretary of the Treasury to admit, for noncommercial purposes, books that might otherwise be prohibited, if they were classics or of recognized literary merit. In June, Lindey had petitioned the Treasury Department to admit a copy of *Ulysses*, maintaining that Joyce's reputation and the universal acclaim accorded the novel justified its designation as a classic. In reply, the Acting Commissioner of Customs ruled that *Ulysses* was "of sufficient literary merit to be entitled to release under the Secretary's discretionary authority."[24] The Treasury ruling placed the government in an embarrassing position. The prosecutors had brought obscenity charges against the book on behalf of United States Customs, which now, in the name of the Secretary of the Treasury, had declared the work a classic.

Fourth, the lawyers for the novel argued that the intention and construction of *Ulysses* were antithetical to the purposes of obscenity. The book lacked illustrations, for example, which could appeal to the vulgar mind. Pornography almost always was published anonymously, but *Ulysses* had carried from the first the name of its author. Even the length of the book was a factor working against assigning the label of obscenity, for *Ulysses* was over seven hundred pages, with the first sexual passages many pages into the work. Calling attention to the replies the lawyers had received from literary figures and librarians, point five informed the court that *Ulysses* had gained broad acceptance in the community of letters.

In their final section the defense lawyers maintained that a book had to be judged "as a whole" and according to its "general purpose and effect." Excerpts out of context were not fair representations of a book's character, and in any event, literary merit overrode occasional obscene expressions. It was true, they admitted, that the book employed "a few Anglo-Saxon words" to represent human organs and functions, but these did not make it obscene. Sex was in the book, but it was only an "insignificant fraction" of the work, for this was a novel of the mind occupied with the "vagaries of consciousness." Although *Ulysses* was too formidable for most readers, it was a classic, and to declare it obscene would earn the derision of future generations, unjustly categorize a work of art as pornography, and degrade the law "under the pretense of asserting it."

After submitting the brief, the attorneys waited for Woolsey and the government lawyers to read it before arranging for oral argument. Weeks passed, but then Lindey discovered that District Attorney Coleman had been putting off an appearance before the judge. Coleman may have been irritated with the defense lawyers for seeking the Secretary of the Treasury's permission to import the book after charges had been brought against it. Whatever the reason, Lindey complained to Ernst that he was "thoroughly sick and tired" of Coleman's excuses and suggested that they press Woolsey to set a date for the hearing. When several more days went by without action, Ernst wrote the judge to remind him that he had been holding the book and the original motion since August. Before that, he noted, *Ulysses* had been held by the government for more than a year. He urged him to end the delays and set a date for the hearing. Pressed by Ernst, Woolsey scheduled the hearing for November 25.[25]

The oral arguments on *Ulysses* took place in no ordinary courtroom, but in the plush accommodations of the New York City Bar Association Building. Interested spectators, including Cerf, John S. Sumner of the New York Society for the Suppression of Vice, and Ernst's wife, Margaret, crowded the room. Mrs. Ernst's presence disturbed prosecutor Coleman. He confided to Ernst that he had planned to read aloud some obscene passages from the book, but now felt too embarrassed to do so.[26]

There is no official record of the proceedings, but according to newspaper accounts, Coleman opened by asking the court not to think of him as a "puritanical censor" because he argued that *Ulysses* was obscene. He conceded the novel's literary importance, but believed that sexual references and questionable language were so woven into its texture that they could not be removed "without destroying essential values of the book."[27] Since the hearing was informal, Judge Woolsey talked freely from the bench. Lighting a cigarette, he declared that it was not an easy case to decide. He was totally against censorship because he believed that "things ought to take their chances in the market place" and because he knew that "as soon as you suppress anything the bootlegger goes to work." Nonetheless, parts of *Ulysses* perplexed him and made him question his attitude against censorship. The courtroom broke into laughter when Woolsey expressed "shocking surprise" that he "perfectly understood" the passages of the book charged obscene by the prosecution. Woolsey briefly laughed too, but then added, "Parts of it are pretty rough, really, but other parts are swell. There are passages of moving literary beauty, passages of worth and power." The book left him "bothered, stirred, and troubled." Ernst seized the opening: "That is exactly the effect of *Ulysses*. You have not used the adjectives 'shocked' or 'revolted'."[28]

Woolsey, Ernst, and Coleman also discussed various definitions of obscenity. Woolsey said that one standard defined an obscene work as one in which the "primary purpose is to excite sexual feeling." Coleman retorted that he did not think obscenity should be so narrowly construed. People could read something and feel it was obscene without feeling sexual excitation. A work could be called obscene according to the "ordinary language used and by what it does to the average reader." Ernst disagreed. He had studied the language, he said, and had not seen a single instance in which it could be proven that reading a book led to a crime of passion. But what about the effect that reading the soliloquy of Molly Bloom might have on a young woman? Woolsey asked. "I don't think that is the standard we should go by," replied Ernst.[29]

During the hearing Woolsey commented on the length and difficulty of *Ulysses*, and Coleman pointed out that many literate people had been unable to finish reading the novel. The judge then asked Ernst if he had read the entire book. Behind the question Ernst sensed the implication that there would be little harm in suppressing a book that appealed to few people. Seized by inspiration, he decided to meet this challenge with a graphic demonstration of stream of consciousness technique. A decade before, he said, he had attempted to read *Ulysses*, but he had found it too difficult. Over the summer, while preparing for the trial, he was again struggling through it at his Nantucket summer home when he was invited to speak at a local church. While talking to the assembly, he said, he realized that he was also thinking on another level of consciousness in which he was reflecting about the domed ceiling of the building, a baby in the audience, and a clock at the back of the room. After his speech, he went back to his reading of *Ulysses* with a new appreciation of Joyce's technique. "And now, your Honor, while arguing to win this case I thought I was intent only on this book, but frankly, while pleading before you, I've also been thinking about that ring around your tie, how your gown does not fit too well on your shoulders, and the picture of George Washington back of your bench." Woolsey responded, "I must confess that while listening to you, I've also been thinking about that Hepplewhite chair behind you." "Judge," Ernst said, "that's the book."[30] With that exchange the court appearance of *Ulysses* came to a close.

On December 6, 1933, Woolsey announced his decision.[31] In a censorship case, the judge said, the first thing to determine was whether the intent of the work was pornographic, "that is, written for the purpose of exploiting obscenity." After reading all of *Ulysses* once, and reading through some passages several times, he had concluded that the novel did not contain the "leer of the sensualist." In Woolsey's view, deciding that *Ulysses* was not pornography did not resolve the case. It remained necessary, for one thing, to discover the author's purpose for using indecent language and images. Woolsey believed that Joyce intended "to show how the screen of consciousness with its ever shifting kaleidoscopic impressions carries, as it were on a plastic palimpsest, not only what is in the focus of each man's observation of the actual things about him, but also in a penumbral zone residua of past impressions, some recent and some drawn up by association from the domain of the subconscious." Such a complex goal brought about two major qualities of the book—its obscurity and its psychological honesty. Of the two, the honesty of the author in revealing his characters' inner thoughts had led to attacks on his book because he necessarily employed certain unsavory words and developed characters who were preoccupied with sex. In Woolsey's view, the objectionable words and episodes were necessary to the book's purpose. He therefore agreed with the defense that verbal and thematic taboos could be overlooked in the proper context.

There remained the problem of determining what effect the book had on its readers. Even if *Ulysses* did not intentionally exploit sex, it could be declared legally obscene if it produced "sexually impure and lustful thoughts." Woolsey rejected the *Hicklin* rule, which judged material by its effect on the most susceptible portion of the population. Instead, he said, the proper standard should be the effect a work had on "a person with average sex instincts." Comparable to the hypothetical "reasonable man" in the law of torts, the "average man" concept provided a middle way in obscenity law between prudery and debauchery. By that standard, *Ulysses* might prove too strong for sensitive persons, but for the average person it was not an aphrodisiac. Considered in its entirety, *Ulysses* was not obscene and was therefore allowed entry into the United States, even for commercial purposes.

As soon as Woolsey announced his decision, Cerf's partner in Random House, Donald Klopfer, telephoned the news to their printers. They had been ready for weeks, and within five minutes the book was in production.[32] In a press conference Cerf declared that the decision was one of the most important ever delivered "from the standpoint of literature and freedom of speech," while an ecstatic Ernst announced that the verdict had "thrust back the narrow frontiers fixed by prudery." Even District Attorney Samuel Coleman praised the decision, adding that he would not recommend a government appeal of the ruling. In Paris, James Joyce pronounced himself pleased. Aside from the vindication, Joyce needed the income.[33]

Beyond the circle of those intimately involved with the case, enthusiasm waned. The *New York Times* reported the results with the remark that interest in the novel would decline now that it no longer offered the romance of illegality. The *Herald-Tribune* approved the decision, calling it a "substantial victory for proportion, common sense and legal flexibility," but the paper added that Ernst overstated the importance of the case.[34]

Was the *Ulysses* decision a milestone in obscenity law? Legal scholars tend to confirm Ernst's opinion. In an interpretive article in the *Minnesota Law Review*, William B. Lockhart and Robert C. McClure describe the decision as a "major attack on the *Hicklin* rule."[35] James C.N. Paul and Murray L. Schwartz maintain that the *Ulysses* opinion "formulated new law designed to explain why such books were not now to be confiscated."[36] Others have challenged that perspective. Eric Larrabee points out that the ruling has fostered the "flattering illusion (for lawyers) that society takes its erotic cues from the bench," an illusion which ignores the assault waged against social prudery for a decade before the *Ulysses* decision.[37] Social and intellectual historian Paul S. Boyer also questions the view that *Ulysses* was a judicial landmark. Boyer calls attention to the increasing literary acceptance of the novel over the decade before the court fight and describes the rise of the "brash publishing generation of the 1920s," which tested the limits of censorship. The *Ulysses* decision, he feels, "only confirmed a change in popular attitudes and standards."[38] These counsels of moderation are correct, but it is important to note that in the tradition-bound legal world, the decision did represent, if not a revolution, at least a substantial development.

Ernst had borrowed arguments from earlier cases, but he used them in a bolder manner than those who preceded him. For Woolsey, the *Ulysses* decision required breaking new legal ground. His ruling had ended a decade of proscription against *Ulysses*. In doing so he advanced three important guidelines for obscenity law. A literary work, he declared, ought to be judged (1) as a whole rather than from isolated passages, (2) for its effect on the average man rather than on the most susceptible portions of the population, and (3) according to the contemporary standards of the community. All of these ideas drew upon the past, but they were given new importance in the *Ulysses* decision by virtue of the widespread publicity attending the case. It was America's first great obscenity trial.[39]

---

First appeared in *Library Chronicle*, 20/21 [1982].

# Notes

1. From 1961 to 1970 HRC received through gift and purchase the personal papers, legal archives, and a portion of the private library of Morris L. Ernst. The Ernst archives are housed in 640 manuscript boxes, folders, and bound volumes, and in addition to voluminous correspondence, there are trial transcripts, briefs, and legal papers dealing with various public movements with which Ernst was involved, including abortion and conception-control rights, censorship, and the right to privacy. Materials on the *Ulysses* case fill sixteen folders and total over 600 pieces of legal briefs, memoranda, and correspondence.

2. Paul S. Boyer, *Purity in Print: The Vice-Society Movement and Book Censorship in America* (New York: Charles Scribner's Sons, 1968), p. 255. On Cerf's early career see his autobiography, *At Random: The Reminiscences of Bennett Cerf* (New York: Random House, 1977), pp. 20-67.

3. Fred Rodell, "Morris Ernst, New York's Unlawyerlike Liberal Lawyer Is the Censor's Enemy, the President's Friend," *Life* 16 (February 21, 1944): 96-98 and passim.

4. Boyer, *Purity in Print*, pp. 146-48; Morris L. Ernst and William Seagle, *To the Pure . . . A Study of Obscenity and the Censor* (New York: Viking Press, 1928); *People* v. *Friede*, 133 Magistrate's Court of New York, 611 (1929); *U.S.* v. *Dennett*, 39 F. 2d, 2d Circuit Court of Appeals, 564 (1930); *U.S.* v. *Married Love*, 48 F. 2d, Southern District of New York Court, 821 (1931).

5. Letter from Lindey to Ernst, August 6, 1931, Box 270, Morris L. Ernst Papers, the Humanities Research Center, The University of Texas at Austin (hereafter cited as Ernst Papers-HRC).

6. Margaret Anderson, *My Thirty Years' War* (New York: Covici, Friede, 1930), pp. 212-30; Jackson R. Bryer, "Joyce, *Ulysses*, and the *Little Review*," *South Atlantic Quarterly* 66 (spring 1967): 148-64.

7. Herbert Gorman, *James Joyce* (New York: Octagon Books, 1974), pp. 306-13. One of the world's more interesting characters, Roth went on to a career as a soft-core pornographer, for which he served several jail terms. From his activities came the Supreme Court's major obscenity ruling, *Roth* v. *U.S.*, 354 U.S. 476 (1957). On Roth, see Leo Hamalian, "Nobody Knows My Names: Samuel Roth and the Underside of American Letters," *Journal of Modern Literature* 3 (April 1974): 889-921; and Robert Antrim, "Sam Roth, Prometheus of the Unprintable," *Eros* 1 (autumn 1962): 24-27.

8. Cerf, *At Random*, pp. 90-92; letter from Cerf to Ernst, March 23, 1932, Box 269, Ernst Papers-HRC.

9. United States Statutes at Large, Vol. XLVI, Part 1, Title III, pp. 688-89.

10. Letter from Cerf to Lindey, April 27, 1932, Box 270; letter from Lindey to Collector of Customs, May 2, 1932, Box 270. Ernst Papers-HRC. See also Cerf, *At Random*, pp. 92-93.

11. Letter from H. C. Stewart (Assistant Collector of Customs) to Lindey, May 13, 1932, Box 270; letter from Lindey to Stewart, May 17, 1932, Box 270; letter from Lindey to Ernst, June 1932, Box 270; letter from Lindey to Ernst, July 30, 1932, Box 270. Ernst Papers-HRC.

12. Undated Proposed Letter to Authors, Critics, Clergymen, Sociologists, Etc., Box 93; Questionnaire to Librarians, April 21, 1932, Box 270. Ernst Papers-HRC.

13. For a reference to Dos Passos's remarks and Lindey's objection, see Lindey to Cerf, May 20, 1932, Box 270, and Cerf to Lindey, June 13, 1932, Box 270. Ernst Papers-HRC.

14. The librarian's comments are in Box 269. Ernst Papers-HRC.

15. Letter from Cerf to Lindey, June 20, 1932, Box 270. Ernst Papers-HRC.

16. Letter from Ernst to [Lindey?], September 27, 1932, Box 270. Ernst Papers-HRC.

17. "United States of America, Libellant, Against One Book Entitled 'Ulysses' by James Joyce," December 9, 1932, and ". . . Claimant's Answer," December 9, 1932. Ernst Papers-HRC.

18. Ernst file memoranda, August 12 and November 11, 1932, Box 270. Ernst Papers-HRC. See also *New York Times*, March 11, 1934.

19. Letter from Lindey to Ernst, January 4, 1933, Box 270; letter from Lindey to Ernst, July 25, 1933, Box 270; letter from Ernst to Jonas Shapiro, August 25, 1933, Box 270. Ernst Papers-HRC.

20. Lindey to Ernst, January 4, 1933, Box 270. Ernst Papers-HRC.

21. "Claimant's Memorandum in Support of Motion to Dismiss Libel," Box 269. Ernst Papers-HRC.

22. *U.S.* v. *Kennerley*, 209 F. 119 (1913).

23. *Regina* v. *Hicklin*, 3 Queen's Bench 360 (1868). The case involved an anti-Catholic pamphlet entitled "The Confessional Unmasked; shewing the depravity of the Romish priesthood, the iniquity of the Confessional, and the questions put to females in Confession."

24. "Petition for Release and Admission of Book into the United States on the Ground That It Is a Classic," [June 1, 1933], Box 93; Frank Dow to Collector of New York, June 16, 1933, Box 93. Ernst Papers-HRC.

25. Lindey to Ernst, November 6, 1933, Box 270; Ernst to Woolsey, November 14, 1933, Box 93; Lindey to Ernst, November 24, 1933, Box 269. Ernst Papers-HRC.

26. Morris L. Ernst, "Reflections on the *Ulysses* Trial and Censorship," *James Joyce Quarterly* 3 (fall 1965): 3-11; Morris L. Ernst, *The Best Is Yet . . .* (New York: Harper, 1945), pp. 115-16.

27. *New York Herald-Tribune*, November 26, 1933.

28. Ibid.

29. Ibid.

30. Ernst, *The Best Is Yet*, pp. 116-17.

31. *U.S.* v. *Ulysses*, 5 F. Supp. 182 (1933).

32. "Planning the Random House 'Ulysses'," *Linotype News* (February 1934); *New York World-Telegram*, January 25, 1934; Boyer, *Purity in Print*, p. 256.

33. *New York Herald-Tribune*, December 7, 1933; Ernst, "Statement," n.d., Box 270. Ernst Papers-HRC. See also Richard Ellmann, *James Joyce* (New York: Oxford University Press, 1959), pp. 677-79.

34. *New York Times*, December 8, 1933; *New York Herald-Tribune*, December 8, 1933.

35. William B. Lockhart and Robert C. McClure, "Literature, the Law of Obscenity, and the Constitution," *Minnesota Law Review* 38 (1954): 327.

36. James C. N. Paul and Murray L. Schwartz, *Federal Censorship: Obscenity in the Mail* (New York: Free Press of Glencoe, 1961), p. 64.

37. Eric Larrabee, "The Cultural Contest of Sex Censorship," *Law and Contemporary Problems* 20 (autumn 1955): 675.

38. Boyer, *Purity in Print*, pp. 254-55, 259.

39. Woolsey's decision did not end efforts to ban *Ulysses*. In December 1933 the government named Martin Conboy, a lawyer formerly associated with the New York Society for the Suppression of Vice, as United States Attorney for the Southern District of New York. Conboy filed an appeal against Woolsey's ruling, but on August 7, 1934, the Circuit Court upheld the earlier decision.

[Commentary 18]

# A Statement by Donald S. Klopfer

Bennett was going to Europe in early 1933 and was going to see James Joyce while in Paris. Both of us had met Joyce several times when we were in Paris—usually through Sylvia Beach. Bennett suggested to Joyce that he pay him a small advance, I think it was $2,500, if he would give us U.S. rights to *Ulysses*, providing we could legalize its publication. The advance was not returnable if we failed in the courts. Joyce was delighted to receive the money, so we signed a contract. We mailed a copy in, thinking it would be seized by the Customs but it came through unscathed. So we had a friend bring a copy in and we went down to the dock to welcome him! The Customs man saw the book and didn't want to do anything about it, but we insisted and got his superior over, and finally they took the book and wouldn't allow us to bring it into the U.S. because it was both obscene and sacrilegious. From that came the case of the government of the U.S. against one copy of *Ulysses*. We got Morris Ernst to defend the book, and Judge John A. Woolsey was the judge before whom it was tried. The trial was held in the Bar Association Building on 43rd Street in a large oval room on the top floor of the building. It was June, 1933, hotter than hell with no air conditioning at that time. The Judge told us to take off our jackets, smoke if we wanted to—and the trial was underway! The U.S. Attorney, Morris Ernst, and the Judge had a three-cornered conversation that lasted until the afternoon. There was no legal nonsense. Both sides seemed intent to get at justice, which doesn't happen very often in trials where I've been a juror. Both Bennett and I felt we were getting a fair shake. The Judge said he'd read the book over the summer and render his opinion in September, and he did just that. We used his opinion as an introduction to the published volume so that it would always be in evidence when the censors tried to attack it. It worked!

September 14, 1983.

# DOCUMENTS

[Doc. 1]

GREENBAUM, WOLFF & ERNST

OFFICE MEMORANDUM

TO: M.L.E.  FROM: A.L.
RE: *Ulysses*  DATE: August 6, 1931.

I have just had quite a lengthy interview with Mrs. Beach Denis, the married sister of Sylvia Beach, who is the Paris publisher of Joyce's *Ulysses*. I learned the following:

1. Sylvia Beach operates a book shop under the name of Shakespeare and Company, at 12 Rue de L'Odeon 12, Paris.

Mrs. Denis tells me that her sister has the sole and exclusive world rights with respect to *Ulysses* and that she has not authorized any publication either in England or in America.

2. Sylvia Beach is tremendously interested in the legalization of *Ulysses* and would be glad to cooperate in every respect if a responsible American publisher could be found.

3. Joyce offered his forthcoming work entitled *Work in Progress* to Sylvia Beach for publication but she is essentially a bookseller and is quite unselfishly interested in Joyce's welfare; and she felt that a regular publisher would be in a much better position to get Joyce the circulation that he deserves. *Work in Progress* therefore will be published by the Viking Press in this country. Mrs. Denis, however, made it quite clear that the Viking Press has no rights whatever in *Ulysses*.

By reason of the connection of Guinzburg and Schwabacher with the Viking Press I realize that you would not be very anxious to see *Ulysses* sponsored by them. Mrs. Denis suggests that I write to her sister and tell her what we propose to do. I don't see any point in this until we line up some American publisher who is willing to undertake publication upon getting the American rights from Sylvia Beach.

I still feel very keenly that this would be the grandest obscenity case in the history of law and literature, and I am ready to do anything in the world to get it started. What do you suggest? By the way, I have stocked in a few copies of the book.

[The following lines appear to be a comment by Ernst.—ED.]

Tell Mrs. Denis that I want to see her when I come down. Leave her address on my desk. I am sure I can get a good publisher.

Be sure not to knock Viking to her. It will get back.

---

[Doc. 2]

GREENBAUM, WOLFF & ERNST

**OFFICE MEMORANDUM**

TO: M.L.E.     FROM: A.L.
RE: *Ulysses*     DATE: August 11, 1931.

I have noted your comments. Mrs. Beach Denis lives in California and was in the city only for a visit. She left on August 6th. We can get in touch with her through the Gotham Book Mart. I did not knock Viking, so you need feel no apprehension.

---

[Doc. 3]

GREENBAUM, WOLFF & ERNST

**OFFICE MEMORANDUM**

TO: M.L.E.     FROM: A.L.
RE: *Ulysses*     DATE: August 13, 1931.

In the book you gave me, called *Censorship and Other Papers* by Bowerman, the librarian, there is a reference to James Joyce, and particularly to an article on Joyce by Edmund Wilson in the *New Republic*. I have just dug up the article from my clipping files and I am sending it to you herewith. [See Doc. 4.—ED.] It is a splendid critical evaluation of Joyce's work. Please return.

[Doc. 4]
[This is an enclosure to Doc. 3.—ED.]

THE NEW REPUBLIC                                             December 18, 1929.

## James Joyce

JAMES JOYCE's first work of fiction, the volume of short stories *Dubliners*, was to have been brought out by a Dublin publisher in 1907, but on account of disrespectful references to Edward VII, on the part of one of the characters in the story called "Ivy Day in the Committee Room," the book was suppressed by the British government, and did not appear until seven years later, when it was published in London. *A Portrait of the Artist as a Young Man* was published first in New York in 1914. Neither of these books had much in common with the English fiction then being written: the typical novelists of that time were H.G. Wells and Arnold Bennett, and Joyce was not in the least like either. In their recent literary renaissance, the Irish had been closer to the Continent than to London; and James Joyce, like George Moore, was working in the tradition, not of English, but of French fiction. *Dubliners* was French in its objectivity, its sobriety and its irony, at the same time that it ran with a music and a grace quite distinct from the mordancy and dryness of Flaubert and Maupassant. And *A Portrait of the Artist as a Young Man*, coming at a time when the public was surfeited with the early histories of sensitive young men—the Edward Ponderevos, the Clayhangers, the Jacob Stahls, the Michael Fanes—had the effect of making most of these books look psychologically superficial and artistically shoddy.

*Ulysses* was published in Paris in 1922. It had originally been conceived as a short story for *Dubliners*, and was to have been called "Mr. Bloom's Day in Dublin," or something of the sort. But this idea was afterwards combined with the further history of Stephen Dedalus, the hero of the autobiographical *Portrait of the Artist as a Young Man*. *Ulysses*, however, in its final form as a volume of seven hundred-odd large pages, took shape as something entirely different from either of Joyce's early books, and it must be approached from a different point of view. The key to *Ulysses* is in the title—and this key is indispensable, if we are to understand what Joyce is really about. Ulysses, as he figures in the *Odyssey*, is a sort of type of the ordinary Greek; among the heroes, he is distinguished for cunning rather than for exalted wisdom, and for common sense, quickness and nerve rather than for the passionate bravery of, say, an Achilles, or for the steadfastness and stoutness of, say, a Hector. The *Odyssey* exhibits such a man in practically every situation and relation of an ordinary human life—Ulysses, in the course of his wanderings, runs the whole gauntlet of temptations and dangers, and by his wits he escapes from them all, to return at last to his family and his home and to reassert himself there as master. Furthermore, the *Odyssey*, by reason of the effectiveness, the strange apparent sophistication, of its form—the wanderings of Ulysses themselves framed between the introductory group of books, in which our interest in Ulysses is aroused by Telemachus' search for his lost father, and the concluding books which describe Ulysses' return home—offers a particularly attractive model for a modern writer attempting an epic.

Now Joyce, in *Ulysses*, has composed a new *Odyssey*, which in form and subject follows closely the classical one; and the significance of the characters and incidents of his ostensibly naturalistic narrative cannot properly be understood without reference to the Homeric poem. Joyce's Telemachus of the opening books is Stephen Dedalus—that is, Joyce himself. The Dedaluses, as we have already learned from *A Portrait of the Artist as a Young Man*, are a shabby-genteel family living in Dublin. Stephen's father, Simon Dedalus, has run through a great variety of employments to end up as nothing in particular, a drinker, a decayed sport, an amateur tenor, a well-known character of the bars. But Stephen has been given a good education at a Jesuit college, and, at the end of the earlier novel, is about to leave for France to follow a literary career. At the beginning of *Ulysses* he has just been brought back from Paris to Dublin, by a telegram that his mother is dying. And with Mrs. Dedalus' death, the family, already reduced to poverty, becomes completely demoralized and disintegrated. While Stephen's young sisters and brothers have hardly enough to eat, Simon Dedalus makes the rounds of the pubs, spending on drink what little money he can get. Stephen, who has always resented his father, feels now that, in effect, he has none. He is more isolated in Dublin than ever. He is Telemachus in search of a Ulysses. His friend, the medical student, Buck Mulligan, with whom he is living in an old tower on the coast and who believes himself to share Stephen's artistic tastes and intellectual interests, really patronizes him unremittingly and turns to ridicule his abilities and ambitions. He is Antinous, that boldest of Penelope's suitors, who tries to make himself master of Ulysses' house in his absence and who mocks Telemachus. Stephen has announced at the end of the earlier book that he is going forth "to forge in the smithy of my soul the uncreated conscience of my race"; and now he has returned to Dublin baffled and disinherited—his life with Mulligan is dissolute and unproductive. Yet, as Telemachus finds friends and helpers, so Stephen is reminded by the old woman, who brings the milk for breakfast in the tower of that Ireland whose uncreated conscience it is still his destiny to forge: "old and secret. . . maybe a messenger." She is Athene in the guise of Mentor who provides Telemachus with his ship; and the memory of Kevin Egan, an Irish exile in Paris, is the Menelaus who speeds him on his way.

The scene now shifts, as it does in the *Odyssey*, to the lost Ulysses himself. Joyce's Ulysses is a Dublin Jew, an advertisement canvasser named Bloom.

Like Stephen, he dwells among aliens: a Jew, the son of a Hungarian father, he is still something of a foreigner among the Irish; a man of genuine, though mediocre, intelligence and sensibility, he has little in common with the other inhabitants of the lower middle-class world in which he lives. He has been married for many years to an Irishwoman, the buxom daughter of an army officer, a professional singer, of prodigious sexual appetite, who has been continually and indiscriminately unfaithful to him. They have had one daughter, who is already growing up and apparently going the way of her mother; and one son, of whom Bloom had hoped that he might resemble, that he might refine upon himself, but who died eleven days after he was born. Things have never been the same between the Blooms since the death of this son; it is now more than ten years since Bloom has attempted complete intercourse with his wife—it is as if the birth of the sickly Rudy had discouraged him and made him doubt his virility. He is aware that his wife has lovers; but he does not complain or try to interfere—he is even resigned to her accepting money from them. He is a Ulysses with no Telemachus and cut off from his Penelope.

We now follow Bloom's adventures on the day of June 16, 1904 (the whole novel takes place in a day). Lotus-eaters allure him; Laestrygonians affright him. He assists at the burial of an Elpenor and descends with him in imagination to the underworld; he suffers from the varying favor of an Aeolus. He escapes by ruse from the ferocity of a Cyclops, as he disengages himself through prudence from the girlish charms of a Nausicaa. And he emerges a man again from the brothel of a Circe who had transformed him into a swine.

The comings and goings of Stephen during the day are woven in and out among the wanderings of Bloom: they encounter each other twice but do not recognize one another. Both men, we become aware, are constantly accompanied and oppressed by ideas which they have tried to dismiss from their minds: the family situation of each is the background of all he does that day. In Stephen's case, his mother, who has just died, had begged him on her deathbed to kneel down and pray for her and, in rebellion against the Catholic education which has disciplined and maimed his spirit, jealous of the independence he has won and in fear of the past to which he has returned, he has implacably refused, and has allowed her to die without the comforting belief that her son has repented of his apostasy. But now that she is dead, this memory tortures him. He has, in the early morning, reproached Mulligan—accusing really himself—for some remark of the latter's about his mother, which Stephen has overheard and resented; and, as he has looked out upon the morning sea, the pathos and horror of her life have become vivid to him—he is dragged back to relive all that she has suffered. Then, "No, mother!" he cries within himself, as he thrusts her memory down out of his mind, "let me be and let me live!" But through his whole aimless and desperate day, it is his helpless feeling of guilt toward his mother, his hopeless conviction of being deprived of a father, which govern all his movements and thoughts. When he teaches school, he brings the class to a close by an hysterical joke about "the fox burying his grandmother under a hollybush," and in a stupid boy who cannot do his sums, he can see now only his own graceless youth which his mother had shielded from the world. After school, he has gone to walk on the beach and has contemplated paying a visit to the family of his maternal uncle, whom he despises, as if he could do penance in this way for his hardness and somehow make it up to his mother by kindness to her wretched relatives; but again that counter impulse which had proved too strong on the former occasion comes into play to block his intention: he thinks of other things and walks beyond where he should have turned. The artist still opposes the son: he sets out to compose a poem, but the poem itself breaks down, and he is left gazing at a silent homing ship. At the library, later in the day, he becomes involved in a long, pretentious lecture on the relation of Shakespeare to his father—a lecture which has little to do with Shakespeare, but a great deal to do with Dedalus.

Now Bloom also is haunted by the situation which he has left behind him at home. At breakfast, his wife has received a letter from Blazes Boylan, a flashy buck about town, who is to manage her coming concert tour. Bloom suspects—and rightly suspects—that Molly is having an affair with him—that he is coming to see her that afternoon. All day he has to change the subject when Boylan's name is mentioned—all day he avoids meeting him in the street. In the afternoon while Bloom is eating at the Ormond Hotel, Boylan comes into the bar, gets a drink and sets off to call on Mrs. Bloom, and when he has gone, Bloom hears the other men laugh about Molly's easy favors. And the conversation later on in the pub, about Boylan's having won money in a boxing match—in spite of Bloom's efforts to induce the company to talk about tennis instead—is one of the incidents which give rise to the antagonism between Bloom and the rest of the company, and eventually to the quarrel between the Cyclops-Citizen and Bloom. At the end of the Nausicaa episode, the cuckoo-clock in the priest's house tells Bloom that he is now a cuckold.

In the evening, Bloom goes to a maternity hospital to inquire after the wife of a friend, who has been having a hard delivery: there he meets and recognizes Stephen, who is drinking with the medical students. In the *Odyssey*, the final shipwreck of Ulysses and his subsequent misfortunes are the result of the impiety of his companions, who, in defiance of all his warnings, have killed and eaten the Oxen of the Sun. So Bloom is pained by the impiety of the medical students as they joke obscenely about childbirth and maternity. On Stephen's part, it is particularly shocking because his own mother has just died, but his own feeling of guilt in this connection makes him particularly blasphemous and brutal. Yet Bloom has himself offended against the principle of fertility in his recent prolonged neglect of Molly: the Calypso who has detained him since his shipwreck is the nymph who hangs in his bedroom, and, whom he makes the subject of amorous fantasies. It is his offense against the principle of fertility which—at the hour when Mrs. Bloom is entertaining Boylan—has landed him on the Phaeacian strand indulging in further amorous fantasies in connection with little Gerty MacDowell, the Nausicaa of the Dublin beach.

When Mrs. Purefoy's child has finally been born, the party rushes out to a public house; and, later on—after a drunken altercation between Dedalus and Buck Mulligan at the station, in which Antinous and Telemachus apparently dispute over the key to the tower and Telemachus goes away homeless— Bloom and Stephen, now deserted by all but one of their former companions, proceed to a brothel. Both, by this time, are pretty drunk—though Bloom, with his invincible prudence, is not so drunk as Stephen. And in their drunkenness, in the sordid gaslight and to the tune of the mechanical piano of the brothel, their respective preoccupations emerge fully for the first time since the morning into their conscious minds. Bloom beholds himself, in a hideous vision, submitting abjectly to being cuckolded by Boylan, the laughing-stock of all the world; and there rises suddenly, in Stephen's imagination, the figure of his mother come back from the grave, reminding him of her love and imploring him to pray for her soul. But again he will not, cannot, acquiesce; in a desperate drunken gesture, intolerably torn by his conflict of impulses, by his emotions which block one another, he lifts his stick and smashes the chandelier, then rushes out into the street, where he gets into a quarrel with two English Tommies and is knocked down by one of them. Bloom has followed and, as he bends over Stephen, beholds a sudden apparition of his own son, little Rudy, who has died, as Bloom would have had him live to be—such a youth as Stephen Dedalus, learned, cultivated, sensitive, he would have had his own Rudy become. Ulysses and Telemachus are united.

Bloom picks Stephen up and takes him first to a coffee-stand, then home to his own house. He tries to talk to him of the arts and sciences, of the general ideas which interest him; but Stephen is morose and exhausted and makes little response. Bloom begs him to spend the night—to come and live with them, but Stephen declines and presently leaves. Bloom goes up, goes to bed with Molly, describes to her his adventures, and soon drops off to sleep. But Bloom's encounter with Stephen is to affect both Stephen's life and the relations between the Blooms. To have rescued and talked with Stephen has somehow restored Bloom's self-respect; a habit in which he has acquiesced in the past has been to cook Molly's breakfast for her and to bring it to her in bed, but tonight he tells her that he expects her to get breakfast next morning herself and to bring it up to him. This amazes and disconcerts Mrs. Bloom, and the rest of the book is the record of her meditations as she lies awake thinking about the conversation. She has been mystified by Bloom's recent behavior, and her attitude toward him now is at first a mixture of jealousy and resentment. She congratulates herself upon the fact that she does not have to depend on him, that her needs are ably supplied by Blazes Boylan. But as she begins to ruminate on the possibility of Stephen's coming to live with them, the idea of Blazes Boylan's coarseness becomes intolerable to her: the thought of Stephen has made her fastidious, and, full of tenderness, she prefigures a relation between them of an ambiguous but intimate character, half amorous, half maternal. But it is Bloom himself who has primarily been the cause of this readjustment in Molly's mind: in telling her about Stephen, he has imposed upon her his own values; in staying away from the house all day, coming back very late at night and asking for his breakfast in bed, he has reasserted his own will. And she goes back in her mind over her experience of him—their courtship, their married life together. She sees again how, when she had promised to marry him, it had been his intelligence and his sympathetic nature—that touch of imagination which he possessed and which distinguished him from other men—which had influenced her in his favor—"because he understood or felt what a woman is and I knew I could always get around him." It is in the mind of his Penelope that this Ulysses has slain the suitors who have disputed his place. As for Stephen, unresponsive as he has been to Bloom's interest and cordiality, he has at last found in Dublin someone sufficiently sympathetic to himself to give him a subject by which to enter artistically into the common life of his race. It is possible that Bloom, as a result of his meeting with Stephen, will resume normal marital relations with Molly; but it is certain that Stephen, as a result of this meeting, will go away and write *Ulysses*. He has told Mulligan that he is going "to write something in ten years": that was in 1904—*Ulysses* is dated at the end as having been begun in 1914.

II

This is the story of *Ulysses* in the light of its Homeric parallel, but to describe it in such a way gives no idea of what the book is really like—of its psychological and technical discoveries or of its magnificent poetry.

*Ulysses* is, I suppose, the most completely "written" novel since Flaubert. The example of the great prose poet of Naturalism has profoundly influenced Joyce—in his attitude toward the modern bourgeois world and perhaps in a contrast implied by the Homeric parallel of *Ulysses* between our own and the ancient world, as well as in an ideal of rigorous objectivity and of adaptation of style to subject—as the influence of that other great naturalistic poet, Ibsen, is obvious in Joyce's single play, *Exiles*. But Flaubert had, in general, confined himself to fitting the cadence and the phrase precisely to the mood or object described; and even then it was the phrase rather than the cadence, and the object rather than the mood, with which he was occupied—for mood and cadence in Flaubert vary little: he never embodies himself in his characters and identifies his voice with theirs, and as a result, Flaubert's own tone of the somber-pompous-ironic becomes, in the long run, a little monotonous. But Joyce has undertaken in *Ulysses* not merely to render, with the last accuracy and beauty, the actual sights and sounds among which his characters move, but to take us into their minds themselves and to find the unique vocabulary and rhythm which will represent the thoughts of each. If Flaubert taught Maupassant to look for the definitive adjective which would distinguish a given hackney-cab from every other hackney-cab in Paris, so Joyce has set himself the task of finding the dialect which will distinguish the thoughts of a given Dubliner from those of every other Dubliner. Thus the mind of Stephen Dedalus is represented by a weaving of bright poetic images and fragmentary abstractions, of things remembered from books, on a rhythm sober, melancholy and proud; that of Bloom by a rapid staccato notation, prosaic but perceptive and alert, jutting out in all directions in little ideas growing out of ideas; the thoughts of Father Conmee, the Rector of the Jesuit college, by a precise prose, perfectly colorless and orderly; those of Gerty-Nausicaa by a combination of school-girl colloquialisms with the jargon of cheap romance; and the ruminations of Mrs. Bloom by a long, unbroken rhythm of brogue, like the swell of some profound sea.

Joyce takes us thus directly into the consciousness of his characters, and in order to do so, he has availed himself of the methods of Symbolism. He has, in *Ulysses*, exploited together, as no writer had thought to do before, the resources both of Symbolism and of Naturalism. His story is naturalistically, as well as objectively, presented: it is documented to the last degree: we know exactly what his people wore, how much they paid for things, where they were at different times of the day, what popular songs they sang and what events they read of in the papers, on June 16, 1904; but when we are admitted to the mind of any one of them, we are in a world as complex and special, a world sometimes as mysterious and vague, as that of a symbolist poet—and a world described in the same sort of language. We are more at home in the minds of Joyce's characters than we are likely to be, except after some study, in the mind of a Mallarmé or an Eliot, because we know more about the circumstances in which they find themselves; but we are confronted with the same sort of confusion between emotions, perceptions and ideas, and we are likely to be disconcerted by the same hiatuses of thought, when certain links in the association of ideas are dropped down into the unconscious mind.

But Joyce has carried the methods of Symbolism further than merely to set a naturalistic scene and then, in that frame, to represent directly the minds of his different characters in symbolistic monologues. And it is the fact that he has not always stopped here which makes parts of *Ulysses* so puzzling when we read them for the first time. So long as we are dealing with internal monologues in realistic settings, we are dealing with familiar elements merely combined in a novel way—that is, instead of reading, "Bloom said to himself, 'I might manage to write a story on some proverb or other. I could sign it, Mr. and Mrs. L.M. Bloom,' " we read, "Might manage a sketch. By Mr. and Mrs. L.M. Bloom. Invent a story for some proverb which?" But as we get further along in *Ulysses*, we find the realistic setting oddly distorting itself and deliquescing, and we are astonished at the introduction of voices which seem to belong neither to the characters nor to the author.

The point is that of each of the episodes Joyce has tried to make an independent unit which shall blend the different sets of elements of each— the minds of the characters, the place where they are, the atmosphere about them, the feeling of the time of day. Joyce had already, in *A Portrait of the Artist*, experimented in making the form of each of the different sections fit the age and phase of Dedalus with which it dealt—from the infantile fragments of childhood impressions, through the ecstatic or terrified reveries of adolescence, to the self-possessed notations of young manhood. But in this book he was writing exclusively about himself, whereas in *Ulysses* he is occupied with a number of different personalities, where not Dedalus but Bloom is the center. In order to understand what Joyce is doing here, one must imagine a set of symbolistic poems which depend, not from the sensibility of the poet speaking for himself, but from an impersonal naturalistic structure. We are not likely to be prepared for this by the early episodes of *Ulysses*: they are as sober and as clear as the morning light of the Irish coast in which they take place: the characters' perceptions of the external world are usually distinct from their thoughts and feelings about them. In the newspaper office, for the first time, a general atmosphere begins to be created, beyond the specific minds of the characters, by a punctuation of the text with newspaper heads which announce the incidents in the narrative. And in the library scene, which takes place in the early afternoon, the setting and people external to Stephen begin to dissolve in Stephen's apprehension, heightened and blurred by some drinks at lunch time and by the intellectual excitement of the conversation amid the dimness and tameness of the library—"Eglinto-neyes, quick with pleasure, looked up shybrightly. Gladly glancing a merry puritan, through the twisted eglantine." Here, however, we see all through Stephen's eyes, but in the scene in the Ormond Hotel, which takes place a couple of hours later—our reveries absorb the world about us progressively as the light fades and as the impressions of the day accumulate—the sights and sounds and thoughts and feelings of the late afternoon, the laughter, the gold-and-bronze hair of the girls at the bar, the jingling of Blazes Boylan's car on his way to visit Molly Bloom, the ringing of the hoofs of the horses of the viceregal cavalcade coming in through the open window, the singing of Simon Dedalus, the sound of the piano accompaniment and the comfortable supper of Bloom—though they are not all, from beginning to end, perceived by Bloom himself—all mingle in a kind of symphony of bright sound, ringing color and declining light. The scene in the brothel, where it is night and where all the men characters are drunk, is like a slowed-up moving-picture, in which the intensified vision of reality is continually lapsing into phantasmagoric visions; and the let-down after the excitement of this, the lassitude and staleness of the scene in the cabmen's shelter where Bloom takes Stephen to get him some coffee, is rendered by a prose as weary and banal as the incidents which it reports. Joyce has achieved here, by different methods, a relativism like that of Proust: he is reproducing in literature the different aspects which things and people take on at different times and under different circumstances.

III

I do not think that Joyce has been equally successful with all these technical devices in *Ulysses*; but before it will be possible to discuss them further, we must approach the book from another point of view.

It has always been characteristic of Joyce to neglect action, narrative drama, even the direct impact on one another of characters, as we get them in the ordinary novel, for a sort of psychological portraiture. There is tremendous vitality in Joyce, but very little movement. Like Proust's novel, his work is symphonic rather than narrative. It has developments, but they are like musical developments rather than dramatic developments. The most elaborate and interesting thing in *Dubliners*—the story called "The Dead"— is simply a record of the modification brought about in the relations of a husband and wife who have come home to bed after a family party, by the husband's becoming aware from the effect produced on his wife by a song which has been sung during the evening, that she has once been loved by another man, who is now dead; *A Portrait of the Artist as a Young Man* is simply a series of pictures of the young man at successive stages of his development; the theme of "Exiles" is the modification in the relations of a husband and wife effected by the reappearance of one of the wife's old lovers. And *Ulysses*, again, for all its vast scale, is simply the story of the modification in the relations between another married couple effected by the impingement on their household of the personality of an only slightly known young man. All these stories cover a relatively brief time, and they are never carried any farther. When Joyce has explored one of these situations, when he has established the small gradual readjustment, he has done all that interests him.

All, that is, from the point of view of ordinary incident. But though Joyce almost entirely lacks appetite for violent conflict or vigorous action, he is prodigiously occupied with enriching and vitalizing his work from other points of view. Joyce's force, instead of following a line, expands itself in every dimension (including that of time!) about a single point. The world of *Ulysses* is animated by a complex inexhaustible life: we revisit it as we do a city, where we come more and more to recognize faces, to feel the force of personalities, to grasp relations, currents and interests. Joyce has exercised considerable technical ingenuity in introducing us to the elements of his story in an order which will enable us to find our bearings: yet I doubt whether any human memory is capable, on a first reading, of meeting the demands of *Ulysses*. And when we reread it, we start in at any point, as if it were indeed something solid like a city which actually existed in space and which could be entered from any direction—as Joyce is said, in composing his books, to work on the different parts simultaneously. More than any other work of fiction, unless perhaps the *Comédie Humaine*, *Ulysses* creates the illusion of a living social organism. We only see it for twenty hours, but we know its past as well as its present. We know Dublin, seen, heard, smelt and felt, brooded over, imagined, remembered.

Joyce's handling of this complex material, his method of giving his book a shape, resembles nothing else in modern fiction. The first critics of *Ulysses* mistook the novel for a "slice of life" and objected that it was too fluid or too chaotic. They did not recognize a plot because they could not recognize a progression: and the title told them nothing. It is now apparent, however, that *Ulysses* suffers from an excess of design rather than from a lack of one. Joyce has drawn up an outline of his novel, of which he has allowed certain of his commentators to avail themselves, but which he has not allowed them to publish in its entirety (though it is to be presumed that the book on *Ulysses* which Mr. Stuart Gilbert has announced will include all the information contained in it); and from this outline it appears that Joyce has set himself the task of fulfilling the requirements of a most complicated scheme—and a scheme which we could never have divined. For even if we had known about the Homeric parallel and had identified its most obvious correspondences— if we had had no difficulty in recognizing the Cyclops in the ferocious professional Fenian or Circe in the brothel-keeper or Hades in the cemetery—we should never have suspected how closely and how subtly the parallel had been followed—we should never have guessed, for example, that when Bloom passes through the National Library while Stephen is having his discussion with the literary men, he is escaping, on the one hand, a Scylla— that is, Aristotle, the rock of Dogma; and, on the other, a Charybdis—Plato, the whirlpool of Mysticism; nor that, when Stephen walks on the seashore, he is reenacting the combat with Proteus—in this case, primal matter, of whose continual transformations Stephen is reminded by the objects absorbed or washed up by the sea, but whose forms he is able to hold and fix, as the Homeric Proteus was held and vanquished, by power of the words which give him images for them. Nor should we have known that the series of phrases and onomatopoetic syllables placed at the beginning of the Sirens episode—the singing in the Ormond Hotel—and selected from the narrative which follows, are supposed to be musical themes and that the episode itself is a fugue; and though we may have felt the ironic effect of the specimens of inflated Irish journalism introduced at regular intervals in the conversation with the patriot in the pub—we should hardly have understood that these had been produced by a deliberate technique of "gigantism"—since, as the Citizen represents the Cyclops, and as the Cyclops was a giant, he must be rendered formidable by a parade of all the banalities of his patriotic claptrap swollen to gigantic proportions. We should probably never have guessed all this, and we should certainly never have guessed at the ingenuity which Joyce has expended in other ways. Not only, we learn from the outline, is there an elaborate Homeric parallel hidden in *Ulysses*, but there is an organ of the human body and a human art or science featured in every episode. We look these up, a little incredulously, but there they all are—buried and disguised beneath the realistic surface, but carefully planted, unmistakably dwelt upon. And if we are tipped off, we are able to discover, in the chapter of the Lotos-Eaters, for example, countless references to flowers; in the Laestrygonians, to eating; in the Sirens, puns on musical terms; and in Aeolus, the newspaper office, not merely many references to wind but—the art featured in this episode being Rhetoric—some hundred different figures of speech.

Now the Homeric parallel in *Ulysses* is in general pointedly and charmingly carried out and justifies itself: it does help give the story a universal significance and it enables Joyce to show us in the actions and the relations of his characters meanings which he perhaps could not indicate easily in any other way, since the characters themselves must be largely unaware of these meanings and since Joyce has adopted the strict objective method, in which the author must not comment on the action. And we may even accept the arts and sciences and the organs of the human body as making the book complete and comprehensive, if a little systematic—the whole of man's experience in a day. But when we get all these things together, and with the variety of technical devices, the result is sometimes baffling or confusing. We become aware, after we have examined the outline, that when we read *Ulysses* for the first time, it was these organs and arts and sciences and Homeric correspondences which sometimes so discouraged our attention and disappointed our enjoyment. We had been climbing over these obstacles, without knowing it, in our attempts to follow Dedalus and Bloom. If, when we read *Ulysses* through, our attention sags, our interest is balked, it is because, beneath the surface of the narrative, too many other subjects—too many different sets of subjects and too many different orders of subjects—are being proposed to our attention.

It seems to me, then, impossible not to conclude that Joyce elaborated *Ulysses* too much—that he tried to put too many things into it. What is the value of all the references to flowers in the Lotos-Eaters chapter, for example? They do not create in the Dublin streets an atmosphere of lotos-eating—they merely puzzle us, if we have not been told to look for them, to know why Joyce has chosen to have Bloom think and see certain things of which the final explanation is that they are pretexts for mentioning flowers. And do not the gigantic interpolations of the Cyclops episode defeat their object by making it impossible for us to follow the narrative itself? The interpolations are funny in themselves, the incident related is a masterpiece of language and of humor, the idea of combining them seems happy, yet the effect is mechanical and annoying: in the end we have to read the whole thing through, skipping the interpolations, in order to find out what has happened. The worst example of the capacities for failure of this too synthetic, too systematic, method seems to me the scene in the maternity hospital. I have described above what actually takes place there as I have worked it out, after several readings and in the light of Joyce's outline. The Oxen of the Sun are "Fertility"—the crime committed against them is "Fraud." But, not content with this, Joyce has been at pains to fill the episode with references to real cattle and to include a long conversation about bulls. As for the special technique, it seems to me in this case to have no real appropriateness to the situation, but to have been dictated by sheer fantastic pedantry: this technique is described as "embryonic," in conformity to the subject, maternity, and it consists of a series of parodies of English literary style from the bad Latin of the early chronicles up through Ruskin and Carlyle, the development of the language corresponding to the development of the child in the womb. Now something important takes place in this chapter—the meeting between Dedalus and Bloom—and an important point is being made about it. But we miss the point because it is all we can do to follow the narrative of the drinking party, itself rather a confused affair, through the medium of the language of the Morte d'Arthur of the seventeenth-century diarists, of the eighteenth-century novelists, and of a great many other things in which we are not at the moment prepared to be interested. If we pay attention to the parodies, we miss the story. The parodies spoil the story, and the necessity of telling the story through them has spoiled the parodies.

Joyce has as little respect as Proust for the capacities of the reader's attention; and one feels, in Joyce's case as in Proust's, that the *longueurs* which break our backs, the mechanical combinations of elements which fail to coalesce, are the result of an effort on the part of a supernormally energetic mind to compensate by piling things up for an inability to make them move.

We have now arrived in the maternity hospital, at the climactic scenes of the story, and Joyce has bogged us as he has never bogged us before. We shall forget the Oxen of the Sun in the wonderful night-town scene which follows it—but we shall be bogged afterwards worse than ever in the interminable let-down of the cabman's shelter and in the scientific question-and-answer chapter which communicates to us through the most uninviting possible medium Dedalus' conversation with Bloom. The night-town episode and Mrs. Bloom's soliloquy, which closes the book, are, of course, among the best things in it—but the proportions of the other three latter chapters, and the jarring effect of the pastiche style sandwiched in with the straight naturalistic, seem to me artistically absolutely unjustifiable. One can understand that Joyce may have intended the colorless and tiresome episodes to set off the rich and vivid ones, but not at the rate of a hundred and sixty-one pages of the former to a hundred and ninety-nine of the latter. Furthermore, Joyce has here half-buried his story under the virtuosity of his technical devices. It is almost as if he had elaborated it so much and worked over it so long that he had forgotten, in the amusement of writing parodies, the drama which he had originally intended to stage—or even as if he did not, after all, quite want us to understand the story, as if he had, in the end, thrown up between us and it a veritable fortification of solemn burlesque prose—almost as if he were shy and solicitous about it, and as if he wanted to protect it from us.

## IV

Yet, even these episodes to which I have objected contribute something to *Ulysses*. In the chapter of parodies, for example, Joyce seems to be saying to us: "Here are specimens of the sort of thing that man has written about himself in the past—how naive and how ludicrous it seems! I have shown you how he must know himself today." And in the question-and-answer chapter, which is written entirely from the point of view of science and where we are supplied with every possible astronomical, physical, statistical and biographical fact about Stephen's visit to Bloom: "This is all that the twentieth-century man thinks he knows about himself and his universe. How brittle and inadequate this reasoning seems when we apply it to Molly and Bloom!"

For one of the most important features of *Ulysses* is its interest as an investigation into the nature of human consciousness and behavior. Its importance from the point of view of psychology has never, it seems to me, been properly appreciated—though its influence on other books and, in consequence, upon our ideas about ourselves, has already been profound. Joyce has attempted to set down as comprehensively, and to render as accurately as it is possible in words to do, what our participation in life is like—or rather, what it seems to us like, as from moment to moment we live. In order to make his record complete, he has been obliged to disregard a number of conventions of literature and taste which, especially in English-speaking countries, have in modern times been pretty strictly observed, even by the writers who have aimed to be most scrupulously truthful. Joyce, in *Ulysses*, has studied the trivial, the base, the dirty elements of our lives with the relentlessness of a modern psychologist; and he has also, what the modern naturalist has seldom been poet enough for, done justice to all those elements in our lives which we have been in the habit of describing by such names as love, nobility, beauty and truth. It is curious to reflect that a number

of critics—including Arnold Bennett—should have found Joyce misanthropic. Flaubert is misanthropic, if you like—and in reproducing his
technique, Joyce sometimes suggests his acrid tone. But Stephen, Mrs. Bloom
and Bloom are certainly not unattractive people—they are even what we
should call good. Stephen and Bloom are played off a little against the duller
and meaner people about them; but even these people can scarcely be said to
be treated with bitterness, even when, as in the case of Buck Mulligan or
Simon Dedalus, Stephen's view of them is bitter: Joyce is remarkable, rather,
for equanimity.

The trouble has really been that the first readers of *Ulysses* were shocked
by the way in which the incongruous elements of our complex human
organism were mingled in Joyce's characters—or rather, by the way in which
Joyce has violated the traditional conventions for representing the mingling
of these elements. But the more we read *Ulysses*, the more we feel its
psychological truth, and the more we are astonished by Joyce's genius in
grasping, not through analysis or generalization, but by the direct representation of life in the process of being lived, the relations of human beings to their
environment and to each other, the nature of their perception of what goes
on about them and of what goes on within themselves, and the interdepend-
ence of their intellectual, their physical, their professional and their
emotional lives. To have traced all these interdependences, to have given
each of these elements its value, yet never to have lost sight of the moral
through preoccupation with the physical, nor to have forgotten the general in
the particular, to have presented us with ordinary humanity without either
satirizing or sentimentalizing it—this would already have been sufficiently
remarkable; but to have turned such material into poetry, and that poetry of
the highest order, is a feat which has hardly been equaled in English in our
age.

In Stephen's diary in *A Portrait of the Artist*, we find this significant entry
apropos of a poem of Yeats:

> Michael Robartes remembers forgotten beauty and, when his arms wrap
> her round, he presses in his arms the loveliness which has long faded
> from the world. Not this. Not at all. I desire to press in my arms the
> loveliness which has not yet come into the world.

And, with *Ulysses*, Joyce has brought into literature a new and unknown
beauty. Some readers have regretted the extinction in the later Joyce of the
charming lyric poet of his two little books of poems and the *fin de siècle* prose
writer of the *fin de siècle* phases of *A Portrait of the Artist as a Young Man*.
This poet is still present in *Ulysses*: "Kind air defined coigns of houses in
Kildare Street. No birds. Frail from the housetops two plumes of smoke
ascended, pluming, and in a flaw of softness softly were blown." But the
conventions of the romantic lyric, of "esthetic" prose, even of the naturalism

of Flaubert, can no longer, for Joyce, be made to accommodate, to contain the reality of experience. The diverse elements of experience are perceived in different relations and they must be differently represented. Joyce has found for this new vision a new language—a language of such vividness and beauty that we no longer feel nostalgia for the old. He is the great poet of a new phase of the human consciousness.

Bloom himself is, in one of his aspects, the typical man of our time—a Jew, he might be an inhabitant of any provincial city of Europe or America. He makes a living by petty business, he leads the life of all the world—and he holds the conventional enlightened opinions of that world: he believes in science, social reconstruction and internationalism. But he is surpassed and illuminated from above by Stephen, who represents the intellect, the creative imagination; and he is upheld by Mrs. Bloom, who represents the body, the earth. Bloom leaves with us in the long run the impression that he is something both better and worse than either of them; for Stephen sins through pride, the sin of the intellect; and Molly is at the mercy of the flesh; but Bloom, though a less powerful personality than either, has the strength of humility. It is difficult to describe the character of Bloom, as it is represented by Joyce in *Ulysses*: it takes precisely the whole of *Ulysses* to describe it. It is not merely that Bloom is mediocre, that he is clever, that he is common-place—that he is comic, that he is pathetic—that he is, as Rebecca West believes, a figure of abject "squatting" vulgarity, that he is, at moments, as Foster Damon indicates, the Christ—he is all these things, and it is the proof of Joyce's greatness, that the more we think about *Ulysses*, the less can we find the formula for Bloom.

Both Stephen and Molly rise to heights which Bloom can never reach. In Stephen's rhapsody on the seashore, in the earlier book, when he realizes his artist's vocation, we have heard the ecstasy of the creative mind. In the soliloquy of Mrs. Bloom, Joyce has given us another ecstasy of creation, the rhapsody of the flesh. Stephen's dream was conceived in loneliness, by a drawing apart from his fellows. But Mrs. Bloom is like the earth, which gives the same life to all: she feels a kinship with all living creatures. She pities the "poor donkeys slipping half asleep" in the steep street of Gibraltar, as well as "the sentry in front of the governor's house . . . half roasted" in the sun; and she gives herself to the bootblack at the General Post Office as readily as to Professor Goodwin. But, none the less, she will tend to breed from the highest type of life she knows: she turns to Bloom, and, beyond him, toward Stephen. This gross body—the body of humanity—upon which the whole structure of *Ulysses* rests—still throbbing with so strong a rhythm amid obscenity and squalor—is laboring to throw up some dignity and some beauty by which it may transcend itself.

These two passages carry off all the ignominies and trivialities through which Joyce has made us live: they seem to me—the soaring silver prose of the one, the deep embedded pulse of the other—among the supreme expressions in literature of the creative power of humanity; they are, respectively, the justifications of the woman and the man.

## V

Since finishing *Ulysses*, Joyce has been engaged upon another work, about half of which has been published in *Transition*. It is not possible to judge this book properly in the imperfect form in which it has appeared. It is a sort of complement to *Ulysses*; Joyce has said of it that, as *Ulysses* deals with the day and with the conscious mind, so his new work is to deal with the night and with the subconscious. The whole of this new production is apparently to occupy itself with the single night's sleep of a single character. Joyce has already exhibited in *Ulysses* a unique genius in the representation of special psychological states. I know of nothing else in literature, for example, like the drunken night-town scene—we are astounded at Joyce's capacity for remembering and reproducing the different phases of drunkenness. His method of rendering the phases of sleep is similar to the methods of the Circe episode, but he is here attempting something even more difficult, and his way of doing it raises an important question in regard to all Joyce's later work. Joyce, as I have said, always nowadays represents the consciousness of his characters directly: but his method of representing consciousness is to let you overhear his characters talking to themselves. Joyce's people think and feel exclusively in terms of words, for Joyce himself thinks in terms of words. This is partly due, no doubt, to his defects of eyesight, which of late years have become so serious as to make it difficult for him to work. There is an interesting passage in *A Portrait of the Artist* in which Joyce himself discusses this aspect of his work:

> He drew forth a phrase from his treasure and spoke it softly to himself:
> —A day of dappled seaborne clouds—
> The phrase and the day and the scene harmonised in a chord. Words. Was it their colors? He allowed them to glow and fade, hue after hue: sunrise gold, the russet and green of apple orchards, azure of waves, the greyfringed fleece of clouds. No, it was not their colors: it was the poise and balance of the period itself. Did he then love the rhythmic rise and fall of words bettter than their associations of legend and color? Or was it that, being as weak of sight as he was shy of mind, he drew less pleasure from the reflection of the glowing sensible world through the prism of a language many colored and richly storied than from the contemplation of an inner world of individual emotions mirrored perfectly in a lucid supple periodic prose.

And in *Ulysses* we hear the characters far more plainly than we see them: Joyce describes them in sparse, scrupulous phrases, one trait here, another there. But the Dublin of *Ulysses* is a city of voices. Who has a clear idea of how

Bloom or Molly Bloom looks?—and should we have a clear idea of Stephen if we had never seen photographs of Joyce? But their eternally soliloquizing voices are as haunting as any in literature.

Joyce already seems sometimes, in *Ulysses*, to go a little beyond the probabilities in the vocabulary which he allows Bloom to dispose of. When Bloom, in the drunken scene, for example, imagines himself giving birth to "eight male yellow and white children" all "with valuable metallic faces" and each with "his name printed in legible letters on his shirt-front: Nasodoro, Goldfinger, Chrysostomos, Maindorée, Silversmile, Silberselber, Vifargent Panargyros"—we have difficulty in believing that he would have been learned enough for this. Yet I do not suppose that Joyce means us to think that Bloom actually formulated these words in his mind: it is the author's way of conveying in words an idea which on the part of Bloom must have been a good deal vaguer than this. Now, in his new book, Joyce has tried to make his hero express directly in words, again, states of mind which do not usually in reality make use of words at all—for the subconscious has no language—the dreaming mind does not usually speak—and when it does, it is more likely to express itself in the looking-glass language of "Jabberwocky" than in anything resembling ordinary speech. Joyce's attempts which, on their large scale and with their greater seriousness, have a good deal in common with those of Lewis Carroll, to find words for the wordless world of sleep—that is, not merely to describe this world, but to let the sleeper communicate it to us directly, are more easily comprehensible to literary people than to people who are not "word-minded." Yet it is worth making an effort to understand this rather formidable-looking new novel of Joyce's, for what he is trying to do is both artistically and psychologically extremely interesting, and it may be that he will turn out to have written the most remarkable piece of dream-literature in existence.

The best way to understand Joyce's method is to note what goes on in one's own mind when one is just dropping off to sleep. Images or words—if one thinks in words like Joyce—which were already in the conscious mind will suddenly take on some quite alien significance—or some vivid incident which may have taken place just before one went to bed will begin to swell with a meaning, an emotion, which at first we do not recognize because it has come up from the submerged part of the mind and assumed the disguise of the more immediate—because it is dissociated from the situation out of which it originally arose. And so the images which our waking mind would keep distinct from one another incongruously mingle in our sleep with an effect of perfect congruity. A single one of Joyce's sentences, therefore, will combine two or three different meanings—two or three different sets of symbols—a single word may combine two or three. We are not to suppose that the hero of his book frames all these sentences to himself—they are merely an equivalent for sleeping states which do not lend themselves to the logic of articulate human thought. We are not to suppose that he knows all the languages or understands all the allusions which Joyce makes him resort to in his dream. We are now at a level below particularized languages—we are in the region whence all languages arise and where the impulses of all acts have their origin.

The hero of the night's sleep in question is, it would appear, a certain H.C. Earwicker, a Norwegian living in Dublin. He seems to have attempted a number of occupations—to have been a postman, to have kept a hotel and a shop—it seems probable that, at the present time, he is working in Guiness's Brewery. He is married and has children, but has apparently been carrying on a flirtation with a girl called Anna Livia. This, along with other lapses from respectability associated with it in his mind, troubles his conscience and his repose. We are introduced, at the very beginning, into Earwicker's drowsing consciousness, and we have to make what we can of the names, the shapes, and above all, of the voices which fill that dim and shifting world—they combine and recombine, they are always changing into one another—but as we go on and we find them recurring, we begin to be able to recognize them— we become familiar with the character of Earwicker—we begin to guess at his condition and history. We identify Maggie and the children, the house in which they live, the four old men with the donkey, Earwicker's drunken misdemeanors and his fear of being caught by the police, the washerwomen gathering up their washing, Anna Livia on the bank of the Liffey, the Hill of Howth, the tree and the stone. But none of these things is presented objectively—they are all parts of Earwicker himself: men and women, old and young, the river, the mountain, the tree and the stone—it is the dreamer speaking through all of them. The old men come to admire him as he is sleeping on the mountainside, but in a moment it is Earwicker himself who is talking about himself; or he splits up into two personalities, one of whom bullies or accuses the other. He is coming out of a pub into the street with a party of drunken companions, many people are standing about but the revelers do not care how much attention they attract: they egg on one of their number to sing and the song turns out to be a recital of all Earwicker's failures and sins—he has made a fool of himself, he has swindled the Dubliners, his wife is going to read him the Riot Act. Or he sets out to explain something by a fable of the Mookse and the Gripes—the Mookse comes swaggering up to the Gripes, who is hanging on a tree—a sort of altercation takes place, and we recognize the incident as one of Earwicker's encounters with the police—but dusk falls and the washerwomen come out and take away the Mookse and the Gripes, who are now merely two pieces of laundry.

One of the most attractive parts which has so far appeared is the "Anna Livia Pluribelle" passage. Here, the stone and the elm have turned into the washerwomen—we hear them gossiping about Anna Livia, who is both the girl with whom the hero is in love and the river Liffey: it is the voice of the river itself, light, rapid, incessant, almost metrical, now monotonously running on one note, now impeded and syncopated, but vivaciously, interminably babbling its indistinct rigmarole story, half unearthly, half vulgarly human, of a semi-lengendary heroine—till, with the final falling of darkness, the voices grow husky and vague and announce the presence of night.

It is early night in this first section of the book, and the shadow of the past, the memory presumably of the day before, darkens the hero's sleep—the vulgarities of his waking life oppress him and pursue him, but after midnight, as dawn approaches, as he becomes dimly aware of the first light, the dream lightens and moves unencumbered—if I am not mistaken, the middle-aged Earwicker reverts to the period of his youth, he becomes carefree, attractive, well-liked—his spirit turns refreshed to the new day. I suppose that the book is to end with his waking up—no doubt we shall see all the fantasies of the dream closed down into the commonplace fate which we have already been able to divine.

This new production of Joyce's exaggerates the qualities we have noted in *Ulysses*. There is even less action than in *Ulysses*. Joyce has set out with certain definite themes and the themes are evidently all to have their developments, but these developments take a long time. We make pro-gress—we pass from night to morning—and no doubt, when the whole book is before us, we shall see that some sort of psychological drama has been played out in Earwicker's mind—but, as we progress, we go round and round. And whereas in *Ulysses*, there is only one parallel, in this new book there are a whole set: Adam and Eve, Tristan and Isolde, Swift and Vanessa, Cain and Abel, Michael and Lucifer, Wellington and Napoleon. It would seem that Joyce has provided plausible reasons for the appearance of all these personages in his hero's mind—but the effect of the superposition, one upon the other, of such a variety of parallels seems sometimes less to enrich the book than to give it a complexity again merely synthetic. Joyce is again trying to do too many things at once. The style he has invented for the purposes of his new book works on the principle of a palimpsest: one meaning, one set of images, is written over another. Now we can grasp a certain number of such suggestions at the same time, but Joyce, with his characteristic disregard for the reader's capacity for attention, apparently works over and over his pages, multiplying allusions and suggestions by the laborious introduction of puns. This appears clearly from the different versions which have been published in various places of the Anna Livia Pluribelle passage. The first of these still seems to me charming and none the worse for being easily intelligible; the second certainly leaves nothing to be desired; but in the third, Joyce has so distorted the words, he has wrenched them to so many double meanings—he has, for example, in the final version, succeeded in introducing plays on words on the names of some five hundred rivers—that instead of conveying as this passage did perfectly before, the dim, ambiguous impression of a dream, it has become too often unpronouncable and impenetrable. As soon as we are aware of Joyce himself systematically embroidering on his text, deliberately inventing puzzles, the illusion of the dream is lost. Yet, on the whole, this illusion is created and kept up with extraordinary success. There is a curious fascination about becoming gradually acquainted with a character whom we know only from the inside and from his dreams. It is, as I say, impossible as yet to judge this new production properly—the account I have given of it may be full of error; but it is safe to say that its best humor and poetry match the best that Joyce has written—that its use of language is an important event in the development of a great master of letters.

EDMUND WILSON

---

[Doc. 5]

October 21, 1931.

Mr. B.W. Huebsch,
18 East 48th Street,
New York City.

Dear Ben:                                    Re: *Ulysses.*

At our conference yesterday, you asked me to drop you a line in regard to possible services that we might render in connection with the legalization of Joyce's *Ulysses.*

This book represents the only volume of literary importance still under a ban in the United States. Any attempt to legalize the volume will be faced at the outset with the condemnation previously ennunciated by various courts against the volume. At this time, the book has no commercial value either to the author, Miss Beach or any publisher. From a monetary point of view, it is now a valueless property in the United States except for a few isolated pirates.

In our opinion the volume can now be tested with the real hope of gaining immunity for it.

I outlined to you in some detail the various legal steps which we would advise taking in order to win a court decision in favor of *Ulysses.* Such proceedings may entail four separate hearings and may necessitate an appeal even up to the United States Supreme Court. Possibly the controversy attending the proceedings will aid the sale.

If we procure through such proceedings the stamp of approval of the Federal Court, there still remains the possibility of any one of our forty-eight states, or even the Post Office Department proceeding independently against the volume. Although such further assaults are legally possible, in our opinion they would be highly improbable.

We have procured admission in the last few years of innumerable volumes for various publishers and in not a single instance has a State, or the Postal authorities, proceeded against a book which had been legalized by the Federal Court. Not since 1915, in the case of *Hagar Revelly*, has any such additional proceeding developed.

The method we have usually employed to retard independent State action is to write a foreword in the American edition, setting forth in full in such foreword the favorable opinion of the Court.

You will note in the American editions of *Married Love*, Putnam; *The Well of Loneliness*, Covici-Friede; *Decameron*, Modern Library, forewords which we have prepared so that the volume itself, if ever hailed into court again would contain within its own pages, legal opinions and literary comment otherwise inadmissible in a court trial. Such forewords, moreover, cause censorship societies to hesitate before commencing proceedings.

We have made no examination in the case of *Ulysses* as to copyrights heretofore granted. It may well be that the volume is part of the public domain. Off-hand, and without examination, it would appear that the injunction in the Roth case is not very impressive.

In an ordinary matter of testing a book against our civil and criminal statutes, where our office is retained, we insist upon a retainer of $1000.00 with an additional fee to be later fixed depending upon the result obtained and the time consumed. If there are several appeals, the total cost, together with printing of briefs, stenographers minutes, etc., can run as high as $7000.00 or $8000.00, should the appeals take us to the United States Supreme Court.

In this case, however, an arrangement such as we have worked out with other leading publishers, might be more acceptable to you and would be agreeable to us. I have in mind a contingency arrangement. I would suggest that you pay a retainer of $500.00 and that an additional $500.00 be paid upon each subsequent appeal, if such subsequent appeals are necessary. It is my impression that there is a very good chance of the case terminating at the time of the second hearing—that is, after argument before the District Court. The maximum, however, which would be payable under such an arrangement in fixed fee, would be $2000.00, provided that the case went even to the United States Supreme Court. In addition to this we expect to be repaid the actual out of pocket disbursements incurred in connection with the printing of briefs, stenographers minutes, etc. You would be at liberty to call the matter off at any stage of the appeals. In addition to the retainer, we would be inclined to gamble with the author and yourselves by accepting as an additional fee, an amount equal to royalties of 4% on the sales. In many cases, leading publishers have adopted some such program and have arranged to split the percentage between the author and themselves. This recommends itself because both the author and the publisher may acquire some wealth by the legalization of the volume and obviously neither the author nor the publisher alone should stand the entire burden of the battle. Moreover, the author is usually held harmless, so that in case the vindication of the book is defeated, he is not called upon to bear one cent of the expense.

To win the case of *Ulysses* involves substantial reversals of opinions laid down by our courts about a decade ago. This is, of course, always an obstacle, but we were confronted with the same situations in the reversals which we have had to obtain in other cases such as the works of Dr. Marie C. Stopes, for the publication of which, ten years ago quite a number of printers and booksellers went to jail.

If there is any further information you desire, kindly communicate with me.

Yours,

MLE-PG

--------

**[Doc. 6]**

December 17, 1931.

Mr. Bennett A. Cerf
The Modern Library, Inc.
20 East 57th Street
New York, N.Y.

Dear Bennett,

Pinker writes from London that he thinks it's hopeless to try to wrench *Ulysses* away from Miss Beach. She refuses even to consider our offer, although, as I need not tell you, I tried to make the offer attractive. Under the circumstances I think that we will have to retire; nevertheless, if no arrangement has been made by the next time that I see Miss Beach, I will of course try again.

You graciously stood aside for us, and naturally we cannot object if you should now determine to try to get the book; but it is my belief that such action may only have the result of keeping the price up.

Yours Cordially,

Ben Huebsch

[Doc. 7]

MODERN LIBRARY, INC.
20 EAST 57th STREET • NEW YORK
BENNETT A. CERF, *President*    Donald S. Klopfer, *Vice-President*

December 22, 1931.

Mr. Morris Ernst,
Greenbaum, Wolff & Ernst,
285 Madison Avenue,
New York City.

Dear Morris:

I hope that we can get together soon after the turn of the year to talk further about *Ulysses*. Ben Huebsch has promised to show me his whole correspondence on this matter. I don't know just what we can do if Sylvia Beach maintains her preposterous stand, but at any rate let's talk the thing over.

Best wishes for a happy new year.

Cordially,

Bennett A. Cerf

bac;pk

———————

[Doc. 8]
[This is a handwritten note, probably by either Ernst or Lindey.—ED.]

March 22/32—Lunch—MLE, AL, Cerf & Klopfer—Cerf gave us contract & letter to consider—went over both—phoned & suggestions.

———————

**[Doc. 9]**

March 22, 1932.

Mr. Robert Kastor,
c/o Sartorius & Smith,
61 Broadway,
New York City.

Dear Bob:

In presenting herewith the contract covering the Random House publication of James Joyce's *Ulysses* [See Doc. 10.—ED.], I have attempted to adhere as closely as possible to the contract presented by Messrs. Pinker & Son, plus the additional contract as drawn up by Mr. Paul Léon.

It is my purpose in this letter to explain fully the causes for any changes or additions that we have suggested in this new contract form. I think it will simplify matters if I deal with each paragraph separately and in chronological order.

Par. 1—I refer to the 9th or subsequent edition of the book because the 9th edition is the last one that we have been able to lay our hands on up to this date. I gather from Mr. Léon's draft that there is now an 11th edition. If this is in any way different from the 9th edition, we of course want to use the latest and best text. If there are any differences between the 11th and 9th editions, we are willing to change the contract to read "11th edition".

Par. 2—No comment necessary.

Par. 3—No comment necessary.

Par. 4—These are the exact terms requested by Mr. Joyce. The only addition I have made to Mr. Léon's phraseology is to ask for the delivery of Mr. Joyce's authenticating letter before we make our initial payment. I am sure that Mr. Joyce can find no objection to this clause. I hope that you will ask Mr. Joyce to make this letter as full and as comprehensive as possible. Obviously we are counting upon this letter not only to establish beyond all doubt the fact that ours is the only authorized edition and the one on which the author is receiving full royalty, but to give a certain first edition value to our edition.

Par. 5—I have changed the period that must elapse before a cheaper edition appears from three years to two, since this is in conformity with present publishing practice in America. The publication of *Ulysses* at this time is not quite the same as though we were publishing a brand new work. Many copies of it have been distributed in America over a period of years, and it seems to us that it will be high time to bring out a popular edition some two years after the publication of the regular trade edition. As far as the reference to a pirated edition is concerned, this is a contingency that must be faced frankly and openly. I regret to say that I not only think it possible that there will be a pirated edition of *Ulysses* if we once succeed in legalizing it in this country, but I think it is distinctly probable. There are three or four firms in New York that are today boldly pirating anything that they possibly can without running afoul of the law. If we have once succeeded in legalizing *Ulysses*, and have made a fine set of plates which these thieves can photograph with the greatest ease, we are setting up far too attractive a target for them to ignore. In the event that this book is pirated, we will of course, do everything that we can to stop them, but as Mr. Joyce and Mr. Léon must realize, we will probably be unable to do anything except fight them on their own grounds. This may mean bringing out an edition just as cheap as theirs in order to compete with them. Obviously, it is just as much to our disadvantage as to the author's to take a step of this sort—possibly even more to our disadvantage, and we will take no such action unless we feel absolutely forced to do so. I do think, however, that the contract should give us the power to take this step if we deem it necessary.

Par. 6—I have already emphasized the importance to us of Mr. Joyce's letter of authentication, and while I make the contract read "not less than 300 words", it is my sincere hope that Mr. Joyce will find it possible to make his letter somewhat longer than this minimum length. This letter would be an ideal place, it seems to me, for Mr. Joyce to give a brief resume of the history of the book. Everybody in the world has wondered how it happened to be brought out by a firm in Paris called Shakespeare & Co.—a firm quite unknown to the American reading public outside of this one publication. Referring to the sentence about the possible inclusion of a foreword by another author in our edition, let me point out that this foreword will be in no sense a criticism of *Ulysses*. It may prove advisable, however, to put in a brief note by a prominent attorney embodying the decision of the judge who legalizes the book. The inclusion of this decision in our volume will protect us in any future court action that may arise in connection with the publication. If the decision is not included, it is possible that on any succeeding action the court would not allow us to introduce previous decisions as evidence. Such a decision obviously would mean that we would have to begin the fight all over again.

Par. 7—The price of $2.50 was reached by us only after long consideration and calculation. Under ordinary circumstances, this book should be priced at as high as $5.00 a copy, and certainly no lower than $3.50, but here again the prime consideration must be fear of these accursed book pirates. To establish a price of anything higher than $2.50 for our edition of *Ulysses* would be simply an engraved invitation to these thieves to pirate the book and peddle it at a substantially lower price. This they could very easily do if they had no plate costs or had to bear absolutely no share of the legal expenses in connection with the book. If our edition is priced at anything like $5.00, and the pirates' edition came out at $2.00, I leave it to you to determine what the reaction of the reading public would be, especially in a period of depression like the present. The fact that our edition was the authorized one containing a letter from Mr. Joyce while the other edition was obviously a pirated one, would not persuade very many buyers, I am afraid, to pay $5.00 for our book when they could get the other one for $2.00. The $2.50 figure, however, will make it as hard as possible for pirates to undersell us by a wide enough margin to excite their cupidity. I am in strong hopes that it may keep them out of the picture entirely.

Par. 8 and 9—No comment necessary.

Par. 10—Our legal counsel tells us that if our fight on this book must be carried up to the Supreme Court, we will have to count on a two year period to settle it. The procedure as I understand it, will be to ship a copy of *Ulysses* at once and inform the U.S. Customs that it is coming. The book will undoubtedly be seized, and will be brought up in the lower court. Within a few months, if the lower court permits the book entry, the matter can very possibly be settled by this Summer. Our counsel thinks there is a very slim chance however, that any judge of a lower court will dare to pass favorably on a book as famous as *Ulysses*. This means that the case will have to go up to the Circuit Court. In this event, the case should go up some time in the Fall of 1932. Our counsel believes that it is in this court that we stand an excellent chance of winning a complete victory. If this indeed is what happens, it means that we will be able to publish the book in the early Spring of 1933. If however, we fail in the Circuit Court, we have no other course open but to carry the case to the Supreme Court and in that event a two year delay will be almost inevitable.

Paragraphs 11, 12, 13, 14, 15, 16, 17, 18, 19, and 20 call for no comment.

Par. 21—We are in strong hopes that we will be able to publish a small limited edition of *Ulysses* to sell to collectors. Obviously this book will have little or no first edition value, but it will after all, be a first edition of Mr. Joyce's authenticating letter, and will be signed by him. Furthermore, we plan to do the book as handsomely as possible. Since Random House was originally organized, after all, to distribute books of typographical interest, I think Mr. Joyce and Mr. Léon can count upon our bringing out a book of which all the parties concerned may be proud. The edition will be a maximum of 200, but whether we do the full 200 or only 100, we propose to give Mr. Joyce $500.00 for his work in signing the books. This $500.00 sum is, of course, in addition to the regular royalties on these special copies.

I think that I have covered everything very fully, and I hope that we may bring this negotiation to a successful conclusion as early as possible, so that we may get to work immediately on the legal battle. This will be a fight that we are proud to wage, and I have not the faintest doubt that we will be able to win. In closing, let me express my appreciation to you for the time and effort that you have devoted to the matter. I hope that I will have an opportunity to repay your kindness some time in the future.

As ever,
Bennett A. Cerf

bac;pk

[Doc. 10]
[This is an enclosure to Doc. 9.—ED.]

MEMORANDUM OF AGREEMENT made this    day of 1932, between
JAMES JOYCE ESQ., c/o James B. Pinker & Son, Talbot House, Arundel
Street, Strand, London, W.C.2, hereinafter called the Author, of the one part
and MESSRS. RANDOM HOUSE INCORPORATED, of 20 East 57th
Street, New York City, U.S.A., hereinafter called the Publishers of the other
part WHEREBY it is mutually agreed as follows:

1. The Publishers will publish in volume form in the U.S.A. a work at
present entitled:

ULYSSES

of which the said James Joyce is the author. The Publishers shall not abridge,
expand, or otherwise alter the said work, but shall publish it as issued in the
9th or subsequent editions of the said work published by the Shakespeare &
Co. Press of Paris.

2. Publication shall be made at the earliest possible date or in other
words, immediately upon legalization.

3. The Publishers hereby undertake that their edition shall be carefully
read through and checked by an expert proof reader, and verified according to
the 9th or subsequent editions of the said work.

4. The Publishers are to pay:

$1000.00 on the signature of the contract by James Joyce and the
delivery of the letter from Mr. Joyce authenticating the publication
(as hereinafter referred to in paragraph 6)

$1500.00 on the day of publication

as advance royalties to be established as follows:

15% on the trade edition up to 25,000 copies

20% on the trade edition after the sale surpasses this figure.

5. Should the Publishers issue an edition of the said work at a price
cheaper than that at which the said work was originally published, they shall
pay to the Author a royalty of 10% of the published price of each and every
copy of the said work, sold in such cheaper form. This popular edition is not
to be published before two years elapse after the publication of the trade
edition, unless a pirated edition at a lower price than the authorized edition
makes its appearance in the U.S.A. prior to the expiration of that two year
period. In this event, the Publishers are authorized to bring out a cheaper
edition immediately in order to compete with this unfair competition.

6. Although it is understood and agreed that there will be no preface by
the Author to the edition of the said work published by the said Publishers,
the Author hereby agrees to write a letter to the Publishers of not less than
300 words, by which he will authenticate the publication. [See Doc. 20.—ED.]
This letter is to be copyrighted according to the laws of the United States and

incorporated in the edition brought out by said Publishers. The Publishers also have the right to include a foreword by another author.

7. The published price of the trade edition of the said work shall not be less than two dollars and fifty cents ($2.50).

8. The author shall be entitled to receive upon publication six (6) presentation copies of the trade edition of the said work, and shall also be entitled to purchase further copies for personal use at the original trade price or less.

9. All steps for the legalization of the book are to be undertaken by the Publishers immediately upon the signature of the contract, and terminated at the earliest possible date. All costs in connection with such legalization are to be borne by the Publishers.

10. The Publishers' right to the publication of the book is to lapse if he fails to publish the book within a period of two years, unless the case is still pending in the courts at the end of that period. This failure will give no right to the Publishers to claim the return of any sums advanced on the book.

11. If at any time in the opinion of the Publishers the said work shall have ceased to have a remunerative sale the Publishers shall be at liberty to dispose of any copies remaining on hand as a remainder and if such copies should not realize more than one-third of the published price, the royalty to be paid by the Publishers to the Author shall be calculated on the actual price obtained and the license of printing and publishing the said work shall then revert to the Author to deal with as he may think fit.

12. Accounts shall be made up the 30th day of June and the 31st day of December of each year and delivered to the Author (or his representative), and settled in cash within 60 days after the 30th day of June and the 31st day of December.

13. So long as this agreement remains in force the said Publishers shall have the exclusive license of printing and publishing the said work in volume form in the United States of America. Should the Publishers at any time by themselves or anyone acting on their behalf fail to fulfill or comply with any of the clauses or conditions herein set forth, or should they commit an act of bankruptcy the Author may forthwith by notice in writing withdraw the license of printing and publishing the said work granted under this agreement and shall have the option of purchasing from the Publisher at cost price the remaining stock of the said work and the moulds or plates if any, at fifty per cent (50%) of the cost of manufacture. Nothing in this clause shall invalidate the Author's claim for damages for any breach of this agreement committed by the Publishers or anyone acting on their behalf.

14. All rights other than those specifically granted under this agreement are retained by the Author.

15. In the event of the Publishers allowing the said work to go out of print and neglecting to publish a new edition within six months the license of

printing and publishing the said work granted under this agreement shall revert to the Author.

16. This agreement may be terminated by either party at any time after the expiration of ten years from the date of publication of the trade edition on giving six months' notice in writing.

17. All difficulties arising out of the said agreement are to be submitted to the decision of the United States Court.

18. The copyright on the new trade edition is to be secured in the name of Random House, and the Author warrants that he is the sole proprietor and has full power to execute this agreement and making the grant, and further warrants that he has executed no agreement in conflict with this contract.

19. This agreement shall ensure to the benefit of, and shall be binding upon, the parties hereto, their legal representatives, successors and assigns.

20. The Publishers shall have such radio rights to the work as may be necessary in connection with sales promotion of the book.

21. The Publishers are authorized to bring out a special edition of not more than 200 copies of said book if they consider conditions favorable for such an edition when and if the book is legalized. In the event that this special edition of not more than 200 copies is actually undertaken, the Author agrees to sign each and every one of these copies, and is to receive therefor an extra remuneration of $500.00, whether the edition consists of 200 copies or less, said sum to be paid in full immediately upon receipt of the signed sheets.

22. The said Author hereby authorizes and empowers his agents, James. B. Pinker and Son of Talbot House, Arundel Street, Strand, London, W.C.2, to collect and receive all sums of money payable to the said Author under the terms of this agreement and declares that the receipt of the said James. B. Pinker and Son shall be a good and valid discharge to all persons paying such monies to them. The said Author also hereby authorizes and empowers the Publishers to treat with James. B. Pinker & Son on his behalf in all matters concerning this agreement in any way whatsoever.

JAMES JOYCE ESQ.

Witness                          By _____

RANDOM HOUSE, INC.

Witness                          By _____

_____

[Doc. 11]

RANDOM HOUSE<br>
20 E. 57<br>
New York

March 23, 1932.

Mr. Morris Ernst,
285 Madison Avenue,
New York City

Dear Morris:

I take pleasure in enclosing herewith for your records a copy of the contract form that was signed by us yesterday and mailed to Mr. Joyce, covering our publication of *Ulysses*. I am also enclosing a carbon copy of the letter that I sent to Mr. Joyce's representative, Robert Kastor, explaining every clause of the contract in as much detail as possible. You will note that I included all the suggestions given to me over the 'phone by Mr. Lindey.

Let me outline here my understanding as to the basis on which you will handle the legal end of this matter.

1. Immediately upon the receipt of the signed contract and the introductory letter of authorization by James Joyce, we are to pay you a retainer of $500.00.

2. In the event that the book is legalized and published by us, you are to receive a straight 5% royalty on our trade edition of the book.

3. You are to receive a 2% royalty on all copies of the book sold in a reprint edition.

4. You are to receive 5% of any net sum realized by Random House from the sale of *Ulysses* to a book club or to a similar organization at a special figure.

5. In the event that the jury trial becomes necessary in this case, it is understood that you are to receive extra compensation. This sum is to be based on the number of days that you are tied up in court, and is to be figured at a rate that is to be agreed on when and if occasion arises.

I will appreciate a note from you covering the above, after which we will consider the matter settled. Needless to say, I am delighted that you are going to take care of this case for us, as I know you will be able to handle it better than anybody else in the country.

Cordially,

Bennett A. Cerf<br>
Random House, Inc.

---

[Doc. 12]

March 24, 1932.

Random House, Inc.,
Bennett A. Cerf, Esq.,
20 East 57th Street,
New York City.

Dear Mr. Cerf:

Mr. Ernst has referred to me your letter of March 23, 1932, together with enclosures. Your statement as to our understanding with respect to our retainer seems to require slight clarification:

1. You are to advance and bear all expenses in connection with the legalization of *Ulysses*, such as the cost of printing briefs, court fees, cables, photostats and the like.

2. With respect to paragraph 5 of your communication, it should be definitely understood, as Mr. Ernst pointed out to you during our conference the other day, that the *per diem* compensation shall in no event be less than $50.00 per day. It is just as well to have this agreed upon even though, in my opinion, a trial does not loom as a serious practical possibility. The United States Attorney would relish spending three weeks in court reading *Ulysses* no more than ourselves.

3. You apparently overlooked the limited edition in specifying our compensation. We are assuming, however, that the limited edition, for the purpose of our 5%, would be treated the same as the trade edition.

It occurs to me that your negotiations with Mr. Joyce may consume some time; and in the meanwhile arrangements might be made for the sending of the proper edition through the customs. This would not involve or commit you to any extent even if your contract with Mr. Joyce fell through. In such event, upon the seizure of the book by the Collector of Customs, you would advise him that you would not contest the detention and you would authorize him to return the book to the sender. If, on the other hand, Mr. Joyce were to sign the contract, you would gain, possibly, as much as a month in point of time.

Mr. Ernst and I have given some time to choice of a sendee. In our opinion, the head of a public or university library would be most desirable, especially if he happens to be a person of national repute. The president of a medical or scientific society would be a good second choice.

Kindly let us hear from you relative to the above. We need not assure you that Mr. Ernst and I look forward with the greatest enthusiasm to working on the case.

Sincerely yours,
Greenbaum, Wolff & Ernst
By Alexander Lindey

AL:JF

**[Doc. 13]**

RANDOM HOUSE
20 E. 57
New York

March 28, 1932.

Mr. Alexander Lindey,
c/o Greenbaum, Wolff & Ernst,
285 Madison Avenue,
New York City.

Dear Mr. Lindey:

I have your letter of March 24th before me, and agree with you that it is best to have every point as well defined as possible before we begin with this *Ulysses* business. Let me take up your points in the order in which you presented them.

1. O.K.

2. Let's decide definitely that the *per diem* compensation for possible time in court be precisely $50.00 a day.

3. O.K.

4. This is a very good point, and I think we should proceed at once with the sending of the proper edition of *Ulysses* through the customs. I still think that the three best names mentioned the other day in this connection are, in the order named, Ex-Justice Holmes, Nicholas Murray Butler, and Roy Howard.

I look forward to hearing further from you on this point.

Cordially yours,

Bennett A. Cerf
Random House, Inc.

---

**[Doc. 14]**

March 28, 1932.

Harry H. Oshrin, Esq.,
1501 Broadway,
New York City.

Re: People v. Wendling
258 N.Y. 451

Dear Mr. Oshrin:

We wish to congratulate you upon your signal victory in the above entitled case. The result is all the more gratifying in view of the recent unexplainable decision of the Court of Appeals in the *Reigen* case.

As you may know, our office has been engaged in several campaigns against the censor. We were counsel in the *Dennett* case, *Married Love* case and the *Contraception* case, all of which were quoted with approval by the Court of Appeals in its opinion in the above entitled case.

We should very much like to obtain a copy of your brief on appeal. We shall appreciate the courtesy.

Yours very truly,

Greenbaum, Wolff & Ernst

AL:JF

---

[Doc. 15]

March 29, 1932.

Random House, Inc.,
Bennett A. Cerf, Esq.,
20 East 57th Street,
New York City

Dear Mr. Cerf:                          Re: *Ulysses*

I have your letter of March 28. I don't want to seem unduly insistent but I am afraid that, in view of all the circumstances, our firm must stand by paragraph 2 of our letter of March 24. As I indicated to you in that communication, the possibility of a jury trial is, in my humble opinion, a remote one; but it is still a possibility. So we may as well leave the question of compensation open, with the understanding as to the minimum.

Any of the sendees indicated in your communication of March 28 would be excellent; and we suggest that you take steps immediately to get in touch with the individuals named.

I believe Mr. Ernst, in the course of our luncheon the other day, mentioned to you that he would secure from Messrs. Chadbourne, Stanchfield & Levy the papers involved in the Roth injunction. We now find that Mr. Joyce has an unpaid bill with the attorneys, and we are therefore experiencing considerable difficulty in enlisting their cooperation. We have secured a copy of the injunction itself; and copies of the pleadings have been promised. This matter of the unpaid bill may be a source of embarrassment later on. If *Ulysses* is cleared and publication proceeds, Chadbourne, Stanchfield & Levy will no doubt take steps to attach Joyce's royalties here.

If you are at all reasonably sure that Mr. Joyce will close with you we suggest that the following matters be attended to as soon as conveniently possible:

1. Testimonials should be secured from prominent critics, librarians, authors, physicians, psychologists, psychoanalysts, welfare workers and the like, who have read the book and who are willing to give a brief statement certifying to its literary, scientific or sociological value, as the case may be.

2. Edmund Wilson had an unusually fine article on James Joyce in the December 18, 1929 issue of the *New Republic*. Undoubtedly he still has in his possession an extensive bibliography of works on Joyce. He should be requested to loan to us whatever data he may have.

3. Aside from testimonials referred to in paragraph 1 above, a compilation should be made of all essays, articles and criticisms of Joyce in general and *Ulysses* in particular. It is possible that Joyce keeps a book of clippings, and if he does not Shakespeare & Co. must have one.

4. In any test case involving the legality of the book, statistics as to its use by educational institutions will have considerable effect. We suggest that you prepare and send out a circular letter to one hundred or more colleges and universities, requesting information as to whether (a) Joyce is considered in any course given by the institution on contemporary literature; and (b) whether *Ulysses* is used as collateral or prescribed reading.

With kindest regards, we are

Yours sincerely,

Greenbaum, Wolff & Ernst

AL:JF

---

[Doc. 16]

RANDOM HOUSE
20 E 57 • NEW YORK
The American Selling Agent for the NONESUCH PRESS Limited Editions

March 30, 1932.

Mr. Alexander Lindey,
c/o Greenbaum, Wolff & Ernst,
285 Madison Avenue,
New York City.

Dear Mr. Lindey:

Thanks for your suggestions about *Ulysses*. I am enclosing herewith a carbon copy of the letter I have just written Ex-Justice Holmes. [See Doc. 17.—ED.] I will let you know as soon as I receive an answer from him.

Meanwhile, I will attempt to get in touch with Edmund Wilson at once, as the first step in going after testimonials from prominent critics and the like. We are also going to work at once to prepare a circular letter to send to the colleges and universities.

Cordially,

Bennett A. Cerf
Random House, Inc.

bac;pk

---

[Doc. 17]
[This is an enclosure to Doc. 16.—ED.]

March 30, 1932.

Hon. Oliver Wendell Holmes,
Washington, D.C.

Dear Sir:

Some two years ago you were kind enough to send us an unsolicited note complimenting the Modern Library on its publication of a one volume edition of *The Philosophy of Spinoza*. We wrote to you at that time telling you how much we appreciated your interest. We are about to embark now on a really exciting publishing venture, and I am writing to you now because you can be of inestimable help to us if you so desire, without the slightest effort on your part.

We want to publish James Joyce's *Ulysses*, complete and unabridged, in America, and with this end in view, have signed a contract with James Joyce, paying him a substantial advance royalty and agreeing to all the expenses of the legal battle that looms in the offing. We have engaged Mr. Morris Ernst as our counsel in our fight to legalize this great book, and all of us feel that now, if ever, is the time to remove the idiotic ban from one of the great works of literature of modern times.

We plan to open our legal battle by having a copy of *Ulysses* mailed to this country from Paris. We will notify the customs authorities that the book is coming, since it is imperative for our purpose that it be seized. We will then be able to fight for the book without having to go through the very expensive procedure of having it printed in America. If the book is once cleared by the U.S. Court, we feel that we will be justified in going ahead with our plan.

If you will permit us to do so, I would like to have this Paris copy of *Ulysses* addressed to you. There is no man in the entire country whose name in connection with this case would be more helpful in swaying any member of the judiciary. By the same token, I feel that there is no man in this country more apt than you to be willing to lend his name to fight to win James Joyce the due that has so long been owing to him on *Ulysses* in the United States.

If you are at all interested in hearing further about our plans for *Ulysses*, I will be delighted to see you personally. I look forward anxiously to your reply.

Very sincerely yours,

Bennett A. Cerf
President
The Modern Library, Inc.

---

**[Doc. 18]**

March 31, 1932.

Random House, Inc.,
Bennett A. Cerf, Esq.,
20 East 57th Street,
New York City.

Dear Mr. Cerf:                    Re: *Ulysses*

I have your letter of March 30, enclosing a copy of the communication sent to Justice Holmes. If he consents to act as sendee it will be a substantial step forward.

It may interest you to know that we have succeeded in obtaining from Messrs. Chadbourne, Stanchfield & Levy copies of the pleadings in the suit which James Joyce instituted against Samuel Roth and Two Worlds Publishing Co., Inc. As we suspected, the action was not predicated upon any copyright. It seems that Roth attempted to secure publicity for his periodical, *The Two Worlds Magazine*, by running *Ulysses* serially therein; and this fact was widely advertised. Under the Civil Rights Law of our state it is unlawful to use the name of an individual, without his express authorization, for advertising or business purposes. Joyce's suit was based on this provision of the Civil Rights Law; and in my opinion his legal position was untenable. If a copyright covering a literary production runs out, or if a literary production has been dedicated to the public, I believe that anyone may publish the production under the name of the author and so advertise it, without incurring any liability under the Civil Rights Law.

It is true that in the Roth suit a sweeping injunction was entered restraining Roth from using Joyce's name, and also from publishing *Ulysses*;

but this was in injunction granted by consent, and of course could have no binding force in any subsequent proceeding.

I have written to you in detail so as to keep the entire situation before you.

Yours very truly,

Greenbaum, Wolff & Ernst

AL:JF

---

[Doc. 19]

1720 Eye Street
Washington, D.C.
April 1, 1932.

Bennett A. Cerf, Esq.,
The Modern Library,
20 East 57th Street,
New York City.

My Dear Sir:

Mr. Justice Holmes asks me to say that he prefers that you do not address to him the copy of *Ulysses* which you plan to send from Paris as the basis of your test case. Regardless of his opinion of the book, the Justice thinks that taking part in the controversy over it, even so slightly as you suggest, would break in upon the complete withdrawal from affairs which he intended by his resignation from the Supreme Court. I am

Very sincerely yours,

Horace Chapman Rose
Secretary to Mr. Justice Holmes

---

[Doc. 20]

2 avenue St. Philibert, Passy.
Paris, April the 2nd. 1932.

Dear Mr. Cerf,

I thank you very much for your message conveyed to me by Mr. Robert Kastor. You ask me for details of the story of the publication of *Ulysses* and since you are determined to fight for its legalisation in the United States and to publish what will be the only authentic edition there, I think it just as well to tell you the history of its publication in Europe and the complications which followed it in America, although I was under the impression that they were already well known. As it is, however, they have given my book in print a life of its own. *Habent sua fata libelli!*

You are surely well aware of the difficulties I found in publishing anything I wrote from the very first volume of prose I attempted to publish: *Dubliners*. Publishers and printers alike seemed to agree among themselves, no matter how divergent their points of view were in other matters, not to publish anything of mine as I wrote it. No less than twenty-two publishers and printers read the manuscript of *Dubliners* and when at last it was printed some very kind person bought out the entire edition and had it burnt in Dublin—a new and private *auto-da-fé*. Without the collaboration of the Egoist Press Ltd. London, conducted by Miss Harriet Weaver, *The Portrait of the Artist as a Young Man* might still be in manuscript.

You can well imagine that when I came to Paris in the summer of 1920 with the voluminous manuscript of *Ulysses* I stood even slenderer chances of finding a publisher on account of its suppression after the publication of the eleventh episode in the *Little Review* conducted by Miss Margaret Anderson and Miss Jane Heap. These two editors were, as you probably remember, prosecuted at the instance of some society and as a result further publication in serial form was prohibited, the existing copies were confiscated and, I believe, the fingerprints of the two ladies were taken. The completed manuscript, however, was offered to one of your colleagues on the American market but I greatly doubt that he even took trouble to glance at it.

My friend Mr. Ezra Pound and good luck brought me into contact with a very clever and energetic person Miss Sylvia Beach who had been running for some years previously a small English bookshop and lending library in Paris under the name of Shakespeare and Co. This brave woman risked what professional publishers did not wish to, she took the manuscript and handed it to the printers. These were very scrupulous and understanding French printers in Dijon, the capital of the French printing press. In fact I attached no small importance to the work being done well and quickly. My eyesight still permitted me at that time to read the proofs myself and thus it came about that thanks to extra work and the kindness of Mr. Darantière the well-known Dijon printer *Ulysses* came out a very short time after the manuscript had been delivered and the first printed copy was sent to me for my fortieth birthday on the second of February 1922.

You are however in error when you think that Shakespeare and Co. never published anything before or after *Ulysses*. As a matter of fact Miss Sylvia Beach brought out a little volume of 13 poems of mine entitled *Pomes Penyeach* in 1927 and also a volume of essays and two letters of protest concerning the book I am engaged in writing since 1922. This volume was brought out in 1929 and it bears the title of *Our Exagmination round his factification for incamination of Work in Progress.*

The continental publication of *Ulysses* proved however to be merely the beginning of complications in the United Kingdom and the United States. Shipments of copies of *Ulysses* were made to America and to Great Britain with the result that all copies were seized and burnt by the Custom authorities of New York and Folkestone. This created a very peculiar situation. On the one hand I was unable to acquire the copyright in the United States since I could not comply with the requirements of the American copyright law which demands the republication in the United States of any English book published elsewhere within a period of six months after the date of such publication, and on the other hand the demand for *Ulysses* which increased every year in proportion as the book penetrated into larger circles gave the opportunity for any unscrupulous person to have it printed and sold clandestinely. This practice provoked a protest signed by one hundred and sixty-seven writers of all nationalities and I even obtained an injunction against one of these unscrupulous persons in a New York Court. I am enclosing copies of both these documents which may interest you. This injunction, however, proved to no avail as the enjoined defendant resumed his practice very soon again under another name and with a different mode of procedure, namely a photographic forgery of the Paris edition which contained the falsification of the Dijon printer's imprint.

It is therefore with the greatest sincerity that I wish you all possible success in your courageous venture both as regards the legalisation of *Ulysses* as well as its publication and I willingly certify hereby that not only will your edition be the only authentic one in the United States but also the only one there on which I will be receiving royalties.

Personally I will be very gratified if your enterprise is successful as it will permit American readers who have always proved very kind to me to obtain the authenticated text of my book without running the risk of helping some unscrupulous person in his purpose of making profit for himself alone out of the work of another to which he can advance no claim of moral ownership.

There may be some other points in which you are interested and I hope that should you be over in Europe again this year you will oblige me by communicating with me either direct or through my son so as to enable me to elucidate any point you may still be in doubt about.

Yours sincerely,

James Joyce

**[Doc. 21]**

RANDOM HOUSE
20 E 57 • NEW YORK
The American Selling Agent for the NONESUCH PRESS Limited Editions

April 13, 1932.

Mr. Morris Ernst,
285 Madison Avenue,
New York City.

Dear Morris:

The enclosed letter was just received from Mr. Howard. It seems final enough.

Have you any other suggestions for us to broach on this subject? What do you think of H.L. Mencken or Henry Seidel Canby?

The signed contract came in from Joyce yesterday, and we have already dispatched him $1000.00 advance. Now I want to get started as soon as we can on the fight.

As ever,

Bennett

P.S. Please send me back the Howard letter when you have read it.

B.A.C.

bac;pk

---

**[Doc. 22]**

April 14, 1932.

Bennett A. Cerf, Esq.,
Random House, Inc.,
20 East 57th Street,
New York City.

Dear Mr. Cerf:                    Re: *Ulysses*

Morris Ernst has turned over to me your letter of April 13, together with Mr. Howard's letter. We are returning the enclosure herewith.

Henry Seidel Canby would be a good bet. Get him, if you can.

Yours very truly,

Greenbaum, Wolff & Ernst

AL:JF

[Doc. 23]

April 19, 1932.

Mr. Paul Léon,
27, Rue Casimer-Périer,
Paris VII$^E$, France.

Dear Mr. Léon:

The contract for the *Ulysses* having been duly signed by all parties, we now want to begin the legal fight on the book at once. We expect to make our fight by having the book seized first by the U.S. Customs authorities, and I ask you to please follow the request I am now making to you, in great detail, so that there can be no possible slip-up in our procedure.

Please buy for us a copy of the latest edition of *Ulysses*. If there has been printed in French any circular containing opinions of prominent men or critics on this book, paste a copy of this circular into the front of the book. It is important that this circular be actually pasted into the book, as if it is separate we may not be able to use it as evidence when the trial comes up, but if these opinions of respected people are actually pasted in the book, they become, for legal purposes, a part of the book, and can be introduced as evidence.

Pack up the book and mail it to us, addressing the package, Random House, Inc., 20 East 57th Street, New York, N.Y. Write on the outside of the package the boat that the book is to come by in very plain letters so that there can be no possible mistake made by the postal service. Then send us a cable as soon as you have shipped the book telling us what boat the book will arrive on.

As soon as we know what boat the book is coming in on, we will notify the Customs authorities here that it is due, so it surely cannot be slipped through without being noticed by them. Obviously, it is necessary that they catch this book or all our efforts in this matter will have been in vain.

I thank you in advance for your help in this matter. Do get us the reprint of critical opinions if you possibly can. Maybe Mr. Joyce himself can help you with this. If no pamphlet has actually been printed, maybe you can have a few important opinions typed and pasted into the book. I suggest that you show this letter to George Joyce and his wife Helen in the event that James Joyce himself has left Paris. Helen may be able to help you in getting excerpts together.

If we can have this book in our hands inside of the next two weeks, there is a chance that the case will come up before the Spring is over. This might make possible the actual publication of the book a full season earlier than would otherwise be the case.

Again thanking you for your help, I remain,

Cordially yours,

Bennett A. Cerf
Random House, Inc.

bac;pk

[Doc. 24]

GREENBAUM, WOLFF & ERNST

## OFFICE MEMORANDUM

TO:  Mr. Lindey                    FROM:  M.L. Ernst
RE:  *Ulysses*                     DATE:  April 20, 1932.

1. It is important that we instruct Random House to send out about 500 letters to eminent people asking their opinion on *Ulysses*. You might draft the letter and submit it to me.

2. I also want a letter to go to about 100 libraries to find out if the book is on their shelves and if so, if open to the public generally.

3. I also want Random House to check up sales on books such as Herbert Gorman and others dealing with *Ulysses*.

4. I suggest that they put somebody on the job also to check up a complete bibliography of magazine articles dealing with *Ulysses*.

5. I think we ought to be able to check up some facts in regard to previous prosecution. I recall no record of the case. I think it was handled by Quinn who is now dead, whose files we might be able to locate.

---

[Doc. 25]

RANDOM HOUSE
20 E 57 • NEW YORK
The American Selling Agent for the NONESUCH PRESS Limited Editions

April 21, 1932.

Mr. Morris Ernst,
285 Madison Avenue,
New York City.

Dear Morris:

I am enclosing the drafts of two letters drawn up more or less in accordance with your suggestion. Are there any changes that you think should be made in either of these letters?

Cordially,

Bennett A. Cerf
Random House, Inc.

bac;pk

[Doc. 26]

April 25, 1932.

Bennett A. Cerf, Esq.,
Random House, Inc.,
20 East 57th Street,
New York City.

Dear Mr. Cerf:                    Re: *Ulysses*

This refers to your letter of April 21, addressed to Mr. Ernst. We have revised the forms which you submitted to us and we hand you herewith the following:

1. Draft of proposed letter to librarians.

2. Draft of proposed questionnaire to be enclosed in the letter to librarians.

3. Draft of proposed general letter to qualified persons.

4. List of prominent individuals whom we have used in past cases. This list is our file copy, and we ask that you be good enough to return it to us at your earliest convenience. No doubt you will be able to secure the missing addresses. You may add such other names as you wish.

We believe that the changes which we have made will be found to be self-explanatory. With respect to the librarians we have borne in mind the important element of inertia, and we have therefore obviated the necessity of placing upon each librarian the onus of sitting down and composing a letter. It is much easier merely to fill in blanks. Unfortunately this cannot be done in connection with the general letter to be sent to physicians, clergymen, etc.

If you have any question as to the enclosures, please get in touch with the undersigned. We may point out at this time, however, that past experience has shown us that there may be meagre response to the first request, and you will therefore have to arrange for a follow-up system of two or three additional letters. This we shall take up with you in due time.

We are sending you herewith our bill covering our retainer in the above matter. We trust that you will find it in order.

With kindest regards, we are

Yours very truly,

Greenbaum, Wolff & Ernst

AL:JF

[Doc. 27]

## PROPOSED LETTER TO AUTHORS, CRITICS, CLERGYMEN, SOCIOLOGISTS, ETC.

### JAMES JOYCE'S *ULYSSES*

Dear Sir:

You will doubtless be interested to hear that we have acquired the American rights to James Joyce's monumental novel, *Ulysses*, and that we propose to publish it in this country in the near future.

In spite of the fact that the book has exerted a profound influence on the literature of the world since its first appearance, decades ago,—there are critics who deem it the most significant prose work of the twentieth century—there still exists in some parts of the United States a legal ban against it. We believe that the ban is unconscionable and vicious, from the point of view of letters, and have been advised that it is unwarranted as a matter of law. We are taking steps to remove it, and have retained Morris L. Ernst, Esq., as counsel, for the purpose.

We realize that the success of the attempt will depend, in this case as in many cases in the past, upon the extent to which intelligent and qualified public opinion can be rallied to the defense of the book. In order to appraise the temper of the community we are sending inquiries identical with this one to a list of representative persons, including newspaper and magazine editors, literary critics, authors, clergymen, members of the bar, sociologists, psychologists, psychiatrists, social workers, teachers and librarians. In this manner we hope to secure a reliable cross-section of critical reaction.

We are addressing this letter to you in the hope that you will give us your frank opinion of *Ulysses*. What we should like to have is not so much a strict literary appraisal, as an estimate of the novel as a social document. We intend to offer your opinion, together with those of other prominent persons, to the authorities as indicative of the preposterousness of the ban which now exists.

It is possible, of course, that you have not read *Ulysses*. Unfortunately there are no copies available for general distribution. If you haven't read it, but know of some qualified person who has and whose opinion might be of value to us, we would appreciate your passing this letter on to him or her. It is understood, of course, that an expression of opinion on your part will not involve you as a witness in any court proceeding, nor in any undue publicity.

We look forward eagerly to your reply, and thank you in advance for your trouble in the matter.

Cordially yours,

Bennett A. Cerf
President
Random House, Inc.

[Doc. 28]

## DRAFT OF LETTER TO BE SENT TO LIBRARIANS

### *ULYSSES*
James Joyce

Dear Sir:

We have just signed a contract with James Joyce for the American publication of his monumental novel *Ulysses*. The book is generally conceded to be a literary work of the first magnitude. It was the first novel to make full use of the so-called stream-of-consciousness method, and it still stands in the forefront of psychological narratives. So profound has been its influence on letters during the past two decades, that it has been acclaimed by many critics as a modern classic: perhaps the most important literary work of the twentieth century.

Only a year ago, George F. Bowerman, Esq., librarian of the Public Library of the District of Columbia, pointed out that the unrestricted circulation of *Ulysses* in this country was merely a matter of time.

We are now endeavoring to appraise the sentiment of representative librarians throughout the country as to the book. The enclosed questions have been prepared for the purpose. They are so arranged as to permit of brief answers which will not consume much of your time. If you will fill in and return the enclosure to us, you will not only render us a great service, but you will be instrumental in aiding the cause of free expression.

We look forward to your reply, and thank you in advance for your trouble. A stamped, self-addressed envelope is enclosed for your convenience.

Cordially yours,

Bennett A. Cerf
President
Random House, Inc.

---

[Doc. 29]

### JAMES JOYCE: *ULYSSES*

1. Have you any copies of *Ulysses* in your library? _____

2. Only one copy, or several? _____

3. If you have no copy, have you made any attempts to secure one or more? _____

124

4. If you have a copy:
    (a) When was it obtained? _____
    (b) Where was it obtained? _____
5. Regardless of whether or not you have a copy:
    (a) Has there been any demand in your library for it? _____
    (b) Much demand in your library for it? _____
    (c) Demand by whom: authors, students, etc? _____
6. Do you believe that an American publication at a reasonable price will be of value? _____
7. What is your estimate of the literary significance of the book?

    _____

8. What is your estimate of its psychological importance?

    _____

9. Have you any other opinion as to the book that you wish to express:

    _____

    _____

    Dated _____

                          _____
                          Name of Librarian

                          _____
                          Position Occupied

                          _____
                          Name of Library

                          _____
                          City and State

                    _____

**[Doc. 30]**
[The next seven letters comprise a sample of the responses to Cerf's appeal (Doc. 27).—ED.]

The Saturday Review
of Literature
25 West 45th Street, New York City

May 7, 1932.

Dear Bennett:

You ask me what I think of your publication of James Joyce's *Ulysses*. I think that *Ulysses* is unquestionably one of the great books of the century. It is already a classic. Its publication in this country is as legitimate as the publication of such classics as Fielding's *Tom Jones*, the works of Rabelais, and other classics. It, also, is a work of genius. In its own way it is as penetrating a study of the human comedy as Balzac ever made. It should be considered in this category. As a social document it is most important. There should be no ban against it.

Very sincerely yours,

William Rose Benét

---

LOUIS UNTERMEYER • ELIZABETHTOWN • ADIRONDACK MOUNTAINS • NEW YORK

May 11th, 1932.

Dear Bennett Cerf:

It seems incredible to me that, in these days of organized lawlessness, there should be a law that can operate against masterpieces of art. But I forget that bigotry has a long and consistent history. *The Impatient Virgins* and *Thirteen Men* have always flourished, as all cheap sensations will, while the works of vital import—works running the centuries from Petronius to Joyce—have had to suffer the not-too-clean hands of the prurient censor.

To say that *Ulysses* is a great work of art would scarcely be a "personal" opinion; it would merely be adding platitude to an axiom. Apart from its literary value, however—and I find it hard to separate the literary from the social aspect—it is a document of these times so revealing, so significant, that it can no more be ignored than the daily depression. What Freud is to modern psychology, or Einstein to our revised notions of time and space, *Ulysses* is to the novel. Joyce has given new dimensions not only to a literary form but to consciousness . . . I don't say that everyone will enjoy the volume—I am certain that not everyone will understand it, and those that fail to comprehend it will be loudest in their condemnation. But I do know that no one who reads it without prejudice can ever quite forget it. And I am equally certain that it is one of the monuments—grotesque and forbidding, if you will, but certainly colossal—of our age.

Of course, I don't mind your "involving" me in the matter. I'd be a coward not only as an author but a human being if I'd do anything else but cry out, whenever the opportunity arose, against such preposterousness.

Cordially,

Louis Untermeyer

Dear Mr. Cerf,

It certainly is good news to hear that somebody is going to publish an honest and complete edition of *Ulysses* in this country. To ban *Ulysses* is as absurd as it would be to ban *The Canterbury Tales* or the Book of Genesis. Banned or not it will remain a great piece of English prose; sooner or later even customs officers will have to regard it as such. Since it deals with human life it can't very well help having some smut in it, but I doubt if the passages that proved so terrifying to Mr. Sumner ten years ago would worry anyone now; except for a few cops and police magistrates the country is definitely less prudish than it was.

I don't see exactly why it should be easier to get it past labelled "social document" than labelled "novel." As a picture of Dublin it's a picture of any modern city, as a picture of Bloom and of Stephen it gives you the very essence of the internal struggle on the dying middle class; that one Dublin day is a microcosm of the lives of hundreds of millions of *hommes moyen sensuels* of Western civilization . . . but essentially it's a piece of imaginative virtuosity, a poem. I think if you try to get it by as an Elsie book, even the dumbest judge will smell a rat. I certainly wish you luck with the project; if there's anything I can do later in the line of written defense or offense, I'll be glad to do it.

Sincerely yours,

John Dos Passos

---

The New
REPUBLIC
421 West 21st Street
New York City

May 6, 1932.

Mr. Bennett A. Cerf, President
Random House, Inc.
20 East 57th Street
New York City.

Dear Mr. Cerf:

James Joyce's position in literature is almost as important as that of Einstein in science. Preventing American authors from reading him is about as stupid as it would be to place an embargo on the theory of relativity.

I heartily sympathize with your plan to publish a complete *Ulysses* in this country.

Sincerely yours,

Malcolm Cowley

MC:B

THEODORE DREISER

Room 709,
1860 Broadway,
New York City,
May 13, 1932.

Bennett A. Cerf, President,
Random House,
20 East 57th Street,
New York City.

Dear Mr. Cerf:

As you and Morris Ernst know, I have always regarded the attempted censorship of any book as one of the most absurd of all unintelligent human actions. I do not need to mention its futility. Books, banned or boosted, are read by those who wish to read them.

But, of course, I despise and deplore the attitude which prompts the censorship of any book, as well as the wholly unnecessary inconvenience and annoyance to which it puts those connected with it.

*Ulysses* is, of course, a highly intellectual work. To read it is to spend a day inside a seeking and profoundly observant human mind, to learn its mysterious wanderings and secret paths. And because it is what it is, some things enter into it which are not generally recorded. But, and for precisely that reason, these things add to its value as an amazing, if not unique, social and literary document.

Naturally, I hope that you are victorious, and promptly, in getting by with it.

Very truly,

Theodore Dreiser

FARRAR & RINEHART
INCORPORATED
PUBLISHERS
NINE EAST FORTY FIRST STREET
Cables-Farrine-New York

17th May 1932.

Bennett A. Cerf, Esq.
Random House
20 East 57th St.
New York City

Dear Bennett:

I am naturally delighted to hear that you are planning to publish *Ulysses*.

Any novel of such really tremendous consequence—a novel which stands not only in the first line of literary acclaim but in the first rank of influence on the writing and thought of a period and which has been so important to the development of psychology in literature—that has been treated in the manner *Ulysses* has by the courts, certainly deserves defense on the part of anyone of sensitiveness and intelligence.

Cordially,
John Farrar

JF:D

---

"La Paix," Rodgers Forge
Towson, Maryland
August 29, 1932.

Mr. Bennett A. Cerf,
20 East 57th Street,
New York, N.Y.

Dear Mr. Cerf:

Of course I think *Ulysses* should be published legally in America. In the first place, time has crept up on *Ulysses* and many people are under the daisies who were horrified ten years ago. In the second place compared to pornography on the news stands *Ulysses* is an Elsie book. And in the third place people who have the patience to read *Ulysses* are not the kind who will slobber over a few little Rabelaisian passages.

Very truly yours,
F. Scott Fitzgerald

[Doc. 31]

April 26, 1932.

Bennett A. Cerf, Esq.,
Random House, Inc.,
20 East 57th Street,
New York City

Dear Mr. Cerf:

This is to supplement our letter of April 25.

No doubt you have already arranged for the sending of the copy into the United States, and for cable advices indicating the date of shipment and the boat. As soon as you receive such advices, we suggest that you communicate with us, so that we in turn may inform the customs authorities of the impending arrival of the book. You will realize, of course, that it is an essential part of our plan that the book be stopped at Customs; and we do not wish it to slip through either by inadvertence or because of lack of advance information.

Yours very truly,

Greenbaum, Wolff & Ernst

AL:JF

---

[Doc. 32]

via S/S *Bremen*, Cherbourg.

27, Rue Casimir-Périer(VII$^E$.)
Paris April the 27-th. 1932.

Bennett A. Cerf, Esq.
c/o Random House, Inc.
20 East 57-th. Street
New York City. U.S.A.

Dear Sir,

I beg to acknowledge receipt of your favour dated April the 19-th. and to inform you that the parcel containing *Ulysses* has been given to day to the post office in a registered Mail (this corresponds to your first class mail I believe) and all measures are taken that it sail to-morrow on the S/S *Bremen*, thus being due in New York five days later, i.e. May the 3-rd.

I have pasted into this copy all the documents possible in order to facilitate your defense and enclosed you will find a list of them [See Doc. 33.—ED.] with the particulars which might be of use to you.

Supplementary copies of all these documents will be mailed to you by the next boat in order that they reach you in time for your counsel to prepare his defense.

I will also add several other articles which even if not admitted as evidence could be used by him in his speech before either the lower or the higher court.

You will certainly be aware of the fact that *Ulysses* has caused a great upheaval and that the number of criticism is enormous. I will be below the truth if I estimate them at a thousand. It is impossible to mail them all to you.

On the other hand you know probably too that *Ulysses* has been placed on the programmes of several Universities, e.g. University of Columbia as also University of Cambridge (England).

I think this covers all I have to tell you.

Believe me,

Yours sincerely,

Paul Léon

Please inform me of the book's arrival. [This is a handwritten postscript, apparently added by Léon.—ED.]

---

**[Doc. 33]**
[This is an enclosure to Doc. 32.—ED.]

LIST OF CRITICAL OPINIONS PASTED IN THE COPY OF *ULYSSES*

1. Immediately after the cover
   Bibliothèque Universelle et Revue de Genève, Mars 1930 Revue Hebdomadaire 20 April 1929 article by Marcel Brion.

2. Next page
   Press extracts on the English edition of *Ulysses*.
   Circular with opinions on the French translation.
   Protest signed by 167 writers.
   Circular of the German translation.

3. Before the title page
   Nouvelle Revue Française 1-er Avril 1922 article by Valéry Larbaud who is a writer of great repute author of *Barnabooth*.

4. Next page

Revue Anglo-Américaine article by Louis Cazamian (the title page of the Review has a misprint saying *Pouis* but the signature of the article should be correct). Cazamian is professor of English literature in a French institution.

5. At the end

Fortnightly Review article by Stuart Gilbert, an Oxford graduate and literary critic of repute.

6. The injunction against Roth.

———————————

[Doc. 34]

April 27, 1932.

Mr. Alexander Lindey,
c/o Greenbaum, Wolff & Ernst,
285 Madison Avenue,
New York City.

Dear Mr. Lindey:

We have ordered a copy of *Ulysses* sent to the United States, and have given explicit instructions as to what procedure was to be followed in this matter. I will notify you at once when I hear what boat the book is being shipped on.

Meanwhile, I enclose herewith a list of the magazine articles on Joyce and a list of the books about him. Is there anything else you would like in this connection?

Cordially yours,

Bennett A. Cerf
Random House, Inc.

———————————

**[Doc. 35]**

April 28, 1932.

Bennett A. Cerf, Esq.,
Random House, Inc.,
20 East 57th Street,
New York City.

Dear Mr. Cerf:                    Re: *Ulysses*

    I have your letter of April 27, together with enclosures. The magazine articles and the books will keep us busy for the time being. I am not sure whether, in the course of our several telephone conversations, I mentioned to you the advisability of ascertaining from Miss Sylvia Beach of Shakespeare & Company whether or not, at the time *Ulysses* appeared or at any later time, a scrapbook of newspaper and magazine reviews was kept. If there is such a scrapbook in existence, and if it is at all complete it may prove invaluable to us.

    Please keep us fully advised of the results that you obtain from the circular letters sent to librarians and representative persons.

Very truly yours,

AL:JF

---

**[Doc. 36]**

April 30, 1932.

Bennett A. Cerf, Esq.,
Random House, Inc.,
20 East 57th Street,
New York City.

Dear Mr. Cerf:                    Re: *Ulysses*

    We herewith acknowledge receipt, with thanks, of your check in the sum of $500.00 in payment of our retainer in the above matter.

Very truly yours,

Greenbaum, Wolff & Ernst

AL:JF

[Doc. 37]

May 1, 1932.

French Cable Company
WL WF 116 Z PARIS 43
WLT RANDOM HOUSE 20 EAST 57 NYK

JAMES JOYCES BOOK ULYSSES FORWARDED YOU AS FIRST
CLASS REGISTERED MAIL DESIGNATED BREMEN SAILED 28 DU
NEW YORK MAY THIRD CONTAINING COPIES PASTED IN
VOLUME OF DOCUMENTS ENUMERATED MY LETTER DES-
PATCHED SAME BOAT CABLE RECEIPT

LEON

---

[Doc. 38]
[This is a handwritten memorandum of uncertain origin from the files of
Greenbaum, Wolff & Ernst.—ED.]
Re: *Ulysses*
May 2/32—Cerf called—just received cable—1st cl. reg. mail—*Bremen*—
sail—Ap. 28—due May 3/32—*Ulysses*—Random House, Inc.—Cerf—

Called up Handler—at Customs House—

---

[Doc. 39]

May 2, 1932.

Collector of Customs,
Customs House,
New York City.

Re: *Ulysses*
by James Joyce

Dear Sir:

We are writing to you on behalf of our client, Random House, Inc. We wish
to advise you that a copy of James Joyce's novel, entitled *Ulysses*, has been
despatched into this country, addressed to our client. We are informed that
the volume left on the *Bremen* on April 28, and is due at the Port of New
York on Tuesday, May 3, 1932.

We are transmitting this information to you because we do not wish the
book to slip through the Customs without official scrutiny. As you may know,

*Ulysses* during the last two decades has been praised by critics as probably the most important contribution to the world literature of the twentieth century. Entirely apart from its profound literary significance, we are convinced that *Ulysses* is not violative of the Tariff Act. In saying this we are not unmindful of the adverse attitude of your Department with regard to the book in the past. We feel, however, that in view of such recent decisions as United States v. Mary Ware Dennett, 39 Fed. (2d) 564; United States v. *Married Love*, 48 Fed. (2d) 821; United States v. *Contraception*, 51 Fed. (2d) 525; Youngs, etc. v. Les, etc., 45 Fed. (2d) 103; and People v. Rendling, 258 N.Y. 461, there is no longer any legal sanction for such attitude.

We request that upon its arrival *Ulysses* be examined by your office in the light of the cases above referred to. We feel confident that you will not hesitate to pass favorably upon it. Should you rule otherwise, we ask that you be good enough to communicate with us before any definite steps are taken.

Kindly address your communication to the attention of the undersigned.

Yours very truly,
Greenbaum, Wolff & Ernst
By Alexander Lindey

AL:JF

---

**[Doc. 40]**

RANDOM HOUSE
20 E 57 • NEW YORK
The American Selling Agent for the NONESUCH PRESS Limited Editions

May 3, 1932.

Mr. Alexander Lindey,
c/o Morris Ernst,
285 Madison Avenue,
New York City.

Dear Mr. Lindey:

I enclose herewith a copy of the list of critical opinions that is pasted in the copy of *Ulysses* that is due to arrive some time today on the *Bremen*. [See Doc. 33.—ED.]

Please let me know definitely when you have news of the arrival of the book.

Cordially yours,
Bennett A. Cerf
Random House, Inc.

bac;pk

[Doc. 41]

RANDOM HOUSE
20 E 57 ● NEW YORK
The American Selling Agent for the NONESUCH PRESS Limited Editions

May 5, 1932.

Mr. Alexander Lindey,
c/o Morris Ernst,
285 Madison Avenue,
New York City.

Dear Mr. Lindey:

In accordance with your request, we are returning herewith the list that you sent us for use in the *Ulysses* matter.

Sincerely yours,
P. Kreiswirth
Random House, Inc.

pk;pf

---

[Doc. 42]

May 6, 1932.

Collector of Customs,
Legal Department,
Customs House,
New York City.

Att: Mr. Handler
Re: *Ulysses*
by James Joyce

Dear Sir:

This refers to our telephone conversation of May 2, and our letter of even date therewith.

Kindly let us know whether the copy of *Ulysses*, addressed to our client Bennett A. Cerf, Random House, Inc., 20 East 57th Street, New York City, has been seized by the Collector of Customs; and if so, what action is being contemplated thereon.

Yours very truly,
Greenbaum, Wolff & Ernst

AL:JF

136

**[Doc. 43]**

May 6, 1932.

Bennett A. Cerf, Esq.,
Random House, Inc.,
20 East 57th Street,
New York City.

Dear Mr. Cerf:                    Re: *Ulysses*

   We wish to acknowledge receipt of your letter of May 3, together with enclosure. We have not yet been officially advised by the Collector of Customs that the book has been seized. We are following up the matter.

Yours very truly,

Greenbaum, Wolff & Ernst

AL:JF

---

**[Doc. 44]**

Treasury Department
A-2
*Ulysses*

United States Custom Service
Port of New York,
5/6, 1932.

Sir:

   I have to acknowledge receipt of your communication of the 2nd.
   It will receive immediate attention, and a full reply will be sent you at the earliest possible moment.
   By order of

PHILIP ELTING
Collector.

B.N. Handler
Act. Deputy Collector.

---

[Doc. 45]

May 7, 1932.

Bennett A. Cerf, Esq.,
Random House, Inc.,
20 East 57th Street,
New York City.

Dear Mr. Cerf:                    Re: *Ulysses*

We tried to reach you Saturday but did not succeed in doing so. In view of the fact that *Ulysses* has been seized by the Customs it is quite important that we proceed with our preparations. Kindly let us know what response you have obtained from librarians and from representative persons. We suggest that you turn over to us all communications received by you, so that they may be photostated. They can then be returned to you.

The undersigned talked with the Solicitor for the Collector of Customs, on Monday. On the basis of this conversation we believe that there is scant likelihood of the Customs Bureau reversing itself with respect to the ban previously imposed on Joyce's book.

Yours very truly,

Greenbaum, Wolff & Ernst

AL:JF

---

[Doc. 46]

RANDOM HOUSE
20 E 57 • NEW YORK
The American Selling Agent for the NONESUCH PRESS Limited Editions

May 9, 1932.

Mr. Alexander Lindey,
c/o Greenbaum, Wolff & Ernst,
285 Madison Avenue,
New York City.

Dear Mr. Lindey:

The last of the letters on *Ulysses* have just gone out to your own list. We added the names of a full hundred other people. Between 800 and 900 letters

138

went out to librarians alone. There should be a sizeable number of responses by Thursday or Friday at which time I will send over the first batch to you to be copied. Will this be satisfactory?

Cordially yours,

Bennett A. Cerf
Random House, Inc.

bac;pk

---

[Doc. 47]

RANDOM HOUSE
20 E 57 ● NEW YORK
The American Selling Agent for the NONESUCH PRESS Limited Editions

May 10, 1932.

Mr. Alexander Lindey,
c/o Morris Ernst,
285 Madison Avenue,
New York City.

Dear Mr. Lindey:

For your records, episode No. 1 of *Ulysses* appeared in the March 1918 issue of the *Little Review*, and the book was continued up through episode No. 14, which appeared in the September-December issue of 1920. All of this material is copyrighted by Margaret Anderson. In the January-March 1921 issue of the *Little Review*, there was a two-page article called "*Ulysses* in Court," written by Margaret Anderson. I take it for granted that we will be able to put "copyright 1918-1920 by Margaret Anderson" in our edition of *Ulysses*, if we ever publish it.

Also, the *Key to Ulysses*, published by Covici-Friede, has sold about 2000 copies to date.

Cordially yours,

Donald S. Klopfer
Random House, Inc.

dsk;pk

[Doc. 48]

May 10, 1932.

Mr. Alexander Lindey,
c/o Greenbaum, Wolff & Ernst,
285 Madison Avenue,
New York City.

Dear Mr. Lindey:

I am enclosing herewith the first batch of replies from both librarians and the general list on the *Ulysses* letters. The librarians' replies I suggest that you keep in your office. The general list I would like to have back after you've had them copied. Is this a satisfactory arrangement?

Cordially yours,

Bennett A. Cerf
Random House, Inc.

bac;pk

[Doc. 49]

RANDOM HOUSE
20 E 57 • NEW YORK
The American Selling Agent for the NONESUCH PRESS Limited Editions

May 11, 1932.

Mr. Alexander Lindey,
c/o Morris Ernst,
285 Madison Avenue,
New York City.

Dear Mr. Lindey:

Here are some more very interesting *Ulysses* letters, and also some valuable stuff mailed to me by Mr. Léon in Paris. I take it that you will return all of these with the other letters when you have a pile of them assembled. Any news?

Cordially,

Bennett A. Cerf
Random House, Inc.

I am also sending some French magazines containing important estimates of *Ulysses*. [This is a handwritten postscript to Cerf's letter.—ED.]

bac;pk

---

[Doc. 50]

**GREENBAUM, WOLFF & ERNST**

**OFFICE MEMORANDUM**

TO: M.L.E.                    FROM: A.L.
RE: *Ulysses*                 DATE: May 12, 1932.

I hand you herewith:
  (a) Sheaf of representative opinions which we have had photostated.
  (b) All the answers of librarians which have been forwarded to us thus far by Mr. Cerf.

Please note:

1. I have retained no record of the answers of librarians.
2. The answers should be analysed by someone with judgment, in the form of a chart. The items of the answers which call for "yes" and "no" will, of course, be easy to compile. However, items 7, 8 and 9 on the questionnaire will require other treatment.
3. The main thing is to have the data furnished in the answers so concentrated as to make the data easy of presentation to the court.
4. This would be a good time for Mr. Cerf to check the answers against the list and to send out a follow-up letter to those who have not responded.
5. You may want to point out to Mr. Cerf that although we have received official acknowledgement from the Customs Bureau of our letter calling attention to the arrival of the book, we have not received any official notification to the effect that it will be held up.

---

**[Doc. 51]**

May 13, 1932.

Mr. Bennett A. Cerf,
The Random House,
20 East 57th Street,

Dear Bennett:                    Re: *Ulysses*

I am returning herewith the letters from so-called experts. We have photostats of those which will be useful. I am also returning herewith the librarian questionnaire. As to this I suggest that you proceed as follows:—

1. Check these up against the list as to which the questions were sent, and send a follow-up letter to those who did not answer.
2. You might write a line of thanks to those who did answer.
3. The answers that have come in should be analyzed and put into the form of a chart in so far as the questions call for "yes" or "no" answers. The items such as 7, 8 and 9 on the questionnaire will require other treatment.

This material should be concentrated so that the data can be presented in easy form to the court. In collating the answers, they might even be analyzed as to number of states in which libraries are anxious for the book.

I wish you could rush this through because we may need it by the end of next week.

Yours,

Encs.
Del.

142

[Doc. 52]

TREASURY DEPARTMENT
United States Customs Service
New York, N.Y.

66241                                                    May 13, 1932.

Messrs. Greenbaum, Wolff & Ernst,
285 Madison Avenue,
New York City.

Att. of Mr. Alexander Lindey

Sirs:

Receipt is acknowledged of your communication of the 2nd and 6th instant, requesting information as to the importation of the book *Ulysses* by James Joyce.

In reply you are advised that the book in question is detained as in violation of Section 305 of the Tariff Act as obscene. For your further information you are advised that the book *Ulysses* was the subject of a Customs Court Decision contained in Treasury Decision 42907 [See Doc. 53.—ED.] in which the Court affirmed the action of the Collector in excluding and refusing to permit entry of this book.

Respectfully,

H.C. Stewart
Assistant Collector

———————

[Doc. 53]

(T.D. 42907)
Excluded merchandise—Obscene books—
*A. Heymoolen* v. *United States*

Books which are offensive to chastity, delicacy, or decency, expressing or presenting to the mind or view something that decency, delicacy, and purity forbid to be expressed, are obscene under section 305(a) of the tariff act of 1922, and were properly excluded from entry.

United States Customs Court, Second Division—protest 266405-G against the decision of the collector of customs at the port of Minneapolis.
(affirmed)                    (Decided August 1, 1928)

Plaintiff not represented by counsel.

Charles D. Lawrence, Assistant Attorney General (James R. Ryan, special attorney), for the United States.

Before Fischer, Weller, and Tilson, Justices; Weller, J., not participating.

Tilson, Justice: The merchandise under consideration in this case consisted of 43 books, as follows:

|  | Vols. |
|---|---|
| *The Ethnology of the Sixth Sense* (Dr. Jacobus) | 1 |
| *The Basis of Passional Psychology* (Dr. Jacobus) | 2 |
| *The Abuses of the Genital Sense* (Dr. Jacobus) | 1 |
| *Crossways of Sex* (Dr. Jacobus) | 2 |
| *The Law Concerning Draped Virginity* (A. Beuerland) | 14 |
| *My First Thirty Years* (G. Beasley) | 10 |
| *Ulysses* (J. Joyce) | 7 |
| *The Strangest Voluptuousness* (Dr. L.R. Dupuy) | 1 |
| *The Vice of Women* (Dr. Confeynon) | 2 |
| *Physiology of Vice* (Dr. Jaf) | 1 |
| *Aphrodite* (Pierre Louys) | 2 |
|  | 43 |

which were sought to be entered at the port of Minneapolis by one A. Heymoolen, the Collector of Customs at said port excluded the books from entry on the ground that they were obscene and seized the same under Section 305(a) of the act of 1922, the pertinent part of which reads as follows:

> That all persons are prohibited from importing into the United States from any foreign country any obscene book, pamphlet, paper, writing, advertisement, circular, print, picture, drawing, or other representation, figure or image on or of paper or other material, or any cast, instrument, or other article of an immoral nature . . . . No such articles, whether imported separately or contained in packages with other goods entitled to entry, shall be admitted to entry; and all such articles shall be proceeded against, seized, and forfeited by due course of law. All such prohibited articles and the package in which they are contained shall be detained by the officer of customs, and proceedings taken against the same, as hereinafter prescribed, unless it appears to the satisfaction of the collector that the obscene articles contained in the package were enclosed therein without the knowledge or consent of the importer, owner, agent, or consignee . . . .

When the case was called for a hearing there was no appearance by the plaintiff, but a rambling argument or brief was filed which throws no light whatever on the subject. Seven samples of the merchandise were introduced in evidence by counsel for the Government, which are now before us for inspection and examination. The only question before this court for determination is whether or not these 43 volumes are obscene and indecent books as contemplated by law.

The word *obscene* is defined in the *Century Dictionary* as "offensive to modesty and decency; impure, unchaste, indecent, lewd, as obscene actions or language; obscene pictures. Obscene publication in law: any impure or indecent publication tending to corrupt the mind and to subvert the respect for decency and morality." The *Standard Dictionary* gives the following definition: "Offensive to chastity, delicacy, or decency, expressing or presenting to the mind or view something that decency, delicacy, and purity forbid to be expressed." The definition given by *Webster* is in the same language. The word *obscene* is defined in *Black's Law Dictionary* as "lewd, impure, indecent."

"The word can not be said to be a technical term of the law, and is not susceptible of exact definition in its juridical uses." (Timmons v. United States, 85 Fed. 204; United States v. Loftis, 12 Fed. 672).

Only a casual glance through the books in evidence is sufficient to satisfy us that they are filled with obscenity of the rottenest and vilest character. If merchandise of this character is to be admitted into the United States, then section 305 of the Tariff Act of 1922 should be erased from the statute books. The plaintiff states in his brief that these books are "books of undoubted merit and literary value." If it could be argued that books abounding in obscenity, filth, and rottenness are "books of undoubted merit and literary value" then all these are masterpieces. By affirmative statement in the plaintiff's brief it is clear that this importation can not be defended as coming under that part of section 305(a) which reads "without the knowledge or consent of the importer, owner, agent, or consignee."

As to all the books which were introduced in evidence, we unhesitatingly affirm the action of the collector in excluding, and refusing to permit entry of the same, and as to those books which were not introduced in evidence, there was no evidence introduced to overcome the presumption of correctness attaching to the action of the collector, and as to those books also the action of the collector is affirmed. The protest is overruled in toto. Let judgment be entered accordingly.

[Doc. 54]

## FILE MEMO

May 16, 1932.

Re: *Ulysses*

Spoke to Fishman of the Collector's office. He told me that *Ulysses* was in his hands, and that as soon as word was received from us that we intended to contest the detention it would be forwarded to the United States attorney.

A.L.

---

[Doc. 55]

RANDOM HOUSE
20 E 57 • NEW YORK
The American Selling Agent for the NONESUCH PRESS Limited Editions

May 16, 1932.

Mr. Morris L. Ernst,
285 Madison Avenue,
New York City.

Dear Morris:

The enclosed letter [See Doc. 52.—ED.] certainly calls for an immediate answer. Do you want to answer or should I? And in the event that you want me to answer the letter, will you please give me all the facts?

We are beginning to compile the librarians' statistics in accordance with your suggestion.

Cordially,

Bennett A. Cerf

bac;pk

146

May 17, 1932.

H.C. Stewart, Assistant Collector,
United States Customs Service,
Custom House,
New York City.

Attention: Mr. I. Fishman
Re: *Ulysses* by James Joyce
Your file #66241

Dear Sir:

We have your letter of May 13, 1932, advising us of the detention of the above entitled book under Section 305 of the Tariff Act, as obscene.

You state that *Ulysses* was the subject of Treasury Department Decision No. 42907, which was handed down in the United States Customs Court in the case of *Heymoolen* v. *United States* on August 1, 1928. You are apparently relying upon this decision.

We have examined the case. We find that there were 43 separate items of merchandise representing 11 different titles; that *Ulysses* did not come up for separate consideration or comment; that the plaintiff was not represented by counsel, and the case went by default; that all the items (insofar as one may judge by the titles) were, unlike *Ulysses*, technical works dealing with unnatural passion; and that if *Ulysses* had been presented for consideration by itself, the result might well have been otherwise. Moreover, the case arose under the Tariff Act of 1922. The Customs Court, as you are doubtless aware, no longer has any jurisdiction in matters of this kind. Hence the decision you refer to is scarcely in point.

However, we do not wish to delay matters, and we ask that you forward the book immediately to the United States Attorney for libel proceedings. Please advise us when this is done.

Yours very truly,

Greenbaum, Wolff & Ernst

AL:JF

[Doc. 57]

May 17, 1932.

Bennett A. Cerf, Esq.,
Random House, Inc.,
20 East 57th Street,
New York City.

Dear Mr. Cerf:                    Re: *Ulysses*

We are returning to you herewith the answers of librarians and the opinions of representative persons, which were sent to us a few days ago. We have kept no record of the answers of librarians, but we have retained photostats of the other opinions.

Have you made any arrangements to follow up the librarians and other persons who have not yet responded?

Robert Briffault, the anthropologist, has considerable standing and it might be a good idea to follow Mr. Crichton's suggestion of getting a letter from him.

Yours very truly,

Greenbaum, Wolff & Ernst

AL:JF

---

[Doc. 58]

May 20, 1932.

Random House, Inc.,
Bennett A. Cerf, Esq.,
20 East 57th Street,
New York City.

Dear Mr. Cerf:                    Re: *Ulysses*

We are returning to you herewith the representative opinions which you sent us May 19. We have had photostats made of the following:

George Jean Nathan
Robert M. Coates
E. Haldeman-Julius
Ben Ray Redman

148

The others are obviously of no help to us.

In regard to John Dos Passos' letter, you will doubtless agree that it would not be politic to submit to a judge testimony which refers to "even the dumbest judge" smelling a rat. Dos Passos' name is valuable and you ought to get in touch with him and secure a revised opinion, with no animadversions on our courts.

Yours very truly,

Greenbaum, Wolff & Ernst

AL:JF

---

[Doc. 59]

May 23, 1932.

I. Fishman, Esq.,
United States Customs Service,
Custom House,
New York City.

Dear Mr. Fishman:                    Re: *Ulysses*

This will confirm our telephone conversation of today. We are sending you herewith a copy of our letter of May 17, which was forwarded to you last week.

We shall sincerely appreciate prompt transmittal of the book to the United States Attorney.

Yours very truly,

Greenbaum, Wolff & Ernst

AL:JF

[Doc. 60]

TREASURY DEPARTMENT
UNITED STATES CUSTOMS SERVICE
NEW YORK, N.Y.

May 24, 1932.

Greenbaum, Wolff & Ernst,
285 Madison Avenue,
New York City.

Att. Mr. Alexander Lindey.

Sirs:

In accordance with your request of the 17th instant with regard to the book *Ulysses* by James Joyce, imported by Random House, Inc., you are informed that the book has this day been transmitted to the United States Attorney Southern District of New York for the institution of proceedings in the District Court for the forfeiture, confiscation and destruction of the book in accordance with the provisions of Section 305a of the Tariff Act of 1930.

Respectfully,

H.C. Stewart
Assistant Collector

---

[Doc. 61]

May 24, 1932.

Mr. Ben Huebsch,
c/o The Viking Press,
18 East 48th Street,
New York City.

Dear Ben:

Your note on *Ulysses* is exactly what I wanted, and I thank you very much for it.

Cordially,

Bennett A. Cerf

150

[Doc. 62]

May 26, 1932.

Bennett A. Cerf, Esq.,
Random House, Inc.,
20 East 57th Street,
New York City.

Dear Mr. Cerf:                        Re: *Ulysses*

We are returning to you herewith the representative opinions of the following:

> Theodore Dreiser
> Robert Briffault
> B.W. Huebsch
> Robert Morss Lovett
> Seth Low Junior College
> Dartmouth College
> Paul Popenoe

We have had photostats made of those which will be of use to us.

Yours very truly,
Greenbaum, Wolff & Ernst

AL:JF

---

[Doc. 63]

May 31, 1932.

Mr. George F. Bowerman,
The Public Library,
Washington, D.C.

Dear Mr. Bowerman:

Many thanks for your note of May 27th. We are carefully tabulating all the replies that we receive from librarians all over the country. These replies are still coming in at the rate of 20 or more a day. When we feel that we have the greater part of them in hand, we will make a very careful analysis of them. I will be very glad to send you a copy of this analysis as soon as it is made.

Cordially yours,
Bennett A. Cerf
Random House, Inc.

bac;pk

[Doc. 64]

RANDOM HOUSE
20 E 57 ● NEW YORK
The American Selling Agent for the NONESUCH PRESS Limited Editions

May 31, 1932.

Mr. Alexander Lindey,
c/o Greenbaum, Wolff & Ernst,
285 Madison Avenue,
New York City.

Dear Mr. Lindey:

I am sending you herewith a few more interesting comments on *Ulysses*, and also a lot of valuable material that was loaned to us by Miss Harriet Weaver. I am enclosing herewith Miss Weaver's letter so as to duly impress upon you the fact that this material must be specially guarded, so that we may return it to her.

I am also sending you a copy of a letter received from Mr. George F. Bowerman, along with a carbon of my reply to him. I think that this takes care of this matter once and for all.

Cordially yours,

Bennett A. Cerf
Random House, Inc.

bac;pk

―――――――――

[Doc. 65]

June 2, 1932.

Bennett A. Cerf, Esq.,
Random House, Inc.,
20 East 57th Street,
New York City.

Dear Mr. Cerf:                    Re: *Ulysses*

We have your letter of May 31, together with enclosures. We are returning to you herewith the testimonials of which we have secured photostats.

We shall take good care of Miss Weaver's material. We are glad that the question raised by Mr. Bowerman has apparently been adjusted to his satisfaction.

As you doubtless know, *Ulysses* is now in the hands of the United States Attorney for this district, and we are awaiting the commencement of libel proceedings. We shall then intervene in your behalf.

Yours very truly,

Greenbaum, Wolff & Ernst

AL:JF

---

**[Doc. 66]**

June 6, 1932.

Bennett A. Cerf, Esq.,
Random House, Inc.,
20 East 57th Street,
New York City.

Dear Mr. Cerf:

In accordance with our telephone conversation of June 3, 1932, we are sending you herewith the questionnaire to be used in connection with booksellers. [See Doc. 67.—ED.] Our suggestion is that the questionnaire be restricted only to the outstanding book stores and book departments, and that instead of sending out the questionnaire with a covering letter (as you did in the case of the librarians) you or your salesmen approach the booksellers in advance.

We believe that forty or fifty responses will be quite sufficient for our purpose.

Yours very truly,

Greenbaum, Wolff & Ernst

AL:JF

**[Doc. 67]**

[This is an enclosure to Doc. 66.—ED.]

## QUESTIONNAIRE

1. Do you believe *Ulysses* is of great literary importance?
2. In your opinion, is it one of the significant books of the age?
3. Do you believe that it should be generally circulated?
4. If the book were declared legal would you stock it for sale, and cooperate in effecting its general distribution?

Dated _____

_____
               Bookseller

By _____

Address _____

_____

**[Doc. 68]**

Certificate of Customs Custody.
United States Customs Service
Collection District No. 10, Port of New York.

Collector's Office 6/8/32.

To the _____

Please report if the goods described below are now, and have been, continually in customs custody since importation.

| Marks and Numbers | Description of Articles |
|---|---|
| | One book *Ulysses* addressed to Random House, Inc., 57th St., N.Y. City. |

_____
Deputy Collector.

The goods described above are now, and have been, in continuous customs custody since their importation.

Date 6/8/32

B.N. Handler,
Act. Dep. Collector.

154

[Doc. 69]

GREENBAUM, WOLFF & ERNST

OFFICE MEMORANDUM

TO:   M.L. Ernst                         FROM:   A. Lindey
RE:   *Ulysses*                          DATE:   June 14, 1932.

Nothing new developed on the book so I telephoned Coleman today.

He said that he was reading the book; that he had covered about 300 pages but was having a difficult time; that he was not in a position to give us definite word; that all he could say at this time was that the book was under consideration.

In view of this I inquired whether there was a possibility that the book would be returned to the Collector of Customs with the recommendation that libel proceedings be abandoned, as had been done in connection with *Enduring Passion*. Coleman said that he was not in a position to commit the U.S. Attorney's office and simply reiterated his statement that the book was under consideration. I then asked him whether there was anything that I could do to assist in his examination of the book, especially in view of his admitted difficulties. I told him that we had several books, notably *A Key to Ulysses*, which were bound to be helpful in the first reading of the book; and I volunteered to send them to him. He indicated that he preferred to plow through the book without external aid the first time but that he might ask me to send him the collateral aids later on. He reminded me of the fact that although his office had taken its time with *Enduring Passion*, the ultimate result, nevertheless, was what we desired. I explained that my telephone call had not been occasioned by any desire on our part to exert undue pressure but was merely an inquiry.

It seems to me that Coleman made a special effort to be cordial and cooperative even though he said that he could not tell at the present time when he would be ready to give his decision. He inquired about you and made a special point of wanting to be remembered to you.

Do you want me to get in touch with Bennett Cerf, and if so, what should I tell him?

**[Doc. 70]**

June 16, 1932.

Bennett A. Cerf, Esq.,
Random House, Inc.,
20 East 57th Street,
New York City.

Dear Mr. Cerf:                    Re: *Ulysses*

Thanks for your note of June 15. We are returning to you herewith the letter from Harriet Weaver. It would be a good idea for you to secure the back number of the Bookman and to send it on to us.

We have been in touch with the office of the United States Attorney for this district. Libel proceedings have not yet been commenced. One of the assistants has the book under consideration and he refuses to commit himself.

Yours very truly,
Greenbaum, Wolff & Ernst

AL:JF

---

**[Doc. 71]**

RANDOM HOUSE
20 E 57 • NEW YORK
The American Selling Agent for the NONESUCH PRESS Limited Editions

June 20, 1932.

Mr. Alexander Lindey,
c/o Greenbaum, Wolff & Ernst,
285 Madison Avenue,
New York City.

Dear Lindey:

Enclosed please find several answers from booksellers on *Ulysses*. There are also a few more replies brought in by the follow-up on our questionnaire to important people. It seems to me that letters like Cabell's and John Watson's might be helpful in that they tend to prove that even many intelligent people can't make head or tail out of *Ulysses*. This should strengthen the point that dumbbells in search of smut will certainly throw down the book in hopeless disgust after trying to wade through the first two chapters.

Cordially yours,
Bennett A. Cerf
Random House, Inc.

bac;pk

**[Doc. 72]**

June 22, 1932.

Bennett A. Cerf, Esq.,
Random House, Inc.,
20 East 57th Street,
New York City.

Dear Cerf:                              Re: *Ulysses*

I have your letter of June 20, together with enclosures.

I am returning the testimonials. Photostats have been made of all of them, excepting the Wise letter, as I quite agree with you that in view of the Canadian decision relative to Feuchtwanger's *Power* a comment on the forbidding dullness of *Ulysses* and its possible discouraging effect on smut-hunters may prove valuable.

For the time being I am retaining the booksellers' responses.

Yours very truly,
Greenbaum, Wolff & Ernst

AL:JF

---

**[Doc. 73]**

July 18, 1932.

Mr. Paul Léon,
27, Rue Casimir-Périer,
Paris, France.

Dear Mr. Léon:

In answer to your query of July 7th, I am pleased to tell you that the Customs authorities lost no time in seizing the special copy of *Ulysses*, exactly in accordance with our expectations and hopes. It was, of course, necessary for them to seize this book before we could make a test case of this situation. Now nothing remains but to wait until the case comes to trial. This will probably be some time in the early Fall and you may rest assured that I will keep you well informed as to developments as soon as they take place.

In Mr. Ernst, we have retained one of the best known and best informed attorneys in the country and I think that we may depend upon him to so arrange affairs that our case comes up before a judge that is as friendly as is possible, under the circumstances.

Cordially,
Bennett A. Cerf,
Random House, Inc.

bac;ref

[Doc. 74]

GREENBAUM, WOLFF & ERNST

OFFICE MEMORANDUM

TO:   Mr. Lindey                 FROM:   Mr. Ernst
RE:                              DATE:   July 23, 1932.

Spoke to Sam Coleman. He is nearly finished with *Ulysses*. He is very much in doubt if he will finish it by August 1st. He will let us know his conclusion. He is going away on his vacation August 1st and I suggest that you communicate with him before August 1st so in case he is going to start proceedings, he commences them before he leaves.

M.L.

---

[Doc. 75]

GREENBAUM, WOLFF & ERNST

OFFICE MEMORANDUM

TO:   M.L.E.                     FROM:   A.L.
RE:   *Ulysses*                  DATE:   July 30, 1932.

I talked to Coleman on Friday. He told me that he had finished the book. He thought that it was a literary masterpiece, but that it was obscene within the meaning of the federal law.

I asked him what he intended to do. Apparently he doesn't want to take upon himself the responsibility of starting proceedings. He said that he had turned over the book, with his opinion, to Medalie, and that he had put the final decision up to Medalie.

I asked him whether he could give me any idea as to when we could accept final, official word. He said that Medalie might want to read the book for himself, and that possibly we would not hear anything for the next two or three weeks. This will carry the matter into my vacation. Anyway, I do not believe that anything is likely to develop until the early part of September.

Coleman said that we should not object to his passing *Ulysses* around in the United States Attorney's office. He said that that was the only way his staff could get a literary education.

I'll see Medalie in town. [This appears to be Ernst's reply to Lindey.—ED.]

[Doc. 76]

GREENBAUM, WOLFF & ERNST

OFFICE MEMORANDUM

TO:  A.L.                         FROM:  M.L.E.
RE:  *Ulysses*                    DATE:  August 12, 1932.

Can you get out today some of the best material on *Ulysses*? I spoke to George Medalie and he is afraid he will have to proceed with the case; thinks it's a very important book and I am pretty sure that we could arrange to have it brought before Judge Woolsey and dispose of it by motion.

He also told me that he got into a lot of trouble because Baum started an action against a medical book, he, Medalie, calling Baum a damn fool. Medalie does not want to get in a jam again because in that case he forced the customs officials to carry the case themselves.

---

[Doc. 77]

September 1, 1932.

Mr. Alexander Lindey,
c/o Greenbaum, Wolff & Ernst,
285 Madison Avenue,
New York City.

Dear Lindey:

Enclosed is a letter from F. Scott Fitzgerald which should be very helpful. [See Doc. 30.—ED.] It is short and to the point.

Is there any news to report?

Cordially,

Bennett A. Cerf
Random House, Inc.

bac;ref

---

**[Doc. 78]**

September 6, 1932.

Bennett A. Cerf, Esq.,
Random House, Inc.,
20 East 57th Street,
New York City.

Dear Mr. Cerf:                    Re: *Ulysses*

I have your letters of August 11, 16 and September 1. I am returning your salesman's letter, as well as F. Scott Fitzgerald's original note. I have had a photostat made of the latter. I am also returning for classification the librarian's questionnaire.

There is no news. The government will probably start libel proceedings this month.

Yours very truly,

Greenbaum, Wolff & Ernst

AL:JF

————————

**[Doc. 79]**

GREENBAUM, WOLFF & ERNST

OFFICE MEMORANDUM

TO:  M.L.E.                    FROM:  A.L.
RE:  *Ulysses*                 DATE:  September 20, 1932.

Bennett Cerf called me up. He says that in view of the various questionnaires that they sent out they are now being deluged with inquiries as to when *Ulysses* is coming out. He says that, with the interest now awakened, a protracted delay will be prejudicial to the sale of the book, as the interest is bound to wane.

I explained to him that you had been in touch with Medalie, and that Medalie had promised to start libel proceedings promptly. I told Cerf that I would do nothing until you return, the early part of next week.

————————

[Doc. 80]

GREENBAUM, WOLFF & ERNST

OFFICE MEMORANDUM

TO:                                    FROM:   M. L. Ernst
RE:   *Ulysses*                        DATE:   September 27, 1932.

Had a long talk with Mr. Medalie. He is worried about the latter part of the book, particularly as to the musings of the wife. He wants to see everything that comes from libraries and particularly from colleges. He says he is not at all worried about the children. He does not want to start anything until Woolsey gets back, which will be October 4th.

There was no use in pressing Medalie in starting a libel action as long as he kept on saying that he did not want to proceed. He was particularly impressed by the *New York Times* letter. We ought to get more letters from the *Times* and the *Tribune*, such as Irita Van Doren, Arthur Crock, etc., particularly those who can write on the *New York Times* or the *New York Tribune* letterheads.

Can you get a letter from Schriftgieser and/or Parker, of the *Boston Transcript*.

We are to send Medalie some of the college-library material and he will get in touch with us by October 10th.

---

[Doc. 81]

GREENBAUM, WOLFF & ERNST

OFFICE MEMORANDUM

TO:   Mr. Lindey                       FROM:   Mr. Ernst
RE:   *Ulysses*                        DATE:   September 27, 1932.

If, as and when a libel action is started in the *Ulysses* matter, make a note to call up Huston, of the *World-Telegram*.

---

[Doc. 82]

27, Rue Casimir-Périer (VII$^E$)
Littre 88-89
September the 27-th., 1932.

B.A. Cerf  Esq.
Random House, Inc.
20 East 57-th. Street
New York City, U.S.A.

Dear Mr. Cerf,

Mr. Joyce has been approached by Warner Bros. First National Films Inc. Paris Office about a project of filming *Ulysses*. Mr. Joyce's health does not permit him at the present moment to go into this matter besides the entire idea seems to be unsettled yet. I have replied them in a dilatory manner, but have had no reply from them yet.

Just in case there might be some pirating idea under this proposal I am writing to you this in order to warn you please to be on your guard and should you hear something please to inform me or if you are in a position to take steps to prevent it.

We are here eagerly expecting the results of your venture.
Believe me,

Yours sincerely,

Paul Léon

---

[Doc. 83]

October 11, 1932.

Mr. Paul Léon,
27, Rue Casimir-Périer,
Paris VII$^E$, France.

Dear Mr. Léon:

Thank you for your letter of September 27th, calling my attention to the fact that Warner Bros. have approached Mr. Joyce with a project for filming *Ulysses*. Let me assure you that there is no pirating idea in this proposal. Warner Bros. are one of the biggest picture producers in the world, and if they could possibly build up some kind of a moving picture based on *Ulysses*, it would help the sale of Mr. Joyce's book in every country in the world. They would also be willing to pay a substantial sum for the moving picture rights, and all in all, Mr. Joyce would profit in every possible way if he could consummate such a sale. Personally, I cannot see how on earth a moving picture could be built out of this book, but that is certainly the problem for Warner Brothers and not for us.

We are in great hopes that our own case on *Ulysses* will come up very soon. Be assured that I will write to you just as soon as there is any news to give you in this matter.

Cordially yours,
Bennett A. Cerf,
Random House, Inc.

bac;pk

---

**[Doc. 84]**

**FILE MEMO**

October 19, 1932.

Re: *Ulysses*

M.L.E. called Coleman, and Coleman promised to take the matter up immediately with Medalie. A.L. likewise phoned Coleman and indicated to him that the matter was of some urgency because of information received by Modern Library to the effect that a pirated edition of *Ulysses* was coming out. Coleman promised to get word to us promptly.

A.L.

---

**[Doc. 85]**

RANDOM HOUSE
20 E 57 ● NEW YORK
The American Selling Agent for the NONESUCH PRESS Limited Editions

October 20, 1932.

Mr. Morris Ernst,
c/o Greenbaum, Wolff & Ernst,
285 Madison Avenue,
New York City.

Dear Morris:

We have pretty definite information that the gentleman who is contemplating a pirated edition of *Ulysses* is one Joseph Meyers, who does business at 100 Fifth Avenue, under the name of Illustrated Editions, Inc. Of course, we have no positive proof that he is planning this book, but since we have had it by word of mouth from two different booksellers, it is reasonably obvious that he is talking about it. I would like to scare him off, if possible, before he actually gets started.

Let me explain that this Meyers is a notorious pirate, and any appeal on purely ethical grounds will fall on deaf ears.

Can we write him some kind of a letter threatening to clap an injunction upon him, and seize any copies of *Ulysses* that he prints as soon as they come off the press? I think he is the type that can be readily frightened into abandoning this project.

Please let me know about this. I consider it of great importance, as obviously a cheap pirated edition will take all the cream off of our own.

Cordially,

Bennett A. Cerf
Random House, Inc.

---

[Doc. 86]

## MEMO

October 21, 1932.

Re: *Ulysses*

Telephoned Cerf re his letter of October 20, and suggested that he send a decoy letter to Meyers. He said he would do so, and let us know.

A.L.

---

[Doc. 87]

### GREENBAUM, WOLFF & ERNST

### OFFICE MEMORANDUM

TO: Mr. Lindey  FROM: M.L.E.
RE: *Ulysses*   DATE: November 11, 1932.

Call up Coleman's secretary and get calendar of judges.

**[Doc. 88]**

November 11, 1932.

Bennett A. Cerf, Esq.,
Random House, Inc.,
20 East 57th Street,
New York City.

Dear Cerf:                              Re: *Ulysses*

Just came from a luncheon at the District Attorney's office, and I am sorry to advise you that we have been unable to get the District Attorney to admit the volume without presentation to the court. The libel proceeding will be started by the United States government within a few days. The case will be disposed of some time between now and March, depending on the calendar.

We have worked out a procedure whereby we can avoid the reading of the book in court. The case will come up for argument on a motion.

We have done everything we could to prevent this long delay, but did not dare to be too dogmatic in our demand for a prompt trial, for fear that the District Attorney would exercise his right to insist upon a reading of the complete book before a jury.

Yours very truly,

MLE:JF

---

**[Doc. 89]**

November 14, 1932.

Mr. Morris Ernst,
c/o Greenbaum, Wolff & Ernst,
285 Madison Avenue,
New York City.

Dear Morris:

I am sorry to hear that we will have to have some court hocus pocus on *Ulysses*. I'd like to hear more about your conversation with the District Attorney in this matter.

Cordially,

Bennett A. Cerf

[Doc. 90]

GREENBAUM, WOLFF & ERNST

OFFICE MEMORANDUM

TO:   Mr. Lindey            FROM:   M.L.E.
RE:                         DATE:   November 17, 1932.

Sam Coleman phoned and said he found that there was a new rule under which trials could be given a preference and he is checking up to find out when Knox or Woolsey are sitting in Trial Term. He will let me know and then we can proceed.

---

[Doc. 91]

UNITED STATES DISTRICT COURT
SOUTHERN DISTRICT OF NEW YORK

UNITED STATES OF AMERICA,

                    Libellant,           A 110-59
     —against—

ONE BOOK entitled *Ulysses*
by James Joyce

TO THE HONORABLES THE JUDGES OF THE UNITED STATES DISTRICT COURT FOR THE SOUTHERN DISTRICT OF NEW YORK.

On December 9, 1932 comes George Z. Medalie, United States Attorney for the Southern District of New York, in a cause of forfeiture, confiscation and destruction under the Tariff Act of 1930, and on information and belief informs the court as follows:

FIRST: That on or about the 8th day of May, 1932, the Collector of Customs at the Port and Collection District of New York did seize on land in the Southern District of New York and within the jurisdiction of this Court, one bound and printed book entitled *Ulysses* by James Joyce, which arrived in the United States from a foreign country, to wit, England, via United States mail, addressed to Random House, Inc., New York City. That on May 24, 1932, pursuant to the provisions of the aforesaid Act, the Collector did transmit information thereof to the District Attorney and that said Collector of Customs now holds said book within the Southern District of New York as forfeited to the United States for the causes propounded as follows:

That said book has been imported into the United States at the Port and Collection District of New York in the Southern District of New York and within the jurisdiction of this Court contrary to the form of the statute of the United States in such cases made and provided, to wit, Section 305 of Title III of the Tariff Act approved June 17, 1930.

SECOND: The United States Attorney on information and belief further informs the Court and says that all the premises are true and that by reason thereof and by force of the statute in such cases made and provided, to wit, Section 305 of Title III of the Tariff Act approved June 17, 1930, the above mentioned book became subject to forfeiture, confiscation and destruction and the United States became and is entitled to a decree of forfeiture directing the destruction of said book.

WHEREFORE the said United States Attorney for the libellant herein prays that due process issue in that behalf as well as a monition to all parties in interest, to appear on the return day of such process and duly intervene herein by claim and plea in the premises, and due proceedings be had thereon that for the causes aforesaid said book be condemned by decree of forfeiture and be destroyed according to law, or such other disposition be made thereof as the Court shall direct.

Dated: New York, N.Y.    December 9, 1932.

> GEORGE Z. MEDALIE, United States Attorney for the Southern District of New York, Proctor for Libellant, Office & P. Address, U.S. Courts and P.O. Bldg., Borough of Manhattan, City of New York.

---

**[Doc. 92]**

State of New York,   }   ss.:
County of New York, }

Harry G. Herman, being duly sworn, deposes and says that he is an Assistant United States Attorney for the Southern District of New York, and as such is in charge of the above-entitled action.

That your deponent has read the foregoing libel and the same is true to his own knowledge, except as to those matters alleged upon information and belief, and as to those matters he believes it to be true.

That the reason this vertification is made by deponent and not by defendant is that the defendant is a corporation sovereign, and your deponent is the Assistant United States Attorney duly authorized to prepare and verify this libel, and the sources of your deponent's knowledge and information consist of letters and documents received in your deponent's official capacity from the Treasury Department.

HARRY G. HERMAN.

Sworn to before me this 7th day of December, 1932.

Catharine M. Conlan,
Notary Public.
Bronx Co. No. 77, Reg. 63-C-33.
Cert. filed in N. Y. Co. No. 493, Reg. 3-C-341.
Commission expires March 30, 1933.

---

[Doc. 93]

UNITED STATES DISTRICT COURT
SOUTHERN DISTRICT OF NEW YORK

UNITED STATES OF AMERICA,

Libellant,

No. A 110-59

—against—

CLAIM

ONE BOOK entitled *Ulysses*
by James Joyce

AND NOW, MORRIS L. ERNST, intervening as agent for the interest of the claimant, Random House, Inc., a corporation with principal place of business in the City, County and State of New York, in the above entitled proceedings, appears before the Honorable Court and makes claim to one book entitled *Ulysses*, by James Joyce, which has been seized by the Collector of Customs at the Port and Collection District of New York; and Morris L. Ernst further avers, on information and belief, that the said book, at the time of the seizure thereof, was and still is in the possession of the Collector of Customs at the Port and Collection District of New York; and Morris L. Ernst further avers that the claimant herein, to wit, Random House, Inc. is the true and bona fide owner of said book; that no other person is the owner thereof;

and that he, Morris L. Ernst, is the true and lawful agent of the claimant in the above entitled proceedings.

WHEREFORE, Morris L. Ernst, as agent for the claimant, prays to make claim to said book accordingly.

GREENBAUM, WOLFF & ERNST,
Proctors for Claimant
Office and P.O. Address,
285 Madison Avenue
Borough of Manhattan,
City of New York.

---

[Doc. 94]

UNITED STATES OF AMERICA
SOUTHERN DISTRICT OF NEW YORK } SS.:
COUNTY AND STATE OF NEW YORK

MORRIS L. ERNST, being duly sworn, deposes and says:

1. I reside at No. 46 West 11th Street, in the Borough of Manhattan, City, County and State of New York, which is in the Southern District of New York.

2. I am the agent of Random House, Inc., the owner of the book mentioned in the foregoing claim, in the proceedings referred to in the claim. The said owner is a corporation having its place of business at 20 East 57th Street, Borough of Manhattan, City, County and State of New York.

3. I have been duly authorized to intervene in these proceedings, and to put in this claim on behalf of the owner of the said book. The foregoing claim is true to my knowledge, except as to matters therein stated to be alleged on information and belief; and as to such matters I believe it to be true.

MORRIS L. ERNST

Sworn to before me this
16th day of December, 1932.

PAULA GROSS
Notary Public

---

[Doc. 95]

## UNITED STATES DISTRICT COURT
## SOUTHERN DISTRICT OF NEW YORK

UNITED STATES OF AMERICA,

|  |  |
|---|---|
| Libellant, | No. A 110-59 |
| —against— | CLAIMANT'S ANSWER |

ONE BOOK entitled *Ulysses*
by James Joyce

The claimant, Random House, Inc., a corporation, owner of the book herein, entitled *Ulysses*, by James Joyce, answering the libel herein, by Greenbaum, Wolff & Ernst, its Proctors, states to the Court as follows:

FIRST: The Claimant admits the importation by the claimant of a bound and printed book, entitled *Ulysses* by James Joyce, into the United States from a foreign country, in May, 1932; and the claimant further admits that on or about the 8th day of May, 1932 the Collector of Customs at the Port and Collection District of New York did seize the said book on land in the Southern District of New York and within the jurisdiction of this Court.

SECOND: The claimant denies that the said book has been imported into the United States at the Port and Collection District of New York, in the Southern District of New York, and within the jurisdiction of this Court contrary to the form of the statute of the United States in such cases made and provided, to wit, Section 305 of Title III of the Tariff Act, Approved June 17, 1930.

THIRD: The claimant further denies that by force of the aforesaid statute or any other statute of the United States that the said book became subject to forfeiture, confiscation and destruction, and that the United States is entitled to a decree of forfeiture directing the destruction of said book.

WHEREFORE, the claimant prays that judgment be entered directing that the said book, *Ulysses*, be admitted into the United States, and for such other and further relief as to the Court may seem just and proper in the premises.

> GREENBAUM, WOLFF & ERNST,
> Proctors for Claimant
> Office & P.O. Address,
> 285 Madison Avenue
> Borough of Manhattan,
> New York City

170

UNITED STATES OF AMERICA
SOUTHERN DISTRICT OF NEW YORK } SS.:
COUNTY AND STATE OF NEW YORK

BENNETT A. CERF, being duly sworn, deposes and says: That he is the President of Random House, Inc., the claimant within named; that he has read and knows the contents of the foregoing answer; that the same is true of his own knowledge, except as to the matters therein stated to be alleged on information and belief, and as to those matters he believes it to be true.

That the reason why this verification is made by deponent and not by claimant is because claimant is a domestic corporation, and deponent is one of its officers, to wit, President.

BENNETT A. CERF

Sworn to before me this
19th day of December, 1932.

T.F. HILBERT
Notary Public

---

UNITED STATES DISTRICT COURT
SOUTHERN DISTRICT OF NEW YORK

UNITED STATES OF AMERICA,

Libellant,                          No. A. 110-59

—against—
                                    STIPULATION FOR
ONE BOOK entitled *Ulysses*         CLAIMANT'S COSTS
by James Joyce                      ENTERED INTO PURSUANT
                                    TO THE RULES IN
                                    PRACTICE IN THIS COURT

WHEREAS, on or about the 9th day of December, 1932, a libel was filed in this court by George Z. Medalie, Esq., United Stated Attorney for the Southern District of New York, on behalf of the United States against one book entitled *Ulysses*, for the alleged reasons and causes set forth in the libel; and

WHEREAS, a claim to the said book has been filed by Random House, Inc., a corporation, through Morris L. Ernst, agent for said corporation; and

WHEREAS, Bennett A. Cerf and Donald S. Klopfer, stipulators, parties hereto, hereby consent and agree that if the libellant recover costs herein, the decree therefor, not exceeding the sum of Two hundred fifty ($250) Dollars, may be entered against them and each of them, and thereupon execution may issue against their and each of their goods, chattels, lands and tenements or other real estate,

NOW, THEREFORE, it is hereby stipulated and agreed for the benefit of whom it may concern, that the undersigned, Bennett A. Cerf, stipulator, residing at 112 West 59th Street, Borough of Manhattan, City, County and State of New York, and the undersigned, Donald S. Klopfer, stipulator, residing at 1112 Park Avenue, Borough of Manhattan, City, County and State of New York, shall be and each of them is, hereby bound in the sum of $250, on condition that they shall pay all costs and expenses which shall be awarded against the claimant herein, and/or the undersigned stipulators or either of them by decree of this court; and in case of appeal, by any appellate court.

BENNETT A. CERF
Bennett A. Cerf, Stipulator

DONALD S. KLOPFER
Donald S. Klopfer, Stipulator

Taken and acknowledged before me
this 19th day of December, 1932.

T.F. HILBERT
Notary Public

UNITED STATES OF AMERICA
SOUTHERN DISTRICT OF NEW YORK } SS.:
COUNTY AND STATE OF NEW YORK

The above stipulator, being duly sworn, deposes and says: I reside at 112 West 59th Street, Borough of Manhattan, City of New York, and I am worth in excess of the sum of $250.00 over and above all my debts and liabilities.

BENNETT A. CERF

Sworn to before me this
19th day of December, 1932.

T.F. HILBERT
Notary Public

UNITED STATES OF AMERICA ⎱
SOUTHERN DISTRICT OF NEW YORK ⎰ SS.:
COUNTY AND STATE OF NEW YORK ⎭

The above stipulator, being duly sworn, deposes and says: I reside at 1112 Park Avenue, Borough of Manhattan, City of New York, and I am worth in excess of the sum of $250.00 over and above all my debts and liabilities.

Sworn to before me this        DONALD S. KLOPFER
19th day of December, 1932.

T.F. HILBERT
Notary Public

---

[Doc. 98]

GREENBAUM, WOLFF & ERNST

OFFICE MEMORANDUM

TO: M.L.E.              FROM: A.L.
RE: *Ulysses*         DATE: December 21, 1932.

Telephoned Coleman. He said that the January assignments were not yet out, but that he would know definitely within a week or ten days. He promised to call me and let me know, before the end of the year.

---

[Doc. 99]

GREENBAUM, WOLFF & ERNST

OFFICE MEMORANDUM

TO: M.L.E.              FROM: A.L.
RE: *Ulysses*         DATE: January 4, 1933.

Called Coleman today relative to the assignment of judges. Coleman and Coxe are sitting in trial term this month. Coleman doesn't feel that either of these two would be suitable for our purposes. He suggests that we hold off until we know what the February assignment will be. His plan in detail, is as follows:

1. The Government will join us in an application to the Court to secure a preference for the trial of the case.

2. The case will then be set down for trial.

3. Since we are entitled to a jury there will be a stipulation as to having a jury of one.

4. At the beginning of the case there will be a motion to dismiss the libel, which will probably be denied because the Judge will not have read the book. The book will then be put in evidence, and the motion will be renewed.

5. When the judge has come to a final decision he will direct a verdict.

Coleman insists on having it done this way. Personally I think that the procedure which we followed in the *Contraception* case was better. However since Coleman insists on this procedure I see no reason to object. He will probably get the same results.

---

January 9, 1933.

Let me know as soon as you know the judge who is sitting next month. See me before you talk further with Coleman.

M.L.E.

---

[Doc. 100]

CLERK'S OFFICE
DISTRICT COURT OF THE UNITED STATES
SOUTHERN DISTRICT OF NEW YORK

New York City   Jan. 12, 1933

Notice is hereby given that the following Calendar number has been assigned to the case listed below.

| DOCKET NO. | TITLE | JURY CALENDAR NO. |
|---|---|---|
| A110-59 | *United States of America* vs. *One Book entitled Ulysses* | 1438 |

Respectfully,

Frank J. Gunner, Jr.
Calendar Commissioner

[Doc. 101]

27, Rue Casimir-Périer (VII$^E$)<br>
Littre 88-89<br>
Paris, February the 9-th. 1933.

B. Cerf, Esq.
Random House Inc.
20 East 57-th., Street
New York City.

Dear Mr. Cerf,

I have received the message concerning the publication of *Ulysses* in the USA you sent through Madame Léon and, since, I have seen the circular note on the same subject. I am glad to learn that the affair is nearing a settlement which should enable the publication at an early date.

May I address a request to you. You wrote to me and also mention in the circular note that you have gathered some 200 different opinions on *Ulysses* for the purposes of the case. As such may or rather will sooner or later come up before the courts in England on the same point it would save considerable time and trouble if you were kind enough to send me a copy of all these opinions with permission to utilise when necessary those among them which you have collected yourself and which have not appeared in print. In case it would be impossible to obtain a complete copy of the material gathered a list of it would also be of use but I hope that you will find your way to send me the copies. I will have to study them and anyhow the use to be made of them, if any, would never be made before you have availed yourself of them.

In the circular note you mention an introduction by Mr. Joyce—the letter he has written can hardly be called an introduction as it relates only to the exterior history of the book. If you need this word for purposes of publicity in circulars and advertisements I do not think Mr. Joyce will have any objection to it. In the book however it might perhaps be more advisable to use a different denomination as e.g. prefatory letter or anything else in this vein. We are however too far yet from the date of the publication to settle this question.

I enclose an announcement of a new edition of *Pomes Penyeach* which coming as it does from the O.U.P. might be added to the list of evidence and prove of use to you.

Believe me,

Sincerely yours,<br><br>
Paul Léon

[Doc. 102]

February 17, 1933.

Mr. Paul Léon,
27, Rue Casimir-Périer,
Paris VII$^E$, France.

Dear Mr. Léon:

We are still waiting for a favorable and liberal judge to sit on the Federal bench in New York before we take the case of *Ulysses* into court. This should come in the near future. In the meantime, our hands are tied.

I realize that Mr. Joyce's letter can hardly be called an introduction. We merely used this word for publicity in circulars and advertisements. In the book we will surely use something nearer the actual vein of the letter, such as "preface" or "prefatory letter".

Thank you for your inclusion of the Oxford University Press announcement. I have sent it down to our lawyer.

With regard to the various opinions on *Ulysses*, I feel sure that our lawyer will have to draw these up in convincing form before we go to court. I hate to duplicate this work, so I should prefer to wait a month or so before sending you a copy of their findings, and copies of the opinions which we have received, that they do not use. I assure you these will be at your disposal once we have settled the matter over here either one way or the other.

Cordially yours,

Donald S. Klopfer
Random House, Inc.

dsk;pk

---

[Doc. 103]

GREENBAUM, WOLFF & ERNST

## OFFICE MEMORANDUM

TO:  A.L.                              FROM:  M.L.E.
RE:  *Ulysses*                         DATE:  March 20, 1933.

Baum called up in re *Ulysses*. Woolsey and Knox are both out of the question for months. I suggested either Patterson or Cox.

[Doc. 104]

GREENBAUM, WOLFF & ERNST

OFFICE MEMORANDUM

TO: M.L.E.          FROM: A.L.
RE: *Ulysses*        DATE: March 23, 1933.

I telephoned Coleman this morning as per your suggestion. He is still on the job and is likely to be indefinitely.

As you know, the case under our present plan will come in jury part. At the present time Bondy is sitting. He was supposed to be followed by Knox, but Knox is ill. At any rate, the present calendar is considerably confused. Coleman says that the jury calendar for April ought to be out in a day or two and we will then be in a better position to know where we stand. I will call him again early next week.

I just received a note from Cerf inquiring concerning the case. Do you want to ring him up or should I?

You do it. [This is Ernst's reply.—ED.]

---

[Doc. 105]

GREENBAUM, WOLFF & ERNST

OFFICE MEMORANDUM

TO: M.L.E.          FROM: A. Lindey
RE: *Ulysses*        DATE: April 20, 1933.

I called Coleman pursuant to your suggestion.

He said that he had hoped, when he spoke to you, to get hold of Woolsey. He now finds that he cannot do it. His plan, as I understand it, was to waive jury trial and to transfer the case from law to equity and to secure a preference. Unfortunately, Cox and Caffey are sitting next month.

I then repeated the suggestion that I made months ago, namely—that instead of a trial, we proceed as we did in *U.S.* vs. *Contraception*; i.e. make a motion to dismiss the libel. This would bring the case up in motion part. However, the situation there is no better. This month Bondy is sitting; next month Coleman.

Coleman wanted to speak to you about something else. I suggest that you call him back.

[Doc. 106]

### FILE MEMO

May 5, 1933.

Re: *Ulysses*

M.L.E. talked with Coleman. Judge Coxe will be sitting in Motion Part the latter part of this month. Coleman will make a motion for judgment on the pleadings, and it will come up before Coxe. He will try to see the Judge in advance, to find out whether the Judge will want to read *Ulysses* before the motion is heard.

A.L.

———————

[Doc. 107]

May 5, 1933.

Collector of Customs,
Customs House,
New York, N.Y.

Att: Mr. H.C. Stewart
Gentlemen:                                        Re: *Ulysses* by James Joyce

This is to advise you that I have just received, through the United States Customs, a copy of *Ulysses*, which was sent to me from Maison du Livre Français, 4, Rue Pelibien, 4, Paris 6$^E$, France.

In view of the fact that the Customs authorities have heretofore seized previous importations of the same book, am I correct in assuming that there has been a change of attitude on your part, and that *Ulysses* is now legal for admission into the United States?

If I am not correct in this assumption, I stand ready to surrender to you for seizure the copy which has just been delivered to me. I then propose to contest the seizure, and to make formal application to the Secretary of the Treasury for the admission of the volume, under that portion of Section 305 of the Tariff Act of 1930 which permits the Secretary in his discretion to permit the importation of the so-called classics, or works of recognized scientific or literary merit.

I shall appreciate your prompt advices.

Yours very truly,
Greenbaum, Wolff & Ernst
By Alexander Lindey

AL:JF

178

TREASURY DEPARTMENT
United States Customs Service
New York, N.Y.

BNH/gh
16166                                                     May 10th, 1933.

Greenbaum, Wolff & Ernst,
285 Madison Avenue,
New York City.

(Attention of Mr. Alexander Lindey)

Sir:

Receipt is acknowledged of your letter of May 5, 1933, in which you advise that you have just received through the Post Office a copy of the book entitled *Ulysses*, which was sent from France. In view of the fact that previous importations of the same book have been seized, you ask whether you are correct in assuming that the book may now be imported into the United States.

In reply you are informed that there has been no change with regard to the admissibility of the book *Ulysses*. Therefore, in accordance with your suggestion, you may surrender the same to the Law Division of this office in the original package in which it was received and, as you further state, make formal application to the Secretary of the Treasury for the admission of the book under that portion of Section 305 of the Tariff Act which permits the Secretary, in his discretion, to release the so-called classics or works of recognized scientific or literary merit.

Respectfully,

H.C. Stewart
Assistant Collector

[Doc. 109]

May 13, 1933.

H.C. Stewart, Esq.,
c/o Collector of Customs,
Customs House,
New York City

Re: *Ulysses* by James Joyce
Dear Sir:                                    File #16166

We wish to acknowledge receipt of your letter of May 10, 1933.

We are sending you herewith, by messenger, a copy of the book entitled *Ulysses*, which was sent to the undersigned from France, and which has apparently slipped through the Customs. You will note that the book is being transmitted to you in the original package.

We assume that in due course we shall receive a notice of seizure. Thereafter we will advise you that we intend to protest the seizure and make a formal application to the Secretary of the Treasury for the admission of the book, under that portion of Section 305 of the Tariff Act which permits the Secretary, in his discretion, to release the so-called classics or works of recognized scientific or literary merit.

Yours very truly,

Greenbaum, Wolff & Ernst

By: Alexander Lindey

AL:JF

---

[Doc. 110]

## UNITED STATES DISTRICT COURT
## SOUTHERN DISTRICT OF NEW YORK

UNITED STATES OF AMERICA,

Libellant,
—against—

1 book entitled *Ulysses* by
James Joyce.

IT IS HEREBY STIPULATED AND AGREED by and between the proctor for the libellant and the proctors for the claimant herein that the book *Ulysses* by James Joyce against which libel proceedings have heretofore been commenced, be annexed to and become part of the libel filed herein and by this reference herein is in the said libel incorporated as if therein entirely restated and re-capitulated, and it is

FURTHER STIPULATED AND AGREED that the claimant hereby waives its right to trial by jury, and it is

FURTHER STIPULATED AND AGREED that both parties hereto will move for judgment herein and that upon such motion the Court may consider, pass upon and decide all questions of law and fact herein involved and that the Court may, after such consideration, render general findings of fact and conclusions of law, and it is

FURTHER STIPULATED AND AGREED that upon such motion the judgment of the Court may be entered herein by either party upon proper notice as if it were judgment after trial.

Dated, N.Y. May 15, 1933   GEORGE Z. MEDALIE
           Proctor for Libellant

           GREENBAUM, WOLFF & ERNST
           Proctors for Claimant

---

[Doc. 111]

UNITED STATES DISTRICT COURT
SOUTHERN DISTRICT OF NEW YORK

UNITED STATES OF AMERICA,

       Libellant,    NOTICE OF MOTION
 —against—        A 110-59

1 book entitled *Ulysses*
by James Joyce.

SIRS:

PLEASE TAKE NOTICE that upon the pleadings and all proceedings heretofore had herein, the undersigned will move this Court at a term for the hearing of motions to be held in and for the Southern District of New York, at the United States Courthouse and Post Office Building, in the Borough of Manhattan, City of New York, on the 23d day of May, 1933, at the opening of Court on that day or as soon thereafter as counsel can be heard, for an order granting judgment in favor of the libellant upon the pleadings and for such other and further relief as to the Court may seem just and proper.
Dated: New York, May 15, 1933.

Yours, etc.,

GEORGE Z. MEDALIE,
United States Attorney for the
Southern District of New York,
Proctor for Libellant,
Office & Post Office Address
U.S. Courts & P.O. Building
Borough of Manhattan
City of New York

TO:
Messrs. Greenbaum, Wolff & Ernst
Proctors for the Claimant
Post Office Address
285 Madison Avenue
City of New York

---

[Doc. 112]

GREENBAUM, WOLFF & ERNST

OFFICE MEMORANDUM

TO: M.L.E.           FROM: A.L.
RE: *Ulysses*        DATE: May 17, 1933.

I called both Coleman and Atlas, his assistant, twice on Tuesday, without getting either of them. I am calling them again today. We have not yet received the stipulation.

---

**[Doc. 113]**

TREASURY DEPARTMENT
United States Customs Service
New York, N.Y.

16166

May 22, 1933.

Greenbaum, Wolff & Ernst,
285 Madison Avenue,
New York City.

Att. Mr. Alexander Lindey

Sirs:

Receipt is acknowledged of your letter of May 13th together with the original package containing a copy of the book entitled *Ulysses* which was sent to you from France and which apparently slipped through the mails.

In reply to the letter I have to inform you in Treasury Decision 42907 of August 1, 1928 the United States Customs Court held that the book was obscene. In view thereof similar action will be taken with respect to the present shipment. The book is subject to detention under the provisions of Section 305 of the Tariff Act and will be seized and forfeited as provided by law.

Your statement is noted that you intend to make a formal application to the Secretary of the Treasury for the admission of the book under that portion of Section 305 of the Tariff Act which permits the Secretary of the Treasury in his discretion to release the so-called classics or books of recognized scientific or literary merit.

With regard to the above your attention is invited to Article 660 (h) of the Customs Regulations of 1931 which provide, with regard to petitions on the ground that the book is a classic, that petitioners must establish their claims by satisfactory evidence. Mere unsupported statements or allegations will not be considered. If you will file such a petition with this office it will be forwarded.

Respectfully,

H.C. Stewart
Assistant Collector

[Doc. 114]

## Claimant's Notice of Motion

### UNITED STATES DISTRICT COURT
### SOUTHERN DISTRICT OF NEW YORK

UNITED STATES OF AMERICA,

Libellant,

against

ONE BOOK entitled Ulysses
by James Joyce.

A 110-59.

Sir:

PLEASE TAKE NOTICE that upon the pleadings and all proceedings heretofore had herein, the undersigned will move this Court at a term for the hearing of motions to be held in and for the Southern District of New York, at the United States Courthouse and Post Office Building, in the Borough of Manhattan, City of New York, on the 23rd day of May, 1933, at the opening of court on that day or as soon thereafter as counsel can be heard, for an order granting judgment in favor of the claimant upon the pleadings and for such other and further relief as to the Court may seem just and proper.

Dated, New York, May 22nd, 1933.

Yours, etc.,

GREENBAUM, WOLFF & ERNST,
Proctors for the Claimant,
Office & P.O. Address,
285 Madison Avenue,
Manhattan Borough,
City of New York.

To:
GEORGE Z. MEDALIE, Esq.,
United States Attorney for the
Southern District of New York,
Proctor for Libellant,
Office & P.O. Address,
U.S. Courts & P.O. Building,
Manhattan Borough,
City of New York.

[Doc. 115]

## Note of Issue

UNITED STATES DISTRICT COURT
SOUTHERN DISTRICT OF NEW YORK

UNITED STATES OF AMERICA,

*v.*

ONE BOOK entitled *Ulysses* by James Joyce.

Admiralty
No. 110-59.

Note of Issue.
Motion for Judgment on the pleadings and a cross-motion for Judgment on the pleadings.

---

Attorney for the Libellant: GEORGE Z. MEDALIE, Esq., U. S. Attorney for the Southern District of N. Y.

Attorneys for the Claimant: GREENBAUM, WOLFF & ERNST, 285 Madison Ave., N. Y. C.  Returnable May 23rd, 1933.

---

[Doc. 116]

May 24, 1933.

Bennett A. Cerf, Esq.,
c/o Random House,
20 East 57th Street,
New York City.

### Re: *Ulysses*

Dear Mr. Cerf:

This will confirm our telephone conversation of yesterday. For technical reasons Judge Coxe declined to entertain the motion for judgment on the pleadings. The motion, therefore, was adjourned until June 16, 1933. We shall know the assignment of judges within the next few days, and advise you.

We have your note about Random House, and also the magazine containing the article on Joyce.

Yours very truly,
Greenbaum, Wolff & Ernst

AL:JF

[Doc. 117]

GREENBAUM, WOLFF & ERNST

OFFICE MEMORANDUM

TO: JOE [Jonas Shapiro]    FROM: A.L.
RE: *Ulysses*    DATE: May 24, 1933.

The motion was adjourned until June 16, at which time we ought to be prepared with our brief and with argument. Within the next few days get in touch with the Clerk of the Court, to find out who will be sitting in motion part around June 16. If the clerk doesn't want to give you information, call up District Attorney Nicholas Atlas.

Inquire about Wednesday 5/31
Probably Judge Woolsey [This is a handwritten notation of uncertain origin.—ED.]

---

[Doc. 118]

June 1, 1933.

Collector of Customs,
Customs House,
New York City.

Att: H.C. Stewart, Esq.
Re: *Ulysses* by James Joyce
File #16166

Gentlemen:

I am sending you herewith my petition, addressed to the Treasury Department, requesting that the above entitled book be admitted into the United States under those provisions of Section 305 of the Tariff Act of 1930, which authorize the Secretary of the Treasury, in his discretion, to admit the so-called classics or works of recognized literary or scientific merit.

In making this application I desire to state specifically that I do not concede that *Ulysses* is not admissible under the general provisions of Section 305.

I trust that in view of the impressive array of evidence appended to the petition (there is scarcely a man of note in American letters who is not represented), the decision of the Secretary will be favorable. Should any further proof be desired I shall be glad to furnish it, as testimonials concerning the literary and psychological importance of *Ulysses* are practically limitless.

Yours very truly,<br>
Alexander Lindey

AL:JF

---

[Doc. 119]

TREASURY DEPARTMENT<br>
UNITED STATES CUSTOMS SERVICE

In the Matter of the Seizure of

*ULYSSES*<br>
by James Joyce

under Section 305 of the Tariff Act<br>
of 1930.

ALEXANDER LINDEY,

Claimant.

PETITION FOR RELEASE AND ADMISSION<br>
OF BOOK INTO THE UNITED STATES ON<br>
THE GROUND THAT IT IS A CLASSIC.

ALEXANDER LINDEY respectfully shows to this Department and alleges:

1. I reside at 670 West End Avenue, in the Borough of Manhattan, City, County and State of New York. I am an attorney-at-law. I am the claimant and consignee in the above matter.

2. On or about May 5, 1933 I received, through the United States Customs, a copy of *Ulysses*, which had been sent to me by Maison du Livre Français, 4, Rue Felibien, 4, Paris, France. On May 5th I wrote to the Collector of Customs at the Port of New York, advising him of the receipt of the book and inquiring whether, in view of the fact that the Customs authorities had theretofore seized previous importations of *Ulysses*, I was correct in assuming that there had been a change of attitude on the Collector's part, and whether *Ulysses* was legal for admission into this country.

3. On May 10, 1933 I received a communication from H.C. Stewart, Assistant Collector, advising me that there had been no change with regard to the admissibility of the book. He suggested that I surrender it to the Law Division of the Customs Service.

4. Accordingly, on May 13, 1933, I relinquished the book to the Law Division, and notified Mr. Stewart that upon receipt of official notification of seizure, I should make formal application to the Secretary of the Treasury for the admission of the book under that portion of Section 305 of the Tariff Act of 1932 which permits the Secretary, in his discretion, to admit the so-called classics or works of recognized scientific or literary merit.

5. On May 22, 1933, Mr. Stewart acknowledged receipt of the book, and stated officially that it was subject to detention under the provisions of the aforesaid section of the Tariff Act, and that it would be seized and forfeited as provided by law.

6. I present this petition for the release of the book under that portion of Section 305 which authorizes the Secretary of the Treasury to admit classics. *However, in doing so I state explicitly that I do not concede that Ulysses is not admissible under the general provisions of the Tariff Act.*

7. I base my application:
   (a)  Generally on the undisputed reputation of James Joyce as a writer of first-rate importance;
   (b)  Generally on the world-wide acclaim which has been accorded to *Ulysses* as the foremost prose masterpiece of the twentieth century; and
   (c)  Specifically on the evidence contained in the exhibits annexed to this petition.

8. Perhaps no other book in the history of letters has created such a stir as *Ulysses*; certainly no other book has been accorded such remarkable eulogies. It has been said by some that *Ulysses* is the most important book that has ever been written; that no other work has had such a profound and far-reaching influence; that Joyce's virtuosity in the manipulation of words has never been surpassed; that when it comes to psychology or realism, beside Joyce "Balzac is beggared and Zola bankrupted"; that there is evident in *Ulysses* "a genius of the very highest order, strictly comparable to Goethe's or Dostoevsky's"; that in power of thought Joyce has no peer but Pascal; that he is the only man in English literature worthy of a place beside Shakespeare. One might be inclined to look askance on such extravagant praise, were it not for the enclosed exhibits which appear to justify the claims made for the book and its author.

9. As evidence of the fact that *Ulysses* is a modern classic of the first magnitude, I present the following exhibits:

   Exhibit A.  Photostatic Copies of Statements Made by Representative Men Concerning *Ulysses*.

   Exhibit B.  Excerpts from Critical Reviews of *Ulysses*.

Exhibit C. Comments of Librarians Concerning
   *Ulysses.*
Exhibit D. List of Books on James Joyce and/or
   *Ulysses.*
Exhibit E. List of Magazine Articles on James Joyce and/
   or *Ulysses.*
   Comments on these exhibits follow:

10. Concerning Exhibit "A". It is to be noted that responsible newspapers, foremost literary critics, educators, publicists, psychologists, authors, publishers, have been unanimous in hailing *Ulysses* as a work of extraordinary literary merit and significance. It would be difficult indeed to secure a more impressive and more varied array of critical judgment than that reflected in the enclosed photostats. The men represented cannot be said to belong to any particular coterie or to express any special shade of opinion. On the contrary, they constitute a trustworthy mirror of all the literate elements in the community.

11. Concerning Exhibit "B". Since the first appearance of *Ulysses*, a vast critical library has grown up about it. It would be impossible to present excerpts from all the published reviews or even to enumerate the reviews. They run into hundreds, possibly thousands. The comments in Exhibit "B" have been selected because in every instance they are by eminent critics and because they present a cross-section of critical opinion.

12. Concerning Exhibit "C". About a year ago the Modern Library, publishers of classics, circulated a questionnaire on *Ulysses* among several hundred of the leading librarians throughout the United States. The librarians were requested to give their opinion of the book. With scarcely a dissenting voice they conceded its greatness. A few of their comments culled at random from hundreds appear in Exhibit "C". The petitioner herein has examined the original questionnaires and hereby vouches for the genuineness of the comments. If the Treasury Department so desires, the petitioner can arrange to have the original questionnaires exhibited to the Department. The illuminating feature of the comments is that they have come from all quarters of the country. It cannot therefore be said that the acclaim of *Ulysses* proceeds from a few ultrasophisticated metropolitan centers.

13. Concerning Exhibits "D" and "E". It is axiomatic that only a man of genius challenges serious attention and critical treatment. The reward of mediocrity is oblivion. One persuasive proof of the significance of *Ulysses* may be found in the fact that important men have written important books and articles about it and its author.

14. *Ulysses* has been translated into French and German: stupendous tasks, when one realizes the length of the book and especially its linguistic idiosyncrasies. To say that only a work of exceptional merit could have prompted such herculean enterprises in translation, is to state a truism which

will bear no denial. The German translation was made by the distinguished scholar, Georg Goyert, and was published by Rhein-Verlag-Basel, a reputable publishing firm with offices at Zurich, Berlin, Leipzig and Strassburg.

15. In introducing the stream-of-consciousness method and developing it to a high degree of perfection Joyce has, in *Ulysses*, made an epochal contribution to letters. There can be no doubt that his book is a modern classic in every sense of the word. It has endured the test of time. After almost a decade of arduous and monastic labor, it was completed in 1914 and during the last two decades it has steadily grown in stature. Even the few myopic reviewers who, bowled over by the terrific impact of the book, decried at the outset its length, its verbal pyrotechnics, its many complexities, have gradually veered around to the view that it is a masterwork. We have long ago repudiated the theory that a literary work must be hundreds or thousands of years old in order to be a classic. We have come to realize that there can be *modern* classics as well as ancient ones. If there is any book in any language today genuinely entitled to be called a "modern classic" it is *Ulysses*.

In view of the foregoing, I respectfully petition that *Ulysses* be released to me under that portion of Section 305 which authorizes the Secretary of the Treasury to admit classics; but in making this application I do not concede that the work here seized should not be released and admitted under the general provisions of Section 305.

Alexander Lindey

---

STATE OF NEW YORK    ⎫
                     ⎬   SS.:

COUNTY OF NEW YORK ⎭

ALEXANDER LINDEY, being duly sworn, deposes and says: That he is the Petitioner in the foregoing Petition; that he has read the foregoing Petition and knows the contents thereof; that the same is true of his own knowledge, except as to those matters therein stated to be alleged on information and belief, and as to those matters he believes it to be true.

Alexander Lindey

Sworn to before me this
2nd day of June 1933
Louis Kerr

## EXHIBIT A

*Photostatic copies of statements made by representative individuals concerning Ulysses.*

The following publicists, critics, psychologists, authors, publishers and others have furnished the annexed testimonials:

| | |
|---|---|
| J. DONALD ADAMS | Editor, *The New York Times Book Review* |
| LEWIS GANNETT | Literary Editor and critic, *New York Herald-Tribune* |
| HARRY HANSEN | Literary Editor and critic, *New York World-Telegram.* |
| WILLIAM ROSE BENÉT | Poet, contributing editor to *The Saturday Review of Literature* |
| HENRY SEIDEL CANBY | Editor, *The Saturday Review of Literature* |
| HARRY EMERSON WILDES | Sociologist, and literary critic of the Philadelphia *Public Ledger* |
| JOHN CLAIR MINOT | Literary Editor and critic, *The Boston Herald* |
| TOM COLLINS | Sunday Editor, *Kansas City Journal Post* |
| HENRY HAZLITT | Literary Editor, *The Nation* |
| HERBERT BAYARD SWOPE | Former executive editor of the *New York World*; director of Brooklyn Manhattan Transit Corporation; director of Columbia Broadcasting System; director of Radio Keith Orpheum; and director of Municipal Art Society |
| JOHN DEWEY | Educator, and head of the Department of Philosophy, Columbia University |
| W. A. NEILSON | President, Smith College, Northampton, Mass. |
| JOHN HAYNES HOLMES | Minister, The Community Church of New York |
| LOUIS S. SHORES | Librarian, Fisk University Library, Nashville, Tennessee |
| WILLARD W. BEATTY | Superintendent, Bronxville Public Schools |
| FREDERIC G. MELCHER | Editor, *The Publishers' Weekly* |
| ZAIDEE B. VOSPER | Editor, *The Booklist* published by American Library Association |

| | |
|---|---|
| ELLIS W. MEYERS | Executive Secretary, American Booksellers Association |
| ROBERT BRIFFAULT | Anthropologist, author of numerous scientific works |
| DR. JOHN B. WATSON | Psychologist and author |
| DOROTHY KENYON | Prominent attorney, active in women's movements for social reform |
| JOHN FARRAR | Of the publishing house of Farrar & Rinehart |
| JAMES HENLE | President, The Vanguard Press, Publishers |
| ALFRED A. KNOPF | President, Alfred A. Knopf, Inc., Publishers |
| GEORGE MACY | Director, The Limited Editions Club, Inc. |
| E. HALDEMAN-JULIUS | Publisher of Little Blue Books, and other publications |
| B. W. HUEBSCH | Of the publishing firm, The Viking Press, Inc. |
| EDMUND WILSON | Eminent critic and contributing editor of *The New Republic* |
| H. L. MENCKEN | Editor, *The American Mercury* |
| ROBERT MORSS LOVETT | Professor in the Department of English, University of Chicago. |
| BEN RAY REDMAN | Critic and author |
| ROBERT M. COATES | Of the Editorial Staff of *The New Yorker* |
| GEORGE JEAN NATHAN | Eminent critic and writer |
| MALCOLM COWLEY | Editor, *The New Republic* |
| HARRY ELMER BARNES | Editorial writer, the *New York World-Telegram* |
| JOHN MACY | Critic, and author of *Story of the World's Literature* |
| BURTON RASCOE | Literary critic |
| GILBERT W. GABRIEL | Dramatic critic of the *New York American* |
| WALTER PRICHARD EATON | Dramatic critic and author |
| THEODORE DREISER | Author |
| JOHN COWPER POWYS | Author |
| LOUIS UNTERMEYER | Author |
| DEEMS TAYLOR | Composer and critic |

| JAMES BRANCH CABELL | Author |
|---|---|
| LEWIS GALANTIERE | Poet and critic |
| F. SCOTT FITZGERALD | Author |
| JOHN DOS PASSOS | Author |
| MICHAEL GOLD | Author, and editor of *New Masses* |
| CARL VAN DOREN | Editor-in-Chief, The Literary Guild of America |

---

## EXHIBIT B

*Excerpts from Critical Reviews of Ulysses*

Arnold Bennett in *The Outlook*, says:

"James Joyce is a very astonishing phenomenon in letters. He is sometimes dazzlingly original. If he does not see life whole he sees it piercingly. His ingenuity is marvellous. He has wit. He has a prodigious humor. He is afraid of naught. And had heaven in its wisdom thought fit not to deprive him of that basic sagacity and that moral self-dominion which alone enable an artist to assemble and control and fully utilize his powers, he would have stood a chance of being one of the greatest novelists that ever lived. The best portions of the novel (unfortunately they constitute only a fraction of the whole) are superb. I single out the long orgiastic scene, and the long unspoken monologue of Mrs. Bloom which closes the book. The former will easily bear comparison with Rabelais at his fantastical finest; it leaves Petronius out of sight. It has plenary inspiration. It is the richest stuff, handled with a virtuosity to match the quality of the material. The latter (forty difficult pages, some twenty-five thousand words without any punctuation at all) might in its utterly convincing realism be an actual document, the magical record of inmost thoughts thought by a woman that existed. Talk about understanding 'feminine psychology' . . . I have never read anything to surpass it, and I doubt if I have ever read anything to equal it. My blame may have seemed extravagant, and my praise may seem extravagant, but that is how I feel about James Joyce. The book is not pornographic . . . "

Ford Madox Hueffer in *The Yale Review*, says:

"I fancy Mr. Joyce is the only artist we have today, who, with an utter composure, regards processes of reproduction, of nourishment, and of physical renewal. But then, Mr. Joyce, the supreme artist, regards with an equal composure—all things. That is why the United States has persecuted his publishers . . . A writer of very beautiful, composed English . . . measures his effects by things immense and lasting . . . *Ulysses* contains the undiscovered mind of man, it is human consciousness analysed as it has never before been analysed."

J. Middleton Murry in *The Nation*, says:

"Unlike any other book that has been written; extraordinarily interesting to those who have patience (and they need it), the work of an intensely serious man . . . indisputably the mind of an artist, abnormally sensitive to the secret individuality of emotions and things, abnormally sensitive also to spiritual beauty . . . In what seems to us the most masterly part of the book, a manifestation of a really rare creativeness, Mr. Joyce stages a Walpurgis-nacht of his chief characters . . . In this part of *Ulysses*—let us say it plainly, in order that we may have our share of the contempt or the glory a hundred years hence—a genius of the very highest order, strictly comparable to Goethe's or Dostoevsky's, is evident. This transcendental buffoonery, this sudden uprush of the *vis comica* into a word wherein the tragic incompatibil-ity of the practical and the instinctive is embodied, is a very great achievement."

Dr. Joseph Collins in the *New York Times Book Review*, says:

"An egocentric genius, whose chief diversion and keenest pleasure is self-analysis and whose lifelong important occupation has been keeping a notebook in which has been recorded incident encountered and speech heard with photographic accuracy and Boswellian fidelity. Moreover, he is determined to tell it in a new way . . . in parodies of classic prose and current slang, in perversions of sacred literature, in carefully metered prose with studied incoherence, in symbols so occult and mystic that only the initiated and profoundly versed can understand—in short, by means of every trick and illusion that a master artificer, or even magician, can play with the English language . . . It will immortalise its author with the same certainty that Gargantua and Pantagruel immortalised Rabelais, and *The Brothers Karamazov* Dostoyevsky . . . comes nearer to being the perfect revelation of a personality than any book in existence . . . I have learned more psychology and psychiatry from it than I did in ten years at the Neurological Institute."

Edmund Wilson in *The New Republic*, says:

"A work of severe and solid architecture . . . Though exercising a rigorous selection which makes the book a technical triumph, Mr. Joyce manages to give the effect of unedited human minds, drifting aimlessly along from one triviality to another, confused and diverted by memory, by sensation and by

inhibition . . . perhaps the most faithful X-ray ever taken of the ordinary
human consciousness . . . as it shifts and shivers behind the front we
present to the world . . . Extraordinary poetic faculty for investing
particular incidents with universal significance . . . a work of high genius
. . . has the effect of making everything else look brassy . . . I cannot
agree that Mr. Joyce has represented the human mind as more disintegrated
or more debased than it actually is . . . one sees the gross ill-drained body of
humanity itself touched divinely by cloudly visions of its creative splendours
yet profoundly shaken and bound by its labouring flesh . . . In the last
pages of the book, when his duty has been sternly discharged by the prosaic,
the base and the absurd, this austere, almost pedantic writer soars to such
rhapsodies of beauty as have probably never been equalled in English prose
fiction."

Gilbert Seldes in *The Nation*, says:

"Possibly the most interesting and the most formidable writer of our
time . . . Among the very great writers only two can be named with him
for the long devotion to their work and for the triumphant conclusion—
Flaubert and Henry James . . . The galvanic fury in which the Walpurgis-
nacht episode is played is, one feels certain, not equalled in literature . . . The parodies I find brilliant . . . they create with rapidity and as
rapidly destroy the whole series of noble aspirations, hopes and illusions of
which the centuries have left their record in prose . . . The innovations in
method and the development in structure, used with a skill approaching
perfection, are going to have an incalculable effect upon the writers of the
future. The book has literally hundreds of points of interest . . . not a
scamped page nor a moment of weakness . . . whole chapters are monuments to the power and glory of the written word . . . a victory of the
creative intelligence over the chaos of uncreated things and a triumph of
devotion, to my mind one of the most significant and beautiful of our time."

Holbrook Jackson in *Today*, says:

"An affront and an achievement. It is not indecent. There is not a salacious
line in it. It is simply naked: naked and unconscious of shame . . . neither
moral nor immoral . . . He simply records like Homer . . . it must claim
the attention of those who look upon fiction as something more than
confectionery. With all its faults it is the biggest event in the history of the
English novel since *Jude*."

Mrs. Mary Colum in *The Freeman*, says:

"A most sincere and cunningly-wrought autobiographical book . . . one of
the most racial books ever written, and one of the most Catholic books ever

written . . . the book presupposes a knowledge of many literatures . . . almost an encyclopedia of odd bits and forms of knowledge . . . humour that is all-embracing, and yet never approaching the extravagant . . . where Rousseau romanticises, Joyce de-romanticises . . . "

Ernest Boyd in the *New York Tribune*, says:

"An imagination which is at once romantic and realistic, brilliant and petty, full of powerful fantasy, yet preserving an almost incredible faculty of detailed material observation . . . rarely in literature has criticism appeared in such harsh and disillusioned guise . . . oscillates between contemptuous Rabelaisian ribaldry and the crude horror and fascination of the body as seen by the great Catholic ascetics . . . wonderful fantastic imagination . . . also has the defects and qualities of naturalism."

*The New York Herald*, says:

"There is to be found in *Ulysses* some of the finest English that has been written . . . To Mr. Joyce the inexpressible does not exist. He proves the suppleness, the flexibility of English . . . The record is monumental, almost staggering and incontestably true to life . . . of an almost diabolic clairvoyance."

Mr. Roscoe Ashworth in *Shadowland* (New York), says:

"The intellectual elite of France, America and England have hailed the Joyce opus as the most sensational literary event of the year, of the decade, of any time within living memory. Whatever else has been said of it, competent opinion is agreed that the book is an achievement stupendous in effort, staggering in the detail, and a little baffling in the contents . . . Unique among books . . . nothing half-way resembling it has been done before in any language."

Mr. George Slocombe in the *Daily Herald*, says:

"As large as a telephone directory or a family Bible and with many of the literary and social characteristics of each . . . A staggering feat which, once attempted and more than half achieved, may never be attempted again."

Mr. Matthew Josephson in *Broom* (Rome), says:

"May be summed up as the work of a man who possess an amazing sensibility for physical qualities, an extraordinary knowledge of English, and an inferior intellect . . . There is a madness in him for *the word*: the play of it, the colour, the tempo of a handful of them . . . Fragments of astonishing poetry . . . Perhaps the sternest charge against *Ulysses* is its sinful length."

*The Times*, says:

"Of the utmost sincerity . . . complete courage."

Mrs. Evelyn Scott in *The Dial* (New York), says:

"A contemporary of the future . . . His technique has developed unique aspects that indicate a revolution of style for the future . . . This Irish artist is recreating a portion of the English language . . . He uses the stuff of the whole world to prove one man."

*The New Age*, says:

"One of the most interesting literary symptoms in the whole literary world, and its publication is very nearly a public obligation."

Mr. Lett-Haines in the *Gargoyle* (Paris), says:

"Its significance in Anglo-Saxon letters is unprecedented, its presage Europe-wide. With calm and forceful elegance it deftly initiates the arrestation of the sugary flow of Irish fiction . . . High pressure condensation of thought and masterly technique . . . thoroughly amusing while deliberatively provocative of illuminating thought. The reading gives intense pleasure."

Miss Kate Buss in the *Boston Evening Transcript*, says:

"A remarkably written human document with its obscurities and its rotten moments just as life has both for each of us . . . a too much suppressed and a too little reflected upon volume."

---

## EXHIBIT C

### Comments of Librarians
### on Ulysses

"I protest against the asininity which bars a work in which I was unable to discover anything as objectionable as the insulting mediocrity in talkies, tabloids and terrible novels . . . Its significance in literary history is of first importance. It is an essential text we feel handicapped at not being able to supply to our professors of comparative literature. No study of literary development in the 20th century can mean anything without *Ulysses*."— Louis Shores, Professor of Library Science, Fisk University, Nashville, Tennessee.

"The most original and characteristic book of this period. The book could do no one any harm and should be available to all those seriously interested in literature."—Susie L. Howard, Head of Circulation Department, Carnegie Library of Atlanta, Georgia.

"*Ulysses* deserves unrestricted circulation as a contribution to literature. Compelling and provocative."—Ethel McVeety, North Dakota Agricultural College, Fargo, N.D.

"Certainly no other 20th century book has exerted so great an influence."—Ward Edwards, State Teachers College Library, Warrensberg, Missouri.

"Important as a new type; should be in every library."—Fred A. Bestow, Free Public Library, New Brunswick, New Jersey.

"An American publication would be of value because it forms the basis and many of the tendencies in recent English and American Literature."—William P. Lewis, Pennsylvania State College Library, State College, Pennsylvania.

"A book which cannot be ignored. Definite place in the historical development of the psychological novel."—Winifred E. Skinner, Pasadena Junior College, Pasadena, California.

"Very influential, monumental work, one of the greatest of the century."—Mary E. Hoyt, Colorado School of Mines, Golden, Colorado.

"The most important of the stream-of-consciousness novels."—Luise F. Kampf, Coburn Library, Colorado College, Colorado Springs, Colorado.

"It is a valuable portrayal of the mind at work beyond the constraining limits of rules or contexts."—Merritt H. Moore, faculty, University of Chicago, Chicago, Illinois.

"Inestimable literary influence."—L.T. Ibbotson, University of Maine, Orono, Maine.

"As the first English novel to use the stream-of-consciousness method, it has had a very considerable influence."—A.B. Metcalf, Wellesley College Library, Wellesley, Massachusetts.

"The book should be in all libraries of a scholarly nature, because of its literary historical importance."—Gilbert H. Doane, Librarian in chief, University of Nebraska Library, Lincoln, Nebraska.

"Think it a stupendous piece of work; of use to authors."—Helen A. Stratloy, Binghamton Public Library, Binghamton, N.Y.

"It is of sufficient importance to be needed wherever courses are given in contemporary literature."—Elizabeth M. Richards, Flora Stone Mather College Library, Cleveland, Ohio.

"Every college library should have a copy of this volume as representative of a trend in literature."—Anne C. Keating, Ohio University Library, Athens, Ohio.

"Outstanding in its literary and psychological contribution."—Alberta Caille, Carnegie Free Public Library, Sioux Falls, South Dakota.

"Regardless of its ethical purport or its literary significance, I think a book so much discussed should be available to students of the new literary movement."—Blanche Prichard McCrum, Washington and Lee University Library, Lexington, Virginia.

"It is honest, therefore psychologically interesting."—J.S. Ibbotson, Colby College Library, Waterville, Maine.

"Apparently a stupendous piece of work; worthy of serious study."—Annie L. Craigie, Denison University Library, Granville, Ohio.

"The book is one of the monuments of modern art. Of the greatest importance both to the cultured reader and all students of the age. It has been nothing short of a crime that the book has been lost to American readers for so many years."—J.F. Marron, Jacksonville Public Library, Jacksonville, Florida.

"I think its influence has been tremendous; a book of such importance as *Ulysses* should be available to adults."—Catherine Beal, South Branch, Omaha Public Library, Omaha, Nebraska.

"I think that every library of any size should have those books which show the trend of modern literature."—Evelyn M. Barrett, Silas Bronson Library, Waterbury, Connecticut.

"It will always be of significance as literary history."—M.E. McClain, University of Oregan Library, Eugene, Oregon.

"One of the greatest contributions to modern literature."—Elizabeth Signlteary, Santa Clara Free Library, San Jose, California.

"It is a work of literary significance. In our opinion the American edition of *Ulysses* ought to be available for University and other scholarly libraries."—W.M. Smith, University of Wisconsin, Madison, Wisconsin.

"It is a masterpiece."—Mrs. Ruth E. Delzell, Free Public Library, Amarillo, Texas.

---

## EXHIBIT D

*List of books dealing with*
*James Joyce and/or Ulysses*

*The Impuritans*
by Harvey Wickham
Dial Press, New York, 1929

*Axel's Castle*
by Edmund Wilson
Scribners, New York, 1931

*Men Seen*
by Paul Rosenfeld
Dial Press, New York, 1925

*James Joyce—His First Forty Years*
by Herbert S. Gorman
Heubsch, New York, 1925

*The Key to the Ulysses of James Joyce*
by Paul Jordan Smith
Covici-Friede, New York

*James Joyce and the Plain Reader*
by Charles Duff
D. Harmsworth, London, 1932

---

## EXHIBIT E

*List of magazine articles dealing with
James Joyce and/or Ulysses*

*The Strange Case of James Joyce*
by Rebecca West
*Bookman*, 1928—Volume 68, pp. 9-23

*Mr. James Joyce and the Modern Stage*
by Ezra Pound
*Drama* (Chicago), 1916—Vol. 6, pp. 122-132

*James Joyce and the New Word*
by Harold J. Salemson
*Modern Quarterly* (Baltimore), 1929—Vol. 5, pp. 294-312

*Some Contemporaries—James Joyce*
by Peter Munro Jack
*Indianapolis*, 1929—Vol. 1, pp. 24-27, 102-108

*James Joyce*
by Michael J. Lennon
*Catholic World* (New York), 1931—Vol. 132, pp. 641-652

*Technik und Thematik von James Joyce*
by Ernst Robert Curtius
*Neue Schweizer Rundschan* (Zurich), 1929—Jahrg.22, Heft.1, pp. 47-68

*Concerning James Joyce's Ulysses*
by Arnold Bennett
*Bookman*, 1922—Vol. 55, pp. 567-570

*James Joyce's Ulysses*
by Bernhard Fehr
*Englische Studien* (Leipsig), 1925—Bd. 60, pp. 180-205

*Zum Ulysses von James Joyce*
by Giedion-Welcker, Carola
*Neuer Schweizer Rundschan* (Zurich), 1928—Jahrg. VI, pp. 18-32

*An Irish Ulysses—The Hades Episode*
by Stuart Gilbert
*Fortnightly Review* (New York), 1929—N.S. Vol. 126, pp. 45-58

*Ulysses and the Handling of Indecencies*
by Ford Madox Hueffer
*English Review* (London), 1922—Vol. 35, pp. 538-548

*James Joyce*
by Edmund Wilson
*The New Republic*, December 18, 1929

*The Ulysses of James Joyce*
by Valéry Larbaud
*Criterion*, (London), 1922—Vol.1, October, pp. 94-103

*Ulysses*
by Leslie Shane
*Quarterly Review* (New York), 1922—Volume 238, pp. 219-234

*The Meaning of Ulysses*
by Edwin Muir
*Calendar of Modern Letters* (London), 1925—Vol. 1, pp. 347-355

*James Joyce et Pecuchet*
by Ezra Pound
*Mercure de France* (Paris), 1922—Annee 33, Tome 156, pp. 307-320

*The Influence of Mr. James Joyce*
by Richard Aldington
*English Review* (London), 1921—Vol. 32, pp. 333-341

*James Joyce in Trieste*
by Silvio Benio
*Bookman*, 1930—Vol. 72, pp. 375-380

*L'Oeuvre de James Joyce*
by Louis Cazamian
*Revue Anglo-Americaine* (Paris), 1924—Annee 2, pp. 97-113

*Homer of Our Time*
by I. Goll
*Living Age*, August 15, 1927, pp. 316-320, 333

*Novel from James to Joyce*
by J. W. Beach
*Nation*, June 10, 1931—pp. 132, 634-6

*Growth of a Titan*
*Saturday Review*, August 2, 1930, pp. 7, 17-19

*Portrait of James Joyce*
by Padraic Colum
*Dublin Magazine* (Dublin), 1932—N.S., Vol. 7, April-June, pp. 40-48

*A Sidelight on James Joyce*
by Louis Golding
*Nineteenth Century* (London), 1933—Vol. 113, pp. 391-497

*Farthest North: A Study of James Joyce*
by Elliott Paul
*Bookman* (Camden), 1932—Vol. 75, pp. 156-163

---

[Doc. 120]

GREENBAUM, WOLFF & ERNST

OFFICE MEMORANDUM

TO:  JOE                    FROM:  A.L.
RE:  *Ulysses*              DATE:  June 3, 1933.

Please find out who will be sitting June 16, re above motion.

Judge Coleman [This is Joe Shapiro's handwritten notation.—ED.]

---

[Doc. 121]

GREENBAUM, WOLFF & ERNST

OFFICE MEMORANDUM

TO:  M.L.E.                          FROM:  A.L.
RE:  *Ulysses*                       DATE:  June 6, 1933.

Please note:

1. I have just received definite word from the Clerk's office that Judge Coleman will be sitting on the 16th.

2. I have made inquiries and find that Judge Coleman is a strait-laced Catholic. Both Atlas and Baum assure me that he is about the worst man on the bench for us.

3. There is a possibility of Woolsey sitting in motion part some time in July. Shall I adjourn the motion? My definite feeling is that we should.

---

[Doc. 122]

GREENBAUM, WOLFF & ERNST

OFFICE MEMORANDUM

TO:  M.L.E.                          FROM:  A.L.
RE:  *Ulysses*                       DATE:  June 13, 1933.

Please note:

1. I have been in touch with Nicholas Atlas, Assistant D.A. We have agreed to put the motion over to July 11.

2. Coleman is still away, and that will be our excuse.

3. Bennett Cerf has been notified. I have explained to him all the circumstances concerning Coleman.

**[Doc. 123]**

53-14/2

June 16, 1933.

Mr. Alexander Lindey,
670 West End Avenue,
New York, N.Y.

Sir:

I inclose herewith a copy of a letter of even date to the Collector of
Customs, containing the Bureau's decision on the case mentioned in your
petition dated June 2, 1933, relative to the importation of the book entitled
*Ulysses* by James Joyce. [See Doc. 124.—ED.]
By direction of the Commissioner.

Respectfully,

E.C. Corkhill,
Chief of Division
Appeals and Protests

Inclosure No. 7288

---

**[Doc. 124]**
[This is an enclosure to Doc. 123.—ED.]

In reply refer to
53-14/2

June 16, 1933.

The Collector of Customs,
New York, N.Y.

Sir:

Receipt is acknowledged of your letter dated June 7, 1933. (BNH/gh)
transmitting a petition by Mr. Alexander Lindey for the release of a copy of
the book entitled *Ulysses*, by James Joyce, under the discretionary authority

granted the Secretary of the Treasury in Section 305 of the Tariff Act of 1930 to admit obscene books. It is understood that the copy of the book in question is held at your office.

The United States Customs Court has held that the above entitled publication constitutes a prohibited importation (Treasury Decision 42907). The Bureau has held in a previous case that it is of sufficient literary merit to be entitled to release under the Secretary's discretionary authority granted in Section 305 of the Tariff Act of 1930.

As it appears that the copy of the book in question is not being imported for commercial purposes, you are hereby authorized to release it to Mr. Lindey, to whom a copy of this letter is being mailed on this date.

Respectfully,

Frank Dow,
Acting Commissioner of Customs.

SR:ALG
6-14-33

---

[Doc. 125]

TREASURY DEPARTMENT
United States Customs Service
New York, N.Y.

18191                                                    June 21, 1933.

Greenbaum, Wolff & Ernst,
285 Madison Avenue,
New York City

Att. Mr. Alexander Lindey

Sirs:

Replying to your letter of June 12th you are advised that your recent petition for release and admission of the book *Ulysses* by James Joyce on the ground that it is a classic, was forwarded to the Commissioner of Customs under date of June 7, 1933. As soon as a reply is received you will be further advised.

Respectfully,

H.C. Stewart
Assistant Collector

[Doc. 126]

June 22, 1933.

Collector of Customs,
Customs House,
New York City

Att. H.C. Stewart, Esq.,
Re: File #18191
*Ulysses* by James Joyce

Gentlemen:

I wish to acknowledge receipt of your letter of June 21, 1933.

On June 16, 1933 I was informed by E.C. Corkhill, Esq., Chief of Division, Appeals and Protests, Treasury Department, Washington, D.C., that my petition of June 2, 1933 in the above matter had been favorably passed upon, and that you had been so instructed by Frank Dow, Esq., Acting Commissioner of Customs, under date of June 16, 1933.

Will you please consult your records, and let me have official word?

Yours very truly,

Greenbaum, Wolff & Ernst

Alexander Lindey

AL:JF

---

[Doc. 127]

## BAN UPON 'ULYSSES' TO BE FOUGHT AGAIN

---

*New York Times*, June 24, 1933

---

### Publisher Seeking to Bring Out Joyce 'Classic' Here Gets One Copy Admitted.

---

### CASE UP IN COURT JULY 11

---

Volumes Bootlegged From Paris Have Brought as Much as $50 in This Country.

For eleven years *Ulysses*, by James Joyce, has had wide recognition as a modern classic, but only bootleg sales in English-speaking countries, where some of the words and situations in the book have been considered obscene. Now Bennett Cerf, head of Random House and The Modern Library, wants to publish the book here. It was learned yesterday that he had won a preliminary victory by obtaining the admittance of one copy of the book.

This was made possible by an exception in the 1930 Tariff Act, presumably made for the benefit of such collectors as J. P. Morgan and the great libraries. Under this exception copies of books otherwise banned but of recognized literary merit and intended for non-commercial use may be allowed entrance at the discretion of the Secretary of the Treasury.

### Case Comes Up July 11.

Alexander Lindey, an attorney with the firm of Greenbaum, Wolff & Ernst, explained that this legal admittance of a single copy of *Ulysses* was a preliminary step in an attempt to make the publication and sale of the book legal here. A case of the *United States* vs. *Ulysses* comes up in Federal court July 11.

Many copies of *Ulysses* have been sold here despite the ban. Some years ago copies brought $50 each. More recently first editions have sold for $25 and second editions for $15. The book was published complete in book form in Paris in 1922. Sylvia Beach brought it out under the imprint "Shakespeare & Co."

Joyce took seven years in writing *Ulysses*, from 1914 to 1921. In March, 1918, *The Little Review* published a first installment here. Ezra Pound sent the part of the manuscript then ready and Margaret Anderson started to bring it out in the magazine. John S. Sumner brought charges and the Post-office Department made a bonfire of the mailed copies of *The Little Review*.

### An Unauthorized Publication.

The book was unprotected by copyright here and Samuel Roth published some of it in his *The Two Worlds Magazine*. The author brought suit against Mr. Roth for the use of his name without authority, claiming $500,000 damages.

About eighteen months ago a curious situation arose in England when a radio critic, talking over the government-owned British Broadcasting Company facilities, recommended in the strongest terms books by James Joyce and D. H. Lawrence that cannot be published or offered for sale in England, any more than they can here.

Recently Mr. Sumner, acting for the New York Society for the Suppression of Vice, has been unsuccessful in three cases brought by him in magistrate's courts against books he considered obscene.

Postmaster General James Farley has declared that he does not consider it the duty of his department to attempt to keep from the people of the United States a knowledge of what is going on in the world.

[Doc. 128]

GREENBAUM, WOLFF & ERNST

OFFICE MEMORANDUM

TO:   M.L.E.                        FROM:   A.L.
RE:   *Ulysses*                     DATE:   June 27, 1933.

Atlas called me up today. Coleman is back on the job. Goddard is sitting. They want another adjournment. They are rather evasive about the real reason. They say they have an accumulation of cases to dispose of, and want ample time to write their brief.

---

[Doc. 129]

GREENBAUM, WOLFF & ERNST

OFFICE MEMORANDUM

TO:   M.L.E.                        FROM:   A.L.
RE:   *Ulysses*                     DATE:   June 30, 1933.

I called up Coleman today to find out why he wanted an adjournment of the motion from July 11th. Please note:

1.  He gives as his reason the outcome of our special petition. He refers to the matter somewhat jocosely but he has intimated that we seemed to have put something over on them. I did my best to dispel this notion, but I have a faint suspicion that I did not entirely succeed. He said in so many words that he thinks we put a fast one over.

2.  They are now trying to get from Washington the complete file on our special application.

3.  Coleman has intimated that since the government has committed itself to the position that *Ulysses* is a classic, and what with the new administration, new Secretary of Treasury and new Postmaster, that the libel proceedings will be dropped and *Ulysses* cleared through the Customs without a court fight.

4.  I have kept Cerf advised.

5.  The motion is going over for about two weeks.

6.  Coleman sends you his regards.

7.  I am sending you a clipping from the *Times*. Did you see it? Please return.

Lets get Coleman to abandon & consent to admission. [This is Ernst's Reply.—ED.]

[Doc. 130]

GREENBAUM, WOLFF & ERNST

OFFICE MEMORANDUM

TO:  M.L.E.                             FROM:  A.L.
RE:  *Ulysses*                          DATE:  July 5, 1933.

Coleman telephoned today. As you know, he had told me several days before that he would get in touch with the Treasury Department and find out the reason for the favorable ruling on my special application and for the adjudication that *Ulysses* was a classic. He had intimated then that if the supporting memorandum given to the Secretary of the Treasury was strong enough he, Coleman, might decide to drop the libel proceedings.

He spoke to me today merely to tell me that he had not yet heard from the Treasury Department. He asked that we put over the motion from the 11th to the 25th. I agreed to do this.

———————————

[Doc. 131]

TREASURY DEPARTMENT
United States Customs Service
New York, N.Y.

16166                                          July 5, 1933.

Mr. Alexander Lindey,
285 Madison Avenue,
New York City.

Sir:

Reference is made to your communication of June 22, 1933, requesting information concerning your petition of June 2 in the matter of the book *Ulysses* by James Joyce.

In accordance with instructions from the Bureau of Customs, in its letter dated June 15, 1933, authority was given for the release of the book to you on the ground that it is a classic and therefore comes within the purview of the Secretary's discretionary authority granted in Section 305 of the Tariff Act of 1930.

The book has been forwarded to the Customs Bureau of the Post Office for delivery to you under date of June 23, 1933.

Respectfully,
H.C. Stewart
Assistant Collector

[Doc. 132]

July 10, 1933.

Hon. Samuel Coleman,
United States Attorney's Office,
Post Office Building,
New York City.

Re: *Ulysses*

Dear Sam:

I am sending you herewith some very precious documents.

I will be down in New York shortly and I hope by that time I will have an opportunity to argue, before Judges Coleman and Atlas, the plea which I have made repeatedly in respect to this matter.

Won't you kindly do me a favor and be in a position to clear up the situation promptly.

Yours sincerely,

Encs.
Del.

P.S. It is imperative that I get these documents back. You will receive copies, no doubt, from the Treasury Department, at which time I would like the return of the enclosed.

M.L.E.

1. Petition for release, etc.
2. Photostatic copies.

---

**[Doc. 133]**

July 11, 1933.

Mr. Bennett A. Cerf,
c/o Random House,
20 East 57th Street,
New York City.

Re: *Ulysses*

Dear Mr. Cerf:

I have your note of July 7 together with enclosure.

The motion scheduled for July 11 will probably go over for two weeks until July 25, for reasons you already know.

I shall keep you informed.

Sincerely,

AL:LS
encl.

P.S. I am sending you herewith a copy of a letter dated July 5, 1933, addressed to me by the Treasury Department. You will note that the enclosure goes much further, and is much more favorable to us, than the official communication a copy of which we sent to you some time ago.

A.L.

––––––––––––

**[Doc. 134]**

July 11, 1933.

Mr. Peter A. Pertzoff
70 Hammond Street,
Cambridge, Mass.

Dear Mr. Pertzoff:

We are the attorneys for Random House, Inc. We are handling the legalization of *Ulysses* for them.

They have turned over to us your kind letter of July 4, 1933, addressed to them. One of the important tasks confronting us in the case which is now pending in the Federal Court for the Southern District of New York, is to convince the court of the respectability of the book. The information set forth in your communication is quite helpful in this connection.

In view of your evident interest we shall impose upon your kindness to the extent of asking you: First, to investigate in what other libraries *Ulysses* may be found; second, to send us the list of items on Joyce referred to in your letter; and, third, to let us have a copy of your thesis, if one is available.

There is a remote chance that we may prevail upon a federal attorney to discontinue the proceedings against *Ulysses*. The information and material above indicated may be useful ammunition for this purpose.

Very truly yours,

Greenbaum, Wolff & Ernst

AL:LS

---

**[Doc. 135]**

July 14, 1933.

Mr. Peter A. Pertzoff,
70 Hammond Street,
Cambridge, Mass.

RE: *Ulysses*

Dear Mr. Pertzoff:

Thanks for sending us your thesis. We should like to hold it for a few weeks, if possible. If you have any sooner need for it, please advise us.

We have merely glanced over it rather hurriedly but it looks like a scholarly and thorough piece of work, and may well be of help to us in our fight for the legalization of the book.

Very truly yours,

Greenbaum, Wolff & Ernst

AL:LS

---

[Doc. 136]

July 17, 1933.

Mr. Peter A. Pertzoff,
70 Hammond Street,
Cambridge, Mass.

RE: *Ulysses*

Dear Mr. Pertzoff:

Many thanks for your letter of July 14th. It is bound to be highly useful to us.

We have been advised that the office of the United States Attorney for this district is considering abandoning the proceeding against *Ulysses*. On this no final decision has been reached. If the Federal Attorney decides to go ahead, we shall place before the court the miscellaneous valuable data which you have been good enough to incorporate in your communication.

It is not likely that your testimony will be required. As the law now stands, opinion testimony on the question of obscenity is inadmissible.

Cordially yours,

AL:LS

---

[Doc. 137]

### GREENBAUM, WOLFF & ERNST

### OFFICE MEMORANDUM

TO: M.L.E.        FROM: A.L.
RE: *U.S.* v. *Ulysses*      DATE: July 25, 1933.

As you know, this case came up on the motion calendar today. I have just heard from the Assistant D.A., Nicholas Atlas.

1. Judge Coleman was sitting.

2. As per our agreement, Atlas asked for an adjournment until August 8.

3. Coleman apparently knew all about the case and said that he would not adjourn it until the 8th because Judge Coxe would then be sitting and Judge Coxe had told him that he did not want the case.

4. Atlas then suggested that the case go over until the 15. Coleman replied that Judge Patterson would be sitting then and he did not want Judge Patterson to get the case because it was rather a "heavy one" and Judge Patterson was just recovering from a severe attack of pneumonia and a child of his is desperately ill.

Nevertheless the case was set down tentatively for August 15, but Coleman instructed Atlas to see Patterson in advance to find out whether Patterson would want the case. If not the case will go over to August 22, at which time— believe it or not—Woolsey will be sitting. I told Atlas that all of the above was just a lot of unnecessary nonsense because he and Coleman would probably decide within the next week or so to discontinue the libel proceedings.

2:45    Since dictating the above I find that Bitz who was in Court, and Atlas, went to see Judge Coleman. Judge Coleman refused to consent to hear the motion on August 15. According to Judge Coleman's directions, therefore, the motion will be heard on August 22.

---

**[Doc. 138]**

July 26, 1933.

Mr. Paul Léon,
27, Rue Casimir-Périer,
Paris, France.

Dear Mr. Léon:

We have received the letter written by Professor Huse in regard to quoting from James Joyce's *Ulysses*, and will take care of same immediately.

The trial on *Ulysses* has been postponed three times now, the last time because the presiding judge flatly refused to read the book. We could have insisted, of course, that he try the case anyway, but this would have been sheer suicide. We now received word that the case is scheduled to be tried on August 22nd before Judge Woolsey, who has the reputation of being the most liberal judge in the particular court where the case comes up. We are very hopeful that we will soon have good news for you.

Cordially yours,

Bennett A. Cerf
Random House

bac;pk

---

**[Doc. 139]**

August 5, 1933.

Memo for Mr. Ernst and Mr. Lindey:

Mr. Atlas, of D.A.'s office phoned; he said the appointment with Mr. Coleman and Atlas will be for Monday morning at 10:30 if convenient to you. If not, we are to phone Mr. Atlas Monday morning and arrange it for some other time during the day.

P.G.

Cort 7-7280

---

**[Doc. 140]**

August 7, 1933.

Nicholas Atlas, Esq.,
United States Attorney's Office,
Post Office Building,
New York City

Re: *Ulysses*
By James Joyce

Dear Mr. Atlas:

Pursuant to our conference of this morning, we are sending you herewith the following:

(a) Nine books as follows:
*Madeleine*—Anonymous
*Mademoiselle de Maupin* by Theophile Gautier
*Casanova's Homecoming* by Arthur Schnitzler
*Eastern Shame Girl*—Anonymous
*Woman and Puppet* by Pierre Louys
*The Adventures of Hsi Men Ching*—Translated from Chinese
*God's Little Acre* by Erskine Caldwell
*Female* by Donald Henderson Clarke
*Flesh*, by Clement Wood
(b) Our brief in *United States* v. *Dennett*
(c) Our brief in *People* v. *Berg*
(d) "James Joyce, a Critical Study", by Peter A. Pertzoff
(e) Leaflet containing critical comments on *Ulysses*, in French
(f) Map of the United States.

Kindly note:

1. Certain material was sent to Mr. Coleman on July 10, 1933. We assume that such material will be considered together with the enclosures.

2. Mr. Coleman wanted a list of recent obscenity cases, so as to enable him to ascertain the present trend of judicial attitude. You will find an itemized list of cases running from 1930 to 1933, on pages 7 and 8 of our brief, *People v. Berg* and additional comments on pages 17 to 19 of the same brief. On the pages last named we call your attention in particular to the cases that were thrown out of the Magistrate's Court, and in connection with which Mr. Sumner tried to get indictments. The fact that the Grand Jury in each instance, *(Casanova's Homecoming, Hsi Men Ching, God's Little Acre)* refused to indict, is in itself eloquent proof of the present mores of the community.

3. The last judicial word in this state on the question of obscenity is to be found in the opinion of the Court of Appeals, in the *Frankie and Johnnie* case, People v. Rendling, 258 N.Y. 451, decided only a few months ago. You will find the full text of the opinion in Exhibit A of the *Berg* brief.

4. The case involving the legality of Erskine Caldwell's *God's Little Acre* has been something of a *cause celebre.* For this reason, and because the case was decided as recently as May 23, 1933, the full text of Magistrate Greenspan's opinion is given in Exhibit B of the *Berg* brief.

5. We have discussed with you the importance of the existence of a bibliography, as one of the determinants of obscenity. This is not a criterion which we have arbitrarily set up. In Halsey v. New York Society, 231 N.Y. 1 the Court of Appeals of this state commented on the general availability of critical opinion, relative to *Mademoiselle de Maupin.* Mr. Pertzoff's treatise, which we are sending you herewith, lists eighteen books and sixty-two magazine articles dealing with Joyce and/or *Ulysses.* We have attached to Mr. Pertzoff's thesis a sheet containing a supplemental bibliography. Apparently the extent and the array of critical comment on Joyce and/or *Ulysses* are *limitless.* We are informed that Mr. Sidney Kellner, 696 Maple Street, Brooklyn, New York, who is compiling a general bibliography of Joyce, for publication, has many items which we have not listed.

6. It seems scarcely necessary to emphasize that the reputation of Joyce has been international. The enclosed leaflet sets forth unqualified praise by such distinguished French critics as Jean Cassau, Marc Chadourne, Auguste Bailly, Rene Lallou, and André Maurois.

7. You are doubtless aware of the fact that *Ulysses* exists in translations by reputable publishing houses, the German (translated by Georg Goyert) by Rheim-Verlag; the French (translated by Auguste Morel and Stuart Gilbert) by Adrienne Mounier. The *Encyclopedia Universal Illustrada* (1932) mentions a Spanish translation by Demaso Alonso; and says that the book has

been translated into nearly all languages. We have recently heard of two rival translations, both unauthorized, in Japan.

8. As a persuasive indication of the rapidly changing mores we call your attention to the photostat which is annexed to our *Berg* brief. Books that were almost universally condemmed less than a generation ago, are now generally distributed without any restrictions whatever.

9. The red dots on the enclosed map of the United States indicate the cities in which city or university librarians have stated that they either have copies of *Ulysses*, or would place the book on their shelves if it were available. The purpose of the map is to show that *Ulysses* has won country-wide recognition, and that it is not being championed only by ultra-radical literary cliques located in large metropolitan centres.

We trust that the enclosures will serve to convince you beyond any doubt that *Ulysses* is a work of genius of the first order, that it has been universally accepted, and that therefore it cannot be deemed to be obscene. If you agree with us as to this, we assume that you will either stipulate to discontinue the libel proceeding, or upon the hearing of the motion, which is now scheduled for August 22, you will make an appropriate recommendation to the court.

Yours very truly,

Greenbaum, Wolff & Ernst

By: Alexander Lindey

AL:JF

P.S. Please note that all the enclosures are our file copies, and should be eventually returned to us.

---

[Doc. 141]

GREENBAUM, WOLFF & ERNST

OFFICE MEMORANDUM

TO:  M.L.E.                    FROM:  A.L.
RE:  *Ulysses*                 DATE:  August 9, 1933.

Please note:

1. All the material that Coleman and Atlas wanted, including books, briefs, etc. was sent to Atlas on August 8, 1933.

2. The motion will come up on August 22. It will probably take the judge a month or six weeks to read the book, and he will certainly have no objection

to giving us some time for the brief. If we do have to go ahead and a brief must be submitted, I ought to be able to have it ready about a week after I return.

3. You will recall that I started working on the brief months ago, and then stopped when it appeared that the libel proceedings might be discontinued.

4. If Coleman does decide to go ahead, we must get back from him and Atlas the miscellaneous material which we turned over to them. We will need the material for our briefs and as exhibits.

---

[Doc. 142]

GREENBAUM, WOLFF & ERNST

OFFICE MEMORANDUM

TO: J.J.S.              FROM: M.L.E.
RE: *Ulysses*          DATE: August 15, 1933.

I just spoke to Sam Coleman, at the United States D.A.'s office. He will either be in charge of the case, or he will have turned it over to Atlas. The case comes up on August 22, having been adjourned from some other day. See Lindey's memo of August 9. I am also sending you herewith the Libel and the Claimant's Answer.

You might check with Coleman and/or Atlas on the 21st. If Woolsey isn't sitting, we don't want to have the papers presented to another judge. Woolsey wants the case. After submission have Woolsey set a date for argument. We don't care how long he wants to read the book. We will then get a week or ten days to submit the brief. You might ask him if he wants the briefs at the time of the argument, or even suggest that we might not need a brief.

I am writing to Coleman today to request the return of various papers which we sent him. These needn't concern you.

---

**[Doc. 143]**

August 15, 1933.

Samuel Coleman, Esq.,
United States Attorney's Office,
Post Office Building,
New York City.

Re: *United States* v. *Ulysses*

Dear Sam:

Will you kindly deliver to our messenger the various questionnaires, exhibits and other material which we sent you? In view of the fact that we have not been able to persuade you as to the validity of the position we are taking, we must have returned the documents we sent down, because we need them in order to do mighty battle with you.

Yours,

MLE:JF

---

**[Doc. 144]**

**WESTERN
UNION**

August 21, 1933.

Morris L. Ernst
Nantucket, Mass.

ULYSSES ADJOURNED ONE WEEK STOP NO COURT ON FRIDAY.

SHAPIRO

---

[Doc. 145]

GREENBAUM, WOLFF & ERNST

OFFICE MEMORANDUM

TO: Jonas Shapiro          FROM:  M. L. Ernst
RE:   *Ulysses*             DATE:   August 25, 1933.

Please follow up the *Ulysses* case next week. Don't let it get away from Woolsey. If they concede that the book is all right, see if you cannot get a stenographic record of their statement and any remarks made by Woolsey. If Woolsey is sitting for another week, there is no objection for further adjournment, but not beyond Woolsey.

———————

[Doc. 146]

August 30, 1933.

Mr. Bennett A. Cerf,
20 East 57th Street,
New York City.

Re: *Ulysses*

Dear Bennett:

*United States* vs. *Ulysses* was at last submitted to Judge Woolsey yesterday morning. We are to exchange briefs on September 25th and to file them with him on October 2nd. We will then decide whether he wishes argument to be made.

Yours sincerely,

———————

[Doc. 147]

GREENBAUM, WOLFF & ERNST

OFFICE MEMORANDUM

TO: M.L.E. and A.L.          FROM: J.J.S.
RE: *U.S.* v. *Ulysses*          DATE: August 30, 1983.

The cross-motions for judgment on the pleadings were submitted to Judge Woolsey today and he will set a date for argument if he feels that argument is necessary. He, however, wants briefs exchanged before October 2nd and the originals with admissions of service submitted to him on October 2nd. I arranged with Mr. Atlas that we would exchange briefs on September 25th and each side could reply by October 2nd.

---

August 30, 1933.

To Mr. Lindey:

1. Will you get your brief out by September 15th or 18th so that I can take a look at it?
2. See Jonas in regard to details of last Tuesday.

M.L.E.

---

[Doc. 148]

GREENBAUM, WOLFF & ERNST

OFFICE MEMORANDUM

TO: Mr. Lindey          FROM: M.L.E.
RE: *Ulysses*          DATE: August 30, 1933.

After dictating the other memorandum, Sam Coleman telephoned and said that he had talked with Woolsey in regard to a shift in the plans, namely— setting the date for argument for October 2nd or thereabouts in chambers, with the submission of briefs after that date. I indicated to Sam that we preferred the other arrangements because possibly Woolsey would not even hear argument. You might clear with Sam on this but in any event, be sure to have the brief ready by the 25th so that we can submit it on the date of argument. We can always submit a supplemental brief in case we think Woolsey wants some more dope.

[Doc. 149]

August 30, 1933.

Mr. Paul Léon,
27, Rue Casimir-Périer,
Paris, France.

Dear Mr. Léon:

The *Ulysses* case is finally under way, after almost innumerable postponements. The last few postponements, as a matter of fact, however, were engineered by our own attorneys for the purpose of getting the case before the most liberal-minded judge on the circuit. This is Judge Woolsey, and the case is now in his hands.

What happened yesterday was that our attorneys formally presented our side of the case, and turned over a copy of the book to Judge Woolsey along with all the testimonials and reports from librarians that we had collected in the past year. There will be no jury trial on the book. Judge Woolsey will go over all the letters and presumably read the book, if he has not already done so, and in the course of the next few weeks will hand down his decision. As soon as this decision becomes known to me, I will cable you.

There was a slight chance for a while that the District Attorney's office would not fight us at all on this case. They informed us finally, however, that they intended to proceed against us because there were too many dirty words in the last section of the book. These are the exact words of the Assistant District Attorney. This is the sort of argument to which there is really no answer. We are only hoping that Judge Woolsey will have a more adult attitude.

Cordially yours,

Bennett A. Cerf
Random House

bac;pk

[Doc. 150]

GREENBAUM, WOLFF & ERNST

OFFICE MEMORANDUM

TO: M.L.E.  FROM: A.L.
RE:  DATE: September 5, 1933.

Just got back from a swell vacation. I have gone over some of the accumulated material. Please note:

1. *Ulysses*: A portion of the brief is already written. I will have ample time to complete it before the end of the month. As soon as you get back I would like to talk to you about the submission of other material, i.e., the commendatory letters, the tabulation of the questionnaire, the opinions of librarians, the map, etc. I spoke to Cerf this morning. He seems to feel quite keenly that the additional material should be turned over to Woolsey before he has a chance to complete his reading of the book.

2. *People* v. *Berg*: Henle called up. He wants to know when you will be back in town. Clarke is in from the Coast, and Henle wants to have a council of war on the possibility of appeal. Berg comes up for sentence on Thursday, September 7. As you may have been informed, I met Magistrate Marvin at the Arcady Country Club, and had quite a talk with him. I learned some interesting sidelights on the case in particular, and on the operations of justice in Queens in general. Incidentally, upon my return I found that Mordecai Konowitz had phoned during my absence. Konowitz was a classmate of mine in college, and is now Assistant D.A. in Queens, in charge of appeals. If we did appeal I don't believe he would be inclined to stress the People's case too much. I have not yet been able to reach him for the purpose of a talk.

3. *Hyde* v. *Hyde*: This is practically complete, except for a few unimportant details. We have received our fee of $1,000, and the Bank of Sicily is holding $500 more in escrow. Did Mrs. Hyde get in touch with you as to the balance of our fee, which we are to collect from her?

4. *Untermeyer* v. *Untermeyer*: This is also nearing the end.

5. Banking Board: Please see the enclosed notice. Will you be in town?

6. Tom Mann: Please see the enclosed letter.

If you are not coming in for the Banking Board meeting, will you please let me know when you propose to be in town?

---

[Doc. 151]

GREENBAUM, WOLFF & ERNST

## OFFICE MEMORANDUM

TO:   M.L.E.                              FROM:   A.L.
RE:   *Ulysses*                           DATE:   September 6, 1933.

I called up Nicholas Atlas again to get the material that we turned over originally to him and Sam Coleman.

Atlas was quite evasive and said that he wanted to keep the material as he needed it in the preparation of his brief. I went over the miscellaneous items and told him that he could not have any conceivable use for any of the stuff. He reluctantly agreed to relinquish the material on Saturday.

I am going to press him from day to day, because he is leaving on his vacation the end of this week, and he may put us in a position where we will be unable to turn over some of the testimonials, etc. to Woolsey, before the date of argument.

My understanding of future arrangements as gathered from Shapiro, was as follows:

1. Briefs were to be exchanged on September 25.

2. Reply briefs would have to be in on or before October 2nd.

3. Woolsey would then decide whether or not he wanted argument in Chambers.

Nicholas Atlas tells me that Coleman has since had another talk with Woolsey. Woolsey has made up his mind that he would in any event want argument on October 2. Atlas suggests that no briefs be filed in advance, but that we get additional time after argument for the purpose.

My own feeling is that we ought to get every available material, including testimonials, brief, etc. to Woolsey before the argument, especially since the material which we have is so impressive. If any points develop during argument, supplemental or reply briefs can always be filed. I have indicated this attitude to Atlas, but I don't want to take a definite position before I know your reaction.

[Doc. 152]

September 6, 1933.

Nicholas Atlas, Esq.,
United States Attorney's Office,
Post Office Building,
New York City.

Re: *U.S.* v. *Ulysses*

Dear Mr. Atlas:

This will confirm our telephone conversation of this morning. Upon going over our file I find the following:

1. On July 10, 1933 Mr. Ernst sent Mr. Coleman:
   (a) The petition which I personally had addressed to the Treasury Department relative to the release of a copy of *Ulysses* to me, under the special provisions of the Tariff Act of 1930; and
   (b) A sheaf of photostatic copies of testimonials of eminent persons concerning the book.
2. On August 7, 1933 I sent you the following:
   (a) Nine books as follows:
   *Madeleine*—Anonymous
   *Mademoiselle de Maupin* by Theophile Gautier
   *Casanova's Homecoming* by Arthur Schnitzler
   *Eastern Shame Girl*—Anonymous
   *Woman and Puppet* by Pierre Louys
   *The Adventures of Hsi Men Ching*—Translated from Chinese
   *God's Little Acre* by Erskine Caldwell
   *Female* by Donald Henderson Clarke
   *Flesh* by Clement Wood
   (b) Our brief in *United States* v. *Dennett*
   (c) Our brief in *People* v. *Berg*
   (d) "James Joyce, a Critical Study," by Peter A. Pertzoff
   (e) Leaflet containing critical comments on *Ulysses*, in French
   (f) Map of the United States.

I have just begun work on our brief, as I feel that briefs should be submitted to Judge Woolsey prior to argument. It is absolutely essential, therefore, that the above enumerated material be returned to us without delay. We have no objection, however, to your keeping copies of our brief in *United States* v. *Dennett* and *People* v. *Berg*.

I am writing to you at this time because, if the material can be returned prior to Saturday, it will help me a great deal.

Yours very truly,
Greenbaum, Wolff & Ernst

AL:JF

[Doc. 153]

September 9, 1933.

File No. 67913
Docket No. S&FM-146

Received from the United States Attorney the following:

1. Leaflet containing critical comments on *Ulysses* in French.
2. Map of the United States marking places where *Ulysses* is had or demanded.
3. "James Joyce, a critical study," by Peter A. Pertzoff.
4. *Flesh* by Clement Wood.
5. *Female* by Donald Henderson Clark.
6. *God's Little Acre* by Erskine Caldwell.
7. *Adventures of Hsi Men Ching*, translated from Chinese.
8. *Woman and Puppet* by Pierre Louys.
9. *Eastern Shame Girl* by George DeMorant, listed by us as anonymous.
10. *Casanova's Homecoming* by Arthur Schnitzler.
11. *Mademoiselle de Maupin* by Theophile Gautier.
12. *Madeleine*—anonymous.
13. A sheaf of photostatic copies, white on black of testimonials of persons concerning *Ulysses*.
14. A copy of the petition of Alexander Lindey for the release of a copy of *Ulysses* to him under special provisions of the Tariff Act of 1930.

Greenbaum, Wolff & Ernst

---

[Doc. 154]

September 12, 1933.

Hon. John M. Woolsey:

I understand from Mr. Coleman that you already have a copy of *James Joyce's Ulysses* by Stuart Gilbert. I take the liberty of sending you herewith Paul Jordan Smith's *The Key to the Ulysses of James Joyce*, and also Herbert S. Gorman's *James Joyce: His First Forty Years*.

I am sending a copy of this letter to Mr. Coleman.

Sincerely yours,

MLE:JF

c/c Samuel Coleman

**[Doc. 155]**

September 12, 1933.

Hon. John M. Woolsey,
235 Broadway,
New York City.

Re: *United States* v. *Ulysses*

Dear Judge:

I am sending you herewith our preliminary memorandum [See Doc. 156.— ED.] in the above matter. You will note that the enclosure contains data of which I trust you will take judicial notice.

My understanding is that originally memoranda of law were to be exchanged on the 25th of this month, and you were to decide thereafter whether or not you wanted to hear argument. I have since been informed by Mr. Coleman that you will hear argument on October 2nd; and he has suggested that we hold in abeyance the matter of submitting memoranda of law until after the argument. This is entirely agreeable to me. I am submitting the enclosure at the present time because I feel that you may nevertheless wish to have some factual material before you prior to the argument.

We have this day served the government with a copy of the enclosure, complete except for the photostats constituting Exhibit 1. These photostats, however, were exhibited to the Government some weeks ago, and I am informed that the Government has had photostatic copies made for its files.

I am also sending you herewith a clipping from *Theatre Arts Monthly*, relative to the case of *Frankie and Johnnie*, (People v. Rendling, 258 N.Y. 451, decided March 3, 1932). The clipping gives the complete text of Judge Pound's opinion. The opinion represents the last word of the highest court of our state on the subject of obscenity. You will note that even though the play was "gross, vulgar and profane," and "the plot cheap and tawdry", and even though the locale was "a St. Louis resort for drinking, gambling and prostitution", depicting "women who carry on a loathsome trade and their male associates" (all of the quotes are from the opinion itself), the Court of Appeals reversed the convictions and dismissed the informations.

You will observe that the Court of Appeals referred with approval to United States v. *Married Love*, 48 Fed. (2d) 821, and United States v. *Contraception*, 51 Fed. (2d) 525. No doubt you will, in determining the issues relative to *Ulysses*, give equal consideration to the *Frankie and Johnnie* opinion.

I understand from Mr. Coleman that you already have a copy of *James Joyce's Ulysses* by Stuart Gilbert. I take the liberty of sending you herewith Paul Jordan Smith's *The Key to the Ulysses of James Joyce*, and also Herbert S. Gorman's *James Joyce: His First Forty Years*.

I am sending a copy of this letter to Mr. Coleman.

Sincerely yours,
Alexander Lindey

[Doc. 156]
[This is an enclosure to Doc. 155.—ED.]

UNITED STATES DISTRICT COURT
SOUTHERN DISTRICT OF NEW YORK

UNITED STATES OF AMERICA,

Libellant,

—against—

1 book entitled *Ulysses* by
James Joyce

PRELIMINARY MEMORANDUM
SUBMITTED ON BEHALF OF
CLAIMANT, WITH EXHIBITS.

Dated: September 12, 1933.

Respectfully submitted,

GREENBAUM, WOLFF & ERNST,
Attorneys for Claimant,
285 Madison Avenue,
Borough of Manhattan,
New York City

Of Counsel:

MORRIS L. ERNST
ALEXANDER LINDEY

---

UNITED STATES DISTRICT COURT
SOUTHERN DISTRICT OF NEW YORK

UNITED STATES OF AMERICA,

Libellant,

—against—

1 book entitled *Ulysses* by
James Joyce

PRELIMINARY
MEMORANDUM SUBMITTED
ON BEHALF OF CLAIMANT,
WITH EXHIBITS.

## Statement

In accordance with the practice which we have followed in the state courts in numerous cases involving the alleged obscenity of books, such practice consisting of submitting to the Court miscellaneous factual data calculated to be of aid to the Court in the course of the Court's reading, we are submitting this preliminary memorandum.

The test of obscenity is a living standard. Any publication must be judged by the *mores* of the day. What is decent or indecent is determined by the sensibilities and moral scruples of a people, as evolved from generation to generation. A thing deemed indecent in one period, may be deemed decent in another, and *vice versa.*

United States v. Kennerley, 209 Fed. 119, 121;

People v. Seltzer, 203 N.Y. Sup. 809, 814;

46 Corpus Juris, 854.

Community morality may be summed up as follows: That which society accepts is moral; that which it rejects is immoral. The law must recognize and give effect to this principle, or else it becomes "not a true mirror of life as it should be, but a bewildering distortion, alike perplexing and misleading, of which the ordinary man or woman becomes properly distrustful." ("The Development of the Law," Prof. Wormser, *Columbia Law Review,* December 1923; reprinted in *Lectures on Legal Topics,* Association of the Bar of the City of New York, Volume 5, page 60.)

This philosophy has been tersely expressed by former Justice Holmes of the United States Supreme Court:

> The first requirement of a sound body of law is, that it should correspond with the actual feelings and demands of the community, whether right or wrong. (Oliver Wendell Holmes, Jr., *The Common Law,* p. 41)

In a magazine article, former Justice Proskauer of the Appellate Division of the Supreme Court of the State of New York said:

> . . . the law does not lead but follows public opinion, and yet it does constantly re-adapt itself slowly but surely to those modifications of life and thought which are soundly established. (*Harper's Magazine,* September 1929, p. 419)

Public opinion furnishes the only true test of obscenity. Such opinion is definitely ascertainable. It is true that people as a mass are inarticulate. The body politic registers its will through representatives chosen at the polls. By the same token the community makes its moral reactions felt and its judgments pronounced, through responsible men who, by reason of their individual integrity and the multiplicity of their respective endeavors, furnish an accurate social mirror.

When newspapers, college professors, critics, educators, authors, librarians, clergymen and publishers rally to the defense of a book, they do more than express their personal views: They speak for the body social.

Public opinion, crystallized in the statements hereto annexed, vigorously repudiates any imputation of obscenity with respect to *Ulysses*. To accept such statements is not to accept opinion evidence; it is to appraise the temper of the community by the only effective means available.

The attached exhibits are presented not as evidence, but rather as general data to aid the Court in its determination. We submit that these exhibits comprise material relevant and pertinent to the issue before the Court; that the material is of such nature as to warrant recognition and acceptance by the Court under the principle of judicial notice; and that the exhibits afford an overwhelming and irrefutable contradiction of the charge of obscenity.

> Respectfully submitted,
>
> GREENBAUM, WOLFF & ERNST
> Attorneys for Claimant,
> 285 Madison Avenue,
> Borough of Manhattan,
> New York City

Of Counsel:

MORRIS L. ERNST
ALEXANDER LINDEY

Dated, September 12, 1933.

-----

## TABLE OF CONTENTS

[Doc. 157]

September 14, 1933.

Bennett A. Cerf, Esq.,
c/o Random House,
20 East 57th Street,
New York City.

Re: *Ulysses*

Dear Cerf:

I am sending you herewith a copy of the preliminary memorandum [See Doc. 156.—ED.] which we have submitted to Judge Woolsey. The original of the enclosure was sent down to the District Court, and I understand that it was forwarded from there to some place in Massachusetts, where Judge Woolsey is vacationing. We were told that the Judge had Stuart Gilbert's book. We sent him Paul Jordan Smith's *Key to Ulysses*, and Gorman's *James Joyce: His First Forty Years*.

The enclosure is a complete copy of the memorandum which went to the Judge, with the exception of the map and the actual photostats of opinions, which are not here included.

Argument is now definitely set for October 20. There will be no briefs submitted prior to that time or thereafter, unless the Judge calls for them. We are nevertheless working on ours so as to be prepared.

Yours very truly,

Greenbaum, Wolff & Ernst

AL:JF

[Doc. 158]

September 16, 1933.

Bennett A. Cerf, Esq.,
c/o Random House,
20 East 57th Street,
New York City.

Re: *United States* v. *Ulysses*

Dear Cerf:

As per your request I am sending you herewith two sets of page proofs of our proposed brief in the above matter.

Will you please go over the enclosure carefully, and let us have whatever suggestions may occur to you.

Thanks for letting us see Mr. Moses' letter, which we are returning to you herewith. You will find that all his comments are already embodied in the brief.

Yours very truly,

Greenbaum, Wolff & Ernst

AL:JF

_____

[Doc. 159]

The Warwick
Locus Street at 17th
Philadelphia

Tuesday—

Dear Lindey:

The brief is swell. Its full of typographical errors, but I presume you've caught them. Be sure *Coleridge* and *Merejkowski* are correctly spelled in the list on page 9. I presume also that your omission of the fact that we publish all of O'Neill was deliberate, although with a man like Woolsey, that might be something in our favor despite the nature of some of his plays.

I'll be back in NY Friday, and will phone you then.

Bennett Cerf

[Doc. 160]

GREENBAUM, WOLFF & ERNST

OFFICE MEMORANDUM

TO:   Mr. Ernst                    FROM:   A.L.
RE:   *Ulysses*                    DATE:   Sept 28, 1933

   Called up Coleman to find out about the motion on Monday. Coleman says that Woolsey is still away and is not due back until Monday. Coleman wants you to call him. He wants to talk to you.

———————

[Doc. 161]

October 2, 1933.

Bennett A. Cerf, Esq.,
c/o Random House,
20 East 57th Street,
New York City.

Re: *U.S.* v. *Ulysses*

Dear Cerf,

   We have just heard from the U.S. Attorney's Office in the above matter. Judge Woolsey's secretary states that the Judge has not yet finished reading the book and he has suggested that we telephone his office later in the week, preferably Friday, relative to the proposed argument.

   We are not proceeding with the printing of our brief in final form until we know definitely when the motion will be heard.

Very truly yours,

Greenbaum, Wolff & Ernst

AL:BBO

———————

[Doc. 162]

October 6, 1933.

Mr. Ernst,

Mr. Atlas phoned at about a quarter to five and gave me the following message for you:

"I spoke to Judge Woolsey on the telephone today. He tells me that during the time he was away he was able to read but a very small part of *Ulysses*; that he is going away again and will return on November 6th. During that time he hopes to be able to conclude the book. After he returns he would appreciate it if we (meaning you and Atlas) could set it down for a convenient Saturday morning for argument, probably at the Bar Association. Judge Woolsey told me that while he was away he was taken up mostly with the motion calendar which he had been hearing before he left."

P.G.

---

[Doc. 163]

October 13, 1933.

Mr. Paul Léon,
27, Rue de Casimir-Périer,
Paris, France.

Dear Mr. Léon:

There are still no new developments to report on the *Ulysses* case. As I told you, we have succeeded in getting this case into the hands of the best judge in the country for our purpose. This is Judge Woolsey, a man who has given favorable decisions in all comparable cases in the past. Unfortunately, however, Judge Woolsey is a pretty old man and takes his own good time about matters of this sort. He took the book with him when he went for his vacation, and all of us confidently expected that we would get a decision on October 2nd. When that day arrived, however, the Judge blandly informed us that he hadn't gotten through with his reading of either *Ulysses* itself, or of some of the books concerning *Ulysses* that he meant to go into before taking up the case officially. Meanwhile, our attorney has prepared a most elaborate brief on the book which we think is such a convincing document that we are having a hundred copies of it printed to send to prominent men throughout the country. This brief will back up all the mass of letters that we collected from critics, librarians, doctors, etc., and that are already in the Judge's hands. We will send you a copy of this brief as soon as it is received from the printers. I am sure that Mr. Joyce and you will approve of it.

Some time ago Mr. Joyce prepared for Mr. Herbert Gorman a most illuminating chart on *Ulysses*, arranged in column form, and showing all the connotations of the various chapters. [See Doc. 169.—ED.] The titles of the various columns read as follows:

Title: Scene: Hour: Organ: Color: Symbol: Technic: Correspondences.

I am sure that Mr. Joyce will recall this chart as soon as you mention it to him, but if he doesn't, I will have a full copy made of it and send it to you. It is my earnest belief that if we can reprint this chart in our edition of *Ulysses* (provided, of course, we ever do get the right to do the edition) we will be rendering a tremendous service to the reading public. I honestly believe, also, that the inclusion of this chart will result in a tremendous number of additional sales. Furthermore, we can copyright this chart, and it will make one more feature of our own edition that cannot possibly be pirated. For all these reasons, we want Mr. Joyce's permission to include his chart in our edition. Will you please let me know about this at your very earliest convenience?

I mention possible pirated editions of *Ulysses* in the above paragraph. Rumors have reached us that some German firm has photographed the pages of the Shakespeare & Co. edition of *Ulysses*, and is prepared to rush copies into this country the very moment that a favorable decision may be rendered. We will exercise all due vigilance in this matter in an attempt to confiscate any such copies that may come in, but as you know, this is a big country with many ports of entry, and it will not be easy to stop this intended business entirely. Consequently, I cannot emphasize too strongly the importance of having as many copyrighted features in our own edition as possible.

I hope you and Mr. Joyce will realize that all these delays in this matter are equally, if not more, distasteful, to us than they are to you. We have invested considerable money and a tremendous amount of time in our fight to legalize *Ulysses* over here, and it should not be necessary to point out to you that we are not overlooking the smallest point in our struggle to get a favorable decision at the very earliest possible moment.

I look forward to hearing from you immediately in the matter of the chart.

Cordially yours,

Bennett A. Cerf
Random House

bac;pk

[Doc. 164]

## UNITED STATES DISTRICT COURT
## SOUTHERN DISTRICT OF NEW YORK

UNITED STATES OF AMERICA,

*Libellant,*

against

One Book Entitled *Ulysses*

————

Random House, Inc.,

*Claimant.*

Index No.
A 110-59.
Cal. No.
1438.
Jury Calendar.

## CLAIMANT'S MEMORANDUM IN SUPPORT OF
## MOTION TO DISMISS LIBEL

Respectfully submitted,

GREENBAUM, WOLFF & ERNST,
Attorneys for Claimant,
285 Madison Avenue,
Borough of Manhattan,
New York City.

MORRIS L. ERNST,
ALEXANDER LINDEY,
Of Counsel.

Dated, New York, October 14, 1933.

————————

## INDEX

Point I. The Test of Obscenity Is a Living Standard and *Ulysses*
Must Be Judged by the Mores of the Day

    A. The Law
    B. The Changing Times
    C. Our Mores

Point II. *Ulysses* Is Not Obscene According to the Accepted Definitions
of Obscenity Laid Down by the Courts

    A. The Question
    B. The Development of the Law
    C. *Frankie and Johnnie*
    D. Some Recent New York Cases Involving Books
    E. *God's Little Acre*
    F. Normal v. Abnormal

Point III. *Ulysses* Is a Modern Classic. The United States Government
Has Officially Acknowledged It as Such. It Cannot, Therefore, Be
Deemed Obscene

    A. The Federal Government Has Officially Paid Tribute to the
       Greatness of *Ulysses*
    B. A Classic Cannot Be Adjudged Obscene

Point IV. The Intrinsic Features of *Ulysses*, as Well as Certain Extrinsic
Facts Connected With It, Negate Any Implication of Obscenity

    A. Intrinsic Characteristics
    B. Extrinsic Circumstances

Point V. *Ulysses* Has Been Generally Accepted by the Community
and Hence Cannot Be Held to Be Violative of the Statute

Point VI. *Ulysses* Must Be Judged as a Whole, and Its General Purpose
and Effect Determined. On That Basis It Must Be Cleared

Conclusion

## TABLE OF CASES CITED

238

## UNITED STATES DISTRICT COURT
## SOUTHERN DISTRICT OF NEW YORK

UNITED STATES OF AMERICA,

|  | |  |
|---|---|---|
| *Libellant,* | } | Index No. |
| against | | A 110-59 |
| One Book Entitled *Ulysses* | | Cal. No. 1438. |
| ———— | | Jury Calendar. |
| Random House, Inc., | | |
| *Claimant.* | | |

## CLAIMANT'S MEMORANDUM IN SUPPORT OF MOTION TO DISMISS LIBEL

The government, at the instance of the Collector of Customs, has libelled a certain book called *Ulysses* by James Joyce, on the ground of obscenity, allegedly pursuant to Section 305 of the Tariff Act of June 17, 1930 (Title 19, United States Code, Section 1305). The book was sent into this country, addressed to the claimant herein. The claimant has interposed an answer admitting the importation of the book, but denying that it contravenes the aforesaid section of the Tariff Act.

The libellant and the claimant have cross-moved for judgment on the pleadings.

The libellant and the claimant have stipulated (1) that *Ulysses* be annexed to and become part of the libel with the same force and effect as if fully set forth therein; (2) that the claimant waive trial by jury; (3) that upon this motion the Court may consider and decide all questions of law and fact, and may render general findings of fact and conclusions of law; and (4) that upon this motion the judgment of the Court may be entered as though it were a judgment after trial.

### Nature of the Case

This case is unique in several respects. It involves a book which has been a *cause célèbre* in literary circles for more than a decade. No other prose work of our times—perhaps no other literary product in the history of the world—has won such enthusiastic critical acclaim and has so profoundly influenced letters. Courts have been often called upon to pass upon books, but never upon a work of the magnitude and newness, of the complexity, of the literary importance of *Ulysses*. The book is unlike any other work that has preceded it. It has been said that in writing it Joyce embarked upon uncharted literary seas. There is every reason, therefore, why the rules of law which are invoked in ordinary cases, should be here applied with exceptional circumspection.

There is a peculiar timeliness about this proceeding. Coming, as it does, in logical sequence after the *Dennett* case, the *Youngs* case, the *Married Love* case, the *Contraception* case, the *Wendling* case,[1] all of which have served to liberalize the law of obscenity and to thrust back the narrow frontiers fixed by prudery, *Ulysses* calls for vindication as a fitting climax to the salutary forward march of our courts.

## The Author

Joyce was born of Roman Catholic parents in Dublin in 1882. His early home life was steeped in an atmosphere of ritual and theology. He was educated at the Jesuit school, Clongowes Wood, and later at Belvedere College and the Royal University, Dublin. His autobiographical novel, *A Portrait of the Artist as a Young Man*, gives a vivid picture of the formative years of a sensitive, brooding child, reared amid incense and colored images and mystical teachings, and torn between religious obsession and doubt.

For some time Joyce studied medicine at the University of Paris. He gave this up, devoted himself to Latin, German, Norwegian and the Romance languages, became a linguist and a teacher. He has lived in Trieste, Switzerland and France. He now resides in Paris.

Though he is the most important figure in world literature today, his works are few in number. *Chamber Music*, a collection of poems, appeared in 1907; *Dubliners*, a series of unforgettable characterizations, intermittently thereafter in periodicals, and in final form in 1914; *A Portrait of the Artist as a Young Man*, a novel,[2] in 1915; *Exiles*, a play, in 1918; and *Ulysses* in 1922. The last-named work, now before the Court, bears the notation "Trieste-Zurich-Paris, 1914-1921" at the conclusion. It took more than seven years to write.

Joyce belongs to that distinguished company of Irish authors which includes such men at Padraic Colum (an ardent champion of Joyce), James Stephens, Sean O'Casey, William Butler Yeats and George Bernard Shaw. Unlike Shaw and others of his countrymen, Joyce has steadfastly scorned ballyhoo and self-exploitation. He has led a monastic existence, and has made no attempt to benefit by the furore created by *Ulysses*. He has delivered no lectures, given no interviews, posed for no newsreels, attached no explanatory prefaces to his works, issued no manifestos, written no magazine articles which might have yielded him easy harvest. Nearly as blind as the Greek master from whose epic he borrowed the name of his novel, he has lived apart, an austere Olympian.[3] His fame has grown. Hailed ten years ago by the untutored and the misguided as a juggler of words, today even his harshest critics concede his greatness.

He has exerted a profound influence on world letters—possibly greater influence than any man before him. There is not a single modern psychological novel worthy of mention which does not bear some trace of the Joycean method.

It is not often that an author, within the span of his lifetime, sees a work of his acclaimed as an enduring classic. Joyce is such an author. He has revolutionized expression. He stands as a kind of Colossus of creative writing, dominating his age. Not since Shakespeare, it is said, has the English language reached such heights as in *Ulysses*. Joyce is a genius of the first rank.

Stuart Gilbert, distinguished American critic, says:

> . . . the genius of James Joyce has an Elizabethan quality, an universality, a gift of reconciling classical, modern and romantic that, Shakespeare excepted, renders it unique. That power of discovering symmetry and coherence in all phenomena, of whatever species and place and epoch, of assimilating the present with the past, passion with intellect and (on the technical side) the utmost verbal freedom with strict precision in the handling of vocabulary, is a power beyond the scope of any but the greatest.[4]

"His prose works," says Rebecca West, "prove him beyond argument a writer of majestic genius."[5]

"No living author," says Paul Rosenfeld, "brings a vocabulary either as crisply, sharply, pungently used, or as vast. Joyce possesses a relatively unlimited knowledge of the resources of the English language . . . Joyce's prose is almost perfect. So utterly faithful to his intuitions has he been, that a marvelous vitality inhabits each of his phrases. . . . It is no petty achievement to have attained with serio-comedy the level upon which Swift and Flaubert stand, and long will stand."[6]

When it comes to psychology or realism, beside Joyce "Balzac is beggared and Zola bankrupted," says Shane Leslie in *The London Quarterly*. In *Ulysses* there is evident, according to J. Middleton Murry, noted English critic, "a genius of the very highest order, strictly comparable to Goethe's or Dostoevsky's."

Arnold Bennett in *The Outlook* finds Joyce "a very astonishing phenomenon in letters. His ingenuity is marvellous. He has wit. He has a prodigious humor."

Ernest Boyd in *The New York Tribune* declares that his imagination is one "which is at once romantic and realistic, brilliant and petty, full of powerful fantasy, yet preserving an almost incredible faculty of detailed material observation."

He is, according to Gilbert Seldes, writing in *The Nation*, "possibly the most interesting and the most formidable writer of our time. . . Among the very great writers only two can be named with him for the long devotion to their work and for the triumphant conclusion—Flaubert and Henry James." He has scored "a victory of the creative intelligence over the chaos of uncreated things and a triumph of devotion, to my mind one of the most significant and beautiful of our time."

"... this austere, almost pedantic writer," says Edmund Wilson in *The New Republic,* "soars to such rhapsodies of beauty as have probably never been equalled in English prose fiction."

It is monstrous to suppose that a man of the stature of Joyce would or could produce a work of obscenity.

## The Book

Dante wrote the *Divine Comedy,* and Balzac the *Comédie Humaine.* It remained for Joyce to write the *Comédie Intellectuelle.*

In some respects *Ulysses* defies accurate description. Although fictional in form, it is not a novel. It is a vast edifice of episode superimposed on episode, a panorama of all the aspects, moods, excesses and torments of the human mind. Despite its heroic proportions,[7] it deals with but one day in the life of Leopold Bloom (Ulysses), advertising solicitor. All the action unfolds itself in Dublin between the early morning hours of June 16, and about three o'clock in the morning, June 17, 1904—about twenty hours altogether. "And yet," says Gorman, "in that short period of time is packed the whole vivid variegated life of Dublin. . . . All the emotions and attributes find their place here. There is birth, love, death, adultery, greed, sloth, drunkenness, anger, chicanery, intrigue, religion, philosophy, spiritual torture, childish ignorance, nationalism, lechery, madness, the list is infinite. Expressing these emotions, hundreds of characters hold forth in the streets, public-houses, cemeteries, shops, libraries, newspaper offices, hospitals, brothels and churches. With this infinite variety of material . . . the author conceives a certain order and in so doing he creates a new form for the novel. . . . The real genius of the book . . . is implicit in the complete revelation and development of two characters, two of the greatest, saddest, most tragic-comic portraits in the entire annals of literary achievement—Stephen Dedalus and Leopold Bloom."[8]

Yet it is neither Dedalus nor Bloom who is the hero of *Ulysses.* The real protagonist is the mind. The arena is not Dublin, but the human skull.

Joyce has patterned his book after Homer's *Odyssey,* but he has not sought to make the parallel perfect. Bloom appears as Ulysses, his wife as Penelope, Blazes Boylan as Antinous, Stephen Dedalus as Telemachus, Bella Cohen as Circe; there are similarities in frame-work; but many details and incidents in Joyce's work have no counterpart in the Homeric story. Whatever discrepancies exist are unimportant. In one significant respect there is a kinship between the two books: the *Odyssey* is a record of journeyings in a physical world; *Ulysses* is the epic of the coursing of the stream of consciousness.

There is no need for us to set forth in this memorandum an analysis of the incidents in *Ulysses.* The Court has read the book; the claimant has heretofore transmitted to the Court Herbert Gorman's *James Joyce,* and Paul Jordan Smith's *A Key to the Ulysses* of *James Joyce.* The last-named work contains a complete outline.

Louis Golding, writing in *The Nineteenth Century*, April 1933, thus indicates the stature of *Ulysses*:

> Among great works of prose we find none that compares in kind with *Ulysses*. When we seek works which compare with it in scope, we cannot stop short this side of the *Inferno*, *Hamlet* and the *Odyssey*, each of which, in point of fact, has the closest bearing on the developing history of Stephen Dedalus and Leopold Bloom during the eternal eighteen hours of the day on which the action of *Ulysses* occurs. But those others are poetry; their compass is between heaven and hell. *Ulysses* is prose. It does not leave the gross stuff of this earth; its journeys are along the grey corridors of mind, among the red chambers of the flesh (p. 491).

### The Claimant[9]

Random House, Inc. was organized several years ago for the purpose of printing and distributing in America books of significant content and typographical distinction. Most of the Random House publications have been printed by the Pynson Printers, one of the finest printers in America.

In the years 1927, 1928 and 1929, Random House published numerous notable books. The first was an edition of *Candide*, with illustrations by Rockwell Kent, which *The New York Times* declared to be the most beautiful book ever produced in America. Other expensive editions were Hawthorne's *The Scarlet Letter*, Emily Brontë's *Wuthering Heights*, Robert Lewis Stevenson's *Dr. Jekyll and Mr. Hyde*, the collected poems of Robert Frost, *Beowulf*, and Mark Twain's *Adventures of Tom Sawyer*. The most elaborate book produced was an edition of four hundred copies of Walt Whitman's *Leaves of Grass*. It sold for $100 a copy.

In addition to publishing books under its own imprint, Random House has acted as exclusive American distributor for three of the outstanding presses in the world, to wit, The Nonesuch Press, and the Golden Cockerel Press of England, and the Cranach Presse of Germany.

The current list of Random House includes the following:

| Title | Author |
| --- | --- |
| *Troilus and Cressida* | Chaucer |
| *Plays and Poems* | W. S. Gilbert |
| *Complete Works* | Coleridge |
| *Romance of Leonardo da Vinci* | Merejkowski |
| *Wuthering Heights* | Emily Brontë |
| *Poetry and Selected Prose* | John Donne |
| *Prose and Poetry* | William Blake |
| *Selected Essays* | William Hazlitt |
| *Moby Dick* (Rockwell Kent) | Herman Melville |
| *Candide* (Rockwell Kent) | Voltaire |

## Recent Cases

The Court's attention is respectfully directed to the fact that in recent years there has not been a single instance where a book generally acclaimed by the press and literary critics was ultimately condemned by the courts, even though prosecuted at the outset for obscenity. This statement is borne out by such books as Theophile Gautier's *Mademoiselle de Maupin* (234 N. Y. 1); the anonymous *Madeleine* (192 App. Div. [N. Y.] 816); *The Satyricon of Petronius* (Magistrate Oberwager, September 27, 1922, New York City); *A Young Girl's Diary* (Magistrate Simpson, September 30, 1922, New York City); Maxwell Bodenheim's *Replenishing Jessica* (Court of General Sessions, New York City, June 1925); Radclyffe Hall's *The Well of Loneliness* (Court of Special Sessions, City of New York, April 19, 1929); *Casanova's Homecoming* (Magistrate Gottlieb, September 25, 1930, New York City); Mary Ware Dennett's *The Sex Side of Life* (39 Fed. (2d) 564); Dr. Marie Stopes' *Married Love* (48 Fed. (2d) 821); Dr. Marie Stopes' *Contraception* (51 Fed. (2d) 525); the Chinese classic *Hsi Men Ching* (Magistrate Brodsky, November 9, 1931, New York City); Clement Wood's *Flesh* (Magistrate Harris, December 18, 1931); Louis Charles Royer's *Let's Go Naked* (Magistrate Van Amringe, December 8, 1932, New York City); and Erskine Caldwell's *God's Little Acre* (Magistrate Greenspan, May 23, 1933, New York City).[10]

## The Law

Section 305 of the Tariff Act of 1930 (Title 19, United States Code, Section 1305), provides in part as follows:

> All persons are prohibited from importing into the United States from any foreign country . . . any obscene book, pamphlet, paper, writing, advertisement, circular, print, picture, drawing or other representation, figure, or image on or of paper or other material . . . .[11]

## Argument

I. The test of obscenity is a living standard, and *Ulysses* must be judged by the *mores* of the day.

II. *Ulysses* is not obscene as a matter of law.

III. *Ulysses* is a modern classic. The United States Government has officially acknowledged it as such. It cannot therefore be deemed obscene.

IV. The intrinsic features of *Ulysses*, as well as certain extrinsic facts, negate any implication of obscenity.

V. *Ulysses* has been generally accepted by the community, and hence cannot be held to be violative of the statute.

VI. *Ulysses* must be judged as a whole, and its general purpose and effect determined. On that basis it must be cleared.

## POINT I

The test of obscenity is a living standard, and *Ulysses* must be judged by the *mores* of the day.

### A. THE LAW

What is decent or indecent is determined by the sensibilities and moral standards of the people, as evolved from generation to generation along with their civilization. A thing deemed indecent in one period may be approved as decent in another.

46 *Corpus Juris*, 854.

It is evident that Judge Learned Hand had this fluidity of standard in mind when he remarked in U.S. v. Kennerley, 209 Fed. 119, at page 121:

> If there be no abstract definition, such as I have suggested, should not the word "obscene" be allowed to indicate the *present critical point* in the compromise between candor and shame at which the community may have arrived *here and now?* . . . Nor is it an objection, I think, that such an interpretation gives to the words of the statute a *varying meaning from time to time*. Such words as these do not embalm the precise morals of an age or place; while they presuppose that some things will always be shocking to the public taste, the vague subject matter is left *to the gradual development of general notions about what is decent.* (Italics ours.)

And so, too, in People v. Seltzer, 203 N. Y. Supp. 809, the Court said, at page 814:

> Moral standards of thought are not of static . . . nature.

In St. Hubert Guild v. Quinn, 64 Misc. 336, the Court insisted that "contemporaneous literature must, of course, be judged by *current* opinion."

To paraphase the words of Justice Holmes,[12] late of the United States Supreme Court, the first requirement of a sane and rational administration of the law is that it should correspond with the actual feelings and demands of the community, whether right or wrong.

Judge Cardozo has said, in his book entitled *The Paradoxes of Legal Science* (p. 10):

> We live in a world of change. If a body of law were in existence adequate for the civilization of today, it could not meet the demands of the civilization of tomorrow.

And he has thus amplified this basic truth in his book *The Growth of the Law*:

There are certain forms of conduct which at any given place and epoch are commonly accepted under the combined influence of reason, practice and tradition, as moral or immoral. If we were asked to define the precise quality that leads them to be so characterized, we might find it troublesome to make answer, yet the same difficulty is found in defining other abstract qualities, even those the most familiar. The forms of conduct thus discriminated are not the same at all times or in all places. *Law accepts as the pattern of its justice the morality of the community whose conduct it assumes to regulate. . . .* The law will not hold the crowd to the morality of saints and seers. It will follow, or strive to follow, the principle and practice of the men and women of the community whom the social mind would rank as *intelligent and virtuous.* (Italics ours.)

On March 16, 1929, the *London Law Journal* wrote:

. . . It must not be forgotten that the standard of obscenity is relative, and must vary from generation to generation; what shocks or corrupts one age will not necessarily shock or corrupt another.

In Redd v. State, 7 Ga. A. 575, the Court said, at page 580:

What is decent and what is indecent is largely a matter of general public opinion.

In his treatise entitled "The Development of the Law," *Columbia Law Review*, December, 1923, Professor Maurice Wormser wrote:

Increasingly—ever increasingly—the community is beginning to require of the law that it justify its own administration of its resources before the bar of public opinion. And in order to justify itself before this critical bar, the law must be brought to evidence the *mores* of the times to which it must conform, or it will fail to fulfill its function as the juridical expression of the community-passion for justice and right dealing.

## B. THE CHANGING TIMES

In Rome remarriage was deemed adulterous and a third marriage was severely punished. Today the notion that remarriage is immoral has been rejected; and the State recognizes, and the Church acquiesces in, the custom of divorce.[13]

Alexander Hamilton, in the early days of our republic, protested against the use of the Maypole in America, claiming that the dance had phallic significance. Now our parks and playgrounds are filled with Maypole parties, and the custom appears obscene to no one.

In 1895, one John B. Wise, of Clay Center, Kansas, was convicted of sending obscene matter through the U. S. mails. The matter consisted of quotations from the Bible.[14]

In 1900 any female who appeared on a bathing beach without sleeves and a long skirt would have been jailed. By 1911 bare knees could be legally displayed at the seashore; but legs still had to be covered, and girls wore stockings rolled down below the knees. A few years ago the one-piece bathing suit came into its own; and today the so-called sunsuits leave very little of the human form concealed. There was a time, not so long ago, when bobbed hair and cigarette-smoking were the signs of a loose woman. It may sound incredible, but Walter Hines Page (back in the days when he was a member of the publishing firm of Doubleday, Page & Company) refused to print a book, because it contained the suggestive word "chaste."[15]

A woman superintendent in the Children's Department of the Brooklyn Public Library once charged that *Tom Sawyer* and *Huckleberry Finn* were corrupting the morals of children.[16]

In 1906 the play *Sappho* was suppressed because Olga Nethersole was carried upstairs in it by a man. To the present generation *Sappho* is an innocuous piece. George Bernard Shaw's *Mrs. Warren's Profession* has had the same history. In 1907 the New England Watch and Ward Society prevented Mary Garden from appearing in Richard Strauss' celebrated opera *Salôme*. Today the opera is in the repertoire of every reputable opera company.

A decade ago *September Morn, Paul and Virginia,* Manet's *Olympia* and similar pictures were deemed pornography; now they hardly elicit a second glance. The *Bacchante* of MacMonnies was once denounced as "a naked woman dancing in her shame."[17] When Goya first painted the Duchess of Alba and called the picture *Maya Desnuda,* the moral sensibilities of his zealous contemporaries were outraged, and for many years the painting was hid from view. Today it has the place of honor in the national gallery at Seville; and at the Ibero-American Exposition which was held in Spain in 1930, thousands of Goya Memorial Stamps were issued by the government bearing miniature reproductions of the painting.

The history of literature affords striking examples of radical changes of opinion concerning the moral content of books. Some works have merely sloughed off the stigma of condemnation; others have run the gamut from vehement denunciation to veneration as classics.

Moxon, the English publisher, was convicted in 1841 for publishing Shelley's works, which included such celebrated pieces as *Queen Mab, The Revolt of Islam, The Cenci, Alastor,* and *Prometheus Unbound* (Moxon's Case, 2 Mod. St. Tr., 356). When first published, Charlotte Brontë's *Jane Eyre* "was pronounced too immoral to be ranked as decent literature"; George Eliot's *Adam Bede* was execrated as "the vile outpouring of a lewd woman's mind"; and Elizabeth Barrett Browning's *Aurora Leigh* was declared to be the "hysterical indecencies of an erotic mind."[18]

Upon the appearance of Hawthorne's *Scarlet Letter*, it was reviewed at length by the Reverend (afterwards Bishop) A. C. Coxe, who fulminated "against any toleration to a popular and gifted writer, when he perpetrates bad morals. Let this brokerage of lust be put down at the very beginning."[19] Hardy's *Tess of the D'Urbervilles* and *Jude the Obscure*, and du Maurier's *Trilby* met with virulent attacks as obscene books. *Leaves of Grass* cost Walt Whitman his position in the Interior Department. Hamlin Garland's *Rose of Dutcher's Coolly*, H. G. Wells' *Ann Veronica* and Theodore Dreiser's *Jennie Gerhardt* all were once considered "bad books." The publication of *Mademoiselle de Maupin* by Gautier in 1834 raised a furor of scandalized protest, and ultimately cost the author the wreath of the Academy. It has since become a classic, and has won generous judicial praise.

Not so many years ago Lewis Carroll (the Reverend Mr. Dodgson), author of *Alice's Adventures in Wonderland*, went to a performance of *Pinafore* given by children, and of the famous "Damme, it's too bad," of the Captain and the chorus he wrote:

> I cannot find words to convey to the reader the pain I felt in seeing those dear children taught to utter such words to amuse ears grown callous to their ghastly meaning. . . . How Mr. Gilbert could have stooped to write, or Sir Arthur Sullivan could have prostituted his noble art to set to music, such vile trash, it passes my skill to understand.

In 1908 the Rev. J. Frank Chase obtained a conviction against a Boston book-dealer for selling Elinor Glyn's *Three Weeks*. (Commonwealth v. Buckley, 200 Mass. 346.) The decision of the Court was promptly nullified by popular acceptance of the book. And seventeen years later the same Mr. Chase remarked to an interviewer, "I know you wouldn't make a fool of me, Mister, but I have been re-reading *Three Weeks* recently. Do you know that I couldn't get a conviction against the book nowadays. I wouldn't dare to take it into court!"[22]

## C. OUR MORES

It is clear that *Ulysses* must be judged in the light of present-day mores. The standards of yesterday, the abhorrence of any mention of certain biological functions, the excessive prudery, the sex taboo, are as definitely dead today as the horsedrawn carriage and the donkey-engines on the Elevated. We have developed sturdier tastes, and grown wiser in the process.

Evidences of our current mores are everywhere around us. Our tabloids carry stories of passion and lust, of crime and perversion, told with a degree of graphic vividness and frankness unheard of a generation ago. Every man, woman and child in the community has easy access to the complete details of torch-murders, of marital infidelities, of boudoir intimacies, kidnappings and abnormalities. The Hall-Mills case, the Snyder-Gray case, and more recently the Winnie Judd case, the Dr. Sylla case, the Jessie Costello case, are but a few of innumerable examples.

For the press of today, a spade is a spade. No longer are such squeamish phrases as "statutory offense" resorted to. The headlines and the columns speak openly of rape, blood-lust and adultery. Such outspokenness would have horrified us in 1900. Today it is accepted as a matter of course.

Even the movies, notwithstanding the prophylaxis of censorship, are now dealing more and more boldly with sex. There was a time when the merest glimpse of the female breast was barred from the screen. Now we have had a whole series of films like *Moana, The Virgins of Bali, Goona-Goona* and *Samarang*, in which the nude human body has been freely revealed. Nor have the movies contented themselves with merely stripping away prudish coverings. They have, in recent years, given us a collection of sex-films, too numerous to mention, culminating in Mae West's frank and unashamed *She Done Him Wrong*.

In "The Facts of Life in Popular Song" (*The American Spectator*, Aug. 1933, Vol. I, No. 10), Dr. Sigmund Spaeth has revealed the extent of forthrightness which our lyricists have come to practice (and the community to accept) in telling of the technique and joys of love-making.

On the stage, we have had plays like *Strictly Dishonorable, Warrior's Husband, Strange Interlude* (abortion, adultery), *Mourning Becomes Electra* (adultery, unnatural passion), *Reunion in Vienna, Frankie and Johnnie* (a dramatic record of happenings in a brothel, cleared of the charge of obscenity by the Court of Appeals in People v. Wendling, 258 N. Y. 451, March 3, 1932), and *Design for Living*, which presented a ménage of two men and a woman, the men alternating in the physical affections of the lady, and finally deserting her because of their fondness for each other.

As for the graphic and plastic arts, it is sufficient to say that the fig-leaf has apparently disappeared forever. William Zorach's *Embrace*, recently exhibited to the general public at the Museum of Modern Art in this city, testifies eloquently to our present-day notions of propriety; Robert Laurent's *Goose Girl* and Gwen Lux's *Eve* stand undraped and unashamed in the lobby of the Roxy Music Hall for New York's millions to behold.

Our current attitude in letters is best illustrated by the kind of books in general circulation. Works like Compton McKenzie's *Extraordinary Women*, Marcel Proust's *Swann's Way*, Thomas Mann's *Death in Venice*, Edouard Bourdet's *The Captive*, Lytton Strachey's *Elizabeth and Essex*, Radclyffe Hall's *The Well of Loneliness*, Arthur Schnitzler's *Casanova's Homecoming*, Octave Mirbeau's *Celestine, Eastern Shame Girl*, Dr. Marie Stopes' *Married Love*, Pierre Louys' *Woman and Puppet*, the Chinese classic *Hsi Men Ching*, Clement Wood's *Flesh*, Erskine Caldwell's *God's Little Acre*, William Faulkner's *Sanctuary* and *Light in August*, Hervey Allen's *Anthony Adverse*,

Albert Cohen's *Solal* and thousands of others dealing with sexual adventures, have all been freely circulated. Some of them have been attacked; none of them has been finally suppressed.

Perhaps the most illuminating proof of our changing mores is an advertisement which was inserted in the *New York Times Book Review* on March 30, 1932, by Macy's. A photostatic copy of the advertisement is annexed to this brief. It proves more eloquently than any amount of argument that the standards of yesterday no longer prevail, and that books which horrified our elders and were branded "forbidden" a decade or so ago, are openly advertised, sold and read today.

Viewed against our contemporary background, *Ulysses* clearly does not violate our obscenity statute.[23]

## POINT II

*Ulysses* is not obscene according to the accepted definitions of obscenity laid down by the Courts.

### A. THE QUESTION

The nature of a proceeding of this kind was clearly indicated by this Court in U.S. v. *Married Love*, 48 Fed. (2d) 821, and U.S. v. *Contraception*, 51 Fed. (2d) 525. The proceeding is one *in rem*, brought under Title 19, U. S. C., Sec. 1305, for the forfeiture of *Ulysses*, on the ground that it falls within the exclusion of the statute.

In view of the stipulation made by the claimant and the government, this Court now sits as judge and jury. To uphold the libel the Court must find not only that there is reasonable ground for believing *Ulysses* to be obscene, but also that it is obscene by a fair preponderance of evidence. The sole evidence is the book.

In the *Married Love* case, this Court, on the authority of *Murray's Oxford English Dictionary*, defined the word *obscene* to mean offensive to modesty or decency, or expressing or suggesting unchaste or lustful ideas; and the word *immoral* to mean not moral, morally evil or impure, unprincipled, vicious or dissolute.[24]

### B. THE DEVELOPMENT OF THE LAW

The ancient test of obscenity was formulated in 1868 in the English case of Regina v. Hicklin, L. R. 3 Q. B. 360. It was "whether the tendency of the matter charged as obscenity is to deprave and corrupt those whose minds are open to such immoral influences and into whose hands a publication of this sort may fall."

Such a criterion was patently unfair, unreasonable and unsound, because it sought to gauge the mental and moral capacity of the community by that of its dullest-witted and most fallible members, and because it sought to withhold from society any material which might conceivably injure its lowest and most impressionable element. The vagueness and absurdity of the mental concept thus created, and the glaring social injustice of its application, necessitated further modification.

Such modification was not long in forthcoming. In U. S. v. Bennett, 16 Blatchf. 338, obscenity was defined as material which "suggests impure and libidinous thoughts." In U. S. v. Kennerley, 209 Fed. 119, at pages 120 and 121, the Court, heedful of the ludicrous result of the early definition, stated:

> Yet, if the time is not yet when men think innocent all that which is honestly germane to a pure subject, however little it may mince its words, still I scarcely think that they would forbid all which might corrupt the most corruptible, or that *society is prepared to accept for its own limitations those which may perhaps be necessary to the weakest of its members. . . .* I hope it is not improper for me to say that the rule as laid down (*i. e.*, in *Regina* v. *Hicklin, supra*), however consonant it may be with mid-Victorian morals, does not seem to me to answer to the understanding and morality of the present time, as conveyed by the words 'obscene, lewd, or lascivious'. I question whether in the end men will regard that as obscene which is honestly relevant to the adequate expression of innocent ideas, and whether they will not believe that truth and beauty are too precious to society at large to be mutilated in the interests of those most likely to pervert them to base uses. Indeed, *it seems hardly likely that we are even today so lukewarm in our interest in letters or serious discussion as to be content to reduce our treatment of sex to the standard of a child's library in the supposed interest of a salacious few . . .* (Italics ours.)

In People v. Muller, 96 N. Y. 408, 411, the Court, referring to the ancient test, sought to limit it in this manner:

> We think it would also be a proper test of obscenity in a painting or statue, whether the motive of the painting or statue, so to speak, as indicated by it, is pure or impure, whether it is naturally calculated to excite in a spectator impure imaginations, and whether the other incidents and qualities, however attractive, were merely accessory to this as the primary or main purposes of the representation.

In People v. Brainard, 192 App. Div. 816, the Court applied the identical test and reversed a conviction in the lower court. In the case of St. Hubert Guild v. Quinn, 64 Misc. 336, Seabury, J., in his illuminating opinion, said, at page 339:

> *The early attitude of the courts upon this subject discloses an illiberality of opinion which is not reflected in the recent cases.* (Italics ours.)

In *St. Hubert Guild* v. *Quinn (supra)*, the Court aptly said, at page 340:

> It is no part of the duty of courts to exercise a censorship over literary productions.

In the case of People vs. Thomas Seltzer, et al. (*New York Law Journal*, September 30, 1922), involving the alleged obscenity of *Casanova's Homecoming*, Magistrate Simpson remarked in part:

> It has been said, with some justice, that the policy of pouncing upon books too frank for contemporary taste, without regard to the motive or purpose for which they were written, or to the use to which they are to be put, *is objectionable and should be curbed.* (Italics ours.)

The obscenity statute does not hinge on any question of good taste. The essence of the crime is sexual *impurity*, not sex (People v. Wendling, 258 N.Y. 451). In Swearingen v. U.S., 161 U. S. 446, the Supreme Court of the United States definitely abandoned the rule laid down in *Regina* v. *Hicklin, supra*. The Court said in connection with the federal law almost identical with our state statute.

> *The words "obscene", "lewd" and "lascivious", as used in the statute, signify that form of immorality which has relation to sexual* IMPURITY . . . (Italics and capitals ours.)[25]

## C. FRANKIE AND JOHNNIE

This Court will doubtless give due consideration to the most recent adjudication of the highest court in this State upon the subject of obscenity. The case is People v. Wendling, 258 N. Y. 451, decided March 3, 1932. It arose out of the dramatization of the folk-song "Frankie and Johnnie," about a country boy, in a St. Louis resort for drinking, gambling and prostitution in the middle of the last century. Here not a book but a stage presentation was involved. This is how the Court of Appeals described the dramatization:

> The language of the play is coarse, vulgar and profane; the plot cheap and tawdry. As a dramatic composition it serves to degrade the stage where vice is thought by some to lose "half its evil by losing all its grossness." "That it is 'indecent' from every consideration of propriety is entirely clear" . . . (at pp. 452-3).

Yet the Court reversed two convictions in the Court of Special Sessions of the City of New York, which had been unanimously affirmed by the Appellate Division. In doing so, the Court of Appeals restated the enlightened definition of obscenity clearly and emphatically, and further extended the liberality of *Halsey* v. *N. Y. Society* which up to that time had been the leading case on obscenity in this State. Said the Court, at page 453:

. . . the court is not a censor of plays and does not attempt to regulate manners. One may call a spade a spade without offending decency, although modesty may be shocked thereby. (People v. Muller, 96 N. Y. 408, 411). The question is not whether the scene is laid in a low dive where refined people are not found or whether the language is that of the bar room rather than the parlor. *The question is whether the tendency of the play is to excite lustful and lecherous desire.* (Italics ours.)

Coarse scenes and vulgar language, the Court insisted (p. 455), do not in themselves create such desire. The Court rejected the argument of the prosecution that the play was obscene because it portrayed the doings of prostitutes. Although the Court admitted that the play was an "uncultured depiction of a phase in the frontier life of the Middle West," it was careful to point out, at page 454:

A coarse realism is its dramatic offense. Perhaps in an age of innocence the facts of life should be withheld from the young, but a theatre goer could not give his approval to the modern stage as "spokesman of the thought and sentiment" of Broadway (Halsey v. New York Society for Suppression of Vice, 234 N. Y. 1) and at the same time silence this rough and profane representation of scenes which repel rather than seduce.

Lastly, the Court considered the possibility that *Frankie and Johnnie* might offend the over-fastidious and the censorious. In disposing of the question, the Court was quite explicit in its definition of the sole test applicable:

The production of such a play may be repulsive to puritanical ideas of propriety as would *Camille* and may be offensive to the more liberal minded as lacking in taste and refinement, as would the morally unobjectionable *Abie's Irish Rose*. The play may be gross and its characters wanting in moral sense. It may depict women who carry on a vicious trade and their male associates. It does not counsel or invite to vice or voluptuousness. It does not deride virtue. Unless we say that it is obscene to use the language of the street rather than that of the scholar, the play is not obscene under the Penal Law, although it might be so styled by the censorious (p. 454).

The opinion of the Court closes by saying:

We hold . . . that the fact that Frankie and Johnnie and their companions were not nice people does not in itself make the play obscene. A history of prostitution or of sexual life is not *per se* indecent . . . (p. 455).

Almost everything that the Court of Appeals had to say in the *Frankie and Johnnie* case is applicable to *Ulysses*. By no amount of exaggeration or distortion can it be said of it—no more than it could be said of *Frankie and Johnnie*—that it suggests unchaste or lustful ideas.

## D. SOME OTHER RECENT NEW YORK CASES
## INVOLVING BOOKS

During the early part of 1931 Mr. Sumner, acting for the New York Society for the Suppression of Vice, instituted proceedings against two books: *Celestine* and *Eastern Shame Girl*. The former was the diary of a chambermaid, and abounded in scenes depicting the sexual temptations of domestic servants and the erotic adventures of their masters and mistresses; the latter was a collection of Chinese folktales portraying the lascivious exploits of singing girls, philanderers, impostors and priests. On May 7, 1931, in the Magistrates' Court, Second District Manhattan, Magistrate William C. Dodge dismissed the complaint, holding that the book did not violate the law.

Subsequently Mr. Sumner proceeded against the Chinese classic *Hsi Men Ching*, an abridged version of the famous *Kin Ping Meh*, which set forth in great detail the amorous adventures of a Chinese Casanova during the Ming dynasty. On November 9, 1931, Magistrate Brodsky dismissed the complaint. Mr. Sumner's proceeding against Pierre Louys' *Woman and Puppet* suffered the same fate at the hands of Chief Magistrate McDonald. Mr. Sumner was not satisfied with Magistrate Brodsky's disposition of *Hsi Men Ching*. He took the case to the district attorney. The grand jury, after hearing Mr. Sumner and the defendant, *refused to indict*.

Toward the latter part of 1931, Mr. Sumner brought a complaint against Clement Wood's *Flesh*, a collection of fifteen short stories, each one dealing graphically and explicitly with a different phase of the psycho-pathology of sex. There was more shocking material in a single one of these stories than in the entire length of *Ulysses*. Magistrate Overton Harris dismissed the complaint.

Early in 1933 Mr. Sumner instituted proceedings against an illustrated volume dealing with nudism, entitled *Let's Go Naked*. Magistrate Van Amringe refused to entertain the charge.

## E. *GOD'S LITTLE ACRE*

Within the last few months Mr. Sumner brought a complaint in the Magistrate's Court, New York City, against Erskine Caldwell's *God's Little Acre*, which set forth in detail the sexual adventures of a Southern family. After mature consideration Magistrate Greenspan exonerated the book, handing down an admirable opinion (not reported) in which he accurately summed up the present status of the law. The following excerpts are peculiarly applicable to *Ulysses*:

> *In order to sustain the prosecution, the Court must find that the tendency of the book as a whole, and indeed its main purpose, is to excite lustful desire and what has been rather fancifully called "impure imaginations."* People v. Muller, 96 N. Y. 408. The statute is aimed at

pornography, and a pornographic book must be taken to be one where all other incidents and qualities are mere accessories to the primary purpose of stimulating immoral thoughts. *The courts have strictly limited the applicability of the statute to works of pornography, and they have consistently declined to apply it to books of genuine literary value.* If the statute were construed more broadly than in the manner just indicated, its effect would be to prevent altogether the realistic portrayal in literature of a large and important field of life. The Court of Appeals has consistently frowned upon such an interpretation of the statute. People v. Wendling, 258 N. Y. 451; Halsey v. N. Y. Society for the Suppression of Vice, 234 N. Y. 1. See also the opinion of the Appellate Division, 1st Dept., in People v. Brainard, 192 App. Div. 816, regarding the book called *Madeleine*, an anonymous autobiography of a prostitute. . . . The book as a whole is very clearly not a work of pornography. It is not necessary for the Court to decide whether it is an important work of literature. Its subject matter constitutes a legitimate field for literary effort and the treatment is also legitimate. The Court must consider the book as a whole even though some paragraphs standing by themselves might be objectionable. . . . The test is whether "not in certain passages, but in its main purpose and construction" (Halsey v. New York Society for the Suppression of Vice, 234 N. Y. 1, at page 10), the book is obscene and lewd, and therefore, violative of the statute. The Court holds that it is not. This is not a book where vice and lewdness are treated as virtues, or which would tend to incite lustful desires in the normal mind. *There is no way of anticipating its effect upon a disordered or diseased mind, and if the courts were to exclude books from sale merely because they might incite lust in disordered minds, our entire literature would very likely be reduced to a relatively small number of uninteresting and barren books.* The greater part of the classics would certainly be excluded. . . . Those who see the ugliness and not the beauty in a piece of work are unable to see the forest for the trees. I personally feel that the very suppression of books arouses curiosity and leads readers to endeavor to find licentiousness where none was intended. (Italics ours.)

### F. NORMAL v. ABNORMAL

In the light of these decisions, the Court, in dealing with *Ulysses* must ask: Is it obscene within the proper definition of the word? Does it express or suggest unchaste or lustful ideas? Is it morally evil or impure? Is it unprincipled, vicious or dissolute? Is its "main purpose and construction to depict sexual impurity?"

Considering all the other influences and stimuli of modern life, the press, the stage, the movies, could the book really hurt a *normal* human being?[26] For it is the *normal* person who must serve as a criterion. This Court has clearly so intimated in the *Married Love* case, at page 824.

*Ulysses* leaves no doubt as to how these questions should be answered. It is a many-faceted crystallization of life and thought. It records the doubts and fears, the joys and torments, the swirling consciousness, of a handful of characters, and informs the experiences of those characters with the quality of universality. Sex is present, to be sure; but sex is part of man's existence. One can no more say that *Ulysses* is obscene than that life or thought is obscene.

## POINT III

*Ulysses* is a modern classic. The United States Government has officially acknowledged it as such. It cannot therefore be deemed obscene.

## A. THE FEDERAL GOVERNMENT HAS OFFICIALLY PAID TRIBUTE TO THE GREATNESS OF *ULYSSES*.

Sometime in May, 1933, a copy of *Ulysses* was sent from Paris, France to Alexander Lindey in New York City. On May 22 the Collector of Customs notified the sendee that the book was subject to detention under Title 19, U.S.C. Sec. 1305. (Sec. 305 of the Tariff Act of 1930.)

On June 2, the sendee addressed a petition to the Treasury Department, requesting that *Ulysses* be admitted into the United States under those provisions of the aforesaid statute which authorized the Secretary of the Treasury, in his discretion, to admit the so-called classics. In the letter that accompanied the application, the sendee wrote:

> In making this application I desire to state specifically that I do not concede that *Ulysses* is not admissible under the general provisions of Section 305.

An identical statement was incorporated in the petition itself.

On June 22 the sendee sent an inquiry to the Collector of Customs concerning the application. The complete answer of the Collector was as follows:

> Reference is made to your communication of June 22, 1933, requesting information concerning your petition of June 2, in the matter of the book *Ulysses* by James Joyce.
>
> In accordance with instructions from the Bureau of Customs, in its letter dated June 16, 1933, authority was given for the release of the book to you on the ground that it is a classic and therefore comes within the purview of the Secretary's discretionary authority granted in Section 305 of the Tariff Act of 1930.
>
> The book has been forwarded to the Customs Bureau of the Post Office for delivery to you under date of June 23, 1933.

In sum, the federal government has accorded *Ulysses* official recognition *as a classic*.

## B. A CLASSIC CANNOT BE ADJUDGED OBSCENE

*Webster's Collegiate Dictionary* (Fourth Edition, Merriam Series) defines a classic as "a work, especially in literature or art, of the highest class and of acknowledged excellence."

The words "classic" and "obscenity" represent polar extremes. They are mutually antagonistic and exclusive. That which is obscene, corrupts and depraves—it cannot be "of the highest class and of acknowledged excellence."

The courts have time and again reaffirmed this, emphasizing the principle that the law of obscenity cannot be invoked to suppress works which have stood the test of time, and have won lasting recognition and acclaim.

> Halsey v. N. Y. Society, 234 N. Y. 1;
> St. Hubert Guild v. Quinn, 64 Misc. 336;
> Stephen's *Digest of Criminal Law*, 7th Ed. (1926), note to Article 247 at p. 456;
> People v. Boni & Liveright, Inc., Magistrate's Court, New York City, September 27, 1922, Judge Oberwager.

On March 16, 1929, the *London Law Journal* published an article[27] reviewing the growth of the obscenity law in England since Regina v. Hicklin, 3 Q. B. 360 (1867), and summarizing practically all the important cases since. Several conclusions were drawn. One of these was that:

> *a classical work is not obscene* unless the circumstances of its sale or exhibition are such as to draw attention to those parts of the work which, if considered out of their historical and literary context, would have a depraving effect. (Italics ours.)

*Ulysses* is a classic. It should be cleared of the charge of obscenity.

### POINT IV

The intrinsic features of *Ulysses*, as well as certain extrinsic facts connected with it, negate any implication of obscenity.

The courts have from time to time given consideration to various elements in weighing the obscenity of any literary work brought before them.

### A. INTRINSIC CHARACTERISTICS

The title of a book, its length, its style and understandableness, the question of whether it has any illustrations, the further question of whether it has been anonymously written or published—all these have a bearing on its possible obscenity.

1. The inclusion of illustrations in a work of fiction may tend to enhance the potency of such work for good or ill. The visual message which can be

conveyed by a graphic representation is instantaneous and complete, and may be absorbed with practically equal quickness by the average and subaverage individual. In exonerating Lion Feuchtwanger's *Power*, the court in Toronto, Canada, commented specifically on the absence of illustrations (Judge Jones, April 30, 1928).

In In re Worthington Co., 30 N. Y. Supp. 361, the court remarked at p. 362:

> The very . . . absence of those glaring and crude pictures, scenes and descriptions which affect the common and vulgar mind, make a place for books of the character in question, entirely apart from such gross and obscene writings as it is the duty of the public authorities to suppress.

There are no illustrations in *Ulysses*.

2. Where a book is offered to the reading public without the name of the author or the publisher, or under a pseudonym, a question may arise as to the integrity of the work, and the motives of publication. As the copy before the Court will indicate, the first edition of *Ulysses* was openly issued by Shakespeare and Company in Paris in February, 1922; the second edition by the Egoist Press in London in October, 1922. The book has always borne Joyce's name as author. The element of concealment—almost invariably present in a work of pornography—is wholly absent here.

U. S. v. Smith, 45 Fed. 476, 478.

3. The length of a book may confer immunity. Said the court in the *Power* case, *supra*:

> The book contains 425 pages, the chapters are mostly 100 pages in length, the type is set in very solid form . . . . A reader looking for obscene matter would get tired of reading the book within the first thirty pages, as the subject is only of interest to students of history, who are endowed with brains and application above the ordinary.

*Ulysses* is a prodigious work of 732 closely-printed pages. The first passage dealing with sex occurs deep in the book. It is difficult reading even for the mature and the intelligent. It is far too tedious and labyrinthine and bewildering for the untutored and the impressionable who might conceivably be affected by it. Such people would not get beyond the first dozen pages.

4. The title of a work may, in some case, be indicative of the questionable nature of the contents, in U.S. v. Janes, 74 Fed. 545, the caption was *Ripe and Unripe Women*; in Shepard v. U.S., 160 Fed. 584, *The Amorous Adventures of a Japanese Gentleman* and *A Lustful Turk*.

The caption of *Ulysses* does not challenge the curiosity of the lascivious. It does not imply that there is anything salacious in the book.

5. But more important than any of the foregoing are style and method. The very definition of obscenity calls for something which will corrupt and

deprave. It is axiomatic that only what is understandable can corrupt. The worst Chinese obscenity is innocuous to anyone not acquainted with the language. If an author's style is incomprehensible to all but a comparatively few who are concededly immune to what the censor calls the suggestive power of words, the work cannot be said to be obscene. The *Jurgen* case is directly in point.

On January 15, 1920, the Grand Jury in New York County handed down an obscenity indictment against Robert M. McBride & Company and Guy Holt, its manager, for publishing James Branch Cabell's *Jurgen*. The case was tried before a jury in the Court of General Sessions of the County of New York. At the close of the People's case, the defendants moved for a direction of acquittal and a dismissal of the indictment on the ground that *Jurgen* was not obscene.[28] Judge Nott granted the motion in a brief but illuminating memorandum decision.

We quote the following excerpts:

> I have read and examined the book carefully. It is by Mr. James Branch Cabell, an author of repute and distinction. From the literary point of view its style may fairly be called brilliant. It is based on the mediaeval legends of Jurgen and is a highly imaginative and fantastic tale. . . .
>
> . . . The most that can be said against the book is that certain passages therein may be considered suggestive in a veiled and subtle way of immorality, but such suggestions are delicately conveyed and the whole atmosphere of the story is of such an unreal and supernatural nature that even these suggestions are free from the evils accompanying suggestiveness in more realistic works. *In fact, it is doubtful if the book could be read or understood at all by more than a very limited number of readers.*
>
> In my opinion the book is one of unusual literary merit and contains nothing "obscene, lewd, lascivious, filthy, indecent or disgusting" within the meaning of the statute and the decisions of the courts of this state in similar cases. (Citing cases. Italics ours.)

The gist of Judge Nott's decision was (1) that an author's reputation was a factor to be weighed; (2) that a consideration of style and literary merit was proper; and (3) that understandableness was likewise a factor. He implied that no book could be hurtful (hence obscene) if it could be read and understood only by a very limited number of persons.

*Ulysses* falls squarely within the *Nott* decision. It is a work of Gargantuan complexity. Beside it, *Jurgen* is a child's primer. It is not only the language that is baffling; the construction is almost unbelievably involved. As Stuart Gilbert has pointed out, each episode of *Ulysses* has its Scene and Hour of the Day, is associated with a given Organ of the human body, relates to a certain Art, has it appropriate Symbol and a specific Technic, and has a title corresponding to a character or episode in the *Odyssey*. Certain episodes also have their appropriate Color.[29] For instance the episode in the office of the *Freeman's Journal and National Press* is entitled Aeolus; its Hour is 12 noon; its Organ the lungs; its Art rhetoric; its Color red; its Symbol editor; its Technic enthymemic.[30]

*Ulysses* taxes a reader's intellectual resources more severely than any other book in English literature. To comprehend it, one must have encyclopedic knowledge.[31]

One must be able to hurdle not only such forbidding polysyllabic barriers as *contransmagnificandjewbangtantiality* (p. 38), and *mahamanvantara* (p. 41), and *weggebobbles* (p. 158), and *theolologicphilolological* (p. 196), and *eppripfftaph* (p. 246), and *honorificabilitudinitatibus* (p. 201), and *inverecund* (p. 366), and *hypsospadia* (p. 465), and *selenographical* (p. 654), and *tetragammation* (p. 676), but also to plod through countless passages which, even after several readings, appear to make no sense whatever.

Here are some words which we have picked at random from the book:

|  | Page |
| --- | --- |
| whelks | 30 |
| cataletic | 37 |
| strandentwining | 38 |
| houyhnhnm | 40 |
| froeken | 43 |
| hismy | 50 |
| quadrireme | 137 |
| fellaheen | 138 |
| crubeen | 140 |
| parallax | 159 |
| cygnets | 180 |
| entelechy | 182 |
| umbrel | 184 |
| yogibogeybox | 184 |
| nookshotten | 185 |
| apocrypha | 188 |
| mavrone | 191 |
| greydauburn | 193 |
| hierophantic | 209 |
| bosthoon | 231 |
| tympanum | 245 |
| henev | 246 |
| demisemiquaver | 276 |
| videlicet | 281 |
| cruiskeen | 283 |
| pralaya | 289 |
| loodheramaun | 293 |

These are not egregious examples; there are thousands of others as difficult in the book. Furthermore, there is constant recurrence of such incomprehensible paragraphs as the following:

> Ineluctable modality of the visible: at least that if no more, thought through my eyes. Signatures of all things I am here to read, seaspawn and seawrack, the nearing tide, that rusty boot. Snotgreen, bluesilver, rust: colored signs. Limits of the diaphane. But he adds: in bodies. Then he was aware of them, sure. Go easy. Bald he was and a millionaire, maestro di color che sanno. Limit of the diaphane in. Why in? Diaphane, adiaphane. If you can put your five fingers through it, it is a gate, if not a door. Shut your eyes and see. (p. 37)

Here is another paragraph:

> That it was not a heaventree, not a heavengrot, not a heavenbeast, not a heavenman. That it was a Utopia, there being no known method from the known to the unknown; an infinity, renderable equally finite by the suppositious probable apposition of one or more bodies equally of the same and of different magnitudes: a mobility of illusory forms immobilised in space, remobilised in air: a past which possibly had ceased to exist as a present before its spectators had entered actual present existence. (p. 654)

There is no reason to multiply illustrations. If one opens *Ulysses* at random almost anywhere, one will confront passages meaningless on the surface, and decipherable only after concentrated study. The book is a treasure-trove, to be sure; but its riches are so well hid in grottoes of recondite learning, of classical allusions, of literary and scientific profundities, that the average seeker—blindly groping about in the surrounding maze—soon tires of the venture and turns back.

"The *Ulysses* of James Joyce," says Paul Jordan Smith,

> is, for most who have turned its curious pages, a puzzle-book to be gazed at and then thrown, somewhat profanely, aside. To some it has proved a challenge; to a few it has been a delight. But the average novel reader expects a work of fiction to be simple, straightforward prose. No amount of talk about expressionism, dadaism, or the subconscious mind, can reconcile him to the unintelligibility of Joyce's unpunctuated pages. He is outraged. Where he expected to find a story of love and ambition and struggle, he finds a bewildering cross-word puzzle. And I am afraid that he cannot be touched by the plea that Joyce has achieved a masterpiece of

modern subjective fiction, that he is a pioneer, breaking his way into strange, new fields of interpretation. He wants a story and that is the end of it.[32]

Smith goes on to say:

> . . . there is no book in the world—unless it be in the *Anatomy of Melancholy*—that requires so much of the reader. To get a clear knowledge of the story, one needs to have read Mr. Joyce's other books—*Dubliners* and *A Portrait of the Artist as a Young Man.* . . . Besides these, one needs a good modern history of Ireland, a comprehensive essay on Dublin, Boyd's *Ireland's Literary Renaissance*, a copy of the Roman Missal, Latin, Hebrew, Greek, French, Italian, Spanish, Gaelic, English, and medical Dictionaries, Grose's *Dictionary of Buckish Slang, University Wit and Pickpocket Eloquence*, Frazer's *Golden Bough*, Handbook of Astronomy, Astrology, Theosophy, and Psychology, and a certain familiarity with modern Shakespearian criticisms; then, and not until then (if one does not skip a single word of the seven hundred and thirty-two pages), one finds in *Ulysses* one of the most fascinating stories ever set down on paper. The English itself has to be translated; what seems at the first glance to be mere jargon turns out to be a coherent and very human story sounding the profound depths of our pitiful souls.[33]

Edmund Wilson writes:

> Joyce has as little respect as Proust for the capacities of the reader's attention; and one feels, in Joyce's case as in Proust's, that the longueurs which break our backs, the mechanical combinations of elements which fail to coalesce, are the result of an effort on the part of a supernormally energetic mind to compensate by piling things up for an inability to make them move.[34]

6. There is no need in this memorandum to analyze the stream-of-consciousness method which Joyce brought to such a high degree of perfection in *Ulysses*. It will suffice to say that the nature of this method in itself is such as would discourage and repel rather than attract the average reader.[35] The latter is interested in action, not in cerebration.

## B. EXTRINSIC CIRCUMSTANCES

Certain collateral facts have a definite bearing on the possible obscenity of a book, and should be given due weight. (U.S. v. Smith, 45 Fed. 476, 477) Among these are the author's literary reputation, the opinions of critics, the attitude of librarians, the acceptance of the book in representative libraries and institutions of learning, and the mode of distribution.

Rosen v. U.S., 161 U.S. 29;
Peabody Book Shop v. U.S., United States Customs Court, Second Division, Protest 298623-G-5556, *et seq.;*

Halsey v. N.Y. Society, 234 N.Y. 1;
*People* v. *McBride, et al.* (not reported);
People v. Muller, 96 N.Y. 408; 413;
St. Hubert Guild v. Quinn, 64 Misc. 336;
In re Worthington Co., 30 N.Y. Supp. 361, 362.

1. In the Preliminary Memorandum, dated September 12, 1933, hereto-fore submitted to the Court, there is conclusive evidence that Joyce is a supreme literary artist (Exs. B, D and I). It has been said of him that his virtuosity in the manipulation of words has never been surpassed; that when it comes to psychology or realism, beside him "Balzac is beggared and Zola bankrupted"; that in *Ulysses* he evidences "a genius of the very highest order, strictly comparable to Goethe's or Dostoevsky's"; that in power of thought he has no peer but Pascal; that he is the only man in English letters worthy of a place beside Shakespeare.

2. When *Ulysses* first appeared in 1922, there were many literary commentators that were staggered and confused by its magnitude and complexities. Today there is scarcely a critic of note who has not paid tribute to the book (Preliminary Memorandum, Exs. A, B, D, E and I). One wonders whether there has ever been a work that has called forth such spirited defense as is evidenced in Exhibit I.

3. About a year ago, the claimant herein circulated a questionnaire on *Ulysses* among hundreds of leading librarians throughout the country. The librarians were requested to voice their opinion of the book freely. With scarcely a dissenting voice they conceded its greatness. Some of their characteristic comments have been placed before the Court. (Preliminary Memorandum, Exs. C. and D.)

4. *Ulysses* has been translated into French, German, Spanish and Japanese. (Preliminary Memorandum, Ex. G.)

5. It goes without saying that pornography finds no place on the shelves of reputable libraries. Many of the librarians answering the questionnaire above referred to, stated that they had copies of *Ulysses*. The catalogues of outstanding libraries reveal the following: the Library of Congress has the English original and the French translation; the Bibliothèque National at Paris has the English original (the catalogue we consulted was not up to date; the French translation is most likely also available by now); the Widener Library at Harvard University has two English copies; the general catalogue of the New York Public Library at 42nd St. and Fifth Avenue, New York City, lists more than thirty items—books, pamphlets, magazine articles—dealing with James Joyce and/or *Ulysses*.

6. It would be absurd to assume that an obscene work would appear as assigned reading in our leading institutions of learning. Yet no course dealing with twentieth century English letters, given at any of our colleges or universities, fails to include Joyce and *Ulysses*. For instance, the book has been

on the reading list at Harvard in connection with English 26, given last year by T. S. Eliot, the distinguished poet (then occupying the Charles Eliot Morton Chair of Poetry), and three years ago by I. A. Richards, Professor at Cambridge and Peking. During his course Professor Richards said:

> *Ulysses* is one of the most heart-shaking of books. It was written, as someone has stated, to put the fear of God into man.[36]

7. Pornography bears the stigma of stealth and secrecy. Printed smut is produced anonymously, is distributed through subterranean channels and is sold at back doors or behind counters.[37] *Contemplated* distribution is a no less reliable and illuminating index. Random House, Inc., the claimant herein, proposes to publish *Ulysses* in this country, openly and under its own imprint. The claimant's reputation, the high character of its list (Preliminary Memorandum, Ex. H), are persuasive indication that what the claimant is eager to do is to add another classic to its roster, not to circulate pornographic material.

## POINT V

*Ulysses* has been generally accepted by the community and hence cannot be held to be violative of the statute.

The law of obscenity is one of changing content.

United States v. Kennerly, 209 Fed. 119, 121;
People v. Seltzer, 203 N. Y. Supp. 809, 814;
46 Corpus Juris, 854.

In each era it is community morality which dictates how and to what extent the obscenity statute should be applied. Community morality may be summed up as follows: That which society accepts is moral; that which it rejects is immoral. The law must recognize and give effect to this principle, or else it becomes "not a true mirror of life as it should be, but a bewildering distortion, alike perplexing and misleading, of which the ordinary man or woman becomes properly distrustful." ("The Development of the Law," Prof. Wormser, *Columbia Law Review*, December 1923; reprinted in *Lectures on Legal Topics*, Association of the Bar of the City of New York, Volume 5, p. 60)

This philosophy has been tersely expressed by former Justice Holmes of the United States Supreme Court:

> "The first requirement of a sound body of law is, that it should correspond with the actual feelings and demands of the community, whether right or wrong." (Oliver Wendell Holmes, Jr., *The Common Law*, p. 41)

In a magazine article, former Justice Proskauer of the Appellate Division of the Supreme Court of the State of New York said:

> . . . the law does not lead but follows public opinion, and yet it does constantly re-adapt itself slowly but surely to those modifications of life and thought which are soundly established. (*Harper's Magazine*, September 1929, p. 419)

Public opinion furnishes the only true test of obscenity. Such opinion is definitely ascertainable. It is true that people as a mass are inarticulate. The body politic registers its will through representatives chosen at the polls. By the same token the community makes its moral reactions felt and its judgments pronounced through responsible men who, by reason of their respective endeavors, furnish an accurate social mirror.

When newspapers, college professors, critics, educators, authors, librarians, clergymen and publishers rally to the defense of a book, they do more than express their personal views. They speak for the body social.

Moreover, *Ulysses* has been placed on the shelves of many of our leading libraries, and has been included in literature courses given in our institutions of learning.

To say that it is obscene is to brand eminent persons in various walks of life as champions of obscenity; and to say that our libraries and universities have been guilty of the criminal offense of disseminating salacious material.[38]

## POINT VI

*Ulysses* must be judged as a whole, and its general purpose and effect determined. On that basis it must be cleared.

A book is to be judged in its entirety, not by isolated fragments. The judicial test is to be applied to the *whole* book, and not to excerpts which may be singled out.

Konda v. United States, 166 Fed. 91, 92;
Clark v. U.S., 211 Fed. 916, 922;
United States v. Dennett, 39 Fed. (2d) 564, 569;
Peabody Book Shop v. United States, U. S. Customs Court, Second
    Division, Court of Baltimore, Protests #298623-G-5556 *et seq.*;
Halsey v. New York Society, 234 N. Y. 1, 4;
St. Hubert Guild v. Quinn, 64 Misc. 336, 339.

In the *Konda* case, *supra*, the plaintiff-in-error was convicted of sending an obscene pamphlet through the mails. The pamphlet was in a foreign language. Merely excerpts of the translation were placed before the jury. The Circuit Court of Appeals reversed the conviction and granted a new trial, saying at page 92:

No translation of it [i. e. the pamphlet] as a whole was in evidence. "A Victim of Circumstances, or Memoirs of a Carniolian Priest" contained 69 pages. In the translation which the judge used in passing upon the character of the work nothing was presented from more than half the pages. From the other pages excerpts were taken here and there. Now these excerpts may have correctly disclosed the scope and tone of the pamphlet. On the other hand, when they were thus taken from their settings and deprived of the support of their full context, it may be that they did not fairly represent the character of the work. For instance, the results of an investigation into the conduct of some of our penal and charitable institutions possibly might be set forth in a way capable of arousing libidinous passions; or the same results might be framed in an attack upon wrongs and an appeal for correction, so that they would stir up, not lecherous thoughts, but only reformative instincts. So in this case, even if it was the function of the judge to decide that the averment in the indictment respecting the character of the pamphlet was proven, it was wrong to base the decision on the untested assumption that the excerpts truly gauged the scope and character of the pamphlet. (Brackets ours.)

The *Peabody* case, *supra*, was quite similar to the proceeding herein, except that it arose in the Customs Court under the Tariff Act of 1922. The Collector of Customs at the Port of Baltimore sought to exclude from the United States *Daphnis and Chloe* by Longus, *Satyrs and Sunlight*, by Hugh McCrea and *The London Aphrodite*. The Court ruled that these works should be admitted and said:

> . . . a careful reading of the works satisfies us that they are not obscene and are not of the class of publications which Congress ordained should not be allowed to enter into this Country. There are passages in the books in question which, published separately and alone, would be considered indecent and their distribution or importation prohibited but a literary work cannot be called obscene, if, here and there may be found some expression which is obscene. If a book can be condemned because of the existence of occasional indecent language, Shakespeare's work would be prohibited. *Books must be considered in their entirety and if they have literary merit and are clearly not published with an object to parade obscenity and attract readers with debased minds, they are not of the class which Congress intended to exclude* . . . While it is true that there are a few passages in the books which might be considered obscene if published alone, the whole work is not obscene and *we must judge each book as a whole.* (Italics ours.)

In *Halsey* v. *New York Society for the Suppression of Vice, supra*,[39] the Court said, at page 4:

> No work may be judged from a selection of such paragraphs alone. Printed by themselves they might, as a matter of law, come within the

prohibition of the statute. So might a similar selection from Aristophanes or Chaucer or Boccaccio or even from the Bible. The book, however, must be considered broadly as a whole.

And in *St. Hubert Guild* v. *Quinn, supra*, the Court, in refusing to brand as obscene certain books, said at page 339:

> The judgement of the court below is based upon a few passages in each of these works . . . These few passages furnish no criterion . . . That some of these passages, judged by the standard of our day, mar rather than enhance the value of these books can be admitted . . . The same criticism has been directed against many of the classics of antiquity and against the works of some of our greatest writers from Chaucer to Walt Whitman. . . .

*Ulysses* should not and cannot be judged on the basis of isolated passages. Granting that it contains occasional episodes of doubtful taste, the fact remains that obscenity is not a question of words nor of specific instances, nor even of whole chapters. It is a question of entirety. To justify the condemnation of *Ulysses* it must be deemed to violate the law as a whole.

The Court has read the book and knows that such portions of it as may conceivably be challenged are a negligible fraction of the whole.

## CONCLUSION

1. It is true that *Ulysses* employs a few Anglo-Saxon words to denote certain human organs and functions. However, this does not render it obscene. Such words recently appeared in Ernst and Seagle's *To the Pure*, Hemingway's *Death in the Afternoon, Lawrence of Arabia* and other books, all of which have been accepted by the community.[40]

2. *Ulysses* is the story of a single day in the life and thought of a man. Though the element of sex is present, it is relegated to a position of relative unimportance. As a matter of actual content it represents an insignificant fraction of the book. It might be said to occupy less relative prominence in *Ulysses* than it would in the actual life of the average individual.

3. *Ulysses* is essentially a novel of the mind, not of actual physical occurrences. It is doubtful if people are influenced by what they read. Assuming that they are, we are constrained to admit that they are influenced by narratives of what other people do and not by what other people *think*. By far the greater portion of *Ulysses* deals with the vagaries of consciousness, not with the actual doings of people.

4. The notion of pornography is wholly inconsistent with an artist's serious effort to mirror and perpetuate truth in literature. Says Herbert S. Gorman:

. . . pornography is as abhorrent to the writer as didacticism
. . . . Truth in itself is not pornographic; it is made so by the unevenly
developed consciousness of the observer. Supreme Art, according to
Joyce, is no more than the white flare of a moment, the bright instant
before a coal begins to fade, an enchantment of the heart, the free and
unimpeded liberation of a rhythm which springs where it will and from
what it will.[41]

Holbrook Jackson has affirmed this in *Today*, saying of *Ulysses*:

It is not indecent. There is not a salacious line in it. It is simply naked:
naked and unconscious of shame . . . neither moral nor immoral. . . . He simply records like Homer.

5. It has been said by some that in *Ulysses*, Joyce depicts the human
consciousness a stream more muddied than it actually is. Edmund Wilson has
answered this:

. . . I cannot agree that Mr. Joyce has represented the human mind
as more disintegrated or more debased than it actually is . . . one sees
the gross ill-drained body of humanity itself touched divinely by cloudly
visions of its creative splendours yet profoundly shaken and bound by its
labouring flesh. . . .

6. Although *Ulysses* is a modern classic it need not be proved to be such in
order to win vindication in this proceeding. Whether we regard it, to use the
words of Shane Leslie, as "an abandonment of form and a mad Shelleyan
effort to extend the known confines of the English language" or as an assault
on human intelligence; whether we concede that its "chapters are monuments to the power and glory of the written word" or contend that they are
the fruit of an "extraordinary and monstrous" undertaking; whether we look
upon Joyce as the peer of Shakespeare and Flaubert and Voltaire or as an
amazing prestidigitator of language—we cannot deny the importance of the
book and the author. Such importance alone is sufficient to confer immunity.

7. It may be that in *Ulysses* Joyce has seen fit to cast light into some of the
murky chambers of the human mind. It is only by such exposure that we can
hope to banish darkness and taint. Joyce's penetration and courage deserve
praise, not condemnation. What Macauley wrote in his essay on Milton
applies with equal force to Joyce:

There is no more hazardous enterprise than that of bearing the torch
of truth into those dark and infected recesses in which no light has ever
shone. But it was the choice and pleasure of Milton to picture the
noisome vapours and to brave the terrible explosion, while, in general,
he left to others the credit of expounding and defending the popular
parts of his religious and political creed. He took his own stand upon this
which the great body of his countrymen reprobated as criminal.

8. "*Ulysses*", says Paul Jordan Smith, "can have no universal appeal; its reading is too formidable a task for that; but as a writer's source book, it is an inexhaustible mine of strange treasures, a veritable encyclopedia of the human soul, and a song of ecstacy. But it does bear a universal message—a weird cry from the very depths of Dublin to the rim of the world—the cry of tortured conscience, 'agenbite of inwit.' "[42]

To bar it from our shores, to brand it obscene, to compel our libraries and universities to sweep it from their shelves, is to assure for ourselves the lasting derision of generations to come.

9. To many of our literary critics, it is incredible that *Ulysses* should now be placed on trial for its life. On May 12, 1932, Lewis S. Gannett, literary editor of the *New York Herald-Tribune*, wrote in that paper:

> It is almost ludicrous to think that such a book still has to fear the hurdles of the obscenity law; if ever there was a serious, earnest book, it is *Ulysses*. Already it has acquired the corpselike color of a "classic." It is discussed for its effect on other writers. It seems, like Anthony Comstock, to be a curious phenomenon of a remote past.

10. If the government prevails on this motion, *Ulysses* will be relegated to the class of smutty French postcards and outright pornography such as *Willie's First Night, Only a Boy*, and the like. The result will be no different than if we were to place Dante's *Inferno* in the same category with *Fanny Hill*.

11. When, more than seventy years ago, a charge of criminal obscenity was brought against several of Shelley's noblest works, his counsel, T. N. Talfourd, delivered an eloquent plea in his defense on June 23, 1841. The case (The Queen v. Moxon, 2 Mod. St. Tr. 356) is referred to in St. Hubert Guild v. Quinn, 64 Misc. 336, by Seabury J, at page 339. Talfourd adjured the court in its justice to reject the charge as "an unexampled attempt to degrade and destroy the law under the pretence of asserting it"; and to "have the courage and the virtue to recognize the distinction between a man who publishes works which are infidel or impure, because they are infidel or impure, and publishes them in a form and at a price which indicate the desire that they should work out mischief, and one who publishes works in which evil of the same kind might be found, but who publishes them because, in spite of that imperfection, they are on the whole for the edification and delight of mankind; between one who tenders the mischief for approbation and one who exposes it for example."

# POINT VII

The libellant's motion should be denied; and the claimant's motion for a dismissal of the libel should be granted.

Dated, New York, October 14, 1933.

Respectfully submitted,

GREENBAUM, WOLFF & ERNST,
Attorneys for Claimant,
285 Madison Avenue,
Borough of Manhattan,
New York City.

Of Counsel:
MORRIS L. ERNST,
ALEXANDER LINDEY.

# *Notes*

1. U. S. v. Mary Ware Dennett, 39 Fed. (2d) 564; Youngs, etc. v. Lee, etc., 45 Fed. (2d) 103; U.S. v. *Married Love*, 48 Fed. (2d) 821; U. S. v. *Contraception*, 51 Fed. (2d) 525; People v. Wendling, 258 N. Y. 451.

2. In *James Joyce: His First Forty Years*, Herbert S. Gorman says that this book "speedily assumed its proper position as the most important experiment in the English-written novel since the influence of Madame Bovary had slipped across the Channel. It was a key to a great door which swung open and revealed an entire new world for the novel." (pp. 99-100)

3. It is this austerity that has prompted McGreevy to say of Joyce that "he writes about human beings as the most enlightened and humane of father confessors might, if it were permitted, write about his penitents." (*Transition*, 1932, p. 254)

4. *Homage to James Joyce*, Stuart Gilbert; *Transition*, 1932.

5. *The Strange Case of James Joyce*, Rebecca West; *The Bookman*, September, 1928.

6. *Men Seen*, Paul Rosenfeld, Dial Press, 1925; pp. 32, 35 and 42.

7. Herbert S. Gorman, well-known critic, estimates that *Ulysses* is as long as seven ordinary novels. (*James Joyce: His First Forty Years*, p. 121)

8. Idem, pp. 121, 122 and 123.

9. It is proper for the Court to give consideration to the character of the claimant and the nature of its business.

10. Mention should be made of Donald Henderson Clarke's *Female*, against which two obscenity proceedings were instituted recently. Magistrate Van Amringe dismissed one complaint in Manhattan; on the other, there was a conviction in Special Sessions in Queens. An appeal is contemplated.

11. It should be noted that the statute is directed only against an obscene book. The word immoral is not used therein in connection with printed matter.

12. *The Common Law*, p. 41.

13. Ernst and Seagle, *To the Pure*, p. 253.

14. Schroeder, *Free Press Anthology*, p. 257.

15. See Lewis S. Gannett's reviews of Ford Maddox Ford's *Return to Yesterday*, *New York Herald-Tribune*, January 15, 1932.

16. Mark Twain's *Autobiography*, Vol. 2, p. 335.

17. Horace M. Kallen, *Indecency and the Seven Arts*, p. 17.

18. Thompson, *Philosophy of Fiction*, p. 191; see also Bowerman, *Censorship and Other Papers*, p. 32.

19. Mordell, *Notorious Literary Attacks*, pp. 122-37.

20. Halsey v. N. Y. Society, 234 N. Y. 1.

21. Dorothy Van Doren, "Mr. Dodgson and Lewis Carroll", *The Nation*, p. 608, December 2, 1931.

22. Ernst and Seagle, *To The Pure*, p. 43.

23. See Stuart Gilbert's scholarly analysis of "indecency" in *Ulysses: James Joyce's Ulysses*, pp. 19-22.

24. See *ante*, p. 11. The statute, in so far as books are concerned, restricts itself to the word obscene; it does not use the word immoral to apply to printed matter. Hence it is not necessary for the Court to inquire into the morality of *Ulysses*; the sole question is, is it obscene?

25. Since the *Swearingen* decision, there has been a long line of cases holding that the material charged must be "calculated to incite to immorality relating to sexual impurity." U. S. v. Journal Co., Inc., 197 Fed. 415; U. S. v. Klauder, 240 Fed. 501; U. S. v. Durant, 46 Fed. 753; U. S. v. Moore, 104 Fed. 78; U. S. v. Reinheimer, 233 Fed. 545; U. S. v. Clarke, 38 Fed. 732; Dysart v. U. S., 4 Fed. (2) 765.

26. In this connection two kinds of abnormal persons may be considered: the morally weak and the prudishly supersensitive.

As to the former, even if this Court were convinced that *Ulysses* might conceivably harm the fatuous and the impressionable, the susceptible and the morally weak, the Court would not be justified in passing adversely on it. Our literature is not to be judged by the standards of morons. Said the Appellate Division of the Supreme Court, First Department in People v. Philip Pesky (230 App. Div. 200); "These matters must be judged by normal people and not by the abnormal. Conditions would be deplorable if abnormal people were permitted to regulate such matters."

As to the prudery-ridden, it does not matter if their sensibilities are offended. As the Court of Appeals pointed out in the *Wendling* case (p. 454) a work "may be repulsive to puritanical ideals of propriety"; it "may be offensive to the more liberal minded as lacking in taste and refinement"; it "may be gross and its characters wanting in moral sense"; it may "depict women who carry on a vicious trade"—yet it cannot be deemed obscene unless it comes within the narrow definition laid down by the courts, that of arousing lustful and lecherous desires.

27. The article was reprinted in the *New York Law Journal*, Editorial Page, April 27, 1929.

28. The Court will note that in effect the *Jurgen* motion was quite similar to the one before this Court.

29. *James Joyce's Ulysses*, pp. 27, 28.

30. Idem, p. 160, *et seq.*

31. Joyce himself has referred to *Ulysses* as a "chafferieng allincluding most farraginous chronicle." *James Joyce's Ulysses*, Stuart Gilbert, p. 42.

32. *The Key to the Ulysses of James Joyce*, p. 15.

33. Idem, p. 60.

34. *James Joyce: The New Republic*, December 18, 1929.

35. ". . . what is the stream of consciousness method? The solitary thoughts of characters in novels have been overheard by god-like authors and yet we do not apply the phrase 'stream of consciousness' to these mappings of thought. The difference is in the word 'stream.' This new method is an attempt through the application of the author's psychological astuteness and intuition and profound knowledge of his character's mind, its depths, its subconscious impulses, inhibitions, and buried urges, to set down the undisturbed flow of thought—not always conscious, perhaps, to the thinker—that pours through the restless mind, a stream that is diverted constantly by a thousand and one extraneous objects, word-connotations, stifled emotions, from the consistent and built-up delineations of thought-processes to be found in the older novelists." Herbert Gorman: *James Joyce: His First Forty Years*, p. viii.

"Men before James Joyce have been aware of the parasitic and independent nature of our upper-story lodger, yet the Irish poet can fairly pretend to being his artistic discoverer and portrayer of his form. The protagonist of his vast novel is no creature of flesh. The hero of the *Odyssey* may have been an individual. But the being whose wanderings are set forth in the modern tragi-comic parallel is no other than 'mind in the making' perceived through types of the flotating dislocated intellect of our time. . . . He has placed the interior soliloquy of the human being on a plane and a parity with his exterior 'action' and boldly mixed the two. . . . He has represented mind's play, the manner of drunken existence led by him, with a queer gusto at once sour and Rabelaisian, with pity, tenderness and Irish mischief, and upon an heroic scale and with heroic richness of illustration. And none of Joyce's coevals, neither Miss

Stein nor Miss Richardson nor Ernest Hemingway, has made it an object of contemplation with a relentlessness and bravery in any way comparable to his. Quite as the painted slides of glass in medical museums give in finest segments the physical aspects of the brain, so does his method render all the strata of mind in their manifold interpenetrations. We are shown the mind we reveal to each other; and the mind full of fears and fantasies, monkey-like preoccupations and ignoble interests which we try to reveal to no one and to keep utterly to ourselves; and through representations of the dreamlike and hallucinatory states in which the activities of the brain assume a definite corporeality, the mind which seeks to conceal itself and its fixations and traumas and outlawed impulses from ourselves, too. We are shown its motion, its rattling activity, broken rhythms, starts, attitudes and relationships, and made to observe it under the influence of bodily states, colored and given form and direction. . ." Paul Rosenfeld, *Men Seen*, pp. 24-26.

36. This information was secured from Peter A. Pertzoff, Esq., of Cambridge, Mass., a Harvard graduate, who took the course with Professor Richards. (Letter dated July 14, 1933, addressed to claimant's attorneys.)

37. Distribution is one of the determinants of obscenity.

> U. S. v. Harmon, 45 Fed. 414;
> U. S. v. Wroblenski, 118 Fed. 495;
> U. S. v. Grimm, 50 Fed. 528;
> Grimm v. United States, 156 U. S. 604;
> Lynch v. U. S., 285 Fed. 162;
> *Stephen's Digest of Criminal Law*, 7th Edition (1926) Article 247;
> U. S. v. Clarke, 38 Fed. 732;
> U. S. v. Smith, 45 Fed. 476, 477;
> U. S. v. Chesman, 19 Fed. 497;
> Burton v. U. S., 142 Fed. 57;
> U. S. v. Dennett, 39 Fed. (2nd) 564;
> People v. Muller, 96 N. Y. 408;
> Halsey v. New York Society, 234 N. Y. 1;
> People v. Boni & Liveright, Inc., Magistrate Oberwager, September 27, 1922;
> In re Worthington Co., N. Y. Supp. 361.

38. Certain portions of the foregoing were embodied in the claimant's Preliminary Memorandum, heretofore submitted to the Court.

39. This case sustained a judgment against Mr. Sumner's society for malicious prosecution growing out of the attempted suppression of *Mademoiselle de Maupin*.

40. Emerson the staid New Englander, philosopher and transcendentalist, lamented that our language lacked earthiness and forthrightness. He said:

> What a pity that we cannot curse and swear in good society! Cannot the stinging dialect of the sailors be domesticated? It is the best rhetoric and for a hundred occasions those forbidden words are the only good ones . . . This profane swearing and barroom wit has salt and fire . . . One who wishes to refresh himself by contact with the bone and sinew of society must avoid what is called the respectable portion of his city and neighborhood. (*New York Herald-Tribune*, April 1, 1932.)

41. *James Joyce: His First Forty Years*, page 93.

42. *The Key to the Ulysses of James Joyce*, page 89.

[Doc. 165]

October 16, 1933.

Hon. John M. Woolsey,
233 Broadway,
New York City.

Re: *United States* v. *Ulysses*

My dear Judge Woolsey,

We are sending you herewith a copy of the claimant's memorandum in support of its motion to dismiss the libel [See Doc. 164.—ED.] in the above entitled proceeding.

We are mindful of the fact that you have indicated that you will not hear argument on the motion until early in November. We feel, nevertheless, that you may wish to be apprised of the claimant's legal contentions in advance of the argument.

We have this day sent a copy of our memorandum to Mr. Coleman.

Very truly yours,

Greenbaum, Wolff & Ernst

AL:BBO
Encl.

---

[Doc. 166]

October 16, 1933.

Samuel Coleman, Esq.,
United States Attorney's Office,
Post Office Building,
New York City.

Re: *U. S.* v. *One Book Entitled Ulysses*
Index No. A 110-59; Cal No. 1438

Dear Sam:

I am sending you herewith two copies of our memorandum in the above case. As I told you the other day, I am arranging to forward a copy of this brief to Judge Woolsey, thinking it might be helpful to him. No doubt you will let me have a copy of your memorandum, if you intend to supply the Judge with one. I suggest that you supply your memorandum to the Judge or to us as long before the argument as possible.

Maybe upon reading the enclosed you will finally convince your Chief to stop this nonsense and consent to the admission of the book.

Yours sincerely,

Encs (2)
Del.

------------

[Doc. 167]

October 17, 1933.

Random House,
20 East 57th Street,
New York City.

Attention: Mr. Bennett A. Cerf
Re: *Ulysses*

Dear Cerf:

We have just received the printer's bill on our memorandum, two hundred copies of which were delivered direct to you. On looking over our records I find that we have accumulated quite a lot of out-of-pocket disbursements. I am quite sure that you will agree that we should be reimbursed. A bill is accordingly herewith enclosed.

The memorandum has been forwarded by the Clerk of the Federal Court to Judge Woolsey, who is away on his vacation.

Very truly yours,

Greenbaum, Wolff & Ernst

By Alexander Lindey

------------

**[Doc. 168]**

October 18, 1933.

Mr. Peter A. Pertzoff,
70 Hammond Street,
Cambridge, Mass.

Re: Ulysses

My dear Pertzoff,

I am sending you herewith a copy of our brief in the above entitled matter. You will find that we have made generous use of the various items and information which you were good enough to furnish us.

Incidentally, we hope that Professor Richards' eyes will never light on the unfortunate typographical error on page 45.

The case will come up for argument before Judge Woolsey of the Federal Court on November 6th. I'll drop you a line as to the result.

Cordially yours,

AL:BBO

[Doc. 169]

| TITLE | SCENE | HOUR | ORGAN |
|---|---|---|---|
| I *Telemachia* | | | |
| 1 Telemachus | : The Tower | : 8 a.m. | : |
| 2 Nestor | : The School | : 10 a.m. | : |
| 3 Proteus | : The Strand | : 11 a.m. | : |
| II *Odyssey* | | | |
| 1 Calypso | : The House | : 8 a.m. | : kidney |
| 2 Lotuseaters | : The Bath | : 10 a.m. | : genitals |
| 3 Hades | : The Graveyard | : 11 a.m. | : heart |
| 4 Eolus | : The Newspaper | : 12 noon | : lungs |
| 5 Lestrygonians | : The Lunch | : 1 p.m. | : esophagus |
| 6 Scylla and Carybdis | : The Library | : 2 p.m. | : brain |
| 7 Wandering Rocks | : The Streets | : 3 p.m. | : blood |
| 8 Sirens | : The Concert Room | : 4 p.m. | : ear |
| 9 Cyclops | : The Tavern | : 5 p.m. | : muscle |
| 10 Nausikaa | : The Rocks | : 8 p.m. | : eye, nose |
| 11 Oxen of Sun | : The Hospital | : 10 p.m. | : womb |
| 12 Circe | : The Brothel | : 12 midnight | : locomotor apparatus |
| III *Nostos* | | | |
| 1 Eumeus | : The Shelter | : 1 a.m. | : nerves |
| 2 Ithaca | : The House | : 2 a.m. | : skeleton |
| 3 Penelope | : The Bed | : | : flesh |

## CORRESPONDENCES

(Stephen—Telemachus—Hamlet: Buck Mulligan—Antinous: Milkwoman—Mentor)

(Deasy: Nestor: Pisistratus: Sargent: Helen: Mrs. O'Shea)

(Proteus—Primal Matter: Kevin Egan—Menelaus: Megapenthus: The Coclepicker)

(Calypso—The Nymph. Dlugacz: The Recall: Zion: Ithaca)

(Lotuseaters: Cabhorses, Communicants, Soldiers, Eunuchs, Bather, Watchers of Cricket)

(Dodder, Grand and Royal Canals, Liffey—The 4 Rivers: Cunningham—Sisyphus: Father: Coffey—Cerberus: Caretaker—Hades—Daniel O'Connell—Hercules: Dignam—Elpenor: Parnell: Agamemnon: Mentor: Ajax)

(Crawford—Eolus: Incest—journalism: Floating Island—press)

(Antiphates—Hunger: The Decoy: Food: Lestrygonians: Teeth)

| ART | COLOUR | SYMBOL | TECHNIC |
|---|---|---|---|
| : theology | : white, gold | : heir | narrative (young) |
| : history | : brown | : horse | catechism (personal) |
| : philology | : green | : tide | monologue (male) |
| | | | |
| : economics | : orange | : nymph | narrative (mature) |
| : botany, chemistry | : | : eucharist | narcissism |
| : religion | : white, black | : caretaker | incubism |
| : rhetoric | : red | : editor | enthymenic |
| : architecture | : | : constables | peristaltic |
| : literature | : | : Stratford, London | dialectic |
| : mechanics | : | : citizens | labyrinth |
| | | | |
| : music | : | : barmaids | fuga per canonem |
| : politics | : | : fenian | gigantism |
| : painting | : grey, blue | : virgin | tumescence, detumescence |
| : medicine | : white | : mothers | embryonic development |
| : magic | : | : whore | hallucination |
| | | | |
| : navigation | : | : sailors | narrative (old) |
| : science | : | : comets | catechism (impersonal) |
| : | : | : earth | monologue (female) |

### CORRESPONDENCES

(The Rock—Aristotle, Dogma, Stratford: The whirlpool: Plato, Mysticism, London, Ulysses, Socrates, Jesus, Shakespeare)

(Bosphorus—Liffey: European bank—Viceroy: Asiatic bank—Conmee: Symplegades: Groups of citizens)

(Sirens—barmaids: Isle—bar)

(Noman—I: Stake—cigar: challenge—apotheosis)

(Phaecia—Star of the Sea: Gerty—Nausikaa)

(Hospital—Trinacria: Lampetie, Phaethusa—Nurses: Helios—Horne: Oxen—Fertility: Crime—Fraud)

(Circe—Bella:)

(Eumeus—Skin the Goat: Sailor—Ulysses Pseudangelos: Melanthius—Corly)

(Eurymachus—Boylan: Suitors—scruples: Bow—reason)

(Penelope—Earth: Web: Movement)

**[Doc. 170]**

27, Rue Casimir-Périer (VII$^E$)
Littre 88-89
Paris, October the 21-St.,1933.

Dear Mr. Cerf,

I beg to confirm the cable sent to you to-night informing you that Mr. Joyce is definitely opposed to the inclusion of the chart you are writing about [See Doc. 169.—ED.] in the American *Ulysses*. I am enclosing a copy of a letter I have written to-day to Mr. Pinker on the same matter which is self-explanatory. The plan which you mention was not made for Mr. Gorman at all but for Mr.Valéry Larbaud in 1920. A copy of it was placed at Mr. Gorman's disposal for the purposes of the biography he intended to write but which it seems he never wrote, and for no other—

Personally I think I can share Mr. Joyce's views on this for two reasons. The inclusion of a chart explaining *Ulysses* in the same book might just as easily deter the reader as it can according to you bring new ones. I imagine an American reader seeing the chart and concluding that since he has to study it before reading it is not worthwhile reading the book. It may defeat its purpose. On the other hand we should not forget that *Ulysses* is a piece of belles lettres, i.e. pure literature; if it needs explanations these belong to the class of critical and historical writings, not to the book itself. If it is destined to remain a classic in English literature, which I have no doubt it will, this work and many others will come and it does not behave to the author to give this indication—it should be the work of the free critic.

I am very glad indeed about what you say concerning the case and I sincerely hope that your expectations will be soon fulfilled.

Believe me,

Sincerely yours,
Paul Léon

---

**[Doc. 171]**

October 30, 1933.

Mr. Paul Léon,
27, Rue Casimir-Périer,
Paris, VII$^E$, France.

Dear Mr. Léon:

I have received your letter of October 21st, stating Mr. Joyce's reason for opposing the inclusion of the chart that we have written to you about in the American edition of *Ulysses*. I urgently beg both Mr. Joyce and yourself to reconsider this decision. Let me assure you, from my ten years experience of selling books in this country, that your idea that the inclusion of this chart will make some readers think it is not worthwhile reading the book, is entirely erroneous. Americans are notorious seekers of short cuts to culture. Thousands of people will want to know about *Ulysses*, especially if we win our legal fight, and they will buy the book if there is some key that will enable them to understand the more obscure portions of the book. Without some guide for their enlightenment, you must know as well as I do that *Ulysses* is not for the general public. I have spoken to the two biggest booksellers in New York, and asked them about this plan, and both of them stated emphatically that they would order twice as many copies of the first edition if this chart is included.

In the second place, I want to stress again the importance of having as much copyrighted material in our edition as is humanly possible, in order to combat possible pirated editions which will undoubtedly come along to vex us all. We are spending a great deal of money, and an infinite amount of time, in order to legalize *Ulysses* here, and I will certainly be disappointed indeed if Mr. Joyce and you cannot take my word on a matter about which all of us feel so very strongly. Bear in mind that this chart does not give away any of the story of *Ulysses*; it simply enables the lay reader to read the book with an infinitely greater amount of intelligent understanding than would otherwise be possible. Your refusal to grant this request will discourage us more than I can say.

I ask you to please take the matter up at once, and let me know at your earliest convenience.

Sincerely yours,

bac;pk

---

[Doc. 172]

GREENBAUM, WOLFF & ERNST

OFFICE MEMORANDUM

TO:  M.L.E.                           FROM:  A.L.
RE:  *Ulysses*                        DATE:  November 6, 1933.

I called Coleman this morning. Woolsey is back, and Coleman and I were supposed to see Woolsey in order to arrange for argument on the motion.

Coleman pleaded the day before election, and put me off till Wednesday. I am getting thoroughly sick and tired of his dilatory tactics, and if he gives me another excuse, as he probably will on Wednesday, I think that we ought to go direct to Woolsey and arrange for the hearing.

[Doc. 173]

November 14, 1933.

Judge John M. Woolsey,
Woolworth Building,
New York City.

Re: *United States* v. *Ulysses*

Dear Judge Woolsey:

The above named book was submitted to you on motion, on August 29, 1933. Some time later you indicated that as soon as you completed your reading of the book, you would set a date for hearing argument on the motion. We have been awaiting your advices accordingly.

In view of the fact that the book was held up by the authorities for more than a year prior to submission to you (*Ulysses* was stopped at the Customs as far back as May 8, 1932), our client Random House, Inc., the claimant in the libel proceedings, is understandably anxious for adjudication. We would deem it a favor, therefore, if you would set the motion down for argument at any time or place that would suit your convenience.

Yours very truly,

MLE:JF

---

[Doc. 174]

27, Rue Casimir-Périer (VII$^E$)
Littre 88-89
Paris, November the 14-th., 1933.

Dear Mr. Cerf,

I have carefully thought over the contents of your letter of the 30-th. of October but am sorry to have to tell you that Mr. Joyce's decision is absolutely definite. *Ulysses'* text must stand on its own feet without any explanation and the introductory letter will authenticate your edition against all others as was arranged in the beginning. Mr. Joyce appreciates greatly the time and money you have invested in your venture and the courage and persistance with which you are handling the matter, and I am sure that the results will prove beneficiary to you as well as to him. Nothing however can be changed in the first arrangement. In fact, Mr. Joyce has been so angry with Mr. Gorman for altogether showing the paper you have referred to that he has withdrawn the authorisation he had previously given him to write the biography, which if it ever is written will appear without his official or unofficial connection with it. Otherwise there is nothing in that paper which was written by Mr. Joyce some eleven years ago for the benefit of Mr. Valéry Larbaud.

Sincerely yours,

Paul Léon

Mr. Joyce has talked the question over with Mr. T.S. Eliot who shares his opinion entirely. What you say about the booksellers may apply to other books but from Mr. Joyce's experience in the last eleven years, he thinks the contrary and is sure that after a year or so you will agree with him.

---

[Doc. 175]

GREENBAUM, WOLFF & ERNST

OFFICE MEMORANDUM

TO:  M.L.E.                     FROM:  A.L.
RE:  *Ulysses*                  DATE:  November 22, 1933.

Called up Coleman again. He said that he spoke to Woolsey on Monday, and Woolsey said he was about to answer our letter. Coleman suggested that we wait until a letter arrives.

---

[Doc. 176]

November 22, 1933.

Mr. Paul Léon,
27, Rue Casimir-Périer,
Paris VII$^E$, France.

Dear Mr. Léon:

We most regretfully take it from your letter of November 14th that Mr. Joyce's decision is final as far as the chart is concerned. We make no effort to conceal our disappointment in this decision. We feel that Mr. Joyce and you are making a great mistake in this matter. We feel that if you both have so little faith in our judgment, it is hard to explain why you ever signed a contract with us for the book in the first place.

I wonder if it might influence you if I gave you the opinions of Mr. Huebsch and a few other American publishers with whom Mr. Joyce is acquainted.

As soon as there is any further news to tell you on this matter, please be assured that I will communicate with you.

Sincerely yours,

Bennett A. Cerf
Random House

bac;pk

---

[Doc. 177]

## Abstract of Minutes

At a Stated Term of the District Court of the United States for the Southern District of New York, held at the Court Room of the Association of the Bar of the City of New York, in the Borough of Manhattan, City of New York, on the 25th day of November in the year of our Lord one thousand nine hundred and thirty-three.

Present: Honorable JOHN M. WOOLSEY,

District Judge

UNITED STATES OF AMERICA,
    Libellant,

*versus*   A. 110-59

One Obscene Book entitled
*Ulysses* by James Joyce.

Now comes the plaintiff by Thomas E. Dewey, Esq., United States Attorney by Samuel C. Coleman and Nicholas Atlas, Esqs., Asst. U. S. Attorneys, of Counsel and moves the trial of this cause. Likewise comes the defendant by Greenbaum, Wolff & Ernst, Esqs. by Morris L. Ernst, Esq., of Counsel for claimant.

The above entitled cause coming on for hearing, Mr. Samuel C. Coleman is heard on behalf of claimant.

An Extract of the Minutes.

CHARLES WEISER,
Clerk

**[Doc. 178]**

43 Manchester Street,
Manchester Square,
London, W.I.

Nov. 25, 1933.

Bennett Cerf, Esq.,
Random House,
New York, N.Y.

Dear Bennett,

Much to my amazement I received a letter from Mr. Paul Léon this morning informing me that I am accused of communicating to you a privately drawn up plan of the parallel episodes between *Ulysses* and the *Odyssey* which was given to me by Mr. Joyce several years ago. As you undoubtedly know I have not been in communication with you or your firm regarding this matter at all, and, for that matter, have neither seen you nor communicated with you regarding anything for years past. Therefore, will you have the goodness to inform Mr. Joyce that (1) I showed you no such plan; (2) that I spoke to you about no such plan; (3) that I never gave you any such plan; and (4) that I gave you no permission at any time to publish any such plan. This plan was privately given to me for my own personal use and if you have secured a copy of it in any way it has certainly been without my permission and knowledge. It is possible that some critic or writer at my studio some time or other copied this plan and if that person has indicated to you in any way that I have agreed to your use or publication of the said plan that critic or person is entirely mistaken. For my own personal satisfaction I should be interested to learn from whom you actually received this plan.

I am sending a copy of this letter along to Mr. Joyce and would thank you if you will write to him as soon as possible and explain that I have nothing whatsoever to do with the plan in question.

Very truly yours,

Herbert Gorman

---

[Doc. 179]

*New York Herald-Tribune*

November 26, 1933

*Ulysses* **Case Reaches Court After 10 Years**

Woolsey Upset Because He Fears He Understands
Debatably Lewd Soliloquy

Read Book on Vacation

Legal 'Spectrum of Adjectives' Complicates Ruling

After a decade of delay, an American court finally convened yesterday to pass judgment on the ban against James Joyce's *Ulysses*, a 735-page book described by its author as "a chaffering all-including most farraginous chronicle." The scene was the tiny oval courtroom on the sixth floor of the Bar Association Building, 42 West Forty-fourth Street, and behind a bench of justice which is said to be one of the most beautifully designed bits of furniture in the United States, sat Judge John Munro Woolsey, of the United States District Court, hearing the case without a jury and pondering over the exact location of that vague line between "candor and shame."

### Defense Pleads for an Hour

Before him, for the government, appeared Samuel C. Coleman, Assistant United States Attorney, who besought the court not to think of him personally as "a puritanical censor" because he contended that *Ulysses* was "obscene" and accordingly should not be permitted to be sold in this country. Defending the book was Morris Ernst, who pleaded for an hour that libraries and the people all over America already had accepted *Ulysses* through bootleg sources as a classic, and that the court should follow the will of the public.

Behind the lawyers, sitting in a row of the finest Colonial chairs in New York, were the rest of the gathering, the press and various persons interested in the fate of *Ulysses*. Among the latter were Mrs. Ernst, Bennett A. Cerf, of Random House, publishers, who is forcing the case and who wants to publish the book in this country; Saxe Commins and Donald Klopfer, also of

Random House, and Whit Burnett, editor of *Story*. By the door stood George, a white-haired Negro whom Judge Woolsey cautioned at the beginning of the hearing not to be "shocked." Above George hung the Thomas Sully portrait of John Marshall.

On the lawyers' tables and on the bench before the judge lay well-thumbed copies of the blue paperbound edition of *Ulysses*, printed by Sylvia Beach, of the Shakespeare Press, in 1922 in Paris. It is this edition that has gone all over the United States by underground channels. In America, the history of *Ulysses*, it was explained, dates to 1918 when *The Little Review* published a part of the manuscript sent here by Ezra Pound. John S. Sumner brought charges and the Post-office Department made such a bonfire of the copies of that magazine that never since has any American publisher dared to print the work.

### Enters U. S. by Exception

Recently, however, Alexander Lindey, an attorney associated with Mr. Ernst, got the Treasury Department to declare *Ulysses* a classic and this decision permitted him to bring in through the customs a copy of the edition printed in Paris. This legal entry was made possible by an exception in the 1930 tariff act, presumably made for the benefit of noted collectors and the great libraries. Under this exception, copies of books otherwise banned, but of recognized literary merit, intended for non-commercial use, are allowed entrance at the discretion of the Secretary of the Treasury.

Mr. Lindey announced that this legal admittance of a single copy was a preliminary to making the publication and sale of the book legal here. Thus, on July 11 was filed the case of the *United States* vs. *Ulysses*.

As the hearing was informal, Judge Woolsey talked freely from the bench and from time to time told of his extremely difficult position in being required to pass on a book that for ten years had evoked the most violent denunciations and praise from all manner of learned men and women.

"This isn't an easy case to decide," said Judge Woolsey, lighting a cigarette in a long holder. "I think things ought to take their chances in the market place. My own feeling is against censorship. I know that as soon as you suppress anything the bootlegger goes to work. The people see about as much of the prohibited article as they otherwise would and the profits go into illegal channels. Still". . . . he broke off, looking perplexed for a few moments, then added: "Still there is that soliloquy in the last chapter. I don't know about that. But, go on with the case."

The courtroom broke into laughter when the judge admitted that to his "shocking surprise" he had found that he "perfectly understood" the passages that had been described constituting the obscene sections of the manuscript. Judge Woolsey laughed himself; then he frowned and talking as though to himself, stated: "Parts of it are pretty rough, really, but other parts are swell.

There are passages of moving literary beauty, passages of worth and power. I tell you" he continued in a louder tone, "reading parts of that book almost drove me frantic. That last part, that soliloquy, it may represent the moods of a woman of that sort. That is what disturbs me. I seem to understand it."

He straightened in his chair, telling wearily of other parts, of reading sections "that are so obscure, so vague, so unintelligible—I didn't know what they were about. I found those parts dull and boring. Take that passage where Stephen was tight and everybody else was tight. They had visions and dreams that to me, were perfectly phantasmal."

### Got Unbelievable Quantity of Mail

Judge Woolsey at one point stopped the proceedings to tell of "the unbelievable" amount of mail he had received since it was published several months ago that he intended to take *Ulysses* with him to read on his vacation. "A man from Lynn, Mass.," he said, "wrote me that this book was the most precious thing in his life and another man wrote me it had seered his soul."

Mr. Coleman said he could cite many such criticisms from famous men. Arnold Bennett, he asserted had been revolted but James Branch Cabell in eight years during which the book had lain by his bedside had never become excited sufficiently to read beyond page forty. Professor John Dewey, he continued, "curiously enough" had called *Ulysses* a great book without "ever reading it at all." Mr. Ernst quoted letters from women librarians in Texas and North Dakota who said they believed *Ulysses* to be "superb," "classically exquisite." Others, another of the lawyers interjected, thought it only "bunk."

Judge Woolsey replied that *Ulysses* left him "bothered, stirred and troubled." Mr. Ernst said, "I think that is exactly the effect of *Ulysses*. You have not used the adjectives 'shocked' or 'revolted.' You have used the adjectives 'bothered,' 'troubled.' "

### That Spectrum of Adjectives

"I think," he continued, "that peculiarly is the power of this book. It is an adventure not in action or in the deeds of men, but it is a weird epitome of what is going on in a human mind." For a time Mr. Coleman and Judge Woolsey engaged in earnest conversation over what should constitute a definition of "obscene" and the judge complained of "the spectrum of adjectives" which bound him by the law—"obscene, lewd, disgusting."

"Mr. Coleman," inquired the judge, "what do you think constitutes obscenity?" Before Mr. Coleman could answer, the judge said, "One definition is a thing may be said to be obscene when its primary purpose is to excite sexual feeling."

Mr. Coleman held, "I do not think that obscenity necessarily should be limited to exciting sexual feeling. I can understand people reading something that does not excite them in such a manner but which they might still pass on as being obscene. I should say a thing is obscene by the ordinary language used and by what it does to the average reader. It need not necessarily be what the author intended. On these grounds, I think there are ample reasons to consider *Ulysses* to be an obscene book."

Mr. Ernst, resuming his plea, said he had made a study of what language in books did to the ordinary reader and he said he had yet to find one single instance where it could be proved that the reading of any book had led to the commission of a crime of passion.

Judge Woolsey apologized for having taken so long to bring the case to a hearing. "I know your client," he said to Mr. Ernst, "is anxious to learn one way or the other about this book. Still I must take a little more time to make up my mind. I must reserve decision."

---

**[Doc. 180]**

November 27, 1933.

Hon. John M. Woolsey,
Room 1542, Woolworth Building,
233 Broadway, New York City.

Re: *United States of America* v. *Ulysses*

Dear Judge Woolsey:

In accordance with your request we are sending you herewith another copy of our printed memorandum of law in the above matter. By tomorrow we hope to have for you a very brief supplemental memorandum [See Doc. 183.—ED.] dealing with the two or three questions which were raised in the course of the argument before you; and we shall also transmit to you a copy of the script of *Frankie and Johnnie* (258 N.Y. 451) which you said that you desired to see.

Sincerely yours,

Alexander Lindey

Enc. (1)
Del.

---

**[Doc. 181]**

November 27, 1933.

Judge John M. Woolsey,
Woolworth Building,
New York City.

Re: *United States* v. *Ulysses*

Dear Judge Woolsey,

We are sending you herewith our supplementary memorandum in the above matter, together with a script of *Frankie and Johnnie* (People v. Wendling, 258 N. Y. 451). In the course of the argument before you you expressed a desire to see the text of this play.

Sincerely yours,

Greenbaum, Wolff & Ernst

By Alexander Lindey

AL:JF

P.S.   The script of *Frankie and Johnnie* was borrowed from the attorney for the defendants in that case. He has requested that the script be returned to him as soon as you are through with it.

---

**[Doc. 182]**

November 27, 1933.

Mr. Ernst:                                    Re: *Ulysses*

Mr. Lindey hopes you will have an opportunity to read the attached [See Doc. 183.—ED.]; he wants to submit a copy to Judge Woolsey sometime during tomorrow.

---

[Doc. 183]

UNITED STATES DISTRICT COURT
SOUTHERN DISTRICT OF NEW YORK

UNITED STATES OF AMERICA,

Libellant,

-against-

One Book Entitled *Ulysses*,

Random House, Inc.

Claimant.

Index No. A 110-59
Calendar No. 1438
Jury Calendar

## CLAIMANT'S SUPPLEMENTARY MEMORANDUM

Upon the argument of the Government's motion for judgment on the pleadings, and of the Claimant's cross-motion to dismiss the libel herein, the Court expressed a desire to see the text of the New York State obscenity statute, and also the text of the play *Frankie and Johnnie*, which was the basis of People v. Wendling, 258 N. Y. 451. Furthermore, since the Court was sitting both as judge and jury, the question arose whether the Government or the Claimant had the burden of proof.

## I. THE NEW YORK STATE STATUTE

Section 1141 of the Penal Law of the State of New York deals with obscene material. The relevant portion of the Section reads as follows:

1. A person who sells, lends, gives away or shows, or offers to sell, lend, give away, or show, or has in his possession with intent to sell, lend or give away, or to show, or advertises in any manner, or who otherwise offers for loan, gift, sale or distribution, any *obscene, lewd, lascivious, filthy, indecent or disgusting* book, magazine, pamphlet, newspaper, story paper, writing, paper, picture, drawing, photograph, figure or image, or any written or printed matter of an *indecent* character; or any article or instrument of *indecent or immoral* use, or purporting to be for indecent or immoral use or purpose, or who designs, copies, draws, photographs, prints, utters, publishes, or in any manner manufactures, or prepares any such book, picture, drawing, magazine, pamphlet, newspaper, story paper, writing, paper, figure, image, matter, article or thing, or who writes, prints, publishes, or utters, or causes to be written, printed, published, or uttered, any advertisement or notice of any kind, giving information, directly or indirectly, stating, or purporting so to do, where, how, of whom, or by what means any, or what purports to be

any *obscene, lewd, lascivious, filthy, disgusting or indecent* book, picture, writing, paper, figure, image, matter, article or thing, named in this section can be purchased, obtained, or had or who has in his possession, any slot machine or other mechanical contrivance with moving pictures of nude or partly denuded female figures which pictures are *lewd, obscene, indecent or immoral, or other lewd, obscene, indecent or immoral* image, article or object, or who shows, advertises or exhibits the same, or causes the same to be shown, advertised, or exhibited, or who buys, owns or holds any such machine with the intent to show, advertise or in any manner exhibit the same . . . Is guilty of a misdemeanor . . . (*Underscoring* ours).

The Court's attention is directed to the fact that the New York law is much broader in scope than Section 305 of the Tariff Act of June 17, 1930 (Title 19, United States Code, Section 1305), under which the libel herein has been brought. The New York Statute is directed against any material that is obscene, lewd, lascivious, filthy, indecent, disgusting or immoral; whereas the Tariff Act merely prohibits the importation of "any *obscene* book . . . " The words lewd, lascivious, filthy, indecent, disgusting or immoral do *not* appear in the Tariff Act. Hence in passing on *Ulysses* the Court may properly restrict itself to the sole consideration as to whether the book is obscene.

The evolutionary phases of the definition of obscenity and the various criteria by which it may be ascertained and measured, have been fully set forth in the claimant's main memorandum heretofore submitted. Nevertheless it may not be amiss to reiterate that a book, in order to be adjudged obscene, must have for its purpose and tendency the excitation of lustful and lecherous desires; that such purpose must be *primary*, not an incidental one; and that such tendency must be a *natural* one. (People v. Muller, 96 N. Y. 408-411). In calculating the possible effect of a book on the community, it is the normal adult that must be considered, not the adolescent or the sub-average individual.

United States v. Kennerley, 209 Fed. 119, 120, 121;
United States v. *Married Love*, 48 Fed. (2d) 821, 824;
People v. Wendling, 258 N. Y. 451, 454.

To contend that the primary purpose of *Ulysses* is the stimulation of lust and lechery, and that its natural tendency will be to corrupt and deprave the normal reader, is either to misapprehend the true meaning of the book, or wilfully to distort it.

## II. *FRANKIE AND JOHNNIE*
### (People v. Wendling, 218 N. Y. 451)

In the course of the argument on the cross-motions, the Court expressed a desire to examine the script of the play *Frankie and Johnnie*. We have secured the script and submit it herewith. It is especially to be noted that the Court of Appeals of this state thus characterized the play:

> The language of the play is coarse, vulgar and profane; the plot cheap and tawdry. As a dramatic composition it serves to degrade the stage where vice is thought by some to lose "half its evil by losing all its grossness." "That it is 'indecent' from every consideration of propriety is entirely clear" . . . (at pp. 452-3).

Yet the Court of Appeals reversed two convictions which had been unanimously affirmed by the Appellate Division, and exonerated the play.

### III. BURDEN OF PROOF

The prosecution has argued—not with too much conviction to be sure—that the burden of proof rests on the claimant and not on the Government. It seems clear from Pooshontas Distilling Company v. United States, 218 Fed. 782-786, and United States v. Regan, 232 U.S. 37, that the burden of proof in a libel proceeding rests on the Government. That this should be so is proper and logical. The Government has attacked a book, contending that it violates the law. The Government should be required in the first instance to prove its case.

The Court is sitting herein as judge and jury. The sole evidence presented is *Ulysses*. The question is: Must the obscenity of the book be proved by a fair preponderance of evidence, or must it be proved beyond a reasonable doubt? It is submitted that it must be proved beyond a reasonable doubt.

It is no abuse of analogy to say that this proceeding is something like a capital case. *Ulysses* stands before the Court as defendant. Charged with being a menace to public morals, it is fighting for its life. If condemned, it faces destruction by a means (i.e., confiscation) no less complete than that of hanging or electrocution. Besides, it is no upstart, no scrubby little churl of the republic of letters that thus faces annihilation. It is a noble citizen whose stature has been almost universally conceded. Before it is turned over to the executioner, its guilt should be shown *beyond a reasonable doubt*.

But there are other persuasive arguments in favor of regarding this case, to a certain extent at least, as one requiring the same measure of proof as a criminal case:

(a) While it would seem that libels under the Tariff Act are in their superficial nature civil proceedings, it must be borne in mind that Section 305 is a prohibitory one; and that a prohibitory statute is necessarily criminal in its effect and implications, even if not in form.

(b) The intent of Section 305, as characterized by its language and by court decisions, is to safeguard "public morality." It is this intent which is at the basis of all criminal statutes.

(c) Section 305 is by its terms confiscatory. It would seem proper not to require the outright destruction of material merely upon a preponderance of evidence.

(d) Section 305 is similar to (though not as broad as) the Federal Postal Statute, which is criminal, and also the New York State obscenity law, which is likewise criminal.

(e) In the civil cases which have heretofore arisen on the subject of obscenity, the Courts have relied on criminal cases for definition and precedent. (United States v. *Married Love*, 48 Fed. (2d) 821; United States v. *Contraception*, 51 Fed. (2d) 525)

(f) It may not be unsound to regard an ordinary libel proceeding, directed against spoiled food-stuffs for instance, as civil in nature. A libel against a book is essentially different. If the Government prevails in such a case, it is not a cargo of maggoty meat or rancid figs that is destroyed. A book is confiscated. Nor does this mean a physical book consisting of a cardboard cover and paper pages. It means that ideas are suppressed, that freedom of expression is fettered. The condemnation of ideas should be much more reluctantly and circumspectly ordered than the destruction of deleterious edibles.

As we have said before, the burden of proof rests on the prosecution. The Government must establish its case in any event, whether it be by a fair preponderance of evidence, if the Court assumes that this is a strictly civil case, or beyond a reasonable doubt, if it is conceded that the case is quasi-criminal.

The Court has stated that its perusal of *Ulysses* has created serious doubt in the Court's mind. It is not likely that such doubt will lessen. If anything, it will grow more persistent and vexing. The doubt should be resolved in favor of the book.

The libel should be dismissed.

Respectfully submitted,

GREENBAUM, WOLFF & ERNST,
Proctors for Claimant,
285 Madison Avenue,
Borough of Manhattan,
New York City.

MORRIS L. ERNST
ALEXANDER LINDEY
Of Counsel

Dated, New York, November 27, 1933.

[Doc. 184]

## UNITED STATES v. ULYSSES

To be included in obscenity record

[The following two memoranda were prepared by Nicholas Atlas, Esq., the Assistant U.S. Attorney who worked with Chief Assistant Samuel C. Coleman on the case. These memoranda were not presented to the court, but were merely used for inter-office purposes by the prosecution.]

### JAMES JOYCE

It is well to begin with the statement made by Valéry Larbaud, French critic, that "during the past two or three years James Joyce has obtained among the men of letters of his generation an extraordinary notoriety." This is from an essay written prior to the publication of Shakespeare & Company's edition of *Ulysses*, an exemplar of which is the *res* in this libel. Larbaud continues, "No critic has as yet occupied himself with his (i.e., Joyce's) work, and it is only now that the most lettered part of the English and American public commences to hear of him; but it is no exaggeration to say that among men of his profession his name is as well known and his works as much discussed as could be among scientists the names and theories of Freud or Einstein."

James Joyce was born in 1882 and is thus but fifty years old. In order to understand his writings it is necessary to have a knowledge of at least the high points of his career and his educational background. He was educated by and under the influence of the Jesuit Order in Jesuit preparatory schools and at the University of Dublin. He continued his education abroad, studying but not completing medicine, and evidencing a great interest in the P.C.N. which he mentions in *Ulysses*, that is to say, physics, chemistry and natural philosophy. In Paris his education broadened, but he did not relinquish the interest of a Jesuit-bred student in the scholastics and he read assiduously Aristotle, St. Thomas Aquinas, and the other great writers of the Middle Ages. The strength of this education and this learning comes fully forth in *Ulysses*, where we are constantly astonished by the depth and breadth of his scholastic learning, as we are also astonished by the scientific insight into the psychology of the human being—using "psychology" in its best accepted scientific sense—and by this thoroughgoing medical learning, which crops up page after page. Joyce eventually lived for many years in Trieste, teaching English and writing and studying and observing human nature. Silvio Benco, in *The Bookman* for December, 1930, writes a sketch of him there that leaves us with the impression of a somewhat gloomy and very modest genius, already beginning to go blind.

Joyce is also the author of *Chamber Music*, a collection of thirty-six poems, which appeared in May, 1907. Of these Larbaud says, "These short poems modestly presented under the title of *Chamber Music* continued or, more exactly, renewed a great tradition, that of the Elizabethan song. . . . What Joyce did in these thirty-six poems was to renew the genre without falling into pastiche."

The production of Joyce most important for us to note in a discussion of *Ulysses*, however, is *A Portrait of the Artist as a Young Man*. In this book we first meet some of the characters who form the ribwork of *Ulysses*. For one, we meet Buck Mulligan who, in this book as well as in *Ulysses*, constantly flits across the scene, a lively young fellow, a medical student and, we strongly suspect, the more amiable and personable and robust side of Joyce himself. For another, we meet Stephen Dedalus, who is undoubtedly Joyce himself, Jesuit-bred, scholarly, a student, and a medium through which Joyce brings forth those things which he as a youth in Dublin must undoubtedly have seen, heard and met. The book is very powerfully written, with strong descriptive passages, and leaves one full of the tone and smell and picture of life in Dublin in the days of "the artist as a young man." Here, too, Joyce for the first time uses the method of writing which is so revealing and also so confusing (to the uninitiated) in *Ulysses*. It is what the critics have called the stream-of-consciousness manner. Without warning, without the handy anchorage of a punctuation mark sometimes, or sometimes only without the conventional punctuation, we are whisked from the contemplation of an external fact like "Dedalus walking," into the chamber of Dedalus' mind, where we can hear Dedalus thinking and where we learn what goes on about Dedalus by what Dedalus is thinking. However, this method is not used to a very large extent in *A Portrait of the Artist*, but is there sufficiently to make one cognizant of the fact that here is a new method of style and as well a new method of writing a novel. In *Ulysses*, this is brought to a full fruition. It might be added that in *A Portrait of the Artist*, those who find obscenity in *Ulysses* might also find many of the same objectionable words. They occur there in the conversation of young and healthy animals at college. They occur in *Ulysses* because they cannot escape being seen and heard in the minds and sometimes in the talk of people who are exposed pitilessly to the scrutiny and hearing of the author, the master scientist researching in life.

There is another book of Joyce's called *Dubliners*, which is a series of fifteen short stories, all about Dublin. In this book the city of *A Portrait of the Artist* and of *Ulysses*, that is, Dublin, is revealed. In the stories Joyce conforms to the method of the Naturalists. Among these stories, at least two deal in a very delicate way, and as Larbaud says, "in a manner perfectly decent and which could not shock a single reader," with delicate subjects. The story, for instance, of two young students, who hear with astonishment and fright the stories of a strange man about corporal punishment and little amorous intrigues between boy and girl students, or the story of two Dubliners of "undecided social position and doubtful profession." Yet this book never suffered by reason of objection to the material treated; on the contrary, it was suppressed for a long time because in one of the stories, "The Anniversary of the Death of Parnell," characters speak freely of many things and in particular of the private life of King Edward VII.

Joyce now lives in Paris, where he writes continuously. His eyesight is very poor and forms the chief concern and trouble of his life. The book upon which he is at present engaged has been called *A Work in Progress*, and here in America when fragments of it were published (it is said, without his permission) *A New Unnamed Work*. It is written in a style much more difficult to understand than *Ulysses*, and what I have seen of it I can scarcely speak of because of the confusion attendant upon my reading of it. Suffice it to say that it carries or seems to carry a step further the psychological stream-of-consciousness writing to which I have already referred.

### ULYSSES

We now proceed to a discussion of the book, the libeled *res*. Let us first clear away the question of possible prejudice by saying that it is not incumbent upon the libellant to approach this book with disrespect, because it is claimed to be obscene. On the contrary, we approach the book with great respect. We realize that the substance of the book is a microcosm, depicted and represented in a most literary, most sensitive, and very scientific way. We admit that the book is to be praised for its style, which is new and startling; for its content, which is narrative in a new manner, analytical with a new precision, and, in its comprehensiveness, exhaustive. We distinguish its method and realize that this is a new method in the creation of the novel and a new system of presenting people to themselves. We know that the book bristles with learning—general learning, esoteric learning. We know that it is an encyclopedia, thorough and classified, of the very substance of two beings, both physical and psychological, external and internal. We realize that it is a deep character study, that even the remotest characters in the book are limned with unmistakable distinctness upon its huge canvas. We know, too, that the book is a scientific discussion and a laboratory process, availing itself of all known science and of its author's perspicacity. Finally, we realize that this is literature and poetry in that it is the communication of the author in the best form which he can find of his reactions to life and nature. But it is not the conventional communication to which we have been accustomed. Rather this is an impromptu communication, avoiding the loss of its full meaning, richness and sense in the stilt-and-stultification of the accepted form of saying things. This does not mean that Joyce dashed the book off. On the contrary, he must have labored greatly to preserve the very last impression, the very last association, the very last reaction, so that it might be communicated.

In brief, *Ulysses* is the story, or, better, the recital of the happenings of eighteen hours in Dublin. It is the recital of happenings pregnant with import for two people: one, Stephen Dedalus, and the other, Leopold Bloom. Each of these characters travels in his own orbit in the city, thinking and encountering and experiencing, until finally their orbits cross. The story is the story of what they see and encounter and think in the course of the travels of each of them and of what happens to them and how they see and think and what they encounter once their orbits have crossed, and how the crossing of their orbits makes changes for them in their own lives and charaters and what they see, encounter and think thereafter. This is the plan of it all. The rest is the material of their thinking and encountering and seeing, meticulously written and in a schemed way set forth so that the reader may know every element, physical and psychological, external and internal, that made up these eighteen hours in the lives of these two people. To that end, the author introduces us to people, scenes and events, bringing before us as much as can be seen by a bird's-eye, but bringing it so close that it is seen with the careful examination of the scientific eye. So, for example, the old milk-woman who brings milk to Dedalus and his companions in the tower where they live is only part of the panorama, yet she is a character who is unforgettable, and that is because Joyce has extracted from her in one of her pithy Irish sayings or in her pithy way of saying nothing the very essence of her character and the very essence of her kind.

Dedalus and Bloom do not commence the day at the same time. Dedalus gets up, converses with his friends, goes to teach, travels again in the circles of his friends and in one of these circles meets Bloom. Bloom gets up, prepares his own breakfast, reflects upon certain things, goes out, attends a funeral, does the regular things that one might expect of an advertising man, goes to a beach, and winds up in the circle where he meets Dedalus, and from that point Dedalus and Bloom go together.

It is not what they do that is so significant; it is what they think and it is the problems of each. Of Stephen Dedalus, if we have read *A Portrait of the Artist*, we already know something. *A Portrait of the Artist* closes with Dedalus leaving for Paris to study. *Ulysses* opens with Dedalus' return from Paris. He comes back to Dublin to a circle of his old friends, particularly to associate again with Buck Mulligan, a hearty, robust and blaspheming medical student. He (Dedalus) has been called home by the death of his mother and it is the crime (in his own mind) that he committed against his mother that oppresses him. Already he is set apart from the rest of his friends and colleagues. He was always different, poetical, sensitive, a man who could say in *A Portrait of the Artist* that he was about to set forth "to forge in the smithy of my soul the uncreated conscience of my race." The props of his religion have been lost to him in the enlightenment which he has attained. He reasons with precision, and reasons away the things that tie man to the society in which he moves. He despises himself. He is bitter over the offense he has given his mother in refusing to pray by her death bedside, in leaving unsatisfied the yearning of her last request to him; and he has no father—that is, no father to speak of, for Simon Dedalus, as we have learned to know him in *A Portrait of the Artist*, is a souse, a weak, inconsequential, little Irishman with a Greek name, a barroom tenor, a rake without dash.

Bloom, too, is an unusual person, a person set apart from his surroundings. He is a patriotic Irishman. He is also a Jew. And he is but one generation removed from being a Hungarian. He is not a cultivated man of the colleges; he solicits "ads" for the journals. But he is perspicacious, he understands people around him, he is intelligent and he is sensitive. He is the instrument used by Joyce for catching and recording the life, the actions and the nature in Dublin during this day. Bloom, too, has his troubles. He is married to an Irishwoman of whom he has reason to believe—and, before the day is done, of whom he is sure—that she commits adultery. He has had a personal grief in that he has lost one of his children, a son. And he moves about Dublin, doing all the things that people do, going to business, preparing his own breakfast in his dissatisfied household, going to funerals, going to the beach, joining in the discussion of groups here and there throughout the town—in the barroom and finally in the ante-room of a hospital, where he meets Stephen. Bloom, with his heavy heart and his unsatisfactory home life, the shabbiness of his sexual relationship with his wife, carries his burden about with him, looking for a son. Dedalus is looking for a father. In the ante-room of the hospital, waiting for the delayed birth of a woman's baby, they meet each other. In a melee in a brothel they find each other. Dedalus goes home with Bloom. His coming is not only the resolution of his own unsatisfied yearnings to be connected with something or somebody. It is the resolution of Bloom's unsatisfied yearnings for the same thing. And the coming of Dedalus creates a difference in the home life of the Blooms, subtly and powerfully illustrated in the lengthy revery of Mrs. Bloom, who lies beside her husband that night, meditating and speaking within herself, shrinking from her husband, planning her design to possess Dedalus too, and going back to her husband. On this note the book closes.

Some critics, notably Edmund Wilson (he is not alone) find significance in the title of the book and feel that they must say that here is another *Odyssey* and go further in drawing the parallel between this book and the classic of Homer, correlating piece by piece the characters, the incidents and the structure of the two works. Bloom becomes Odysseus (Ulysses), Stephen is Telemachus—the first wandering back to Ithaca, the second setting forth in search of his father. And *Ulysses* is also endowed by these critics with its own Antinous, in the person of Buck Mulligan, its own Nausicaa, in the person of Gertie McDowell, and so on. For one who has the patience to go through the book I doubt whether this analysis is necessary, although when called to the attention the similarities are striking. It is sufficient to say that this is, if it is an odyssey, an odyssey of two spirits carried about in a circumscribed urban circle by their respective bodies. To me, the courses each of Dedalus and Bloom are the courses and progress of pilgrims (not holy), both proceeding through the maze of their lives, carrying with them their respective taints, deficiencies and burdens, and encountering the forces and bodies about them.

Of course, it is not all as simple as this. The skein of this story is unwound from and traced through the network of all that Joyce has written, a network of conversations, snatches of popular songs, political talk, platitudes, philosophy and all the "ologies" of scholastic logic, great splashes of medical knowledge and medical information (as, for example, the conversation through the medium of Joyce between Dedalus and Bloom), great patches of emotion and feeling and perceptions and reactions wrested from the minds of his chief characters by a more than psychological analysis, by intuition, by living in his characters. There is rare poetry, like

> Woodshadows floated silently by through the morning peace from the stairhead seaward where he gazed. Inshore and farther out the mirror of water widened, spurned by lightshod hurrying feet. White breast of the dim sea. The twining stresses, two by two. A hand plucking the harpstrings merging their twining chords. Wavewhite wedded words shimmering on the dim tide.

In this we find an echo of the old songs of the sea, of old Anglo-Saxon chanters, an echo of "The Seafarer." There are exercises in prose as, for example, in the description of the period of time—one cannot say he describes the scene—spent by Bloom and Dedalus with the medical students in the ante-room of the hospital waiting for the birth of Mrs. Purefoy's baby. Here the reflections made upon the birth are written progressively in the various forms of English style. We read Anglo-Saxon in English, and Old English, and Chaucerian English, and Elizabethan English, and Eighteenth Century English, and Modern English and slang English. Some critics see in this method an effort to trace the embryological development of that child in the development of English prose. There are trick spellings in the prose, there is the response of the linguist in Joyce to the sound of words, and throughout we find the tendency to speak a word and to rhyme the word in one's mind, to vary a word, to change the suffixes and the prefixes around the root, to speak words giving them their original etymological significance and connotation, to play with derivatives, to recognize relationships between English words and words of other languages—the writing of a linguist run riot. Greek and Hebrew, Yiddish and Hungarian, words in Erse and Latin crop up and stare at us. There is dialogue, the ribald dialogues of the students speaking among themselves, making ribald couplets, singing blasphemous songs, writing ribald titles for plays never written that lie in their ribald minds. There is the deep dialogue in the brothel.

Like Sterne, Joyce uses typographical tricks. There are sentences without punctuation and unusual punctuation and boldfaced type in astounding places, and the thoughts of Mrs. Bloom, at the end of the book, are written for over forty pages without a single mark of punctuation to distinguish one sentence from the other. There is rare and obscure learning, snatches from church rituals and the Mass, computation of household expenses. The chapter written to show what Bloom and Dedalus had between them in common (really the examination of Dedalus by Bloom who seeks Stephen's qualifications for the post of being Bloom's son) which is next to the last chapter of the book, is in question and answer form, replete with all learning, medicine, music, astronomy, the classics, and vulgar learnings, catalogues of books, snatches of personal description, a maze in which each of the characters reveals to the other how fit he is for the friendship of the other. Even the Zionist anthem, quaintly transliterated from the original Hebrew of Imber, finds place in this agglomeration of knowledge. There are the political opinions of the day, and the comment of one man upon the other, and the platitudes one speaks of the things in life that are inexplicable, life and death. There is endless blasphemy, coupled with a great love for the church and all it gave. In short, accompanying his characters, Joyce steps up to each man and removes the veil of his mind, showing to us what is there, and invades the secret places of the imagination, bringing forth those things even which we dare not say to ourselves.

Is this book readable? No more than Rabelais to the average men. To read it, to understand it and to appreciate it, it is necessary to have, in preparation, at least some of the learning which it embodies and at least some of the intuition, imagination and perception of its author. It is necessary to know Stephen Dedalus with his background and Bloom and his background and Joyce and his background. The theme of the story as outlined is simple, but it is bowed down and hidden under the weight and covering of the voluminous and exhaustive theme of life in which it is made to run. That is its chief fault literarily.

## ANALYSIS OF BOOKS SUBMITTED TO US BY THE CLAIMANT IN THE *ULYSSES* CASE FOR COMPARISON

### I. Re: *Madeline*

The book purports to be the autobiography of a prostitute. It is written in a whining and self-pitying tone, and describes the misfortunes of a prostitute passing from man to man, and hand to hand, and house to house. There is no obscenity in this book. We find descriptions of life in houses of prostitution. We learn that the author of the book is afflicted with a venereal disease. We find the kind of material which has been repeated hundreds of times since the day of *Madeline*. There are no obscene words. There are no incidents that are double entendres. There are no bawdy jokes. If one could say of the book that it was truly written by a prostitute, whether now reformed or not, it might even be said that it indicates the danger of a life of immorality and certainly makes such a life most unattractive and forbidding. It is no worse than the preachings of an evangelist well started, and full of his theme, and whether authentic or not, would be a deterrent from vice to those who read it.

## II. Re: *Mademoiselle de Maupin*

This is Gautier's classic. The book abounds in passionate and amorous description. It is true that the central figure is a woman in man's clothes, who, by reason of her position of moving among men, and of her handsomeness in her disguise, appeals to the women whom she meets. A great many strange situations naturally occur. At the end of the book she finally gives up her disguise and gives herself to a man whom she truly loves. One must consider that the book was written before the world generally understood homosexuality, and one can, therefore, not attribute to the author a desire to portray any such relationship. The story is written in the rich, romantic and imaginative style of Gautier, and the passionate, and I admit, sometimes exciting language that he uses is no different than the language used in his *Le Capitaine Fracasse* or in his brilliant short stories. Certainly the book contains no such obscenities as *Ulysses*, there being no bawdy words, no bawdy scenes. Even the description of the sexual encounter between the heroine and her finally chosen lover is written in a style of great linguistic reserve, though, in a manner passionately romantic. One calls to mind Gautier's own statement in which he refers to the French language as "si chaste, si pure."

## III. Re: *Casanova's Homecoming*

This is a story by the most delicate of contemporary Austrian prose artists, of the return of Casanova, and the impression he makes upon the society (of his day) to which he returns, and of how his entrance into the home of a friend affects a young woman there, and of his encounter with this young woman and of the murder in a duel of his friend. There is not a single bawdy scene or word in this book according to my present recollection. It may be said with respect to this book, as with respect to *Mademoiselle de Maupin*, that descriptions of nudity certainly are not obscene. This book describes emotions, which, I take it, have long been known not only to authors and poets and bards, but to all humanity, and while the relationship described may be irregular from our view of matrimony, certainly there is nothing new in the book, the chief joy of which lies in its delicate style. If one cannot call *Mademoiselle de Maupin*, where the relationship fringes upon a sexual irregularity, obscene, one certainly cannot call this description of that which is sexually regular, obscene. It should be added that in *Mademoiselle de Maupin*, the passion evoked is not evoked by a *girl* but by one supposed to be a *man*.

IV. Re: *Eastern Shame Girl*
and
V. Re: *Adventures of Hsi Men Ching*

These two books are old Chinese stories. In their own country they are classics, and there is no reason why they should not be in ours. They are written as far as one can tell from the excellent English translations in a style most elegant, and there is nothing in them of any lurid description, but only the charming, unadorned, beautiful and naked language needed artistically to convey the thought. The incidents are out of the social life of the China and the dynasty contemporary with their occurrence. The boldest incidents in these stories are much more delicately treated than similar incidents to be found in the "Heptameron" of Marguerite of Navarre and the stories of Boccaccio, Aretino and Masuccio, all accepted reading matter, and in some instances, assigned secondary reading in colleges. As an example, one might resume a story out of the second volume mentioned. It concerns the love of a young man for a young woman and relates what transpires when he is assigned to the same bedroom with the girl he adores. It is all treated with the usual Chinese sophistication and delicacy. Another story deals with the manner in which a young man travelling in a river boat fell in love with a young lady travelling in another river boat and of how he contrived to go aboard the boat she was on and of how they made love and of how their parents regularized their love by the age-old Chinese arrangements for marriage.

VI. Re: *Woman and Puppet*

I suppose this book first came under the eye of the authorities chiefly by reason of the fact that its author, Pierre Louys, was also the author of *Aphrodite*. The story is that of the deep, burning, inevitable and disastrous love which a Spanish gentleman has for a girl of doubtful ancestry and no social standing. It reveals, in fine language, a woman deeply passionate, yet maddeningly reserving of her sexual favors. It shows how this conduct on her part broke the will power on the part of the Spanish gentleman and finally made him her abject slave despite the numberless indignities and trials she heaped upon him. These indignities include a seemingly actual sexual encounter with another man in his presence and her constant refusal at the ripe and poignant moment to give herself to him. But he finally possesses her, yet he is forced to leave her because she is so fearfully jealous and suspicious. The book reveals his last note to her in which he shows her quite plainly that, whatever she does, he is her puppet. This book has in it not a single obscene or bawdy word. Even the description of the mentioned sexual encounter is accomplished by circumlocution. The book merely accepts, as all Continental people accept, the fact that people are passionate; that a beautiful woman attracts; that a bachelor gentleman may have his diversions; that sometimes a passion lodges in the bones and will not be dislodged. The story is very strongly written in the clear style for which its author is noted.

## VII. Re: *God's Little Acre*

This book is a picture of life in South Carolina, not far from the border of Georgia, and we are taken across the border several times during the story. On the one hand we have a family of benighted, superstitious peasantry consisting of a father, two sons, two daughters and a daughter-in-law. One of the daughters is married to a Georgia millhand. There are other incidental characters. The story concerns their lives and superstitions. First we are taught to understand the abysmal ignorance and native shrewdness of the peasant folk, their superstitions, beliefs with respect to God and gold, their manner of living, their thinking and desires which revert from time to time to thoughts of sex and sexual unions.

The old man cannot refrain from noting his daughter-in-law's pair of "rising beauties" and suggesting perversion of sex with respect to her. The daughter, Darling Jill, runs around like a free mare receiving the sexual attentions and salute of those whom she desires, and who, without fail, seem to desire her too. The husband of the daughter, Rosamond, on the other hand, symbolizes the oppressed Southern mill-hand and it is he who dies in an effort to start the mills running during a lock-out of the working men there. As one shot in the back by a company officer, he is made to be a symbol of downtrodden labor. To his peasant relations he is a strange man, passing understanding. To the women folk he is the aboriginal, primitive, violent incarnation of the male sex, and also the lover of each. He is married to Rosamond, he possesses in his indolent way the sister Darling Jill who invites him thereto and the night before his fatal adventure in the mill, in a scene tense, stark and forceful, he possesses the daughter-in-law Griselda, the sister of his wife's brother. When he is dead the negro servants of his wife's family say, "Trouble in the house, male man is dead." This book is a serious study. There is nothing in it intended to be obscene. Nevertheless, we cannot say that the jabberings of the old man are not obscene and calculated to incite to lust. The scene of sexual encounter between Will, the mill-hand, and Griselda is written to show the inevitable force that drove these two turbulent spirits together—the girl within herself, and in a way not known even to her, the man turbulent always, and known by all to be turbulent.

Magistrate Greenspan, in his opinion, which can be made available, held that the book was a serious effort to describe the lives of people in a given locality and that, the things written being part of their lives, he could not hold that the book was obscene. Magistrate Greenspan said of the book:

> This is not a book where vice and lewdness are treated as virtues or which would tend to incite lustful desires in the normal mind.

Apparently the Court felt that the book as a whole was not obscene and could not by reason of certain obscene passages be held so to be.

## VII. Re: *Female*

This is a book written for popular consumption and not intended to joy the discriminating mind. The effort of the author is to describe the life, the millieu and the doings of that kind of woman who is the product at the same time of a desire for money, a desire for adventure and passion, and of the age of clandestine drinking.

Maggie Kane, later Margie Kane, is a country girl who early gives evidence of her propensities towards sex. She is endowed with beauty and in her mother she finds adequate antecedent for the life she lives throughout the book with the exception that she is well paid where her mother wasn't. The book consists chiefly of dialogue and the dialogue is in the vernacular of today, so that a great many of the words used are words that can be heard upon the street from the mouths of little children as well as in some of our best social circles where the standards have been let down by the informality of the age. All there is to say about the chief character of the book is that she is an exclusive prostitute who grows rich. The author has no thought anywhere to make any character studies or to show any developments or changes of character. In accord with modern popular taste he has given this prostitute the traditional heart of gold and she reaches the zenith of her career in protecting innocent young girlhood. It is a sentimental story and is written to sell well. It has nothing to recommend to the intellectual mind and undoubtedly has a great deal to recommend it to the prurience of shop-girls, grocers' wives, and probably some stenographers. An occasional word is offensive to general taste, but according to the standards of the law, the book cannot be held to be obscene. Even the amorous passages are not in detail,— the author being in so great a hurry to pile up words and to finish his job. The demimondaine circle he describes might well be the subject for a better hand. I think, therefore, that this volume by what it fails to disclose and by reason of the fact that it is written in a language easily understood by people of the type it is intended to appeal to, is more calculated to incite to lust than almost any of the others mentioned herein.

## VIII. Re: *Flesh*

This author will write on any given subject from anthropology to sexual perversion. This time he has apparently taken several cases out of Krafft-Ebing and made them into so-called short stories. They are sketches of perversions in most instances. There is the story of the killing of a cat by a dog in the presence of a man and a woman and how they are by this sadistic display encouraged to an encounter of their own. There is the story of a wayside rape and murder told in a brutal manner. There is the story and description of a "necking party" between two very young people. The stories are not very well written and often rendered obscure by the injection of supposed witticisms and references over which the author seems to delight. Most of the stories are calculated even in a free and understanding mind to arouse a revulsion of feeling. Partly this comes about because one can see that the author himself so evidently enjoys the stories he is telling. This book of all those mentioned is the most clearly obscene. As far as I can now remember there is not one word in it which per se is obscene or filthy. It is one book the public could very well dispense with, especially because the material is not artistically treated.

. . . .

In *Ulysses* we have to deal with a book highly serious in its purpose but permeated throughout with expressions, allusions, clichés and situations which even in this day and age could not be mentioned in any society pretending to call itself polite, and certainly not in mixed company, no matter how free that mixed company may be.

---

**[Doc. 185]**

November 28, 1933.

Bennett A. Cerf, Esq.,
c/o Random House,
20 East 57th Street,
New York City.

Re: *U.S.* v. *Ulysses*

Dear Cerf:

I am sending you herewith a copy of our supplementary memorandum, which we are this day submitting to Judge Woolsey.

You will recall that he wanted to see the text of *Frankie and Johnnie*. We managed to get hold of it with considerable difficulty.

With kind regards, I am

Yours very truly,

Greenbaum, Wolff & Ernst

AL:JF

---

[Doc. 186]

RANDOM HOUSE
20 E 57 • NEW YORK
The American Selling Agent for the NONESUCH PRESS Limited Editions

November 29, 1933.

Mr. Alexander Lindey,
c/o Greenbaum, Wolff & Ernst,
285 Madison Avenue,
New York City.

Dear Lindey:

Thanks for sending me a copy of your supplementary memorandum to Judge Woolsey. It seems to me that you and Morris have done everything possible in this case. Whether we win or lose, I think, you ought to be congratulated for your efforts in the matter.

Cordially,

Bennett A. Cerf

bac;pk

----

[Doc. 187]

December 1, 1933.

Mr. Bennett A. Cerf,
c/o Random House,
20 East 57th Street,
New York City.

Dear Bennett:

Thanks for your letter of November 29th, particularly your comment as to congratulations even if we lose. I am hoping that your mood on this point will continue even if we are defeated. At this stage of the proceedings you represent a prevalent state of mind of all clients. Call us up the day after the decision.

I do think that we put in our case at full strength.

Yours,

MLE-PG

**[Doc. 188]**

December 1, 1933.

Mr. Paul Léon,
27, Rue Casimir-Périer,
Paris, France.

Dear Mr. Léon:

The *Ulysses* hearing finally took place, and I am enclosing herewith two newspaper clippings which will pretty well tell you the story. The judge has reserved decision, and we hope for early word from him. He was quite evidently still very much in doubt when he left us and it is impossible to predict what his final decision will be. We are hoping for the best.

Cordially yours,

Bennett A. Cerf
Random House

bac;pk

---

**[Doc. 189]**

December 4, 1933.

Harry H. Oshrin, Esq.,
1519 Broadway,
New York City.

Re: *United States* v. *Ulysses*

Dear Mr. Oshrin:

Many thanks for letting us have the script of *Frankie and Johnnie*, and also a copy of the printed case on appeal.

We have submitted *Frankie and Johnnie* to Judge Wollsey, as per his request. We have pointed out to him that the script is not our property and is to be returned. We feel certain that good care will be taken of it. We shall follow it up and see that it gets back to you.

Yours very sincerely,

Greenbaum, Wolff & Ernst

AL:JF

[Doc. 190]

27, Rue Casimir-Périer (VII$^E$)
Littre 88–89
Paris, December the 5-th., 1933.

Bennett Cerf, Esq.,
Random House, Inc.,
20 East 57-th. Street,
New York City.

Dear Mr. Cerf,

I beg to acknowledge receipt of your favour of the 22-nd of November 1933 and I hasten to reply to you in order to dispel whatever doubts you may have entertained as to a possible absence of faith of Mr. Joyce concerning your judgement as to the value of your publication. As I have written to you, the reasons for the non-inclusion in the text of the chart referred to [See Doc. 169.—ED.] are purely literary but they are the more absolute and Mr. Joyce could not let any commercial consideration interfere with them. I have tried to make the commercial aspect clear in a letter I wrote to Mr. Kastor who has probably shown it to you.

In order to prove to you that there is no question of distrust I think that should Mr. Gorman abandon his idea to write Mr. Joyce's biography and return the documents which he obtained from him, I think Mr. Joyce will see no objection to the incorporation of the chart in any publication you might envisage about *Ulysses*, i.e. in any criticism or history of *Ulysses* you may be interested in publishing, except in the text of *Ulysses* itself.

I hope I have made myself clear and dispelled your doubts.
Believe me,

Sincerely yours,

Paul Léon

308

[Doc. 191]

GREENBAUM, WOLFF & ERNST

OFFICE MEMORANDUM

TO:  M.L.E.                    FROM:  A.L.
RE:   *U. S.* v. *Ulysses*      DATE:   December 6, 1933.

I have already called up Atlas who seemed genuinely pleased over the result. [See Doc. 192.—ED.] Don't you think that you ought to drop a line to Coleman or Atlas (or both) in your usual friendly vein?

---

[Doc. 192]

UNITED STATES DISTRICT COURT

Southern District of New York

---

United States of America,

       Libellant

          v.

One Book called *Ulysses*
Random House, Inc.,

       Claimant

OPINION
A. 110-59

On cross-motions for a decree in a libel of confiscation, supplemented by a stipulation—hereinafter described—brought by the United States against the book *Ulysses* by James Joyce, under Section 305 of the Tariff Act of 1930, Title 19 United States Code, Section 1305, on the ground that the book is obscene within the meaning of that Section, and, hence, is not importable into the United States, but is subject to seizure, forfeiture and confiscation and destruction.

United States Attorney—by Samuel C. Coleman, Esq. and Nicholas Atlas, Esq., of counsel—for the United States, in support of motion for a decree of forfeiture, and in opposition to motion for a decree dismissing the libel.

Messrs. Greenbaum, Wolff & Ernst—by Morris L. Ernst, Esq., and Alexander Lindey, Esq., of counsel—attorneys for claimant Random House, Inc., in support of motion for a decree dismissing the libel, and in opposition to motion for a decree of forfeiture.

WOOLSEY, J:

The motion for a decree dismissing the libel herein is granted, and, consequently, of course, the Government's motion for a decree of forfeiture and destruction is denied.

Accordingly a decree dismissing the libel without costs may be entered herein.

I. The practice followed in this case is in accordance with the suggestion made by me in the case of United States v. One Book Entitled *Contraception*, 51 F. (2d) 525, and is as follows:

After issue was joined by the filing of the claimant's answer to the libel for forfeiture against *Ulysses*, a stipulation was made between the United States Attorney's office and the attorneys for the claimant providing:

1. That the book *Ulysses* should be deemed to have been annexed to and to have become part of the libel just as if it had been incorporated in its entirety therein.

2. That the parties waived their right to a trial by jury.

3. That each party agreed to move for decree in its favor.

4. That on such cross-motions the Court might decide all the questions of law and fact involved and render a general finding thereon.

5. That on the decision of such motions the decree of the Court might be entered as if it were a decree after trial.

It seems to me that a procedure of this kind is highly appropriate in libels for the confiscation of books such as this. It is an especially advantageous procedure in the instant case because on account of the length of *Ulysses* and the difficulty of reading it, a jury trial would have been an extremely unsatisfactory, if not an almost impossible, method of dealing with it.

II. I have read *Ulysses* once in its entirety and I have read those passages of which the Government particularly complains several times. In fact, for many weeks, my spare time has been devoted to the consideration of the decision which my duty would require me to make in this matter.

*Ulysses* is not an easy book to read or to understand. But there has been much written about it, and in order properly to approach the consideration of it, it is advisable to read a number of other books which have now become its satellites. The study of *Ulysses* is, therefore, a heavy task.

III. The reputation of *Ulysses* in the literary world, however, warranted my taking such time as was necessary to enable me to satisfy myself as to the intent with which the book was written, for, of course, in any case where a book is claimed to be obscene it must first be determined whether the intent with which it was written was what is called, according to the usual phrase, pornographic—that is, written for the purpose of exploiting obscenity.

If the conclusion is that the book is pornographic that is the end of the inquiry and forfeiture must follow.

But in *Ulysses*, in spite of its unusual frankness, I do not detect anywhere the leer of the sensualist. I hold, therefore, that it is not pornographic.

IV. In writing *Ulysses*, Joyce sought to make a serious experiment in a new, if not wholly novel, literary genre. He takes persons of the lower middle class living in Dublin in 1904 and seeks not only to describe what they did on a certain day early in June of that year as they went about the city bent on their usual occupations, but also to tell what many of them thought about the while.

Joyce has attempted—it seems to me, with astonishing success—to show how the screen of consciousness with its ever-shifting kaleidoscopic impressions carries, as it were on a plastic palimpsest, not only what is in the focus of each man's observation of the actual things about him, but also in a penumbral zone residua of past impressions, some recent and some drawn up by association from the domain of the subconscious. He shows how each of these impressions affects the life and behavior of the character which he is describing.

What he seeks to get is not unlike the result of a double or, if that is possible, a multiple exposure on a cinema film which would give a clear foreground with a background visible but somewhat blurred and out of focus in varying degrees.

To convey by words an effect which obviously lends itself more appropriately to a graphic technique, accounts, it seems to me, for much of the obscurity which meets a reader of *Ulysses*. And it also explains another aspect of the book, which I have further to consider, namely, Joyce's sincerity and his honest effort to show exactly how the minds of his characters operate.

If Joyce did not attempt to be honest in developing the technique which he has adopted in *Ulysses* the result would be psychologically misleading and thus unfaithful to his chosen technique. Such an attitude would be artistically inexcusable.

It is because Joyce has been loyal to his technique and has not funked its necessary implications, but has honestly attempted to tell fully what his characters think about, that he has been the subject of so many attacks and that his purpose has been so often misunderstood and misrepresented. For his attempt sincerely and honestly to realize his objective has required him incidentally to use certain words which are generally considered dirty words and has led at times to what many think is a too poignant preoccupation with sex in the thoughts of his characters.

The words which are criticized as dirty are old Saxon words known to almost all men and, I venture, to many women, and are such words as would be naturally and habitually used, I believe, by the types of folk whose life, physical and mental, Joyce is seeking to describe. In respect of the recurrent emergence of the theme of sex in the minds of his characters, it must always be remembered that his locale was Celtic and his season Spring.

Whether or not one enjoys such a technique as Joyce uses is a matter of taste on which disagreement or argument is futile, but to subject that technique to the standards of some other technique seems to me to be little short of absurd.

Accordingly, I hold that *Ulysses* is a sincere and honest book and I think that the criticisms of it are entirely disposed of by its rationale.

V. Furthermore, *Ulysses* is an amazing tour de force when one considers the success which has been in the main achieved with such a difficult objective as Joyce set for himself. As I have stated, *Ulysses* is not an easy book to read. It is brilliant and dull, intelligible and obscure by turns. In many places it seems to me to be disgusting, but although it contains, as I have mentioned above, many words usually considered dirty, I have not found anything that I consider to be dirt for dirt's sake. Each word of the book contributes like a bit of mosaic to the detail of the picture which Joyce is seeking to construct for his readers.

If one does not wish to associate with such folk as Joyce describes, that is one's own choice. In order to avoid indirect contact with them one may not wish to read *Ulysses*; that is quite understandable. But when such a real artist in words, as Joyce undoubtedly is, seeks to draw a true picture of the lower middle class in a European city, ought it to be impossible for the American public legally to see that picture?

To answer this question it is not sufficient merely to find, as I have found above, that Joyce did not write *Ulysses* with what is commonly called pornographic intent; I must endeavor to apply a more objective standard to his book in order to determine its effect in the result, irrespective of the intent with which it was written.

VI. The statute under which the Libel is filed only denounces, in so far as we are here concerned, the importation into the United States from any foreign country of "any obscene book." Section 305 of the Tariff Act of 1930, Title 19 United States Code, Section 1305. It does not marshal against books the spectrum of condemnatory adjectives found, commonly, in laws dealing with matters of this kind. I am, therefore, only required to determine whether *Ulysses* is obscene within the legal definition of that word.

The meaning of the word *obscene* as legally defined by the Courts is: tending to stir the sex impulses or to lead to sexually impure and lustful thoughts. Dunlop v. United States, 165 U. S. 486, 501; United States v. One Book Entitled *Married Love*, 48 F. (2d) 821; United States v. One Book Entitled *Contraception*, 51 F. (2d) 525, 528; and compare Dysart v. United States, 272 U. S. 655, 657; Swearingen v. United States, 161 U. S. 446, 450; United States v. Dennett, 39 F. (2d) 564, 568 (C.C.A.2); People v. Wendling, 258 N. Y. 451, 453.

Whether a particular book would tend to excite such impulses and thoughts must be tested by the Court's opinion as to its effect on a person with average sex instincts—what the French would call *l'homme moyen sensuel*—who plays, in this branch of legal inquiry, the same role of hypothetical reagent as does the "reasonable man" in the law of torts and "the man learned in the art" on questions of invention in patent law.

The risk involved in the use of such a reagent arises from the inherent tendency of the trier of facts, however fair he may intend to be, to make his reagent too much subservient to his own idiosyncrasies. Here, I have attempted to avoid this, if possible, and to make my reagent herein more objective than he might otherwise be, by adopting the following course:

After I had made my decision in regard to the aspect of *Ulysses* now under consideration, I checked my impressions with two friends of mine who in my opinion answered to the above stated requirement for my reagent.

These literary assessors—as I might properly describe them—were called on separately, and neither knew that I was consulting the other. They are men whose opinion on literature and on life I value most highly. They had both read *Ulysses*, and, of course, were wholly unconnected with this cause.

Without letting either of my assessors know what my decision was, I gave to each of them the legal definition of obscene and asked each whether in his opinion *Ulysses* was obscene within that definition.

I was interested to find that they both agreed with my opinion: that reading *Ulysses* in its entirety, as a book must be read on such a test as this, did not tend to excite sexual impulses or lustful thoughts but that its net effect on them was only that of a somewhat tragic and very powerful commentary on the inner lives of men and women.

It is only with the normal person that the law is concerned. Such a test as I have described, therefore, is the only proper test of obscenity in the case of a book like *Ulysses* which is a sincere and serious attempt to devise a new literary method for the observation and description of mankind.

I am quite aware that owing to some of its scenes *Ulysses* is a rather strong draught to ask some sensitive, though normal, persons to take. But my considered opinion, after long reflection, is that whilst in many places the effect of *Ulysses* on the reader undoubtedly is somewhat emetic, nowhere does it tend to be an aphrodisiac.

*Ulysses* may, therefore, be admitted into the United States.

December 6, 1933.

John M. Woolsey
United States District Judge

[Doc. 193]

NA42 16 CABLE VIA FRENCH

PARIS 1625 DEC 7 1933

LC CERF

20 EAST 57 NEW YORK NY

THANKS CONGRATULATIONS TO YOU COLLEAGUES

COUNSEL SUCCESSFUL CASE

JAMES JOYCE

1239 P

---

[Doc. 194]

December 7, 1933.

Mr. Paul Léon,
27, Rue Casimir-Périer,
Paris, France.

Dear Mr. Léon:

As I cabled you yesterday, the final decision has come through on *Ulysses*, and it could not possibly be more sweepingly favorable. I am enclosing herewith a complete copy of the decision. We are planning to publish *Ulysses* immediately, and hope to have the book on sale throughout the United States by the 25th of January, 1934.

Sincerely yours,

Bennett A. Cerf
Random House

bac;pk

**[Doc. 195]**

27, Rue Casimir-Périer (VII$^E$)
Littre 88–89
Paris, December the 7-th., 1933.

Bennett Cerf, Esq.,
Random House, Inc.,
20 East 57-th. Street,
New York.

Dear Mr. Cerf,

In great haste in order to catch the outgoing boat and thank you for your cable containing the very good news as well as to send you Mr. Joyce's congratulations and thanks to all concerned with the success of the *Ulysses* case.

Let me add my own congratulations on the success of the first stage of your courageous venture which I am sure will be crowned by a further success in the issue and sale of your edition.

Sincerely yours,

Paul Léon

---

**[Doc. 196]**

December 7, 1933.

Random House, Inc.,
20 East 57th Street,
New York City.

Re: *United States* v. *Ulysses*

Gentlemen:

We are sending you herewith:

1. 100 mimeographed copies of Judge Woolsey's opinion.

2. Copy of the statement which Mr. Ernst gave to the press. [See Doc. 201.—ED.]

3. A list of the people who gave you testimonials for presentation to the court.

As you must have noticed from the press this morning, the material went out last night to all the morning papers. We are assuming that you are taking care of the afternoon papers.

We think it will be an act of courtesy for you to send a copy of the opinion to every one of the persons who gave us testimonials. You ought to thank them for their assistance. Even with Judge Woolsey's salutary decision it is within the realm of possibility that you may need them again.

Yours very truly,

Greenbaum, Wolff & Ernst

AL:JF

---

[Doc. 197]

GREENBAUM, WOLFF & ERNST

OFFICE MEMORANDUM

TO: Joe        FROM: A.L.
RE: *United States* v. *Ulysses*        DATE: December 7, 1933.

Will you please prepare and enter up a decree in accordance with Judge Woolsey's opinion. Make sure that we get the copy of *Ulysses* which was sent in from Europe.

[The following lines are a handwritten notation of uncertain origin.—ED.]

(1) If decree is signed, confirm copy
(2) See that it is entered
(3) Get Certified copy (of confirmed copy)
(4) How do we get the book?
—Serve certified copy to Collector of Customs, Customs House

**[Doc. 198]**

December 7, 1933.

Samuel Coleman, Esq.,
U.S. Attorney's Office,
Old Post Office Building,
New York City.

Dear Sam:

Please include Atlas in this memorandum. I only want to say that I hope you will stay in the District Attorney's Office for life, so that in the future we can meet in similar pleasant matters. This is a case that no person won or lost. The book spoke for itself.

Yours,

[Morris Ernst]

---

**[Doc. 199]**

December 7, 1933.

Mr. Ernst:

Mr. Lindey said that altho' he spoke to you about the foreword, he would like you to please read this memo [See Doc. 200.—ED.] as it contains other information, besides the request for the foreword.

---

**[Doc. 200]**

### GREENBAUM, WOLFF & ERNST

### OFFICE MEMORANDUM

TO:  M.L.E.             FROM:  A.L.
RE:  *United States* v. *Ulysses*     DATE:  December 7, 1933.

### VERY IMPORTANT

Bennett Cerf is rushing to press with *Ulysses*. He would like to have a foreword by you. I think it would be swell if you could give him a couple hundred words. It might be quite amusing for you to place side by side the opinion of Judge Fischer of the Customs Court (Treasury Department opinion 42907, in the case of Heymoolen, 2 U.S.) and Judge Woolsey's opinion.

In the *Heymoolen* case, 11 books were ordered excluded. One of them was *Ulysses*. Judge Fischer said:

> Only a casual glance through the books in evidence is sufficient to satisfy us that they are filled with obscenity of the rottenest and vilest characters.

The *Heymoolen* case arose under the Tariff Act, but this makes no difference.

If you are too busy to write the foreword let me know what you would like to say and I will write it out for you. As a matter of fact I don't see why we cannot use your so-called statement to the press [See Doc. 201.—ED.] with some slight changes. I hand you a copy of it herewith.

I have had several pleasant conversations with Bennett on miscellaneous things. I told him, among other things, to send a nice letter to Bowerman, the Washington Librarian, and to Pertzoff, the Harvard student, who gave us such handsome assistance. I urged him to send a gift of books to Pertzoff.

Bennett Cerf found out the names of the two persons whom Judge Woolsey consulted on *Ulysses*. The names are Henry Seidel Canby and Charles E. Merrill, Jr.

---

**[Doc. 201]**
[This is an enclosure to Docs. 196 and 200.—ED.]

Statement of Morris L. Ernst, of the Firm of
Greenbaum, Wolff & Ernst,
Upon the Handing Down of Judge Woolsey's
Opinion in the *Ulysses* Case

Judge Woolsey's decision exonerating *Ulysses* under the Customs Law has cleared the last important book suppressed by the censors as obscene. In the past men have gone to jail for circulating *Ulysses*. Joyce's masterpiece may now freely enter this country.

But the decision means more than that a great prose work has been made available for the general reading public. It means that squeamishness and circumlocution have been banished from literature. It means that authors, writing with integrity concerning common aspects of daily life, need no longer seek refuge in euphemisms. It means the good old Anglo-Saxon words known to every child may now be read by adults.

Judge Woolsey says that in the course of his consideration of *Ulysses* he checked his impressions with two friends of his. He states that he turned to these men as "literary assessors" because he valued their opinions on literature and life. This procedure on the Judge's part is a confirmation of the soundness and validity of the method used by Modern Library, who will publish *Ulysses* here, in presenting its case to the Court. Modern Library, too, relied on the reactions of men whose opinions of "literature and life" were worthy of consideration, and presented to Judge Woolsey an imposing array of "literary assessors"—authors, publishers, critics, publicists, educators, etc.—all of whom acclaimed the book as a significant literary achievement. In addition, Modern Library presented a map of the United States showing the location of libraries, public institutions and colleges which already had copies of *Ulysses* on their shelves, or desired to put the book there. In this case the legal result has been completely in accord with and has fully vindicated enlightened public opinion.

The first week of December 1933 will go down in history for two repeals, that of Prohibition and that of squeamishness in literature. We may now imbibe freely of the contents of bottles and forthright books. It may well be that in the future the repeal of the sex taboo in letters, inherent in Judge Woolsey's decision, will prove to be of the greater importance. Perhaps the intolerance which closed our breweries was the intolerance which decreed that basic human functions had to be treated in books in a furtive, leering, hypocritical manner.

Happily, both of these have now been repudiated. The *Ulysses* case is the culmination of a long and determined struggle against the literary censor dating back to the victory over the New York Vice Society in the famous *Mademoiselle de Maupin* case in 1922. Coming as it does in logical sequence after *The Well of Loneliness* case, the *Dennett* case, the cases involving Dr. Stopes' books, the *Casanova's Homecoming* case, the *Frankie and Johnnie* case, and the *God's Little Acre* case, all of which have served to liberalize the law of obscenity and to thrust back the narrow frontiers fixed by prudery, the victory of *Ulysses* is a fitting climax to the salutary forward march of our courts.

---

[Doc. 202]

RANDOM HOUSE
20 E 57 • NEW YORK
The American Selling Agent for the NONESUCH PRESS Limited Editions

December 7, 1933.

Mr. Morris L. Ernst,
285 Madison Avenue,
New York City.

Dear Morris

I simply would like to go on record to the effect that we are delighted with the successful conclusion to the *Ulysses* case, and deeply impressed with the way the matter was handled both by you and Alexander Lindey.

Cordially,

Bennett

bac;pk

---

[Doc. 203]

*New York American*
December 7, 1933

**Ulysses Gets Right of Entry**

---

In a classical literary opinion, Federal Judge Woolsey held yesterday that James Joyce's *Ulysses* is not pornographic and is therefore admissible to this country. He ordered customs officials, who had impounded a copy of the book sent from England, to turn it over to Random House, Inc.

After studying the book for several weeks. Judge Woolsey said he did not detect anywhere the "leer of the sensualist." He added:

"The words which are criticized as dirty are old Saxon words known to almost all men and, I venture, to many women, and are such words as would be naturally and habitually used, I believe, by the types of folk whose life, physical and mental, Joyce is seeking to describe.

"In respect to the recurrent emergence of the theme of sex in the minds of his characters, it must always be remembered that his locale was Celtic and his season Spring."

[Doc. 204]

*New York Herald-Tribune*
December 7, 1933

*Ulysses* Ban Is Removed by Federal Court

---

Joyce's Book Not Obscene, Is a Sincere Work of Art,
Declares Judge Woolsey

---

Decision Called Epochal

---

Publishers Plan to Issue Unabridged Edition Soon

---

James Joyce's *Ulysses*, highly praised by some and much abused by others, but generally regarded as a modern classic, got a clean bill of health and was admitted to the United States yesterday by Federal Judge John Munro Woolsey in a decision which is expected to have far-reaching effect in judicial definition of the word *obscene*.

Judge Woolsey has studied the book since August and said yesterday that he had read it once in its entirety and had read several passages, of which the government complained in its suit to confiscate and destroy the book, several times. He found that while it might be "somewhat emetic" to some readers, "nowhere does it tend to be an aphrodisiac."

*Ulysses* was brought into court last July after it had been circulated through bootleg channels in America for eleven years. Bennett Cerf, head of Random House, publishers, and The Modern Library, who wanted to publish the book here, ordered from abroad an unexpurgated copy which was seized by customs agents and turned over to the United States Attorney's office for prosecution and prohibited from entry on the ground that it was "immoral and obscene."

Judge Woolsey decided that the book was not obscene but that it was a sincere work of art, accomplishing, "with astonishing success," a venture into a new literary genre.

### "Old Saxon Words" Defended

"The words which are criticized as dirty," Judge Woolsey wrote, "are old Saxon words known to almost all men and, I venture, to many women, and are such words as would be naturally and habitually used, I believe, by the types of folk whose life, physical and mental, Joyce is seeking to describe. In respect of the recurrent emergence of the theme of sex in the minds of his characters, it must always be remembered that that his locale was Celtic and his season Spring."

Judge Woolsey admitted that the book was, in parts, obscure and difficult reading, but held that it was a "sincere and honest book" and "an amazing tour de force when one considers the success which has been in the main achieved with such a difficult objective as Joyce set for himself."

The case was presented in behalf of the government by Samuel C. Coleman, Assistant United States Attorney in charge of the civil division, who said last night that he welcomed the decision and would recommend to the United States Attorney and to the Attorney General that no appeal be taken from the decision of Judge Woolsey. He said that he regarded the decision as fair to the publishers and that neither he nor George Z. Medalie, who was United States Attorney when the case was opened, had any desire to be considered as "persecuting censors."

### Coleman Agrees With Court

"I feel just as Judge Woolsey does about the book." Mr. Coleman said. "The result is, I think, a wholesome one. I welcome the decision and am satisfied with it. The reason for the action was that there had been so much adverse criticism of the book and such adulation of it, on the other hand, that the government felt that there should be an authoritative ruling at this time as to whether or not the book was 'obscene'."

Morris L. Ernst, counsel for Random House, hailed the decision as more important, perhaps, than Prohibition repeal which came the day before.

"The first week of December, 1933," he said, "will go down in history for two repeals, that of Prohibition and that of squeamishness in literature. We may now imbibe freely of the contents of bottles and forthright books. It may well be that in the future the repeal of the sex taboo in letters, inherent in Judge Woolsey's decision, will prove to be of the greater importance.

"The victory of *Ulysses* is a fitting climax to the salutary forward march of our courts."

Mr. Cerf said that an unabridged edition of *Ulysses* would be published at "all possible speed" by Random House. "From the standpoint of literature and freedom of speech," he said, "we consider this one of the most important decisions ever rendered."

### Judge Woolsey's Decision

Judge Woolsey's decision follows in part:

"I have read *Ulysses* once in its entirety and I have read those passages of which the Government particularly complains several times. In fact, for many weeks, my spare time has been devoted to the consideration of the decision which my duty would require me to make in this matter.

"*Ulysses* is not an easy book to read or to understand. But there has been much written about it, and in order properly to approach the consideration of it, it is advisable to read a number of other books which have now become its satellites. The study of *Ulysses* is, therefore, a heavy task.

"The reputation of *Ulysses* in the literary world, however, warranted my taking such time as was necessary to enable me to satisfy myself as to the intent with which the book was written, for, of course, in any case where a book is claimed to be obscene it must first be determined whether the intent with which it was written was what is called, according to the usual phrase, pornographic, that is, written for the purpose of exploiting obscenity.

"If the conclusion is that the book is pornographic that is the end of the inquiry and forfeiture must follow."

### No "Leer of the Sensualist"

"But in *Ulysses*, in spite of its unusual frankness, I do not detect anywhere the leer of the sensualist. I hold, therefore, that it is not pornographic.

"In writing *Ulysses*, Joyce sought to make a serious experiment in a new, if not wholly novel, literary genre. He takes persons of the lower middle class living in Dublin in 1904, and seeks not only to describe what they did on a certain day early in June of that year as they went about the city bent on their usual occupations, but also to tell what many of them thought about the while.

"Joyce has attempted—it seems to me, with astonishing success—to show how the screen of consciousness with its ever-shifting kaleidoscopic impressions carries, as it were on a plastic palimpsest, not only what is in the focus of each man's observation of the actual things about him, but also in a penumbral zone residua of past impressions, some recent and some drawn up by association from the domain of the subconscious. He shows how each of these impressions affects the life and behavior of the character which he is describing.

"What he seeks to get is not unlike the result of a double or, if that is possible, a multiple exposure on a cinema film which would give a clear foreground with a background visible but somewhat blurred and out of focus in varying degrees."

### Obscurity Accounted For

"To convey by words an effect which obviously lends itself more appropriately to a graphic technique, accounts, it seems to me, for much of the obscurity which meets a reader of *Ulysses*. And it also explains another aspect of the book which I have further to consider, namely, Joyce's sincerity and his honest effort to show exactly how the minds of his characters operate.

"If Joyce did not attempt to be honest in developing the technique which he has adopted in *Ulysses* the result would be psychologically misleading and thus unfaithful to his chosen technique. Such an attitude would be artistically inexcusable.

"It is because Joyce has been loyal to his technique and has not funked its necessary implications, but has honestly attempted to tell fully what his characters think about, that he has been the subject of so many attacks and that his purpose has been so often misunderstood and misrepresented. For his attempt sincerely and honestly to realize his objective has required him incidently to use certain words which are generally considered dirty words and has led at times to what many think is a too poignant preoccupation with sex in the thoughts of his characters."

### Enjoyment Matter of Taste

"Whether or not one enjoys such a technique as Joyce uses is a matter of taste on which disagreement or argument is futile, but to subject that technique to the standards of some other technique seems to me to be little short of absurd.

"Accordingly, I hold that *Ulysses* is a sincere and honest book and I think that the criticisms of it are entirely disposed of by its rationale.

"Furthermore, *Ulysses* is an amazing tour de force when one considers the success which has been in the main achieved with such a difficult objective as Joyce set for himself. As I have stated, *Ulysses* is not an easy book to read; it is brilliant and dull, intelligible and obscure by turns. In many places it seems to me to be disgusting, but although it contains, as I have mentioned above, many words usually considered dirty, I have not found anything that I consider to be dirt for dirt's sake. Each word of the book contributes like a bit of mosaic to the detail of the picture which Joyce is seeking to construct for his readers.

"If one does not wish to associate with such folk as Joyce describes, that is one's own choice. In order to avoid indirect contact with them one may not wish to read *Ulysses*; that is quite understandable. But when such a real artist in words, as Joyce undoubtedly is, seeks to draw a true picture of the lower middle class in a European city, ought it to be impossible for the American public legally to see that picture?

"To answer this question it is not sufficient merely to find, as I have found above, that Joyce did not write *Ulysses* with what is commonly called pornographic intent. I must endeavor to apply a more objective standard to his book in order to determine its effect in the result irrespective of the intent with which it was written.

"The statute under which the libel is filed only denounces in so far as we are here concerned, the importation into the United States from any foreign country of 'any obscene book.' Section 305 of the Tariff Act of 1930, Title 19 United States Code, Section 1305. It does not marshal against books the spectrum of condemnatory adjectives found, commonly, in laws dealing with matters of this kind. I am, therefore, only required to determine whether *Ulysses* is obscene within the legal definition of that word."

## Word *Obscene* Defined

"The meaning of the word *obscene* as legally defined by the courts is: tending to stir the sex impulses or to lead to sexually impure, and lustful thoughts. Dunlop v. United States, 165 U. S. 486, 501; United States v. One Book Entitled *Married Love*, 48 F. (2d) 821, 824; United States v. One Book Entitled *Contraception*, 51 F. (2d) 525, 528; and compare Dysart v. United States, 272 U.S. 655, 657; Swearingen v. United States, 161 U.S. 446, 450; United States v. Dennett, 39 F.(2d) 564, 568 (C.C.A.2); People v. Wendling, 258 N.Y. 451, 453.

"Whether a particular book would tend to excite such impulses and thoughts must be tested by the court's opinion as to its effects on a person with average sex instincts—what the French would call *l'homme moyen sensuel*—who plays, in this branch of legal inquiry, the same role of hypothetical reagent as does the 'reasonable man' in the law of torts and 'the man learned in the art' on questions of invention in patent law.

"The risk involved in the use of such a reagent arises from the inherent tendency of the trier of facts however fair he may intend to be, to make his reagent too much subservient to his own idiosyncrasies. Here I have attempted to avoid this, if possible, and to make my reagent herein more objective than he might otherwise be, by adopting the following course."

## Check-up With Friends

"After I had made my decision in regard to the aspect of *Ulysses* now under consideration I checked my impressions with two friends of mine who in my opinion answered to the above stated requirement for my reagent.

"These literary assessors—as I might properly describe them—were called on separately, and neither knew that I was consulting the other. They are men whose opinion on literature and on life I value most highly. They had both read *Ulysses* and, of course, were wholly unconnected with this case.

"Without letting either of my assessors know what my decision was, I gave to each of them the legal definition of *obscene* and asked each whether in his opinion *Ulysses* was obscene within that definition.

"I was interested to find that they both agreed with my opinion, that reading *Ulysses* in its entirety, as a book must be read on such a test as this, did not tend to excite sexual impulses or lustful thoughts but that its net effect on them was only that of a somewhat tragic and very powerful commentary on the inner lives of men and women.

"It is only with the normal person that the law is concerned. Such a test as I have described, therefore, is the only proper test of obscenity in the case of a book like *Ulysses* which is a sincere and serious attempt to devise a new literary method for the observation and description of mankind.

"I am quite aware that owing to some of its scenes *Ulysses* is a rather strong draught to ask some sensitive, though normal, persons to take. But my considered opinion, after long reflection, is that while in many places the effect of *Ulysses* on the reader undoubtedly is somewhat emetic, nowhere does it tend to be an aphrodisiac.

"*Ulysses* may, therefore, be admitted into the United States."

John M. Woolsey,

United States District Judge

December 6, 1933.

---

[Doc. 205]

*New York Times*
December 7, 1933

**Court Lifts Ban on *Ulysses* Here**

---

**Woolsey Holds Joyce Novel is Not Obscene—
He Finds It a Work of Literary Merit**

---

**Ignores Single Passages**

---

**His Judging of Volume as a Whole,
Not in Isolated Parts, Establishes a Precedent**

---

James Joyce's *Ulysses*, a novel which has been banned from the United States by customs censors on the ground that it might cause American readers to harbor "impure and lustful thoughts," found a champion yesterday in the United States District Court.

Federal Judge John M. Woolsey, after devoting almost a month of his time to reading the book, ruled in an opinion which he filed in court that *Ulysses* not only was not obscene in a legal sense, but that it was a work of literary merit.

Under the ruling the book will be published here in unexpurgated form on Jan. 20 by Random House. It will contain an introduction expecially written for it by Joyce and also the full decision of Judge Woolsey, which was considered here to establish a precedent in an interpretation of "obscenity."

Judge Woolsey held in brief that single passages could not be isolated from a literary work in determining whether or not the work as a whole was pornographic.

He defended Joyce's purpose in writing *Ulysses* and suggested that attacks against the book had been occasioned because "Joyce has been loyal to his technique and has not funked its necessary implications."

The court, expressing its own reaction to a reading of the book, found it to be "brilliant" and at the same time "dull." It had not been "easy to read," he noted, nor had it been clear in all places, though in other places it was thoroughly intelligible.

### No "Dirt for Dirt's Sake"

"In many places," Judge Woolsey wrote, "it seems to me to be disgusting," but nothing, he added, had been included in it as "dirt for dirt's sake."

Before announcing his decision Judge Woolsey noted that he had read the whole book and had given special attention to passages singled out by the government as objectionable.

"I am quite aware," he concluded, "that owing to some of its scenes *Ulysses* is a rather strong draught to ask some sensitive, though normal, persons to take. But my considered opinion, after long reflection, is that whilst in many places the effect of *Ulysses* on the reader undoubtedly is somewhat emetic, nowhere does it tend to be an aphrodisiac.

"*Ulysses* may, therefore, be admitted into the United States."

Judge Woolsey directed that a copy of the book which the customs censors had seized as it entered this port from Europe be surrendered to Random House, Inc., the assignee. Samuel C. Coleman, Assistant United States Attorney, who brought the matter to the court's attention, said that the decision, in his opinion, was a masterpiece and "thoroughly wholesome."

Judge Woolsey began his opinion by saying that he believed *Ulysses* to be "a sincere and serious attempt to devise a new literary method for the observation and description of mankind."

He explained that in arriving at his conclusions he had also weighed the merits of other books of the same school. He described these books as "satellites of *Ulysses*."

## Holds Purpose Not Obscene

The principal question he had to solve, the court suggested, was whether or not Joyce's purpose in writing the book had been pornographic.

"In spite of its unusual frankness," he wrote, "I do not detect anywhere the leer of the sensualist. I hold, therefore, that it is not pornographic.

"In writing *Ulysses* Joyce sought to make a serious experiment in a new if not wholly novel literary genre.

"Joyce has attempted—it seems to me, with astonishing success—to show how the screen of consciousness with its ever-shifting kaleidoscopic impressions carries, as it were on a plastic palimpsest, not only what is in the focus of each man's observation of the actual things about him, but also in a penumbral zone residua of past impressions, some recent and some drawn up by association from the domain of the subconscious.

"The words which are criticized as dirty are old Saxon words known to almost all men, and, I venture, to many women, and are such words as would be naturally and habitually used, I believe, by the types of folk whose life, physical and mental, Joyce is seeking to describe.

"If one does not wish to associate with such folks as Joyce describes, that is one's own choice."

---

**[Doc. 206]**

December 8, 1933.

Mr. Bennett Cerf,
20 East 57th Street,
New York City.

Dear Bennett:

Thanks for your letter of the 7th. Lindey certainly did a swell job.

Yours,

[Morris Ernst]

---

[Doc. 207]

December 8, 1933.

H. C. Stewart, Esq.,
Collector of Customs,
Customs House,
New York City.

Re: United States v. Ulysses

Dear Sir:

We are sending you herewith a copy of Judge Woolsey's opinion in the above matter.

Your office has indicated to us on a number of occasions that it has not been your intention to enforce the censorship provisions of the Tariff Act beyond the degree necessitated by court decisions. As a result, you will doubtless be glad to note the sane and liberal interpretation of the Tariff Act inherent in Judge Woolsey's opinion, and will be guided by it in the future in connection with matters referred to you.

Sincerely yours,<br>Greenbaum, Wolff & Ernst

AL:JF

---

[Doc. 208]

December 8, 1933.

B. N. Handler, Esq.
Office of the Collector,
Customs House,
New York City.

Re: United States v. Ulysses

Dear Mr. Handler:

I am sending you herewith a copy of Judge Woolsey's opinion in the above matter. I think you will be as gratified over the result as we have been.

Sincerely yours,<br>Greenbaum, Wolff & Ernst

AL:JF

**[Doc. 209]**

December 8, 1933.

Harry H. Oshrin, Esq.,
1619 Broadway,
New York City.

Re: *United States* v. *Ulysses*

Dear Mr. Oshrin:

We are returning to you herewith the script of *Frankie and Johnnie* which you were good enough to let us have. No doubt by this time you know the happy result.

We wish to express our appreciation of your courtesy in enabling us to present the script to Judge Woolsey.

Yours very truly,

Greenbaum, Wolff & Ernst

AL: JF

---

**[Doc. 210]**

GREENBAUM, WOLFF & ERNST

## OFFICE MEMORANDUM

TO:  A. Lindey          FROM:  M.L.E.
RE:                     DATE:  December 8, 1933.

Can you call up Lewis Gannett soon, and give him the following information, if possible. Don't spend too much time on it.

1. Date of *Mademoiselle de Maupin*.

2. Date when *Ulysses* was originally barred in respect to *Little Review*, or Margaret Anderson.

3. Some facts in regard to the Customs case against *Ulysses*.

NOTE: Before you give him this information, can you see me for a minute?

[Doc. 211]

*New York Herald-Tribune*
December 9, 1933

## BOOKS AND THINGS
### by Lewis Gannett

Ezra Pound sent Margaret Anderson, editor of *The Little Review*, the manuscript of James Joyce's *Ulysses* back in 1918, and Miss Anderson, spotting a good thing, printed the first installment in the issue for March, 1918. The post office called it filthy and seized and burned all copies that were put into the mails.

### When *Ulysses* Was Banned

Margaret Anderson continued publishing *Ulysses*, and sent out her magazine by express. In 1920 John S. Sumner, of the Society for the Prevention of Vice, had her indicted, and in 1921 she and her co-editor, Jane Heap, were found guilty of publishing indecent matter by the Court of General Sessions, were fined $50 each and fingerprinted as criminals.

*Ulysses* was printed as a book in Paris. It was translated into French, German, Spanish and Japanese. It was discussed and imitated all over the world. Copies were bootlegged into the United States; college professors told their students about it, though the boys could not buy copies. (Some thirty thousand copies were sold in Paris, probably most of them to American tourists.) And whenever the customs officials or the postal authorities caught copies headed into pure America they seized them. As late as 1928 a United States judge gave himself an idiotic immortality by declaring that "only a casual glance" was sufficient to satisfy him that the book was "filled with obscenity of the rottenest and vilest character."

### Comment by Judge Woolsey

Now, in 1933, United States Judge John M. Woolsey has ruled that *Ulysses* is not pornographic and may be admitted into the United States, in a decision which read like an exceptionally intelligent and enthusiastic book review. He called *Ulysses* "a sincere and honest book," "an amazing tour de force," "a true picture of the lower middle class in a European city," "a serious experiment in a new literary genre" and "a tragic and very powerful commentary of the inner lives of men and women." Parts of it were "disgusting," he said; and it included words which, though familiar to all men and many women, are generally regarded as "dirty"; but they were essential parts of the mosaic whole, and Joyce would have been artistically dishonest and "psychologically misleading" had he left them out.

So, on January 25, 1934, Random House will publish the first American edition of *Ulysses*—10,000 copies in the edition—with a new foreword by James Joyce and the text of Judge Woolsey's great decision.

## The Censors, Only Yesterday

Censorship was in its prime in the United States in 1920. Dreiser's *The Genius* had been suppressed in 1916; it was not to reappear until 1923. Cabell's *Jurgen* was declared "indecent" in January, 1920, and was not to be given a clean bill of health until July 1922. *Madeleine* had just been cleared by the Appellate Division; but most of the publishers were cowed. Horace Liveright and Thomas Seltzer fought bravely as did McBride, for *Jurgen*, but many of the others withdrew books attacked by the vice society. Among others, Floyd Dell's innocuous *Janet March* was withdrawn. And even Mr. Seltzer, after a long fight for Schnitzler's *Casanova's Homecoming*, D. H. Lawrence's *Women in Love* and *A Young Girl's Diary*, agreed in the face of strong political pressure, not to reprint those books after he had sold out his current editions (a strange official morality which held that one edition of a book was inoffensive but a second would corrupt!)

## Morris Ernst, Crusader Against Censorship

The tide really turned about the time that Morris Ernst, attorney, who has fought most of the historic censorship cases of the last five years (he was counsel for Random House in the *Ulysses* case), published his *To the Pure . . . A Study of Obscenity and the Censor* (Viking Press, 1928; William Seagle, coauthor). Mr. Ernst had lost a censorship case the previous year. John Herrman's *What Happens* would seem mild in 1933, but it included a word which shocked the 1927 jury. (In those days *The Evening Post* regularly substituted "blood lust" for what it deemed the indecent word "sadism"; and a court officially ruled that it was obscene to use the word "Lesbianism" in a newspaper.) That defeat aroused a crusading zeal in Morris Ernst. He dug into the history of censorship, published his books exposing its absurdities and contradictions, and emerged as the logical and fearless defender of frank, honest literature.

In 1929, with Mr. Ernst as defending counsel in both cases, Radclyffe Hall's *The Well of Loneliness* was cleared of the charge of obscenity in General Sessions and Magistrate Gottlieb gave *Casanova's Homecoming* a clean-cut indorsement. In 1930 the Circuit Court of Appeals reversed an adverse verdict of a lower court on Mary Ware Dennett's "The Sex Side of Life," and Judge Woolsey, in the first of three decisions which have become historic, ruled in favor of Dr. Marie Stopes's *Married Love*. Mr. Ernst was counsel in both cases. In 1931 Dr. Stopes's *Contraception* was declared admissible by Judge Woolsey, the Chinese classic *Hsi Men Ching* was cleared by Magistrate Brodsky, Clement Wood's *Flesh* by Magistrate Harris and Octave Mirbeau's *Celestine* by Magistrate Dodge, now District Attorney-elect—all with Mr. Ernst defending them. Last year Louis Charles Royer's *Let's Go Naked* successfully survived attack by the Comstockites, and this year a victory for Erskine Caldwell's *God's Little Acre* preceded the *Ulysses* case, and Schnitzler's *Reigen*, three years ago ruled obscene by part of the Court of

Appeals, was republished, in the Modern Library, without attack. An amazing series of amazing victories for Morris Ernst. The *Ulysses* decision is the culmination of a long struggle for sanity. Judge Woolsey's decision is not necessarily binding on the state courts of this and still less of other states, nor are the little censors of the Post Office Department officially bound by it. But the large scope, the careful wording and thinking of Judge Woolsey's previous decisions have had their effect on other courts, and the *Ulysses* decision is sure to prove a monument. Perhaps it may even encourage Secretary Morgenthau to economize by dropping some of the meddlesome customs officials who have been paid by Uncle Sam to hunt for erotic passages in incoming books.

### Boldness Becomes Boring

Some sincere people deplore the new freedom of literature. I think time will prove that the Comstock kind of people are responsible for the attention paid to erotic passages. Censorship creates titillation. Familiarity breeds boredom, with good things and bad. People who see nude women bathing in the open river in Moscow, in Japan or in Scandinavia are not excited by the sight, only those whose eyes have been sealed. A merely stockingless bathing beauty once seemed dangerously provocative; but today. . . . Most of us, in our college days, waded through a good many reams of Balzac and Boccaccio hunting for the passages which had led censors to seek to suppress them. I doubt if we are the worse for it; and we soon became bored.

---

[Doc. 212]

*New York World-Telegram*
December 9, 1933

### It Seems to Me
### by Heywood Broun

Morris L. Ernst, the young lawyer who beat a pathway for *Ulysses* to come back to this country, says that the decision of Judge Woolsey constitutes a repeal of squeamishness. In the eyes of Mr. Ernst this is rather more important than the repeal of prohibition.

Perhaps there is something too impetuous in this attitude of Mr. Ernst. My guess would be that fifty years from now he will still find himself engaged in the practice of defending some printed words from the fear of those inclined to ban them. But, naturally, I have not the slightest hesitation in agreeing that the present court victory marks a new high in judicial liberalism.

## The Principle of the Thing

It is merely the principle of the matter which interests me. I can't read *Ulysses*. I can't even get through page—whatever the number is. I mean the one to which you are referred by Joyce enthusiasts about the time you complain, "But when does the blame thing begin to get dirty?"

Wiser men and women have assured me that the novel belongs to the ages, and no doubt they are right. I will grant, of course, that it is a serious work of art, even though it bores me. Possibly I should have written "and therefore" in place of "even though."

I am pleased by the decision chiefly because it is a step toward the liberation of certain words which are highly essential if the gusto of speech is ever to be accurately represented on the printed page. At the present time it is quite impossible to give anything like faithful color to stories about stevedores, stokers, prizefighters, newspaper columnists or children's hour broadcasters.

## Noble in Purpose

Somebody may object that the words I am thinking about are evil in intent and ugly in sound. I hold no brief for—well, any of the Anglo-Saxon brevities. I didn't invent any of these words, and I use very few of them since I swore off playing poker.

But, as far as intention goes, I have never been able to understand why a long, fancy word should be accepted as in some ways cleaner than a short and simple one. As for sound, one man's mate may be another man's dash-dash-dash-blinkety-blinkety-b. It all depends upon what sounds you happen to like.

The question of mere verbal limitations has practically nothing to do with moral intent or lack of it. Evil conduct might be encouraged in words all of which were of the utmost propriety. But I have no intention of quibbling. I would rather boldly take the stand that anybody who restricts his reading to moral books will miss much delightful literature.

When I was in college a book agent came around with a combination offer. You could get the works of Ralph Waldo Emerson and also Guy de Maupassant illustrated. The price was $5 down and $1 a month for quite a long time.

Emerson was without pictures, but the agent showed me a prospectus of the de Maupassant illustrations, which were in five colors—chiefly pink. He assured me that Emerson had actually made an enduring contribution to the philosophic thought of America. When the books arrived I found that some of the illustrations were missing. I have a suspicion that the works of Ralph Waldo Emerson were less than complete, but on this point I never did make a wholly complete checkup.

## A Taste for Literature

The books revived in me a taste for literature which at that time was rather dormant. I read them all and one volume of Emerson. De Maupassant was just as great a master of the short story as the agent had informed me.

The next year I bought Thomas Hardy complete, with Balzac's *Droll Tales* as a bonus. I think that book agent did just about as much to encourage literature at Harvard University as anybody in the faculty. In spirit I owe him much.

I have heard a great deal—far too much, in fact—about books which are calculated to inspire love of country or clean living or a passion for gardening. All these things are excellent in moderation, but it is a great pity there is not more being done for books the only purpose of which is to encourage reading.

---

**[Doc. 213]**

December 9, 1933.

Mr. Heywood Broun,
Hotel des Artistes,
1 West 67th Street,
New York City.

Dear Heywood:

I never said that the *Ulysses* decision constituted a repeal of squeamishness. I said only that it repealed the squeamishness arising out of words and phrases. I indicated that no longer did authors of integrity have to use a phrase like "they slept together". This decision legalized the more direct Anglo-Saxon words. In fact a phrase like "they slept together" was a dishonest phrase. It was far from the illusion which the author intended to create.

> Yours,
> Morris Ernst

---

**[Doc. 214]**

### GREENBAUM, WOLFF & ERNST

### OFFICE MEMORANDUM

TO:  M.L.E.            FROM:  A.L.
RE:  *Ulysses*         DATE:  December 11, 1933.

I hand you herewith the *Ulysses* foreword. [See Doc. 215.—ED.] Please change it any way you see fit.

[Doc. 215]
[This is an enclosure to Doc. 214.—ED.]

The new deal in the law of letters is here. Judge Woolsey has exonerated *Ulysses* of the charge of obscenity, handing down an opinion that bids fair to become a major event in the history of the struggle for free expression. Joyce's masterpiece, for the circulation of which people have been branded criminals in the past, may now freely enter this country.

It would be difficult to overestimate the importance of Judge Woolsey's decision. For decades the censors have fought to emasculate literature. They have tried to set up the sensibilities of the prudery-ridden as a criterion for society, have sought to reduce the reading matter of adults to the level of adolescents and subnormal persons, and have nurtured evasions and sanctimonies.

The *Ulysses* case marks a turning point. It is a body-blow for the censors. The necessity for hypocrisy and circumlocution in literature has been eliminated. Writers need no longer seek refuge in euphemisms. They may now describe basic human functions without fear of the law.

The *Ulysses* case has a three-fold significance. The definition and criteria of obscenity have long vexed us. Judge Woolsey has given us a formula which is lucid, rational and practical. In doing so he has not only charted a labyinthine branch of the law, but has written an opinion which raises him to the level of former Supreme Court Justice Oliver Wendell Holmes as a master of juridical prose. His service to the cause of free letters has been of no lesser moment. But perhaps his greatest service has been to the community. The precedent he has established will do much to rescue the mental pabulum of the public from the censors who have striven to convert it into treacle, and will help to make it the strong, provocative fare it ought to be.

The first week of December 1933 will go down in history for two repeals, that of Prohibition and that of the legal compulsion for squeamishness in literature. It is not inconceivable that these two have been closely interlinked in the recent past, and that sex repressions found vent in intemperance. At any rate, we may now imbibe freely of the contents of bottles and forthright books. It may well be that in the future the repeal of the sex taboo in letters will prove to be of the greater importance. Perhaps the intolerance which closed our distilleries was the intolerance which decreed that basic human functions had to be treated in books in a furtive, leering, roundabout manner. Happily, both of these have now been repudiated.

The *Ulysses* case is the culmination of a protracted and stubborn struggle against the censors dating back to the victory over the New York Vice Society in the *Mademoiselle de Maupin* case in 1922. Coming in logical sequence after *The Well of Loneliness* case, the *Dennett* case, the cases involving Dr. Stopes' books, the *Casanova's Homecoming* case, the *Frankie and Johnnie* case, and the *God's Little Acre* case, all of which have served to liberalize the law of obscenity, the victory of *Ulysses* is a fitting climax to the salutary forward march of our courts.

Under the *Ulysses* case it should henceforth be impossible for the censors legally to sustain an attack against any book of artistic integrity, no matter how frank and forthright it may be. We have travelled a long way from the days of Bowdler and Mrs. Grundy and Comstock. We may well rejoice over the result.

Morris L. Ernst

New York, December 11, 1933.

---

**[Doc. 216]**

December 11, 1933.

Random House, Inc.,
20 East 57th Street,
New York City.

Attention: Mr. Bennett Cerf.

Re: *Ulysses*

Dear Bennett:

In accordance with our telephone conversation this morning, I am sending you herewith Morris' Foreword. I think it is short and to the point. I hope you will like it.

With kind regards, I am

Sincerely yours,

AL:JCG
Enc.

---

**[Doc. 217]**

December 12, 1933.

Mr. Morris L. Ernst,
285 Madison Avenue,
New York City.

Dear Morris:

The foreword for *Ulysses* is swell and is already in the process of being put into type.

As ever,

bac;pk

---

**[Doc. 218]**

27, Rue Casimir-Périer (VII$^E$)
Littre 88–89
Paris, December the 12-th., 1933.

Bennett Cerf, Esq.,
The Random House,
20 East 57-th. Street,
New York City.

Dear Mr. Cerf,

I beg to thank you again for your cable informing us of the satisfactory conclusion of the American case of *Ulysses* as well as for your letter containing the cuttings about the first hearing. At the same time I am extremely interested to know the details of the proceedings as well as those especially of the judge's argumentation. I hope that you will find it possible to let me have these in extenso as well as the brief of the case which you referred to in one of your letters as having been printed and circulated.

I would be greatly obliged to you if you could let me have these documents at your earliest convenience.

Believe me,

Sincerely yours,

Paul Léon

**[Doc. 219]**

December 12, 1933.

Mr. James Joyce,
c/o Paul Léon,
27, Rue Casimir-Périer,
Paris, France.

Dear Mr. Joyce:

We were delighted with your congratulations on the successful culmination of the *Ulysses* case. The decision has resulted in a tremendous amount of favorable publicity, and we have high hopes that the book will get off to a magnificent start. It would have been marvelous, of course, if we could have had books ready to deliver the moment the decision was rendered so that we could have taken full advantage of all the publicity. Naturally, this was impossible. We are rushing production of the book with all possible speed, however, and have announced our publication date definitely as January 25, 1934.

Have you made final arrangements as yet for the publication of *Work in Progress* in America? We should dearly like to publish this book and bring it out possibly in the format that will duplicate that of *Ulysses*. If you are free to discuss this matter with us, we will be glad to send you a format proposition.

Looking forward to early word from you, I remain,

Cordially yours,

Bennett A. Cerf
Random House

---

**[Doc. 220]**

December 12, 1933.

Mr. Herbert Gorman,
43 Manchester Street,
Manchester Square,
London, W.I.

Dear Herbert:

First let me dispose of this *Ulysses* chart business. I am terribly sorry that you should have been drawn into this controversy in any way, shape, or form, and I am writing to Paul Léon at once [See Doc. 221.—ED.] telling him that it was no fault of yours that this chart fell into our hands. At the time the chart was shown to me I thought it such an excellent piece of work that I immediately wrote to Paul Léon and asked him to get Joyce's permission for us to include this chart in the American edition of *Ulysses*. I expected his permission to come as a matter of course, and was amazed at the vehemence with which he refused. I still think that the publication of such a chart could only result in increased sales of the book, and what is more important, in increased understanding on the part of the people who actually read the book. There was no arguing with either Joyce or Léon in this matter, however, so we dropped the whole idea. In light of the fact that they became so angry about the whole business, I don't think it would be fair for me to tell where I saw this chart. I can only say that the man who showed it to me was acting in perfect good faith and never had the slightest intention of betraying anybody's confidence. I am enclosing a copy of my letter to Léon about this matter, and I hope that you will suffer no further inconvenience because of it. You must believe that I never dreamed you would be drawn into this matter in any way. As a matter of fact, the first time I had the faintest knowledge that you were involved in the business was when Léon seemed to take for granted the fact that it was you who had given the chart to me.

I cabled you this morning asking whether or not you had made definite plans for the publication of the biography you are doing of James Joyce. I suppose I am much too late in this business and that you have already signed a contract with somebody, but if you have not, I want to emphasize how interested we would be in arranging with you for the publication of this book. Now that the *Ulysses* case was decided in our favor, we could sell the biography and *Ulysses* hand in hand. Probably one book would help the other.

It occurs to me that you might be interested in seeing the historic decision that Judge Woolsey handed down on the *Ulysses* case, and I am enclosing a copy of it for you. It was a great victory and has been hailed as such by every newspaper in New York. We will publish the book complete and unabridged on January 25, 1934, and at last Joyce will receive some royalties on the American edition of his masterwork.

Looking forward to hearing from you I remain,

Cordially,

Bennett A. Cerf

bac;pk

---

**[Doc. 221]**

December 12, 1933.

Mr. Paul Léon,
27, Rue Casimir-Périer,
Paris, France.

Dear Mr. Léon:

I was very much surprised to receive a letter from Herbert Gorman this morning in which he told me that you had accused him of turning over to us the *Ulysses* chart about which we have had so much correspondence in the last few weeks. I am writing to you at once to assure you that I have neither seen nor heard a word from Mr. Gorman in the last two years. The chart was shown to me some weeks ago by someone who did not tell me where he had gotten hold of it. Furthermore, he asked for no money for this chart and was convinced that he was doing Mr. Joyce and ourselves a great favor in letting us see it because he felt that its inclusion in our edition of the book would result in greater sales and what was even more important, would help clarify the book for every reader. It is unnecessary for me to repeat again that I thoroughly agree with this opinion, and regard it as extremely unfortunate that Mr. Joyce would not give us permission to use this chart.

The purpose of this letter, however, is not to reopen this question. It is simply to assure you and Mr. Joyce once and for all that Mr. Gorman had no knowledge whatever that this chart was given to us, or for that matter, that a copy of it even existed here in New York.

Cordially yours,

Bennett A. Cerf
Random House

bac;pk

[Doc. 222]

*New York World-Telegram*
December 13, 1933

## Judge Woolsey, Who Searched *Ulysses* But Could Find No Wooden Horses, Has Traits of His Ancestors—George, a Tapster, and Theodore, President of Yale

### Here and in His Summer Home He Devotes Himself to the Study of Architecture, Woodwork and Furniture

By Forrest Davis

The first male ancestor in New York of John Munro Woolsey—United States District Judge, antiquarian, authority in Admiralty law, collector of Johnsoniana, author of the celebrated *Ulysses* decision and the freest literary critic in the land—bore the name George and kept a porter house at Pearl St., then the East River waterfront, and Coenties Slip.

Accounted a hospitable tapster (he was licensed in 1740), George Woolsey did not long confine himself to ladling potables. He dealt in more solid commodities and in time came to represent as agent the Yankee colonies of New England among the Dutch in New York.

By stages the Woolseys expanded their energies into wider fields. William Walton Woolsey, great-grandfather of the literary Judge, a worthy merchant of the town, retired as president of the Merchants' Exchange in 1833, two years before the great fire of 1835.

Presently thereafter Mr. Woolsey betook himself, family, carriage and pair, gold-headed canes, beaver hats and a tidy fortune to New Haven, where his son, the Augustan Theodore Dwight Woolsey—named for the great Theodore Dwight, poet, Calvinist, Federalist, president of Yale and Thomas Jefferson's most irksome "hair shirt"—himself was settled as president of the University. The Woolsey clan in that generation gradually gathered at New Haven, centering about President Woolsey, a theologian and legal scholar of vast learning, who wrote the first standard work in America on international law.

### His Word Is Law

Thus the Woolseys, swinging down the generations from tapster George through pundit Theodore, have contributed in this time to the forming of Judge Woolsey, the most eminently-placed of book critics; a reviewer whose word quite literally is law.

The Judge, whose precise prose flowed melodically through the *Ulysses* decision, partakes, one suspects of the qualities of the earlier Woolseys. Well-fleshed, ruddy cheeks, the gold ring around the cravat, the ivory cigaret holder, the long-stemmed pipe, an easy twinkle in the eye no doubt represent the good cheer of Ancestor George.

Judge Woolsey, in New York and at his summer estate outside Petersham, Mass., devotes himself to the study and appreciation of Colonial and republican architecture, woodwork, furniture, glassware, etc. His library, on a hilltop near his dwelling at Petersham, is the restored Town Hall of Prescott, Mass., a village near Amherst, a building bought to prevent its demolition by the Boston Waterworks District.

### Held Weekend Court

The Judge copied pre-Revolutionary paneling in the Dauntless Yacht Club, at Essex, Conn., for the walls, and this summer held weekend court there in a copyright case. At the intermissions, counsel, principals and witnesses spread out over the Woolsey pastures to pick blueberries.

It was in this charming hilltop study that Judge Woolsey plowed through *Ulysses* last summer reading the eleven "satellite" books he said were necessary to give him completer understanding of that erudite Joyce's classic and mythological allusions.

In his preoccupation with traditional objects, the Judge may be thought to approximate Merchant Woolsey's interest in tangibles.

And in his scholarship at the law—Judge Woolsey founded the *Columbia Law Review* and was American associate editor of *Revue de Droit Maritime Compare*, Paris—he indubitably stems from the Jovian Theodore Dwight Woolsey, who preached regularly, ruled Yale with iron grip from 1846 to 1872 and yet found time to establish American principles in international law.

### Admiralty Lawyer First

Judge Woolsey, an admiralty lawyer before he went on the federal bench in 1929, by appointment of President Hoover, has been hearing the important literary cases in this district pretty much since 1931. He it was who assessed $17,500 in costs against George Lewys when the author of *The Temple of Palias Athene* lost her plagiarism suit against Eugene O'Neill. He did so, he said, to discourage unjustified nuisance suits against successful authors and playwrights.

He admitted Dr. Marie Stopes' books, *Married Love* and *Contraception*, to this country, holding, in the case of the former, that while it contained little that was novel, it seemed unlikely to incite to "obscene or immoral conduct."

### Widely Hailed

His decision in the *Ulysses* case—chiming as it did with repeal—electrified publishers, authors, editors and critics. Morris Ernst, attorney for the firm which hoped at last to rescue James Joyce's innovative novel from the bootleg shelves of bookstores, hailed it as a knell to squeamishness and a greater civilizing force than repeal. Telegrams and letters of approbation reached Judge Woolsey by the dozens.

A Daniel come to judgment; moreover, a literate Daniel, able to express himself in felicitous, not to say elegant prose.

Judge Woolsey accepted the plaudits on his style modestly. He disclaims for himself the title "well-read man," but confesses that from youth he has read steadily, appreciatively, in current fiction as well as the lawbooks. His favorite period is the late eighteenth century; Dr. Johnson is his demigod. He has, he hopes, every Johnson first edition available to him since he took up collecting.

### Reserves Judgment

Upon the work of contemporaries, he reserves critical judgment. He enjoys Cather, parts of Hemingway, for example; Dreiser's unstudied form vaguely annoys him.

The Judge, who as critic is free from pressure of author, publisher, friends, literary teas, etc., relishes the literary litigations that come before him.

By preference he does not read works suspected of being obscene. But his tastes are catholic. A candid old Anglo-Saxon phrase, encountered on a moving page, does not bring him up standing. He holds that an author should have a "rationale;" that is, a scheme or frame of reference.

If that inevitably carries him, or his characters, into bawdy situations which may only be expressed bawdily then the author must carry on.

### Anyone Can Tell

And, he holds, that anyone may determine for himself whether the author has followed his gleam where it led or whether he has inserted a phrase or passage for the purpose of shocking the sensitive or exploiting sex interest.

As a critic the Judge is unprejudiced and empirical.

Judge Woolsey was graduated from Yale in 1898. All the Woolseys have been going to Yale except William Walton, the rich merchant, since Tapster George's son went up to New Haven. He was born in Aiken, S. C., while the family sojourned there in search of health for his father.

The Judge prepared at Phillips Andover, studied law at Columbia, received a Doctor of Laws degree there in recent years, was admitted to the New York bar in 1901, taught at the law school for several years and practiced from 1920 until 1925 as a member of Kirlin, Woolsey, Campbell, Hickox & Keating. He is a Republican, an Episcopalian and lives in Manhattan at 131 E. 66th St.

[Doc. 223]

December 14, 1933.

Forrest Davis, Esq.,
c/o *The World-Telegram*,
125 Barclay Street,
New York City.

Re: *United States* v. *Ulysses*

Dear Mr. Davis:

Felicitations to you on your swell story on Judge Woolsey.

So many of our judges are virtually illiterate (one of them sitting in an obscenity case, confessed in open court that he had not read a book in ten years), so many of them are timid or reactionary or both, so many of them are cursed with a prose style that renders their opinions all but unintelligible, that when a judge does emerge who is enlightened and courageous and is able to express himself gracefully and intelligibly, the press should not be niggard of praise. I cannot think of a more gracious gesture in this direction than your article.

Sincerely yours,

AL:JF

---

[Doc. 224]

UNITED STATES DISTRICT COURT

SOUTHERN DISTRICT OF NEW YORK

United States of America,

Libellant,

v.

One Book called *Ulysses*
Random House, Inc.,

Claimant.

DECREE
A. 110-59

Issue have been joined by the service and filing of the Claimant's answer herein on December 19, 1932; and a stipulation having been entered into between the parties on May 15, 1933, which provided, among other things, that trial by jury be waived, and that the parties cross-move for decrees in their favor; and the Libellant having moved this Court by notice of motion dated May 15, 1933 for a decree of forfeiture and destruction; and the Claimant having cross-moved this Court by notice of motion dated May 17, 1933 for a decree dismissing the libel herein; and the aforesaid motions having duly come on to be heard before Hon. John M. Woolsey, one of the Judges of this Court, on November 23, 1933.

NOW, on reading and filing the libel dated December 9, 1932, the answer verified December 19, 1932, the above-mentioned stipulation dated May 15, 1933, the Libellant's notice of motion dated May 17, 1933; and Samuel C. Coleman, Esq. and Nicholas Atlas, Esq., Assistant United States Attorneys, appearing for the Libellant in support of the motion for a decree of forfeiture and destruction and in opposition to the motion to dismiss the libel; and Morris L. Ernst and Alexander Lindey, Esqs., of Greenbaum, Wolff & Ernst, attorneys for the Claimant herein, appearing for the Claimant in support of the motion to dismiss the libel and in opposition to the motion for a decree of forfeiture and destruction; and the Court having handed down its opinion dated December 6, 1933,

NOW, on motion of Greenbaum, Wolff & Ernst, attorneys for the Claimant, it is

ORDERED AND ADJUDGED that the book entitled *Ulysses* is not of the character the entry of which is prohibited under the provisions of Section 305 of the Tariff Act of 1930, and Title 19, United States Code, Section 1305, and should not be excluded from entry to the United States of America under the provisions thereof; and it is further

ORDERED AND ADJUDGED that the motion for a decree dismissing the libel herein is granted without costs, and the libel dismissed; and it is further

ORDERED AND ADJUDGED that the motion for a decree of forfeiture and destruction is denied; and it is further

ORDERED AND ADJUDGED that the book entitled *Ulysses*, heretofore seized by the Collector of Customs of the United States at the Port and Collection District of New York, be released to the Claimant herein.

Dated: New York, N.Y., December 15, 1933.

[Judge John M. Woolsey]

**[Doc. 225]**

27, Rue Casimir-Périer (VII$^E$)
Littre 88–89
Paris, December the 16-th., 1933

Bennett Cerf, Esq.,
The Random House, Inc.,
20 East 57-th. Street,
New York City.

Dear Mr. Cerf,

I beg to acknowledge receipt of the brilliant brief of your case which I received the other day as well as of the copy of the judge's decision enclosed in your letter of the 7-th. and to renew once more my compliments and congratulations on the deserved success of your venture.

The receipt of these documents annuls my previous letter to you but, as it seems all my letters are begging letters, may I try your patience once more asking you if you would kindly let me have a copy of the Preliminary Memorandum referred to in the brief; what interests me most in it are naturally the exhibits referring to the general question outside the purely American issue, as well as the opinions expressed on *Ulysses*. Should there be any expenses in the copying of this, I gather, rather voluminous material, I will naturally refund them to you.

Thanking you in advance,
Believe me,

Sincerely yours,

Paul Léon

---

**[Doc. 226]**

December 16, 1933.

Hon. John M. Woolsey,
Woolworth Building,
New York City.

Re: *Ulysses*

Dear Judge:

I am sending you herewith the clipping from *The Nation* that I mentioned to you yesterday. I am also enclosing a copy of Lewis Gannett's column of today, clipped from the *New York Herald-Tribune*.

I am wondering whether you listened in on the *March of Time* yesterday, over Station WABC. They reenacted a part of the argument on the motion, and read generous portions of your opinion, placing special emphasis on the now celebrated sentence dealing with springtime, Celtic characters and recurrent sex.

Sincerely yours,

AL:JF

---

[Doc. 227]

December 16, 1933.

Miss Saul,
*Time* Magazine,
Chrysler Building,
New York City.

Dear Miss Saul:

Thanks for sending me a copy of *Time*, containing your piece on *Ulysses*.

I want to congratulate you on the fairness, clarity and completeness of the article. I was with Judge Woolsey yesterday afternoon, and I can tell you that he was very much pleased with it. He did wonder where you obtained the information that he plays golf "wearing a peculiar oriental cap to keep the sun from shining into his spectacles," but it may interest you to know that he did not deny it.

My faith is restored.

Sincerely yours,

AL:JF

---

**[Doc. 228]**

December 16, 1933.

"March of Time,"
*Time* Magazine,
New York City.

Gentlemen:

I wish to congratulate you upon the effective fashion in which you reenacted the *Ulysses* court incident last night. It seems to me that you managed, with singular success, to bring out all the highlights of the case, and to do so with considerable dramatic force.

Sincerely yours,

AL:JF

---

**[Doc. 229]**

### GREENBAUM, WOLFF & ERNST

### OFFICE MEMORANDUM

| TO: Joe | FROM: A.L. |
|---|---|
| RE: *Ulysses* | DATE: December 18, 1933. |

The judgment must have been entered Saturday or today. Get a certified copy and make inquiries at the Clerk's office as to who is supposed to serve the copy of the judgment on the Collector of Customs. No service may be necessary, but we do want to get back the detained copy of *Ulysses* which the Collector is holding.

It might be a good idea to get a copy of the final judgment, to turn over to Random House.

[Doc. 230]

UNITED STATES DISTRICT COURT

JUDGE WOOLSEY'S CHAMBERS

1542 WOOLWORTH BUILDING

NEW YORK

December 18, 1933.

Alexander Lindey, Esq.,
285 Madison Avenue,
New York City.

Dear Mr. Lindey:

I acknowledge with appreciation your letter of December 16th with its enclosed clipping from Lewis Gannett's column and from *The Nation*. I am much obliged to you for sending them to me.

On thinking over the question which we were discussing the other afternoon as to what part of my opinion should be published in connection with the book *Ulysses*, it seems to me that what appeared in the last number of the *Saturday Review of Literature*, which covered all my opinion except the practice part and the citations would perhaps be the most appropriate form, but, as I said before, there may be reasons why they wish to put the whole opinion in and it makes not the slightest difference to me; I am merely mentioning this to you because it seemed to me that the way in which the Saturday Review dealt with the opinion might be very appropriate in connection with the book.

Very truly yours,

John Woolsey

---

[Doc. 231]

*Time* Magazine

Week of December 18th, 1933

### A Welcome to *Ulysses*

"A chaffering, all including most farraginous chronicle" is James Joyce's definition of his *Ulysses*, a book which many a critic considers the most important novel of its generation. Whether *Ulysses* is also "immoral and obscene" and therefore unfit for U.S. readers was the question which Manhattan's Federal Judge John M. Woolsey last week was ready to answer in the extraordinary case of *The U. S.* vs. *One Book Entitled Ulysses.*

The U. S. Customs started the case in May, 1932 when it seized an unexpurgated copy sent to Publisher Bennett A. Cerf from Paris. Last fortnight there was a hearing in the small, elegantly informal courtroom of the Bar Association Building. Publisher Cerf's lawyer, Morris Ernst, who makes a specialty of fighting censorship cases, contended that he had yet to find a single instance which proved that reading any book had led to the commission of a crime. Assistant U. S. Attorney Samuel C. Coleman asked the court not to regard him as a "puritanical censor," said he found "ample grounds to consider *Ulysses* an obscene book." Fat, bald-headed Judge Woolsey who spent his vacation last summer on *Ulysses* [          ].

" . . . [          ] be disgusting but although it contains, as I have mentioned above, many words usually considered dirty, I have not found anything that I consider to be dirt for dirt's sake. If one does not wish to associate with such folk as Joyce describes, that is one's own choice. . . . But when such a real artist as Joyce undoubtedly is, seeks to draw a true picture of the lower middle class in a European city, ought it to be impossible for the American public legally to see that picture?

"The meaning of the word *obscene* as legally defined by the courts is: 'Tending to stir the sex impulses or to lead to sexually impure and lustful thoughts'. . . . After I had made my decision in regard to the aspect of *Ulysses* now under consideration I checked my impressions with two friends. . . I was interested to find that they both agreed with my opinion: that reading *Ulysses* in its entirety . . . did not tend to excite sexual impulses or lustful thoughts but that its net effect on them was only that of a somewhat tragic and very powerful commentary on the inner lives of men and women. . . .

"My considered opinion after long reflection is that while in many places the effect of *Ulysses* on the reader undoubtedly is somewhat emetic, nowhere does it tend to be an aphrodisiac.

"*Ulysses* may, therefore, be admitted into the United States."

Last week's opinion was not the first of its kind for Judge Woolsey. A shy, scholarly, ponderous, blunt devotee of literature, the law, and what he calls "the art of small delights," he has been concerned with the legal nature of obscenity since 1931. In that year he ruled in favor of Dr. Marie Stopes' *Married Love*. Three months later he rendered a favorable decision on her *Contraception*. He was the judge in famed plagiarism suits over *Strange Interlude* and *Of Thee I Sing*, in both of which he rendered decisions for the defendants. He earned the vacation he devoted to *Ulysses* by presiding last spring at the longest criminal case in the history of U. S. jurisprudence, the 109-day fraud trial of the promoters of the National Diversified Corp. who bilked Roman Catholic clergymen and others out of $3,000,000 to make talkie pictures (*Time*, July 17).

Born in Aiken, S.C., 56 years ago, John Munro Woolsey went to Phillips Andover, Yale, Columbia Law School. For hobbies [    ] Anderson indicted for publishing indecent matter, caused her and her co-Editor Jane Heap to be fined $50. Thirty thousand copies of *Ulysses* have been sold in France, mostly to U. S. tourists to smuggle home.

Immediate results of last week's decision were two. Publisher Cerf's Random House announced a forthcoming unabridged edition of *Ulysses* ($3.50) for general sale. In Paris, where he was waiting for another operation on his right eye, Author Joyce said he was "pleased with the judgment," hoped to get some much needed cash out of the U. S. edition.

---

**[Doc. 232]**

December 19, 1933.

Hon. John M. Woolsey,
Woolworth Building,
New York City.

Re: *Ulysses*

Dear Judge Woolsey:

Thanks for your kind letter of December 18.

With respect to the form in which your opinion is to be incorporated in the forthcoming American edition of *Ulysses*, I am passing your thought on to Random House. I believe, as you do, that the intelligent reader will find the entire opinion, excepting only the practice part and the citations, of much interest and enlightenment.

During the last eight years I have had the good fortune to be associated with Morris Ernst in the handling of several dozen literary censorship cases. It is only fair to state that the three cases in which you have sat—the *Married Love* case, the *Contraception* case, and now the *Ulysses* case—stand out in my mind as the most pleasant experiences I have had in court. I am sincere when I say that my reaction would have been the same even if one or more of the cases had gone against us. Nothing, I believe, can be more exasperating and discouraging to an attorney who has painstakingly prepared his case, than a closed mind on the part of the court. To be sure, all of us want to win cases. But whether we win them or not, we do hope to encounter three things: a judicial receptiveness, a grasp of the issue involved, and a disposition based on mature consideration; and whenever we have appeared before you, we have been assured of all three.

Yours very truly,

AL:JF

[Doc. 233]

December 19, 1933.

Bennett A. Cerf, Esq.,
c/o Random House, Inc.
20 East 57th Street,
New York City.

Dear Cerf:

I am sending you herewith a letter I have just received from Judge Woolsey. I saw him Friday of last week, and we were discussing the form in which his opinion would be incorporated in the American edition of *Ulysses*. The enclosure is self-explanatory.

Yours sincerely,

AL:JF

---

[Doc. 234]

December 21, 1933.

Bennett A. Cerf, Esq.,
c/o Random House, Inc.,
20 East 57th Street,
New York City.

Re: *Ulysses*

Dear Cerf:

I am sending you herewith a copy of the final decree in the above matter. Legally it is this document, and not the opinion, which clears *Ulysses*.

I direct your attention to the marked paragraph on page 2 of the decree. The district attorney opposed the inclusion of this paragraph, and there was a final argument before Woolsey on the point. As might be expected, we won.

I suppose that you sent James Joyce and Sylvia Beach a copy of Woolsey's opinion.

Yours very truly,

AL:JF

---

[Doc. 235]

December 27, 1933.

Mr. Paul Léon,
27, Rue Casimir-Périer,
Paris VII<sup>E</sup>,
France.

Dear Mr. Léon:

The preliminary memorandum referred to in our *Ulysses* brief consisted of a portfolio containing letters from hundreds of critics, professional men, librarians, authors, and so forth, about the book, as well as long excerpts from books and magazines that had previously been written about *Ulysses*. It will be simply impossible to send you a copy of this entire portfolio. Be assured that every important fact presented by us is contained in the brief that I have already sent you.

I am glad that you and Mr. Joyce are pleased with the work we have done on the book. I am enclosing herewith a rough sample of a poster that we are preparing to send to bookstores all over the country. This poster will, of course, be mounted on stiff cardboard and will be displayed, I am sure, very widely. We are planning our advertising campaign for the book now and I will be sure to send you copies of our more important advertisements as soon as they appear. The case has been receiving tremendous publicity, and we have high hopes that the book will achieve a really fine sale.

We would like to have some pictures of Mr. Joyce for publicity purposes. Will you please send me a few characteristic poses at once so that we can have reproductions made to send to all newspapers along with copies of the book.

Hoping that you will give this matter your immediate attention, I remain,

Cordially yours,

Bennett A. Cerf
Random House

bac;pk

———————————

[Doc. 236]

GREENBAUM, WOLFF & ERNST

OFFICE MEMORANDUM

TO:   Mr. Lindey          FROM:   Hy
RE:   *Ulysses*           DATE:   December 28, 1933.

I have done the following work towards getting back the copy of *Ulysses* seized by the Collector of Customs.

12/19—Served a certified copy of the decree on the Collector of Customs by
       Dr. Handler's office (Law Div.) They said that they would let you
       know when the book would be ready for delivery.
12/28—I called on Mr. Fishman of Mr. Handler's office to make inquiry as to
the whereabouts of the book. He told me that the U.S. Attorney General
intended to appeal the decision of Judge Woolsey. Dr. Fishman wants you to
call him up.

---

[Doc. 237]

December 29, 1933.

Don Wharton, Esq.,
c/o *The New Yorker*,
25 West 45th Street,
New York City.

My dear Wharton:

I have before me your note of December 27, addressed to Morris Ernst. Since he is not coming back until some time next week, I am taking the liberty of answering it.

We may have another case before Judge Woolsey, but it is not likely to break for some months. If you want to capitalize on the *Ulysses* episode while it is still fresh in the minds of your readers, it will probably be better for you to run your "Talk of the Town" story on him now, rather than later.

Morris Ernst may have different ideas. As soon as he comes back I will show him your note.

Sincerely yours,

AL:JF

[Doc. 238]

27, Rue Casimir-Périer (VII$^E$)
Littre 88–89
Paris, January the 2-nd., 1934.

Bennett Cerf, Esq.,
The Random House,
20 East 57-th. Street,
New York City.

Dear Mr. Cerf,

Mr. Joyce wishes me to write to you on the following matter. If you are definitely certain to bring out your edition of *Ulysses* on the 25-th of this month, would you very kindly send one copy ahead of time to Mr. Joyce himself so that it reaches him on the 2-nd of February (this being the anniversary of the publication of *Ulysses* in Europe).

Very sincerely yours and with renewed good wishes for the coming year.

Paul Léon

---

[Doc. 239]

January 2, 1934.

Bennett A. Cerf, Esq.,
c/o Random House,
20 East 57th Street,
New York City.

Re: *Ulysses*

Dear Cerf:

B. N. Handler and Fishman (I don't know his initials), both of the office of the Solicitor to the Collector of Customs, gave us willing cooperation in clearing *Ulysses*. I think it would be a generous gesture for you to send each of them a copy of the book when it comes off the press. They may both be reached at the office of the Collector of Customs, Customs House, New York City.

Sincerely yours,

AL:JF

**[Doc. 240]**

RANDOM HOUSE
20 E 57 • NEW YORK
The American Selling Agent for the NONESUCH PRESS Limited Editions

January 3, 1934.

Mr. Alexander Lindey,
c/o Greenbaum, Wolff & Ernst,
285 Madison Avenue,
New York City.

Dear Lindey:

Handler and Fishman will each receive copies of *Ulysses*. I am sending you a dummy of our edition of the book under separate cover. I hope that you and your high-powered associates will talk up the sales on this book. I don't suppose I need remind you that you're in on the royalties.

As ever,

Bennett

bac;pk

---

**[Doc. 241]**

January 11, 1934.

Mr. Paul Léon,
27, Rue Casimir-Périer,
Paris VII$^E$, France.

Dear Mr. Léon:

We are certain to bring out *Ulysses* on the 25th of this month, and I assure you that Mr. Joyce will have copies by the 2nd of February.

It gives me great pleasure to be able to get them to him on or before the anniversary of the publication of *Ulysses* in Europe.

Cordially,

Donald S. Klopfer
Random House

dsk;ref

[Doc. 242]

January 17, 1934.

Mr. Paul Léon,
27, Rue Casimir-Périer,
Paris VII$^E$, France.

Dear Mr. Léon:

The first copies of *Ulysses* have just arrived in this office and in accordance with our promise, six of them go off today for Mr. Joyce. We hope that all of you will be pleased with the appearance of this book, as we are ourselves.

The tremendous publicity continues to attend the publication of *Ulysses*. We will have the whole front page of this Sunday's *Tribune Book Review* and next week we think we have persuaded the *Times* to follow suit. The position of their *Review* is still in doubt. The advance sale is now somewhere in the neighborhood of 12,000, a really phenomenal figure for a $3.50 book in times like these, and one that frankly we did not expect to reach for months. If the public will react to the book as booksellers all over the country expect them to, all of us may have cause for additional rejoicing in the months to come.

My partner, Donald Klopfer, and I would both appreciate it tremendously if Mr. Joyce would inscribe copies of *Ulysses* for us. Naturally we would like to treasure these volumes in our private libraries. If Mr. Joyce will send us two of these inscribed copies we will, of course, send him other copies of the book to replace those sent, immediately.

I am surely coming to Europe this Spring, probably early in May, and look forward to the pleasure of meeting you personally.

Cordially yours,

Bennett A. Cerf

bac;pk

---

[Doc. 243]

FILE MEMO

January 24, 1934.

Telephoned Atlas relative to the following:

1. *Japanese Pessaries*: He said that he would look over the proposed stipulation today, and let us know.

2. *Story Teller's Holiday*: He said that he had already prepared a recommendation against libel proceedings, and that he would turn over the recommendation to Coleman within the next few days.

3. *Ulysses*: He said that his recommendation against appeal was in Coleman's hands.

A.L.

---

**[Doc. 244]**

January 24, 1934.

Bennett A. Cerf, Esq.,
c/o Random House, Inc.,
20 East 57th Street,
New York City.

Re: *Ulysses*

Dear Cerf:

I am informed that the United States Attorney's office here in New York has now under consideration a recommendation against appeal. I have no way of knowing whether this recommendation will go forward to Washington.

Please do not forget to send copies of the book to Samuel C. Coleman and Nicholas Atlas, both Assistant United States Attorneys, U.S. Courts and Post Office Building, New York City.

Here's hoping that your sales exceed your rosiest expectations.

Sincerely yours,

AL:JF

---

[Doc. 245]

January 27, 1934.

Peter A. Pertzoff, Esq.,
70 Hammond Street,
Cambridge, Mass.

Re: *Ulysses*

Dear Mr. Pertzoff:

No doubt by this time you have seen the first American edition of *Ulysses*, in connection with the legalization of which you rendered generous assistance.

We are ready to return your thesis if you wish it. If you can spare the copy we should like to retain it as part of our records on the case.

Many thanks.

Sincerely yours,
Greenbaum, Wolff & Ernst

AL:JF

---

[Doc. 246]

January 28, 1934.

Bennett A. Cerf, Esq.,
c/o Random House, Inc.,
20 East 57th Street,
New York City.

Re: *Ulysses*

Dear Cerf:

Now that you are all excited about the forthcoming American edition I hate to dampen your ardor, but just as a matter of record I must advise you that the Government has ninety days to appeal from Judge Woolsey's decision. The period of ninety days starts running from the date of the entry of judgment, which was December 19, 1933. Accordingly the prosecution has until March 19 to appeal.

I have been informed that the United States Attorney's office here in New York has made or will make a recommendation against appeal. However, the Government's course of conduct is not guided necessarily by the people here. Some official in the Treasury Department in Washington may insist upon testing out the book in the Circuit Court of Appeals.

Sincerely yours,

AL:JF

[Doc. 247]

FILE MEMO

February 8, 1934.

Re: *Ulysses*

Spoke to Atlas today. He said that Coleman has written to the Attorney General, making a recommendation with respect to appeal. He refused to divulge the nature of the recommendation.

A.L.

---

[Doc. 248]

*N. Y. Herald-Tribune*
March 13, 1934

**U.S. Will Carry *Ulysses* Ruling
To High Court**

---

**Conboy, Who Read Joyce's Book Carefully,
to Handle Obscenity Case Appeal**

---

The United States government will file an appeal from the decision of Federal Judge John M. Woolsey which permitted the importation of James Joyce's *Ulysses*. Martin Conboy, United States Attorney, who will present the government's case, said yesterday he had read the book carefully. The appeal papers must be filed before Saturday, which is three months from the entry of the final decree of Judge Woolsey.

Mr. Conboy's decision to appeal does not coincide with statements of Samuel C. Coleman, chief of the civil division, who represented the government before Judge Woolsey at hearings in the Bar Association Building, or of Nicholas Atlas, Assistant United States Attorney, who helped Mr. Coleman prepare the motion to exclude and confiscate the book.

Both Mr. Coleman and Mr. Atlas said when the decision was handed down last December that a recommendation would be made to the United States Attorney General that no appeal be taken. George Z. Medalie was Federal prosecutor in the Southern District at that time.

*Ulysses* became the subject of prosecution in July, 1933, after it had been bootlegged in this country since 1922. An imported copy was prohibited from entry on the ground that it was "immoral and obscene." In his opinion Judge Woolsey wrote that the book was not obscene, but a sincere and honest work of literary art, and "a serious experiment in a new, if not wholly novel, literary genre."

It is expected that the government's appeal will be based on the assertion that Judge Woolsey erred in holding *Ulysses* to be admissible under Section 305 of the Tariff act of 1930, Title 19 United States code, Section 1305, the statute under which the libel was filed. This statute, Judge Woolsey said in his opinion, "only denounces, in so far as we are here concerned, the importation into the United States from any foreign country of 'any obscene book.' It does not marshall against books the spectrum of condemnatory adjectives found commonly in laws dealing with matters of this kind. I am, therefore, only required to determine whether *Ulysses* is obscene within the legal definition of that word.

"The meaning of the word *obscene* as legally defined by the courts is: tending to stir the sex impulses or to lead to sexually impure and lustful thoughts."

### Admittedly Difficult to Read

Judge Woolsey held that the book was not pornographic, nor "written for the purpose of exploiting obscenity." He held that although to ask some sensitive, though normal, persons to read the book might prove "rather a strong draught," it was his opinion that "while in many places the effect of *Ulysses* on the reader undoubtedly is somewhat emetic, nowhere does it tend to be an aphrodisiac."

The court admitted that *Ulysses* was not an easy book to read or understand and that its study was an arduous task, in that "a number of other books which have now become its satellites" had to be considered for a proper approach to consideration of the work named in the government's complaint.

Morris L. Ernst, attorney for Random House, publishers of the book in this country, informed of the government's action, said: "It is a new point of departure for the government. In this case the judge sat as a jury and found that as a matter of law and as a matter of fact that the book was legal. We are confident that the Circuit Court of Appeals will sustain us."

———

**[Doc. 249]**

To: Mr. Lindey
From: Mr. Kaplan                                        March 16, 1934.

Re: United States v. Ulysses

There is no extraordinary system of appeal provided for in the case of libels *in rem* against obscene books under the Customs Duties Law, so that Section 230 of the Judicial Code seems clearly to apply.

Under 19 U.S.C., Section 135, the importation of obscene books is prohibited. Under Section 136 of the same title, provision is made for a proceeding *in rem* "which shall be conducted in the same manner as other proceedings in the case of municipal seizure, and with the same right of appeal or writ of error." The action is properly brought in the District Court of the applicable district.

Under 28 U.S.C. Section 41 (5) (10), general jurisdiction is confirmed to the district court in cases arising under internal revenue, customs and tonnage laws. Under Section 225 (a) (1) of the same title, the Circuit Courts of Appeal are given appellate jurisdiction to review by appeal or writ of error final decisions in all district courts in all cases, save where a direct review may be had in the Supreme Court under Section 345. As there is no direct appeal to the highest court in cases of libels *in rem* against obscene books, it follows that Circuit Courts of Appeal have the usual appellate competency in cases of this kind. Therefore, 28 U.S.C. 230 applies as a limitation on time of appeal.

---

**[Doc. 250]**

## CITATION

**By the Honorable John M. Woolsey, One of the United States District Judges for the Southern District of New York, in the Second Circuit to Random House, Inc., Claimant.**

Greeting:

You are hereby cited and admonished to be and appear before a United States Circuit Court of Appeals for the Second Circuit, to be holden at the Borough of Manhattan, in the City of New York, in the District and Circuit above named on the 2nd day of April, 1934, pursuant to an appeal filed in the Clerk's office of the District Court of the United States for the Southern District of New York, wherein the United States of America is appellant and you are appellee, to show cause, if any there be, why the order and judgment entered in said cause mentioned should not be corrected and why speedy justice should not be done to the parties in that behalf.

> Given under my hand at the Borough of Manhattan, in the City of New York, in the District and Circuit above named, this 16th day of March, in the year of our Lord One Thousand Nine Hundred and Thirty-four and of the Independence of the United States the One Hundred and Fifty-eighth.

> John M. Woolsey
> United States District Judge for the Southern District of New York in the Second Circuit.

---

[Doc. 251]

UNITED STATES DISTRICT COURT

SOUTHERN DISTRICT OF NEW YORK

UNITED STATES OF AMERICA,

Libellant

-against-

ONE BOOK ENTITLED *ULYSSES* BY JAMES JOYCE, RANDOM HOUSE, INC.,

Claimant.

PETITION FOR APPEAL AND ALLOWANCE

TO THE HONORABLE JUDGES OF THE UNITED STATES DISTRICT COURT FOR THE SOUTHERN DISTRICT OF NEW YORK

Your petitioner, United States of America, the libellant above named, feeling itself aggrieved by the order and judgment herein of this Court entered December 18, 1933, does hereby appeal from said order and judgment to the United States Circuit Court of Appeals for the Second Circuit for the reasons specified in the assignment of errors which is filed herewith, and prays for an order allowing it to prosecute an appeal, and that a transcript of record, papers and proceedings upon which said order and judgment was made and entered may be duly authenticated and sent to the Circuit Court of Appeals for the Second Circuit and that a citation be issued as provided by law.

Dated, New York, N.Y., March 16th, 1934.

> MARTIN CONBOY,
> United States Attorney for the
> Southern District of New York,
> Proctor for Libellant,
> Office and Post Office Address
> U.S. Courts and P.O. Bldg.,
> Borough of Manhattan,
> City of New York.

It is ordered that the appeal above prayed for be, and it hereby is, allowed.

Dated: New York, N.Y., March 16, 1934.

> John M. Woolsey
> United States District Judge
> for the Southern District of
> New York in the Second
> Circuit.

---

[Doc. 252]

UNITED STATES DISTRICT COURT
SOUTHERN DISTRICT OF NEW YORK

UNITED STATES OF AMERICA,
                    Libellant,

—against—

ONE BOOK ENTITLED *ULYSSES*        ASSIGNMENT OF ERRORS
BY JAMES JOYCE,
RANDOM HOUSE, INC.,
                    Claimant.

Comes now the above named libellant, United States of America, by its proctor, Martin Conboy, United States Attorney for the Southern District of New York, and makes and files the following assignment of errors upon which it will rely upon the prosecution of its appeal to the United States Circuit Court of Appeals for the Second Circuit filed by it herein to review the errors committed in the above-entitled cause in the United States District

Court for the Southern District of New York in the proceedings had herein and against it in said court:

That the said District Court erred as follows:

1. In ordering and adjudging that the book *Ulysses* is not of the character, the entry of which is prohibited under the provisions of Section 305 of the Tariff Act of 1930 (Title 19, U.S. Code, Section 1305) and that it should not be excluded from entry into the United States under the provisions thereof.

2. In not ordering and adjudging that the book *Ulysses* is of the character, the entry of which is prohibited under the provisions of Section 305 of the Tariff Act of 1930 (Title 19, U.S. Code, Section 1305), and that it should be excluded from entry into the United States under the provisions thereof.

3. In not ruling as a matter of law that the book *Ulysses* is obscene within the meaning of Section 305 of the Tariff Act of 1930 (Title 19, U.S. Code, Section 1305).

4. In ruling that the book *Ulysses* is not obscene within the meaning of Section 305 of the Tariff Act of 1930 (Title 19, U.S. Code, Section 1305).

5. In denying the motion of libellant for a decree of forfeiture and destruction.

6. In not granting the motion of the libellant for a decree of forfeiture and destruction.

7. In granting the motion of the claimant for a decree dismissing the libel.

8. In not denying the motion of the claimant for a decree dismissing the libel.

9. In dismissing the libel herein.

10. In directing that the book *Ulysses* be released to the claimant.

WHEREFORE, the said United States of America, the libellant herein, prays that the order and judgment for the errors aforesaid and for the errors in the record and proceedings herein may be reversed and that the libellant be restored to all things which it has lost by reason of said order and judgment and for such other and further relief as to the court may seem proper.

Dated, New York, N.Y., March 16, 1934.

MARTIN CONBOY,
United States Attorney for the
Southern District of New York,
Proctor for Libellant,
Office and Post Office Address,
U.S. Courts and Post Office Building,
Borough of Manhattan,
City of New York.

[Doc. 253]

UNITED STATES DISTRICT COURT
SOUTHERN DISTRICT OF NEW YORK

THE UNITED STATES,

-versus-

ONE BOOK ENTITLED *ULYSSES*
BY JAMES JOYCE.

ORDER AND CONSENT
110-59

Upon reading and filing the annexed consent, and upon motion of MARTIN CONBOY, United States Attorney for the Southern District of New York, it is

ORDERED that the Dec. 1933 Term of this Honorable Court be and the same hereby is extended to and including the 17th day of April 1934, for the purpose of filing Bill of Exceptions in the above entitled action.

Dated: New York, N.Y., March 16, 1934.

We hereby consent to the entry of the above order without further notice.

GREENBAUM, WOLFF & ERNST
Attorneys for Claimant

MARTIN CONBOY
Attorneys for Libellant

To:
Greenbaum, Wolff & Ernst, Esqs.,
285 Madison Avenue,
New York City.

[Doc. 254]

UNITED STATES DISTRICT COURT
SOUTHERN DISTRICT OF NEW YORK

UNITED STATES OF AMERICA,

Libellant,

-against-                                    ORDER

ONE BOOK ENTITLED *ULYSSES*
by JAMES JOYCE,
RANDOM HOUSE, INC.

Claimant.

Upon the application of the United States of America, libellant, herein by its attorney, Martin Conboy, United States Attorney for the Southern District of New York, and upon the consent of the claimant by its attorneys, Greenbaum, Wolff & Ernst, Esqs., it is hereby

ORDERED that the term of court herein, for the purpose of perfecting an appeal, be and the same hereby is extended to and including the 18th day of April, 1934.

Dated: New York, N.Y., March 16, 1934.

JUDGE JOHN M. WOOLSEY

United States District Judge

[Doc. 255]

*New York Herald-Tribune*
March 18, 1934

U. S. Files *Ulysses* Appeal

Bill of Exceptions Holds Court
Erred in Allowing Import

The United States government filed its appeal yesterday from the decision of Federal Judge John M. Woolsey which permitted the importation of James Joyce's *Ulysses*. Martin Conboy, United States Attorney, filed the appeal in person. Yesterday was the last day an appeal could be made since it is three months from the entry of the final decree of Judge Woolsey.

The bill of exceptions, drawn by Francis H. Horan, Assistant United States Attorney, sets forth that the court erred in adjudging the book as not prohibited under the provisions of Section 305 of the Tariff Act of 1930, Title 19 U.S. Code, Section 1305: in adjudicating that the book is not obscene within the meaning of that section; in denying a decree of forfeiture and destruction; in granting the motion to dismiss the libel, and in directing that the book be released to the importer.

---

[Doc. 256]

UNITED STATES CIRCUIT
COURT OF APPEALS
FOR THE SECOND CIRCUIT

UNITED STATES OF AMERICA,

Libellant-Appellant,

-against-

ONE BOOK ENTITLED *ULYSSES*,
BY JAMES JOYCE,
RANDOM HOUSE, INC.,

Claimant-Appellee.

STIPULATION DISPENSING
WITH PRINTING OF
BOOK IN RECORD

The *res* involved in the libel herein, to wit, the book *Ulysses* by James Joyce, having heretofore by a stipulation dated May 15, 1933 been annexed to and made a part of the libel herein,

It is hereby STIPULATED AND AGREED by and between the parties hereto that the appellant, the United States of America, may dispense with the printing of the said book *Ulysses* in the record on appeal herein, and that three copies of the said book of the so-called Random House Edition, which, it is hereby stipulated, contain all of the printed matter contained in the *res* herein, may, in lieu of said printing, be filed with the Court upon the argument of the appeal herein.

Dated, New York, March 23, 1934.

MARTIN CONBOY
United States Attorney
Proctor for Libellant-Appellant

GREENBAUM, WOLFF & ERNST
Proctors for Claimant-Appellee

[Doc. 257]

## UNITED STATES CIRCUIT COURT OF APPEALS
Second Circuit
Post Office Building, Park Row
New York

April 21, 1934.

### UNITED STATES

vs.

### ONE BOOK ENTITLED *ULYSSES*
### BY JAMES JOYCE,
### RANDOM HOUSE, INC.

In accordance with the provisions of General Rule 34 of this court, the above-entitled case has been added to the calendar, its number being 459.

Very truly yours,

Clerk.

Will be reached early in May and no applications for adjournment will be entertained.

---

[Doc. 258]

## UNITED STATES CIRCUIT COURT OF APPEALS
## FOR THE SECOND CIRCUIT

UNITED STATES OF AMERICA,

Libellant-Appellant,

-against-

ONE BOOK ENTITLED *ULYSSES* BY
JAMES JOYCE,
RANDOM HOUSE, INC.,

Claimant-Appellee.

### BRIEF FOR LIBELLANT-APPELLANT

## Statement

Appeal from a decree of the District Court for the Southern District of New York, granting the claimant-appellee's motion to dismiss the libel, denying the libellant-appellant's motion for a decree of forfeiture and destruction, adjudging that the book entitled *Ulysses* is not of the character the entry of which is prohibited under the provisions of Section 305 of the Tariff Act of 1930, and ordering that said book be released by the Collector of Customs to the claimant-appellee (Record, p. 32).

The action was commenced in the United States District Court for the Southern District of New York by the filing of a libel on December 9, 1932, against the book *Ulysses*, which was then in Customs custody (Record, pp. 3, 6). On December 21, 1932 the claim of Random House, Inc., the claimant's answer, and the claimant's stipulation as to costs were filed (Record, pp. 7, 10, 12).

On May 15, 1933, a stipulation was entered into incorporating the libelled book in the libel, waiving trial by jury, and agreeing that each party should move for judgment on the pleadings, and that upon such motions the Court might decide all question of law and fact involved and that judgment might be entered as if it were a judgment after trial (Record, p. 15).

Thereupon the libellant moved for an order granting it judgment on the pleadings and the claimant moved for an order granting judgment in favor of claimant upon the pleadings, both motions being made returnable on May 23, 1933 (Record, pp. 17, 18).

After several adjournments, both motions were argued before Judge Woolsey on November 25, 1933 (Record, p. 21). On December 6, 1933, Judge Woolsey filed his opinion that *Ulysses* might be admitted into the United States, and on December 18, 1933, the decree was entered from which this appeal is taken (Record, pp. 22, 30).

## Issues Involved

The question presented by this appeal is whether the book entitled *Ulysses* is "obscene" within the meaning of Section 305 (a) of the Tariff Act of 1930, 19 U.S.C.A. Sec. 1305 (a), which reads in part as follows:

"All persons are prohibited from importing into the United States from any foreign country . . . any obscene book, pamphlet, paper, writing, advertisement, circular, print, picture, drawing, or other representation, figure or image on or of paper or other material . . .

"Upon the appearance of any such book or matter at any Customs office, the same shall be seized and held by the Collector to await the judgment of the District Court as hereinafter provided . . . Upon the seizure of such book or matter the Collector shall transmit information thereof to the District Attorney of the district in which is situated the office at which such seizure has taken place, who shall institute proceedings in the District Court for the forfeiture, confiscation, and destruction of the book or matter seized . . .

"In any such proceeding any party in interest may upon demand have the facts at issue determined by a jury and anybody may have an appeal or the right of review as in the case of ordinary actions or suits."

## Summary of Argument

I. The District Court erred in determining that *Ulysses* is not obscene.

II. The decree appealed from should be reversed in all respects.

## Point I

### The District Court Erred in Determining that *Ulysses* is not Obscene

The determination of the District Court that *Ulysses* is not obscene within the meaning of Section 305 (a) of the Tariff Act of 1930 was erroneous.

The pleadings in a suit *in rem* brought by the United States for the forfeiture of property are to be according to the course in admiralty. They are not within the scope of the Conformity Act, and for that reason are not governed by the practice in the state courts. Coffey v. United States, 116 U.S. 427; Id. 117 U.S. 233. When that case first came before the Supreme Court, the Court said at page 435:

> The first court of the amended information is in substantial compliance with Rule 22 of the Rules of Admiralty. That Rule prescribes regulations for the form of informations and libels of information on seizures for the breach of the laws of the United States on land or water; and the general rules of pleading in regard to admiralty suits *in rem* apply to a suit *in rem* for a forfeiture, brought by the United States, after a seizure on land. The Sarah, 8 Wheat. 391; Union Ins. Co. v. United States, 6 Wall. 759; 765; Armstrong's Foundry, 6 Wall. 766, 769; Morris' Cotton, 8 Wall. 507, 511.

Upon petition for rehearing, the Court said at pages 233, 234:

> On the hearing in this court, the claimant contended that, as there was no traverse of the answer, it must be taken to be true. But this court held that no reply or replication to the answer was necessary to raise an issue of fact on the matters averred in it; that the proceedings, so far as the pleadings were concerned, were kindred to those in a suit in admiralty *in rem*; that the general rules of pleading in regard to admiralty suits *in rem* apply to suits *in rem* for a forfeiture, brought by the United States, after a seizure on land, as laid down in the cases . . . ; [citing decisions referred to in its former opinion]; that Rule 22 of the Rules of Admiralty prescribes regulations for the form of informations and libels of information on seizures for the breach of the laws of the United States on

land or water; that by Rule 51 in Admiralty, new matter in an answer is considered as denied by the libellant; . . . and that no question in regard to the defense set up could be raised. . . .

Such suits *in rem* are peculiar in their practice, pleadings and forms of procedure, and so long as there is ample scope for the operation of Section 914 of the Revised Statutes (the Conformity Act) in regard to civil suits *in personam*, and no intention is manifest to change the established practice in such suits *in rem*, and any change in practice is limited to 'like causes,' we must continue to regard the former practice as applicable to the present suit.

While the foregoing case arose under the internal revenue laws of the United States, its reasoning is equally applicable to forfeiture proceedings arising under the customs laws. And in United States v. Fourteen Pieces of Embroidery, 155 Fed. 651, it was specifically held that an action by the United States for the forfeiture of goods smuggled in violation of the customs laws was a statutory proceeding assimilated to an action *in rem* in admiralty and that the Conformity Act was therefore not applicable.

A similar course of procedure is prescribed by statute with respect to the forfeiture of prohibited articles under the Pure Food and Drug Law and under the Insecticides Act (21 U.S.C.A., Section 14; 7 U.S.C.A., Section 133).

The parties below recognized and followed the forms of admiralty pleading in filing, respectively, the libel, claim, claimant's answer, and stipulation for claimant's costs.

Since the procedure in this type of action conforms to that employed in suits in admiralty (see *Coffey* v. *United States, supra*), the Circuit Court of Appeals can review the District Court's determination of questions of fact. The Africa Maru, 54 Fed. (2d) 265 (C.C.A 2nd), cert. denied 285 U.S. 556; The Perry Setzer, 299 Fed. 586 (C.C.A. 2nd); The Mason, 249 Fed. 718 (C.C.A. 2nd).

Even if the practice followed should be the same as in ordinary actions at law, this Court can nevertheless review the determination of the District Court on the facts. This is so because the parties in the Court below agreed upon all the facts. There was no conflicting testimony, and no question involving the credibility of witnesses. The only evidence adduced by either party was the book itself. In Lumbermen's Trust Company v. Town of Ryegate, 61 F. (2d) 14 (C.C.A. 9th), the Court said at page 16:

In an action at law where the parties waive a jury the power of this Court to review or consider the facts on appeal is extremely limited. *Where there is an agreed set of facts, the power is more ample.* (Italics supplied.)

In order of United Commercial Travelers v. Shane, 64 F. (2d) 55 (C.C.A. 8th), the beneficiary of an accident insurance policy brought an action at law.

The parties waived a jury by stipulation, and the District Court rendered findings of fact and conclusions of law. Upon appeal the Circuit Court of Appeals held that it could review the facts determined by the District Court, and said at page 57:

> It is provided by statute, where a jury is waived and the case tried to the Court, that "the finding of the Court upon the facts, which may be either general or special, shall have the same effect as the verdict of a jury" (28 U.S.C.A., Sec. 773). This statutory provision does not prevent a review of questions of law; and, where the primary facts are either stipulated or established by uncontradicted evidence, and the Court solely from these primary facts, finds an ultimate fact upon which the judgment rests, such finding is in the nature of a conclusion of law, and as such is reviewable on appeal to determine whether the primary facts support it.

In the foregoing case the undisputed primary facts disclosed that the insured had died as the result of the administration of a local anaesthetic. The District Court found, as a fact within the meaning of the insurance policy, that the death had resulted from "accidental means" and not from "medical" or "surgical treatment." Upon appeal both of these findings of fact were reversed.

Similarly, in St. Paul Abstract Co. v. Commissioner of Internal Revenue, 32 F. (2d) 225 (C.C.A. 8th) where the Board of Tax Appeals found as a fact that the taxpayer was a "personal service corporation" within the meaning of Section 200 of the Revenue Act of 1918, upon review by the Circuit Court of Appeals, the Court said at page 226:

> Where the facts are undisputed there remains no question of fact in the usual sense of the term, but where the primary facts are agreed it is a question of law whether such facts justify the finding of the ultimate fact required by the statute. Botany Worsted Mills v. U.S., 278, U.S. 282. . . . The ultimate fact required by this statute to be found is whether the taxpayer is a personal service corporation within the meaning of that statute. This requires a construction of the meaning of the statute and its application to a set of primary facts. We think that we must examine the stipulated facts and determine whether they justify the conclusion that the petitioner is not a personal service corporation within the meaning of the statute.

By a parity of reason, in the present case, where there is no dispute as to the primary facts, this Court can determine for itself the ultimate question of fact involved: namely, whether Ulysses is "obscene" within the meaning of Section 305 (a) of the Tariff Act of 1930.

Among the leading cases in the Supreme Court upon the question of obscenity are Rosen v. United States, 161 U.S. 29, and Dunlop v. United States, 165 U.S. 486.

In Rosen v. United States, the Supreme Court approved a charge by the trial court in language almost identical with that used by Lord Cockburn in Regina v. Hicklin, L.R. 3 Q.B. 369. The charge that was approved was as follows:

> The test of obscenity is whether the tendency of the matter is to deprave and corrupt the morals of those whose minds are open to such influence and into whose hands a publication of this sort may fall.

The test laid down in *Regina* v. *Hicklin* has been repeatedly enunciated as the proper rule in a great number of cases in the Federal Courts.

> United States v. Bennett, Fed. Cas. No. 14571;
> United States v. Bebout, 28 Fed. 522;
> United States v. Wightman, 29 Fed. 636;
> United States v. Clarke, 38 Fed. 733;
> United States v. Smith, 45 Fed. 476;
> United States v. Harmon, 45 Fed. 417;
> United States v. Dennett, 39 Fed. (2d) 564 (C.C.A. 2nd).

In the last named case, this Court said at page 568 that:

> The test most frequently laid down seems to have been whether it would tend to deprave the morals of those into whose hands the publication might fall by suggesting lewd thoughts and inciting sensual desires.

It seems clear beyond question, therefore, that the rule of *Regina* v. *Hicklin* is established as the yardstick by which books are to be measured in the Federal Courts.

It does not require lengthy argument to establish that *Ulysses* is obscene under this test. It is sufficient to read pages 173, 213, 214, 231–233, 318, 359–364, 398–399, 423–424, 434, 443, 458, 467–468, 489–491, 500, 508, 522–525, 527, 552–553, 555–556, 718–720, 724–727, 731, 738–739, 744–745, 754–755, 761–762, 765.*

It cannot be argued that the test enunciated in *Regina* v. *Hicklin, supra,* was abandoned by the federal courts by virtue of the decisions in the cases of

---

*The page references are to the so-called Random House Edition which, as has been stipulated, contains all of the printed matter contained in the *res* herein and has been filed with the Court (Rec. p. 40).

The corresponding pages in the *res* are as follows:

167, 168, 207, 208, 225–227, 310, 349–354, 386, 387, 409, 410, 420, 428, 442, 450, 451, 471, 473, 481, 489, 502–505, 507, 530, 531, 533, 534, 689–691, 694–697, 700, 701, 708, 709, 714, 715, 722–724, 729, 730, 733.

Swearingen v. United States, 161 U.S. 446; United States v. Kennerley, 209 Fed. 119 and United States v. Bennett, Fed Cas. No. 14, 571. In *Swearingen* v. *United States*, the Supreme Court incorporated that test in its opinion. In *United States* v. *Kennerley*, the Court stated that "that test has been accepted by the lower Federal Courts until it would be no longer proper for me to disregard it," and accordingly held that a demurrer to an indictment would be overruled since certain parts of the book there in question might well be found obscene under the test. In *United States* v. *Bennett*, the Court expressly approved a charge to the jury in the language set forth in *Regina* v. *Hicklin*.

The decisions in United States v. One Book entitled *Contraception*, 51 Fed. (2d) 525; United States v. One Obscene Book entitled *Married Love*, 48 F. (2d) 821 and *United States* v. *Dennett, supra*, are clearly distinguishable from the present case. The books involved in those cases were of a medical nature and described certain physical and biological facts. They are in no way comparable with a work of fiction such as *Ulysses*, either in language or in the impression sought to be created.

No argument may be based upon the purpose of the author, his literary importance or unimportance or psychological truthfulness or falsity. The statute does not make intent an essential element of its violation. It is well settled that the object or motive in publishing a questioned book is immaterial. See *United States* v. *Dennett, supra; United States* v. *Bennett, supra*. The same is true of the opinion or belief of the author or publisher as to the obscenity of the publication. See *Rosen* v. *United States, supra*, at page 41, *United States* v. *Harmon, supra*. A book that is obscene is not rendered less so by reason of the fact that the matter complained of is in fact truthful. Burton v. United States, 142 Fed. 57 (C.C.A. 8th).

The fact that some portions of the book are unobjectionable under the statute is immaterial. It is not necessary that every incident and every experience described in it shall be obscene to justify a conviction of obscenity. Taking the test of obscenity which has been established in the Federal Courts and applying it to the numerous passages of grossly obscene matter with which this book fairly reeks, there can be no doubt that the District Court erred in its determination that *Ulysses* is not obscene.

Indeed its obscenity is so indisputable that it is submitted that the Court erred in its decision not only as a matter of fact, but also as a matter of law, because no reasonable man applying the proper rule of law could come to any conclusion other than that *Ulysses* is obscene. The District Court erred, therefore, not only in its determination that this book did not violate the federal laws on obscenity but also in its failure to grant the libellant's motion for judgment on the pleadings.

One further consideration should be mentioned. Taking the claimant's contentions as a whole it becomes evident that its position is not that *Ulysses* should not be found obscene within the meaning of the statute, but that the statute itself is a bad one. The thesis advanced is in substance the same one set forth in *To the Pure* by Morris L. Ernst, one of the counsel for claimant herein. That thesis is "that obscenity is only a superstition of the day—the modern counterpart of ancient witchcraft" (*To the Pure*, Introduction, p. X). The discussion of the truth or falsity of this idea is beyond the scope of the question presented to the court by the present case. We have a statute upon the books forbidding the importation of obscene books. "The word *obscene* as used in that statute has received a meaning from the decisions of the Federal Courts in a great number of cases. Within that meaning *Ulysses* is clearly obscene and its importation should not be permitted.

### Point II
The Decree Appealed from Should Be Reversed in all Respects.

Respectfully submitted,

MARTIN CONBOY,
United States Attorney for the
Southern District of New York,
Attorney for Libellant-Appellant.

MARTIN CONBOY
and
FRANCIS H. HORAN,
JOHN F. DAVIDSON,
Assistant U.S. Attorneys,
of Counsel.

---

[Doc. 259]

To: Mr. Lindey
From: Mr. Kaplan                                    April 26, 1934.

Where the question of obscenity is tried before judge and jury the respective functions of these branches of the court may be summarized as follows:

  I. It is the duty of the judge to determine whether the book libeled is:

    (a) obscene as a matter of law, in which case it may be withdrawn from jury or;

    (b) whether the inference of obscenity is so remote that it must be withdrawn from jury or;

    (c) whether the inference of obscenity is permissible, in which case it must be left to the jury.

II. It is the jury's duty to make or decline to make the inferences. This fundamental analysis is not destroyed by virtue of the fact that a jury trial is waived and the judge thereby performs the functions both of a judge and of a jury. Hence Judge Woolsey, in ruling that *Ulysses* was not obscene, may have been holding:

(a) That the inference of obscenity was not even permissible; or
(b) That the inference was permissible; but he, acting as the jury, chose to make the inference that the book was not obscene.

On appeal the function of the Circuit Court of Appeals is restricted to one thing, namely, is it a permissible inference of fact, on the basis of a judicial interpretation of the word *obscenity* as contained in section 305, that the book is not obscene.*

The government has sought to avoid the force of this reasoning by insinuating that an action to condemn a book must be analogized to an action to forfeit under the Customs Law; or an ordinary action in Admiralty. Here what I suspect to be the law in customs forfeiture and admiralty must be noticed. My suspicion is that in both these branches of the law the jury trial, when permissible (and this is a rare case), is restricted to an advisory capacity only. In most cases I think jury trials may not be demanded as a matter of right and I think the law is not different even where it is demandable as of right. In the obscenity statute there is no indication that the jury is to be used in an advisory capacity, and the whole pressure of history in this field (compare libel) is to give the jury verdict persuasive and even absolutely binding effect. If this is so, the picture of the law presented above is unimpeachable.

---

*Assuming that W[oolsey] was convinced of II.a., there would be no sense in reversing if the inference of obscenity was merely permissible.

[Doc. 260]

## United States Circuit Court of Appeals
## for the Second Circuit

UNITED STATES OF AMERICA,
            Libellant-Appellant,

*against*

ONE BOOK ENTITLED *ULYSSES* BY
            JAMES JOYCE

RANDOM HOUSE, INC.,
            Claimant-Appellee.

### BRIEF FOR CLAIMANT-APPELLEE.

Respectfully submitted,

GREENBAUM, WOLFF & ERNST,
Attorneys for Claimant-Appellee,
285 Madison Avenue,
Borough of Manhattan,
New York City.

Morris L. Ernst,
Alexander Lindey,
Of Counsel.

Dated, New York, May 1, 1934.

----------

## INDEX

Point I. The Judgment Below Should Be Affirmed

    A. The Ancient Test of Obscenity Urged by the Appellant No Longer Applies

    B. In the Court Below, the Legality of *Ulysses* Has Been Established in Law and Fact

    C. Only Questions of Law Are Involved in This Appeal

    D. The Decision of the Lower Court, Acclaimed Throughout the Country, Reflects Public Opinion and Should Not Be Disturbed

Point II. The Test of Obscenity Is a Living Standard and *Ulysses* Must be Judged by the Mores of the Day

    A. The Law

    B. The Changing Times

    C. Our Mores

Point III. *Ulysses* Has Been Generally Accepted by the Community and Hence Cannot Be Held to Be Violative of the Statute

Point IV. *Ulysses* Is Not Obscene According to the Accepted Definitions of Obscenity Laid Down by the Courts

    A. The Question

    B. The Development of the Law

    C. *Frankie and Johnnie*

    D. Some Recent New York Cases Involving Books

    E. Normal v. Abnormal

Point V. *Ulysses* Is a Modern Classic. The United States Government Has Officially Acknowledged It as Such. It Cannot Therefore Be Deemed Obscene

    A. The Federal Government Has Officially Paid Tribute to the Greatness of *Ulysses*

    B. A Classic Cannot Be Adjudged Obscene

Point VI. The Intrinsic Features of Ulysses, as Well as Certain Extrinsic Facts Connected With It, Negate Any Implication of Obscenity

    A. Intrinsic Characteristics

    B. Extrinsic Circumstances

Point VII. *Ulysses* Must Be Judged as a Whole, and Its General Purpose and Effect Determined. On That Basis It Must Be Cleared

Conclusion

## Appendices

Note on the Appendices

### United States Circuit Court of Appeals
### for the Second Circuit

UNITED STATES OF AMERICA,
  Libellant-Appellant,

*against*

ONE BOOK ENTITLED *ULYSSES*
BY
JAMES JOYCE,

RANDOM HOUSE, INC.,
  Claimant-Appellee.

### BRIEF FOR CLAIMANT-APPELLEE

#### Statement

This is an appeal from a judgment of the District Court for the Southern District of New York, adjudging that *Ulysses* is not obscene and is therefore entitled to enter the United States (Transcript, fol. 94).

The book was sent to this country, addressed to the claimant herein. At the instance of the Collector of Customs, the government filed a libel against it on December 9, 1932. On December 21, Random House, Inc. filed its claim, answer and stipulation as to costs (fols. 20–44).

On May 15, 1933, the parties entered into a stipulation (1) that *Ulysses* be annexed to the libel; (2) that the claimant waive trial by jury; (3) that both parties move for judgment; (4) that upon such judgment the Court consider and decide all questions of law and fact; and (5) that upon the motion judgment be entered herein as if it were judgment after trial (fols. 45–48). Thereafter the parties cross-moved as stipulated (fols. 49–56).

The motions were argued before Judge Woolsey on November 25, 1933. On December 6 he handed down his memorable opinion exonerating the book. The judgment embodying his decision was signed on December 15 and filed three days later.

## Nature of the Case

This case is unique in several respects. It involves a book which has been a *cause célèbre* in literary circles for more than a decade. No other prose work of our times—perhaps no other literary product in the history of the world— has caused so much controversy, has won such enthusiastic critical acclaim and has so profoundly influenced letters. There is every reason, therefore, why the rules of law which are invoked in ordinary cases should be applied here with exceptional circumspection.

There is a peculiar timeliness about this appeal. Coming, as it does, in logical sequence after the *Dennett* case, the *Youngs* case, the *Married Love* case, the *Contraception* case, the *Wendling* case,[1] all of which have served to liberalize the law of obscenity to meet prevailing notions of morality, *Ulysses* calls for an affirmance of its vindication as a fitting climax to the salutary forward march of our courts.

The decision of the court below has met with overwhelming public approval such as has rarely been accorded in recent years to a judicial disposition.[2] It is this decision that the appellant seeks to upset on appeal.

## The Author

Joyce was born of Roman Catholic parents in Dublin in 1882. His early home life was steeped in an atmosphere of ritual and theology. He was educated at the Jesuit school, Clongowes Wood, and later at Belvedere College and the Royal University, Dublin. His autobiographical novel, *A Portrait of the Artist as a Young Man*, gives a vivid picture of the formative years of a sensitive, brooding child, torn between religious obsession and doubt.

After studying medicine at the University of Paris, Joyce devoted himself to Latin, German, Norwegian and the Romance languages, and became a linguist and a teacher. He has lived in Trieste, Switzerland and France. He now resides in Paris.

Though he is the most important figure in world literature today, his works are few in number. *Chamber Music*, a collection of poems, appeared in 1907; *Dubliners*, a series of unforgettable characterizations, intermittently thereafter in periodicals, and in final form in 1914; *A Portrait of the Artist as a Young Man*, a novel,[3] in 1915; *Exiles*, a play, in 1918; and *Ulysses* in 1922.

The last-named work, now before the Court, bears the notation "Trieste-Zurich-Paris, 1914–1921" at the conclusion. It took more than seven years to write.

Joyce belongs to that distinguished company of Irish authors which includes such men at Padraic Colum (an ardent champion of Joyce), James Stephens, Sean O'Casey, William Butler Yeats and George Bernard Shaw. Unlike Shaw and others of his countrymen, Joyce has steadfastly scorned ballyhoo and self-exploitation. He has led a monastic existence, and has made no attempt to benefit by the furore created by *Ulysses*. He has delivered no lectures, given no interviews, posed for no newsreels, attached no explanatory prefaces to his works, issued no manifestos, written no magazine articles which might have yielded him easy harvest. Nearly as blind as the Greek master from whose epic he borrowed the name of his novel, he has lived apart, an austere Olympian.[4] Hailed ten years ago by the untutored and the misguided as a juggler of words, today even his harshest critics concede his greatness.

He has exerted a profound influence on world letters—possibly greater influence than any man before him. There is not a single modern psychological novel worthy of mention which does not bear some trace of the Joycean method.[5]

It is not often that an author, within the span of his lifetime, sees a work of his acclaimed as a classic. Joyce is such an author. He stands as a kind of Colossus of creative writing, dominating his age. He is a genius of the first rank.

Stuart Gilbert, distinguished American critic, says:

> . . . the genius of James Joyce has an Elizabethan quality, an universality, a gift of reconciling classical, modern and romantic that, Shakespeare excepted, renders it unique.[6]

"His prose works," says Rebecca West, "prove him beyond argument a writer of majestic genius."[7]

"No living author," says Paul Rosenfeld, "brings a vocabulary either as crisply, sharply, pungently used, or as vast. Joyce possesses a relatively unlimited knowledge of the resources of the English language. . . . It is no petty achievement to have attained with serio-comedy the level upon which Swift and Flaubert stand, and long will stand."[8]

When it comes to psychology or realism, beside Joyce "Balzac is beggared and Zola bankrupted," says Shane Leslie in *The Quarterly Review*, October, 1922. In *Ulysses* there is evident, according to J. Middleton Murry, noted English critic, "a genius of the very highest order, strictly comparable to Goethe's or Dostoevsky's."

He is, according to Gilbert Seldes, writing in *The Nation*, "possibly the most interesting and the most formidable writer of our time. . . .Among the very great writers only two can be named with him for the long devotion to their work and for the triumphant conclusion—Flaubert and Henry James." He has scored "a victory of the creative intelligence over the chaos of uncreated things and a triumph of devotion, to my mind one of the most significant and beautiful of our time."

". . . this austere, almost pedantic writer," says Edmund Wilson in *The New Republic*, "soars to such rhapsodies of beauty as have probably never been equalled in English prose fiction" (December 18, 1929).

It is monstrous to suppose that a man of Joyce's stature would or could produce a work of obscenity.

## The Book

Dante wrote the *Divine Comedy*, and Balzac the *Comédie Humaine*. It remained for Joyce to write the *Comédie Intellectuelle*.

In some respects *Ulysses* defies accurate description. Although fictional in form, it is not a novel. It is a vast edifice of episode superimposed on episode, a panorama of all the aspects, moods, excesses and torments of the human mind. Despite its heroic proportions,[9] it deals with but one day in the life of Leopold Bloom (Ulysses), advertising solicitor. All the action unfolds itself in Dublin between the early morning hours of June 16, and about three o'clock in the morning, June 17, 1904—about twenty hours altogether. "And yet," says Gorman, "in that short period of time is packed the whole vivid variegated life of Dublin. . . . All the emotions and attributes find their place here. There is birth, love, death, adultery, greed, sloth, drunkenness, anger, chicanery, intrigue, religion, philosophy, spiritual torture, childish ignorance, nationalism, lechery, madness, the list is infinite. Expressing these emotions, hundreds of characters hold forth in the streets, public-houses, cemeteries, shops, libraries, newspaper offices, hospitals, brothels and churches. With this infinite variety of material . . . the author conceives a certain order and in so doing he creates a new form for the novel. . . . The real genius of the book . . . is implicit in the complete revelation and development of two characters, two of the greatest, saddest, most tragi-comic portraits in the entire annals of literary achievement—Stephen Dedalus and Leopold Bloom."[10]

Yet it is neither Dedalus nor Bloom who is the hero of *Ulysses*. The real protagonist is the mind. The arena is not Dublin, but the human skull.

Joyce has patterned his book after Homer's *Odyssey*, but he has not sought to make the parallel perfect. Whatever discrepancies exist are unimportant. In one significant respect there is a kinship between the two books: the *Odyssey* is a record of journeyings in a physical world; *Ulysses* is the epic of the coursing of the stream of consciousness.

There is no need for us to set forth in this brief an analysis of the incidents in *Ulysses*. The Court will read the book; upon the argument of the appeal the claimant will offer to the Court Herbert Gorman's *James Joyce*, and Paul Jordan Smith's *A Key to the Ulysses of James Joyce*. The last-named work contains a complete outline.

Louis Golding, writing in *The Nineteenth Century*, April 1933, thus indicates the stature of *Ulysses*:

> Among great works of prose we find none that compares in kind with *Ulysses*. When we seek works which compare with it in scope, we cannot stop short this side of the *Inferno, Hamlet* and the *Odyssey*, each of which, in point of fact, has the closest bearing on the developing history of Stephen Dedalus and Leopold Bloom during the eternal eighteen hours of the day on which the action of *Ulysses* occurs. (p. 491)

## Recent Cases

The Court's attention is respectfully directed to the fact that in recent years there has not been a single instance where a book generally acclaimed by the press and literary critics was ultimately condemned by the courts, even though prosecuted at the outset for obscenity. This statement is borne out by such books as Theophile Gautier's *Mademoiselle de Maupin* (234 N.Y. 1); the anonymous *Madeleine* (192 App. Div. [N.Y.] 816); *The Satyricon of Petronius* (Magistrate Oberwager, September 27, 1922, New York City); *A Young Girl's Diary* (Magistrate Simpson, September 30, 1922, New York City); Maxwell Bodenheim's *Replenishing Jessica* (Court of General Sessions, New York City, June 1925); Radclyffe Hall's *The Well of Loneliness* (Court of Special Sessions, City of New York, April 19, 1929); *Casanova's Homecoming* (Magistrate Gottlieb, September 25, 1930, New York City); Mary Ware Dennett's *The Sex Side of Life* (39 Fed. [2d] 564); Dr. Marie Stopes' *Married Love* (48 Fed. [2d] 821); Dr. Marie Stopes' *Contraception* (51 Fed. [2d] 525); the Chinese classic *Hsi Men Ching* (Magistrate Brodsky, November 9, 1931, New York City); Clement Wood's *Flesh* (Magistrate Harris, December 18, 1931); Louis Charles Royer's *Let's Go Naked* (Magistrate Van Amringe, December 8, 1932, New York City); and Erskine Caldwell's *God's Little Acre* (Magistrate Greenspan, May 23, 1933, New York City).[11]

## The Law

Section 305 of the Tariff Act of 1930 (Title 19, United States Code, Section 1305), provides in part as follows:

> All persons are prohibited from importing into the United States from any foreign country . . . any obscene book, pamphlet, paper, writing, advertisement, circular, print, picture, drawing or other representation, figure, or image on or of paper or other material. . . .[12]

## Argument

I. The judgment below should be affirmed.

II. The test of obscenity is a living standard, and *Ulysses* must be judged by the mores of the day.

III. *Ulysses* has been generally accepted by the community, and hence cannot be held to be violative of the statute.

IV. *Ulysses* is not obscene as a matter of law.

V. *Ulysses* is a modern classic. The United States Government having officially acknowledged it as such, it cannot be deemed obscene.

VI. The intrinsic features of *Ulysses*, as well as certain extrinsic facts, negate any implications of obscenity.

VII. *Ulysses* must be judged as a whole, and its general purpose and effect determined. On that basis it must be cleared.

## Table of Cases Cited

387

## POINT I

### The judgment below should be affirmed

A. THE ANCIENT TEST OF OBSCENITY URGED BY THE APPELLANT NO
LONGER APPLIES.

The appellant urges this Court, in the face of Judge Woolsey's memorable decision, to declare *Ulysses* obscene; and in support of its position it advances the ancient case of Regina v. Hicklin, L.R., 3 Q.B. 360. It is worthy of note that this case was decided in 1868—*sixty-six years ago*. The appellant also relies on Rosen v. United States, 161 U.S. 29, and on Dunlop v. United States, 165 U.S. 486. The former case was decided in 1896, thirty-eight years ago; the latter in 1897, thirty-seven years ago. (Aplt.'s Br., p. 9)

The appellant concludes by saying (idem., p. 10) that "it seems clear beyond question that the rule of *Regina* v. *Hicklin* is established as the yardstick by which books are to be measured in the Federal Courts."

The contrary is true. In U.S. v. Bennett, 16 Blatchf. 338, the unsound English rule was modified; in U.S. v. Kennerley, 209 Fed. 119, 120, twenty-one years ago, Judge Learned Hand all but repudiated it when he said:

> I hope it is not improper for me to say that the rule as laid down [in *Regina* v. *Hicklin*], however consonant it may be with mid-Victorian morals, does not seem to me to answer to the understanding and morality of the present time. . . . (Brackets ours.)

We are unwilling to believe that the appellant is seriously urging this Court to apply to a present-day book an obsolete rule of law which was enunciated more than three generations ago on a subject as variable as obscenity, and which has been substantially revised by our courts.[13]

The opinion of the lower Court represents a succinct and lucid crystallization of the law as it now exists, and is fully supported by the cases therein cited.

B. IN THE COURT BELOW, THE LEGALITY OF *ULYSSES* HAS BEEN
ESTABLISHED IN LAW AND IN FACT.

The Court's attention is directed to the stipulation which was signed on behalf of the libellant and the claimant in the lower Court prior to adjudication (Transcript, fols. 45-48). It was agreed that the Court would sit as judge and jury; that upon the cross-motions of the parties, it might consider and decide *all questions of law and fact*; and that the Court's judgment might be entered as if it were a judgment after trial (Idem., fol. 47). This stipulation was necessary because the Tariff Act of 1930 provides for trial by jury.

Judge Woolsey has found, as a matter of law and as a matter of fact, that *Ulysses* is not obscene since it does "not tend to excite sexual impulses or lustful thoughts" (fol. 87), and that it is therefore entitled to entry into this country (fol. 88).

The question presented on this appeal is not whether Judge Woolsey has ruled properly on some point of law in connection with a motion preliminary to trial. There *has* been a trial; *Ulysses* has been cleared in law and in fact. Accordingly, this Court should have the same reluctance to disturb the result as if it had been reached by a jury.

The position of the appellant is thus set forth on page 12 of its brief:

> . . . There can be no doubt that the District Court erred in its determination that *Ulysses* is not obscene. Indeed its obscenity is so indisputable that it is submitted that the court erred in its decision not only as a matter of fact, but also as a matter of law, because *no reasonable man* applying the proper rule of law could come to any conclusion other than that *Ulysses* is obscene. (Italics ours.)

What the appellant is saying in effect is that in ruling on the book below, Judge Woolsey did not act as a reasonable man.

In its brief filed in the Circuit Court of Appeals in connection with United States v. Dennett, 39 Fed. (2d) 564, the government made the following statement at page 27:

> . . . the question of whether the pamphlet was obscene, lewd and lascivious rested squarely on the shoulders of the jury, and so far as their decision of this question is concerned, it is foreclosed on this appeal.

The Federal appellate courts have time and again held that they will not pass on the "weight of the evidence."

Hederley v. United States, 193 Fed. 561 (C.C.A. 9);
Crompton v. United States, 138 U.S. 363;
Cohen v. United States, 214 Fed. 23 (C.C.A. 9);
Looker v. United States, 240 Fed. 942 (C.C.A. 2);
Fraina v. United States, 255 Fed. 28, 34 (C.C.A. 2);
Felder v. United States, 9 Fed. (2d), 872, 875 (C.C.A. 2).

In *Felder* v. *United States, supra*, this Court, Judge Hough writing, said in part:

> That we cannot investigate it to pass on the weight of the evidence is a point too often decided to need citation; nor can we, after investigation, use such doubts as may assail us to disturb the verdict of the jury. That reasonable doubt which often prevents conviction must be the jury's doubt, and not that of any court, either original or appellate. Looker v.

United States, 240 F. 932, 153 C.C.A. 618. Cf. Fraina v. United States, 255 F. 28, at page 34, 166 C.C.A. 356. Our duty is but to declare whether the jury had the right to pass on what evidence there was.

In other words, if this Court upon reading *Ulysses* comes to the conclusion that *two* inferences may reasonably be drawn as to the legality of its contents, the judgment must stand even though this Court may be inclined to disagree with Judge Woolsey's inference.

We have considered this problem at length because a considerable portion of the appellant's brief has been devoted to it. We do not desire to convey the impression that we are endeavoring to exculpate *Ulysses* on hypertechnical legalistic grounds. We submit that even if this Court were to sit as a jury in considering the book, it would still hold that it is not obscene.

C. ONLY QUESTIONS OF LAW ARE INVOLVED IN THIS APPEAL.

As we have stated above, the parties waived a jury in the lower court, and agreed that the judge hearing the cross-motions might render "general findings of fact and conclusions of law" (fol. 47). This was done (fols. 90-96).

It is provided by statute, where a jury is waived and the case tried to the Court, that "the finding of the Court upon the facts, which may be either general or special, shall have the same effect as the verdict of a jury." 28 U.S.C.A. Sec. 773.

The verdict or the findings of a jury will not be disturbed where the case was properly submitted to it. (N.Y. Cent. etc. R.R. v. Fraloff, 100 U.S. 24); nor where the verdict is supported by inferences reasonably deducible from the evidence (U.S. v. Metropolitan Club, 11 App. Div. [D.C.] 180); nor where reasonable men may differ in their conclusions (4 C.J. 854).

In Carter-Crume Co. v. Peurrung, 86 Fed. 439, the Circuit Court said:

> . . . where there is any substantial evidence upon which a jury could reasonably find, this court will not disturb the verdict . . . This is too long and well settled to need other authority than *Railway Co.* v. *Lowry,* cited heretofore. (The citation of the last named case is 43 U.S. App. 408).

See also,

Herencia v. Guzman, 219 U.S. 44; and
Petrie v. N.Y. Cent. etc. R.R. Co., 63 App. Div. (N.Y.) 473.

On appeal the reviewing court must take the view of the evidence most favorable to the verdict.

Zang v. Joline, 159 App. Div. [N.Y.] 885.

Under the circumstances no issue of fact may be reviewed on this appeal. This Court is not sitting as a jury; it may condemn *Ulysses* only if it finds, as a matter of law, that the book is so flagrantly objectionable as to be virtually indefensible.

The appellant argues at length to the contrary (Aplt.'s Br., pp. 4-8). Yet the very cases cited by it contradict its contention. In Lumbermen's Trust Co. v. Town of Ryegate, 61 Fed. (2d) 14, Circuit Court Judge Wilbur expressly stated that the power of the Circuit Court to review or consider the facts on appeal was extremely limited (p. 16). "Where there is an agreed state of facts," said the Judge, "the power is more ample."

The appellant strives to bring this appeal within the purview of Judge Wilbur's qualification by saying (Alpt.'s Br., p. 6) that "the parties in the court below agreed upon all the facts." *Such is not the case.* What the parties did agree upon was the *evidence* (Transcript, fol. 46). Whether or not a book is obscene is a question partly of law and partly of fact.[14] Had the parties below agreed on the *facts*, there would have been nothing for the lower court to determine.

So, too, in Order of United Commercial Travelers v. Shane, 64 Fed. (2d) 55, 57, the Circuit Court held that only questions of law (and "ultimate" facts in the nature of conclusions of law) were reviewable.

Unless this Court is ready to stamp Judge Woolsey's verdict as unreasonable and irrational, the judgment below must stand.

D. THE DECISION OF THE LOWER COURT, HAVING WON ACCLAIM THROUGHOUT THE COUNTRY, REFLECTS PUBLIC OPINION AND SHOULD NOT BE DISTURBED.

When on December 6, 1933, Judge Woolsey handed down his opinion clearing *Ulysses*, it was greeted with praise and approval in every quarter of the United States.[15] Literary critics, authors, editors of newspapers ranging from liberal to conservative, lawyers and judges, all joined in saying that rarely had there been an opinion so lucid in its statement of the law, so balanced in its reasoning, so felicitously phrased and so completely consonant with the social temper.

Judge Woolsey held that Joyce's epic of the human mind was not obscene—

(1) Because, despite its unusual frankness, one could not detect in it "the leer of the sensualist" or any "pornographic" intent[16] (fols. 72-73);

(2) Because it was "a sincere and honest book", in the composition of which Joyce had been faithful "to his chosen technique", so that criticisms of it were "entirely disposed of by its rationale" (fols. 76, 79);

(3) Because it drew "a true picture" of life (fol. 81);

(4) Because, regardless of intent, it did not come within the accepted definition of obscenity, since it "did not tend to excite sexual impulses or lustful thoughts" (fol. 87); and

(5) Because its effect on the normal person—*"l'homme moyen sensual,"* who played the role of hypothetical reagent (fol. 84)—was bound to be that of an emetic instead of an aphrodisiac (fol. 88).

A reversal of the judgment below would mean not only the disapproval of these sane principles, but also the repudiation of public opinion. And it is certain that in the case of no other literary work has society voiced its enthusiasm with such articulate emphasis.

The law is not a petrified system of rules, nor does it develop in a vacuum. It is a living organism, subject to growth and change in precisely the same manner as society itself, whose conduct it seeks to regulate. Public approval should mean—and must mean—legal vindication.

## POINT II

The test of obscenity is a living standard, and *Ulysses* must be judged by the mores of the day

### A. THE LAW

What is decent or indecent is determined by the sensibilities and moral standards of the people, as evolved from generation to generation along with their civilization. A thing deemed indecent in one period may be approved as decent in another.

> 46 *Corpus Juris,* 854;
> People v. Seltzer, 203 N.Y. Supp. 809, 814.

It is evident that Judge Learned Hand had this fluidity of standard in mind when he remarked in U.S. v. Kennerley, 209 Fed. 119, at page 121:

> If there be no abstract definition, such as I have suggested, should not the word *obscene* be allowed to indicate the *present critical point* in the compromise between candor and shame at which the community may have arrived *here and now?* . . . Nor is it an objection, I think, that such an interpretation gives to the words of the statute a *varying meaning* from time to time. Such words as these do not embalm the precise morals of an age or place; while they presuppose that some things will always be shocking to the public taste, the vague subject matter is left *to the gradual development of general notions about what is decent.* (Italics ours.)

In St. Hubert Guild v. Quinn, 64 Misc. 336, the Court insisted that "contemporaneous literature must, of course, be judged by *current* opinion."

Judge Cardozo has said, in his book entitled *The Paradoxes of Legal Science* (p. 10):

> We live in a world of change. If a body of law were in existence adequate for the civilization of today, it could not meet the demands of the civilization of tomorrow.

In his *The Growth of the Law*, he has reiterated this basic truth, saying:

> *Law accepts as the pattern of its justice the morality of the community whose conduct it assumes to regulate.* . . . The law will not hold the crowd to the morality of saints and seers. (Italics ours.)

In his treatise entitled "The Development of the Law," *Columbia Law Review*, December 1923, Professor Maurice Wormser wrote:

> Increasingly—ever increasingly—the community is beginning to require of the law that it justify its own administration of its resources before the bar of public opinion. And in order to justify itself before this critical bar, the law must be brought to evidence the mores of the times, to which it must conform, or it will fail to fulfill its function as the juridical expression of the community-passion for justice and right dealing.

## B. THE CHANGING TIMES

In Rome remarriage was deemed adulterous and a third marriage was severely punished. Today the notion that remarriage is immoral has been rejected; and the State recognizes, and the Church acquiesces in, the custom of divorce.[17]

Alexander Hamilton, in the early days of our republic, protested against the use of the Maypole in America, claiming that the dance had phallic significance. Now our parks and playgrounds are filled with Maypole parties, and the custom appears obscene to no one.

In 1895, one John B. Wise, of Clay Center, Kansas, was convicted of sending obscene matter through the U.S. mails. The matter consisted of quotations from the Bible.[18]

In 1900 any female who appeared on a bathing beach without sleeves and a long skirt would have been jailed. By 1911 bare knees could be legally displayed at the seashore; but legs still had to be covered, and girls wore stockings rolled down below the knees. A few years ago the one-piece bathing suit came into its own; and today the so-called sunsuits leave very little of the human form concealed. There was a time, not so long ago, when bobbed hair and cigarette-smoking were the signs of a loose woman. It may sound incredible, but Walter Hines Page (back in the days when he was a member of the publishing firm of Doubleday, Page & Company) refused to print a book, because it contained the suggestive word *chaste*.[19]

A woman superintendent in the Children's Department of the Brooklyn Public Library once charged that *Tom Sawyer* and *Huckleberry Finn* were corrupting the morals of children.[20]

In 1906 the play *Sappho* was suppressed because Olga Nethersole was carried upstairs in it by a man. To the present generation *Sappho* is an innocuous piece. George Bernard Shaw's *Mrs. Warren's Profession* has had the same history. In 1907 the New England Watch and Ward Society prevented Mary Garden from appearing in Richard Strauss' celebrated opera *Salôme*. Today the opera is in the repertoire of every reputable opera company.

A decade ago *September Morn*, *Paul and Virginia*, Manet's *Olympia* and similar pictures were deemed pornography; now they hardly elicit a second glance. The *Bacchante* of MacMonnies was once denounced as "a naked woman dancing in her shame."[21] When Goya first painted the Duchess of Alba as *Maya Desnuda*, the moral sensibilities of his zealous contemporaries were outraged, and for many years the painting was hid from view. Today it has the place of honor in the national gallery at the Prado; and at the Ibero-American Exposition which was held in Spain in 1930, thousands of Goya Memorial Stamps were issued by the government bearing miniature reproductions of the painting.

The history of literature affords striking examples of radical changes of opinion concerning the moral content of books. Some works have merely sloughed off the stigma of condemnation; others have run the gamut from vehement denunciation to veneration as classics.

Moxon, the English publisher, was convicted in 1841 for publishing Shelley's works, which included such celebrated pieces as *Queen Mab*, *The Revolt of Islam*, *The Cenci*, *Alastor*, and *Prometheus Unbound* (Moxon's Case, 2 Mod. St. Tr., 356). When first published, Charlotte Brontë's *Jane Eyre* "was pronounced too immoral to be ranked as decent literature"; George Eliot's *Adam Bede* was execrated as "the vile outpouring of a lewd woman's mind"; and Elizabeth Barrett Browning's *Aurora Leigh* was declared to be the "hysterical indecencies of an erotic mind."[22]

Upon the appearance of Hawthorne's *Scarlet Letter*, it was reviewed at length by the Reverend (afterwards Bishop) A.C. Coxe, who fulminated "against any toleration to a popular and gifted writer, when he perpetrates bad morals. Let this brokerage of lust be put down at the very beginning."[23] Hardy's *Tess of the D'Urbervilles* and *Jude the Obscure*, and du Maurier's *Trilby* met with virulent attacks as obscene books. *Leaves of Grass* cost Walt Whitman his position in the Interior Department. Hamlin Garland's *Rose of Dutcher's Coolly*, H.G. Wells' *Ann Veronica* and Theodore Dreiser's *Jennie Gerhardt* all were once considered "bad books." The publication of *Mademoiselle de Maupin* by Gautier in 1834 raised a furor of scandalized protest, and ultimately cost the author the wreath of the Academy. It has since become a classic, and has won generous judicial praise.[24]

In 1908 the Rev. J. Frank Chase obtained a conviction against a Boston book-dealer for selling Elinor Glyn's *Three Weeks*. (Commonwealth v. Buckley, 200 Mass. 346.) The decision of the Court was promptly nullified by popular acceptance of the book. And seventeen years later the same Mr. Chase remarked to an interviewer, "I know you wouldn't make a fool of me,

Mister, but I have been re-reading *Three Weeks* recently. Do you know that I couldn't get a conviction against the book nowadays. I wouldn't dare to take it into court!"[25]

### C. OUR MORES

Evidences of our current mores are everywhere around us. Our tabloids carry stories of passion and lust, of crime and perversion, told with a degree of graphic vividness and frankness unheard of a generation ago. Every man, woman and child in the community has easy access to the complete details of suicides, sash-weight murders, or torch murders, or marital infidelities, of boudoir intimacies, kidnappings and abnormalities. The Hall-Mills case, the Snyder-Gray case, and more recently the Winnie Judd case, the Dr. Sylla case, the Jessie Costello case, the Dr. Wynekoop case, are but a few of innumerable examples.

For the press of today, a spade is a spade. No longer are such squeamish phrases as "statutory offense" resorted to. The headlines and the columns speak openly of rape, blood-lust and adultery. Such outspokenness would have horrified us in 1900. Today it is accepted as a matter of course.

Even the movies, notwithstanding the prophylaxis of censorship, are now dealing more and more boldly with sex. There was a time when the merest glimpse of the female breast was barred from the screen. Now we have had a whole series of films like *Moana*, *The Virgins of Bali*, *Goona-Goona* and *Samarang*, in which the nude human body has been freely revealed. Nor have the movies contented themselves with merely stripping away prudish coverings. They have, in recent years, given us a collection of sex films, too numerous to mention, culminating in Mae West's frank and unashamed *She Done Him Wrong*.

In "The Facts of Life in Popular Song" (*The American Spectator*, Aug. 1933, Vol. I, No. 10), Dr. Sigmund Spaeth[26] has revealed the extent of forthrightness which our lyricists have come to practice (and the community to accept) in telling of the technique and joys of love-making.

On the stage, we have had plays like *Strictly Dishonorable*, *Warrior's Husband*, *Strange Interlude* (abortion, adultery), *Mourning Becomes Electra* (adultery, unnatural passion), *Reunion in Vienna*, *Frankie and Johnnie* (a dramatic record of happenings in a brothel, cleared of the charge of obscenity by the Court of Appeals in People v. Wendling, 258 N.Y. 451, March 3, 1932), and *Design for Living*, which presented a ménage of two men and a woman, the men alternating in the physical affections of the lady, and finally deserting her because of their fondness for each other; and more recently the homosexual *Green Bay Tree*, the thoroughly rowdy *Sailor Beware!* and the stark *Tobacco Road*.

As for the graphic and plastic arts, it is sufficient to say that the fig-leaf has apparently disappeared forever. William Zorach's *Embrace*, recently exhibited to the general public at the Museum of Modern Art in this city, testifies eloquently to our present-day notions of propriety; Robert Laurent's *Goose Girl* and Gwen Lux's *Eve* stand undraped and unashamed in the lobby of the Rockefeller Center Music Hall for New York's millions to behold.

Our current attitude in letters is best illustrated by the kind of books in general circulation. Works like Compton McKenzie's *Extraordinary Women*, Marcel Proust's *Swann's Way*, Thomas Mann's *Death in Venice*, Edouard Bourdet's *The Captive*, Lytton Strachey's *Elizabeth and Essex*, Radclyffe Hall's *The Well of Loneliness*, Arthur Schnitzler's *Casanova's Homecoming*, Octave Mirbeau's *Celestine, Eastern Shame Girl*, Dr. Marie Stopes' *Married Love*, Pierre Louys' *Woman and Puppet*, the Chinese classic *Hsi Men Ching*, Clement Wood's *Flesh*, Erskine Caldwell's *God's Little Acre*, William Faulkner's *Sanctuary* and *Light in August*, Hervey Allen's *Anthony Adverse*, Albert Cohen's *Solal* and thousands of others dealing with sexual adventures, have all been freely circulated. Some of them have been attacked; none of them has been finally suppressed.

Perhaps the most illuminating proof of our changing mores is an advertisement which was inserted in the *New York Times Book Review* on March 20, 1932, by Macy's.[27] A photostatic copy of the advertisement is annexed to this brief, showing that books which horrified our elders and were branded "forbidden" a decade or so ago, are openly advertised, sold and read today. One could scarcely desire more persuasive proof of the variableness of moral concepts.

*Ulysses* must be judged in the light of present-day mores. The standards of yesterday, the abhorrence of any mention of certain biological functions, excessive prudery, the sex taboo are as definitely dead today as the horse-drawn carriage and the donkey-engines on the Elevated. We have developed sturdier tastes, and grown wiser in the process.

Viewed against our contemporary background, *Ulysses* clearly does not violate our obscenity statute.[28]

### POINT III

*Ulysses* has been generally accepted by the community and hence cannot be held to be violative of the statute

In each era it is community morality which dictates how and to what extent the obscenity statute should be applied. Whatever society approves and accepts is moral; whatever it frowns upon and rejects is immoral. The law must recognize and give effect to this principle, or else it becomes "not a true mirror of life as it should be, but a bewildering distortion, alike perplexing and misleading, of which the ordinary man or woman becomes properly distrustful." ("The Development of the Law," Prof. Wormser, *Columbia Law Review*, December 1923; reprinted in *Lectures on Legal Topics*, Association of the Bar of the City of New York, Volume 5, p. 60.)

To paraphrase the words of Justice Holmes, late of the United States Supreme Court, the first requirement of a sane and rational administration of the law is that it should correspond with the actual feelings and demands of the community, whether right or wrong. (*The Common Law*, p. 41)

Public opinion, then, furnishes the only true test of obscenity. Such opinion is definitely ascertainable. It is true that people as a mass are inarticulate. The body politic registers its will through representatives chosen at the polls. Similarly the community makes its moral reactions felt and its judgments pronounced through responsible men who, by reason of their individual integrity and the multiplicity of their respective endeavors, furnish an accurate social mirror.

When newspapers, college professors, critics, educators, authors, librarians, clergymen and publishers rally to the defense of a book or express their gratification over its exoneration in court, they do more than express their personal views. They speak for the body social.[30]

Moreover, *Ulysses* has been placed on the shelves of many of our leading libraries, and has been included in literature courses given in our institutions of learning.

To say that it is obscene is to brand eminent persons in various walks of life as champions of obscenity; and to say that our libraries and universities have been guilty of the criminal offense of disseminating salacious material.

## POINT IV

*Ulysses* is not obscene according to the accepted definitions of obscenity laid down by the Courts

### A. THE QUESTION

The nature of a proceeding of this kind was clearly indicated by Judge Woolsey in U.S. v. *Married Love*, 48 Fed. (2d) 821, and U.S. v. *Contraception*, 51 Fed. (2d) 525. The proceeding is one in *rem*, brought under Title 19, U.S.C., Sec. 1305, for the forfeiture of *Ulysses*, on the ground that it falls within the exclusion of the statute.

In the *Married Love* case, the word *obscene* was defined, on the authority of *Murray's Oxford English Dictionary*, to mean offensive to modesty or decency, or expressing or suggesting unchaste or lustful ideas; and the word *immoral* to mean not moral, morally evil or impure, unprincipled, vicious or dissolute.[29]

### B. THE DEVELOPMENT OF THE LAW

The ancient test of obscenity was formulated in 1868 in the English case of Regina v. Hicklin, L.R. 3 Q.B. 360. It was "whether the tendency of the matter charged as obscenity is to deprave and corrupt those whose minds are open to such immoral influences and into whose hands a publication of this sort may fall."

Such a criterion was patently unfair, unreasonable and unsound, because it sought to gauge the mental and moral capacity of the community by that of its dullest-witted and most fallible members, and because it sought to withhold from society any material which might conceivably injure its lowest and most impressionable element. The vagueness and absurdity of the mental concept thus created, and the glaring social injustice of its application, necessitated further modification.

Such modification was not long in forthcoming. In U.S. v. Bennett, 16 Blatchf. 338, obscenity was defined as material which "suggests impure and libidinous thoughts." In U.S. v. Kennerley, 209 Fed. 119, at pp. 120 and 121, Judge Learned Hand wrote:

> Yet, if the time is not yet when men think innocent all that which is honestly germane to a pure subject, however little it may mince its words, still I scarcely think that they would forbid all which might corrupt the most corruptible, or that *society is prepared to accept for its own limitations those which may perhaps be necessary to the weakest of its members.* . . . I hope it is not improper for me to say that the rule laid down (i.e., in *Regina* v. *Hicklin, supra*), however consonant it may be with mid-Victorian morals, does not seem to me to answer to the understanding and morality of the present time, as conveyed by the words "obscene, lewd, or lascivious." I question whether in the end men will regard that as obscene which is honestly relevant to the adequate expression of innocent ideas, and whether they will not believe that truth and beauty are too precious to society at large to be mutilated in the interests of those most likely to pervert them to base uses. Indeed, *it seems hardly likely that we are even today so lukewarm in our interest in letters or serious discussion as to be content to reduce our treatment of sex to the standard of a child's library in the supposed interest of a salacious few.* . . . (Italics ours.)

In United States v. Mary Ware Dennett, 39 Fed. (2d) 564, this Court said:

> The statute we have to construe was never thought to bar from the mails everything that might stimulate sex impulses. If so, much chaste poetry and fiction, as well as many useful medical works, would be under the ban. Like everything else, this law must be construed reasonably with a view to the general objects aimed at.

In People v. Muller, 96 N.Y. 408, 411, the Court, referring to the ancient test, sought to limit it in this manner:

> We think it would also be a proper test of obscenity in a painting or statue, whether the motive of the painting or statue, so to speak, as indicated by it, is pure or impure, whether it is naturally calculated to

excite in a spectator impure imaginations, and whether the other incidents and qualities, however attractive, were merely accessory to this as the primary or main purposes of the representations.

In People v. Brainard, 192 App. Div. 816, the Court applied the identical test and reversed a conviction in the lower court. In the case of St. Hubert Guild v. Quinn, 64 Misc. 336, Seabury, J., in his illuminating opinion, said, at pages 339 and 340:

> The early attitude of the courts upon this subject discloses an illiberality of opinion which is not reflected in the recent cases. . . . It is no part of the duty of courts to exercise a censorship over literary productions. (Italics ours.)

The obscenity statute does not hinge on any question of good taste. The essence of the crime is sexual *impurity*, not sex (People v. Wendling, 258 N.Y. 451). In Swearingen v. U.S., 161 U.S. 446, the Supreme Court of the United States abandoned the rule laid down in *Regina* v. *Hicklin, supra*. The Court said in connection with the Federal law almost identical with our state statute:

> The words "obscene", "lewd" and "lascivious", as used in the statute, signify that form of immorality which has relation to sexual IMPUR-ITY . . . (Italics and capitals ours.)[31]

## C. *FRANKIE AND JOHNNIE*

This Court will doubtless give due consideration to the most recent adjudication of the highest court in this State upon the subject of obscenity.

The case is People v. Wendling, 258 N.Y. 451, decided March 3, 1932. It arose out of the dramatization of the folk-song "Frankie and Johnnie", about a country boy in a St. Louis resort for drinking, gambling and prostitution in the middle of the last century. Here not a book but a stage presentation was involved. This is how the Court of Appeals described the dramatization:

> The language of the play is coarse, vulgar and profane; the plot cheap and tawdry. As a dramatic composition it serves to degrade the stage where vice is thought by some to lose "half its evil by losing all its grossness." "That it is 'indecent' from every consideration of propriety is entirely clear" . . . (at pp. 452-3)

Yet the Court reversed the two convictions in the Court of Special Sessions of the City of New York, which had been unanimously affirmed by the Appellate Division. In doing so, the Court of Appeals restated the enlightened definition of obscenity clearly and emphatically, and further extended the liberality of *Halsey* v. *N.Y. Society* which up to that time had been the leading case on obscenity in this State. Said the Court, at page 453:

. . . the court is not a censor of plays and does not attempt to regulate manners. One may call a spade a spade without offending decency, although modesty may be shocked thereby. (People v. Muller, 96 N.Y. 408, 411) The question is not whether the scene is laid in a low dive where refined people are not found or whether the language is that of the bar room rather than the parlor. *The question is whether the tendency of the play is to excite lustful and lecherous desire.* (Italics ours.)

Coarse scenes and vulgar language, the Court insisted (p. 455), do not in themselves create such desire. The Court rejected the argument of the prosecution that the play was obscene because it portrayed the doings of prostitutes. Although the Court admitted that the play was an "uncultured depiction of a phase in the frontier life of the Middle West," it was careful to point out, at page 454:

A coarse realism is its dramatic offense. Perhaps in an age of innocence the facts of life should be withheld from the young, but a theatregoer could not give his approval to the modern stage as "spokesman of the thought and sentiment" of Broadway (Halsey v. New York Society for Suppression of Vice, 234 N.Y. 1) and at the same time silence this rough and profane representation of scenes which repel rather than seduce.

Lastly, the Court considered the possibility that *Frankie and Johnnie* might offend the over-fastidious and the censorious. In disposing of the question, the Court was quite explicit in its definition of the sole test applicable:

The production of such a play may be repulsive to puritanical ideas of propriety as would *Camille* and may be offensive to the more liberal minded as lacking in taste and refinement, as would the morally unobjectionable *Abie's Irish Rose*. The play may be gross and its characters wanting in moral sense. It may depict women who carry on a vicious trade and their male associates. It cannot be said to suggest, except "to a prurient imagination," unchaste or lustful ideas. It does not counsel or invite to vice or voluptuousness. It does not deride virtue. Unless we say that it is obscene to use the language of the scholar, the play is not obscene under the Penal Law, although it might be so styled by the censorious. (p. 454)

The opinion of the Court closes by saying:

We hold . . . that the fact that Frankie and Johnnie and their companions were not nice people does not in itself make the play obscene. A history of prostitution or of sexual life is not *per se* indecent . . . (p. 455)

Almost everything that the Court of Appeals had to say in the *Frankie and Johnnie* case is applicable to *Ulysses*.

### D. Some Other Recent New York Cases Involving
### Books (Unreported)

During the early part of 1931 Mr. Sumner, acting for the New York Society for the Suppression of Vice, instituted proceedings against two books: *Celestine* and *Eastern Shame Girl*. The former was the diary of a chambermaid, and related the sexual temptations of domestic servants; the latter was a collection of bawdy Chinese folktales. On May 7, 1931, in the Magistrates' Court, Second District, Manhattan, former Magistrate William C. Dodge—now District Attorney of New York County—dismissed the complaint, holding that the book did not violate the law.

Subsequently Mr. Sumner proceeded against the Chinese classic *Hsi Men Ching*, an abridged version of the famous *Kin Ping Meh*, which set forth in great detail the amorous adventures of a Chinese Casanova during the Ming dynasty. On November 9, 1931, Magistrate Brodsky dismissed the complaint. Mr. Sumner's proceeding against Pierre Louys' *Woman and Puppet* suffered the same fate at the hands of Chief Magistrate McDonald. Mr. Sumner was not satisfied with Magistrate Brodsky's disposition of *Hsi Men Ching*. He took the case to the district attorney. The grand jury, after hearing Mr. Sumner and the defendant, *refused to indict*.

Toward the latter part of 1931, Mr. Sumner brought a complaint against Clement Wood's *Flesh*, a collection of fifteen short stories, each one dealing graphically with a different phase of the psychopathology of sex. There was more shocking material in a single one of these stories than in the entire length of *Ulysses*. Magistrate Overton Harris dismissed the complaint.

Early in 1933 Mr. Sumner instituted proceedings against an illustrated volume dealing with nudism, entitled *Let's Go Naked*. Magistrate Van Amringe refused to entertain the charge.

In May 1933, the Vice Society met a similar rebuff at the hands of Magistrate Greenspan in connection with Erskine Caldwell's *God's Little Acre*, which set forth in detail the sexual adventures of a Southern family.

In short, the tendency of the New York courts has been to reject with increasing emphasis the role of censor, and to permit a wide latitude of expression consistent with our times.

### E. Normal v. Abnormal

In the light of these decisions, the Court in dealing with *Ulysses* must ask: Is it obscene within the proper definition of the word? Does it express or suggest unchaste or impure ideas? Is it morally evil or impure? Is it unprincipled, vicious or dissolute? Is its "main purpose and construction to depict sexual impurity?"

Considering all the other influences and stimuli of modern life, the press, the stage, the movies, could the book really hurt a *normal* human being?[32] For it is the *normal* person who must serve as a criterion. Perhaps the most cogent portion of Judge Woolsey's opinion affirms this rule, saying:

> Whether a particular book would tend to excite such impulses and thoughts [i.e. sexually impure and lustful thoughts (fol. 83)] must be tested by the Court's opinion as to its effect on a person with average sex instincts—what the French could call *l'homme moyen sensuel*—who plays, in this branch of legal inquiry, the same role of hypothetical reagent as does the "reasonable man" in the law of torts and "the man learned in the art" on questions of invention in patent law. (fol. 84)

*Ulysses* leaves no doubt as to how the above questions should be answered. It is a many-faceted crystallization of life and thought. It records the doubts and fears, the joys and torments, the swirling consciousness, of a handful of characters, and informs the experiences of those characters with the quality of universality. Sex is present, to be sure; but sex is part of man's existence. *Ulysses* is no more obscene than human life or thought. And, as Judge Woolsey has pointed out, "it must always be remembered that his [Joyce's] locale was Celtic and his season Spring." (fol. 78)

## POINT V

*Ulysses* is a modern classic. The United States Government having officially acknowledged it as such, it cannot be deemed obscene.

### A. THE FEDERAL GOVERNMENT HAS OFFICIALLY PAID TRIBUTE TO THE GREATNESS OF *ULYSSES*

Sometime in May 1933, a copy of *Ulysses* was sent from Paris, France to Alexander Lindey in New York City. On May 22 the Collector of Customs notified the sendee that the book was subject to detention under Title 19, U.S.C. Sec. 1305 (Sec. 305 of the Tariff Act of 1930.)

On June 2, the sendee addressed a petition to the Treasury Department, requesting that *Ulysses* be admitted into the United States under those provisions of the aforesaid statute which authorized the Secretary of the Treasury, in his discretion, to admit the so-called classics. In the letter that accompanied the application, the sendee wrote:

> In making this application I desire to state specifically that I do not concede that *Ulysses* is not admissible under the general provisions of Section 305.

An identical statement was incorporated in the petition itself.

On June 22, the sendee sent an inquiry to the Collector of Customs concerning the application. The complete answer of the Collector was as follows:

> Reference is made to your communication of June 22, 1933, requesting information concerning your petition of June 2, in the matter of the book *Ulysses* by James Joyce.
>
> In accordance with instructions from the Bureau of Customs, in its letter dated June 16, 1933, *authority was given for the release of the book to you on the ground that it is a classic* and therefore comes within the purview of the Secretary's discretionary authority granted in Section 305 of the Tariff Act of 1930.
>
> The book has been forwarded to the Customs Bureau of the Post Office for delivery to you under date of June 23, 1933. (Italics ours.)

In sum, the federal government has accorded *Ulysses* official recognition *as a classic.*

## B. A CLASSIC CANNOT BE ADJUDGED OBSCENE

*Webster's Collegiate Dictionary* (Fourth Edition, Merriam Series) defines a classic as "a work, especially in literature or art, of the highest class and of acknowledged excellence."

The words *classic* and *obscenity* represent polar extremes. They are mutually antagonistic and exclusive. That which is obscene corrupts and depraves—it cannot be "of the highest class and of acknowledged excellence."

The courts have time and again refused to suppress works which have stood the test of time and have won lasting recognition.

> Halsey v. N.Y. Society, 234 N.Y. 1;
> St. Hubert Guild v. Quinn, 64 Misc. 336;
> Stephen's *Digest of Criminal Law*, 7th Ed. (1926), note to Article 247 at p. 456;
> People v. Boni & Liveright, Inc., Magistrate's Court, New York City, September 27, 1922, Judge Oberwager (unreported).

On March 16, 1929, the *London Law Journal* published an article[33] reviewing the growth of the obscenity law in England since Regina v. Hicklin, 3 Q.B. 360 (1868), and summarizing practically all the important cases since. Several conclusions were drawn. One of these was that:

> *a classical work is not obscene* unless the circumstance of its sale or exhibition are such as to draw attention to those parts of the work which, if considered out of their historical and literary context, would have a depraving effect. (Italics ours.)

*Ulysses* is a classic. Judge Woolsey intimated as much. It cannot be held obscene.

## POINT VI

The intrinsic features of *Ulysses*, as well as certain extrinsic facts connected with it, negate any implication of obscenity.

The courts have from time to time given consideration to various elements in weighing the obscenity of any literary work brought before them.

A. INTRINSIC CHARACTERISTICS

The title of a book, its length, its style and understandableness, the question of whether it has any illustrations, the further question of whether it has been anonymously written or published—all these have a bearing on its possible obscenity.

1. The inclusion of illustrations in a work of fiction may tend to enhance the potency of such work for good or ill. The visual message which can be conveyed by a graphic representation is instantaneous and complete, and may be absorbed with practically equal quickness by the average and subaverage individual. In exonerating Lion Feuchtwanger's *Power*, the court in Toronto, Canada commented specifically on the absence of illustrations (Judge Jones, April 30, 1928). In In re Worthington Co., 30 N.Y. Supp. 361, at p. 362, like comment was made. There are no illustrations in *Ulysses*.

2. Where a book is offered to the reading public without the name of the author or the publisher, or under a pseudonym, a question may arise as to the integrity of the work, and the motives of publication. The *res* itself shows that the first edition of *Ulysses* was openly issued by Shakespeare and Company in Paris in February 1922; the second edition by the Egoist Press in London in October 1922. The Random House Edition, published by the claimant and made part of the record by stipulation (fols. 118-120), has been issued under the claimant's imprint, and has been openly advertised and sold.[34] The book has always borne Joyce's name as author. The element of concealment—almost invariably present in a work of pornography—is wholly absent here.

U.S. v. Smith, 45 Fed. 476, 478.

3. The length of a book may confer immunity.
Said the court in the *Power* case, *supra*:

> The book contains 425 pages, the chapters are mostly 100 pages in length, the type is set in very solid form. . . . A reader looking for obscene matter would get tired of reading the book within the first thirty pages, as the subject is only of interest to students of history, who are endowed with brains and application above the ordinary.

*Ulysses* is a prodigious work of 732 closely printed pages. The first passage dealing with sex occurs deep in the book. It is difficult reading even for the mature and the intelligent. It is far too tedious and labyrinthine and bewildering for the untutored and the impressionable who might conceivably be affected by it. Such people would not get beyond the first dozen pages.[35]

4. The title of a work may, in some case, be indicative of the questionable nature of the contents. In U.S. v. Janes, 74 Fed. 545, the caption was *Ripe and Unripe Women*; in Shepard v. U.S., 160 Fed. 584, *The Amorous Adventures of a Japanese Gentleman* and *A Lustful Turk*. The caption of *Ulysses* does not challenge the curiosity of the lascivious.

5. But more important than any of the foregoing are style and method. The very definition of obscenity calls for something which will corrupt and deprave. It is axiomatic that only what is understandable can corrupt. The worst Chinese obscenity is innocuous to anyone not acquainted with the language. If an author's style is incomprehensible to all but a comparatively few who are concededly immune to the purported suggestive power of words, the work cannot be said to be obscene. The *Jurgen* case is directly in point.

On January 15, 1920, the Grand Jury in New York County handed down an obscenity indictment against Robert M. McBride & Company and Guy Holt, its manager, for publishing James Branch Cabell's *Jurgen*. The case was tried before a jury in the Court of General Sessions of the County of New York. At the close of the People's case, the defendants moved for a direction of acquittal and a dismissal of the indictment on the ground that *Jurgen* was not obscene.[36] Judge Nott granted the motion in a brief but illuminating memorandum decision. We quote the following excerpts:

> I have read and examined the book carefully. It is by Mr. James Branch Cabell, an author of repute and distinction. From the literary point of view its style may fairly be called brilliant. It is based on the mediaeval legends of Jurgen and is a highly imaginative and fantastic tale. . . .
> . . . The most that can be said against the book is that certain passages therein may be considered suggestive in a veiled and subtle way of immorality, but such suggestions are delicately conveyed and the whole atmosphere of the story is of such an unreal and supernatural nature that even these suggestions are free from the evils accompanying suggestiveness in more realistic works. *In fact, it is doubtful if the book could be read or understood at all by more than a very limited number of readers.* (Italics ours.)

*Ulysses* falls squarely within the *Nott* decision. It is a work of Gargantuan complexity. Beside it, *Jurgen* is a child's primer. It is not only the language that is baffling; the construction is almost unbelievably involved. As Stuart Gilbert has pointed out, each episode of *Ulysses* has its Scene and Hour of the Day, is associated with a given Organ of the human body, relates to a certain Art, has its appropriate Symbol and a specific Technic, and has a title corresponding to a character or episode in the *Odyssey*. Certain episodes also have their appropriate Color.[37] For instance, the episode in the office of the

*Freeman's Journal and National Press* is entitled Aeolus; its Hour is 12 noon; its Organ the lungs; its Art rhetoric; its Color red; its Symbol editor; its Technic enthymemic.[38]

*Ulysses* taxes a reader's intellectual resources more severely than any other book in English literature. To comprehend it, one must have encyclopedic knowledge.[39]

One must be able to hurdle not only such forbidding polysyllabic barriers as *contransmagnificandjewbangtantiality* (p. 38), and *mahamanvantara* (p. 41), and *weggebobbles* (p. 158), and *theolologicphilolological* (p. 196), and *eppripfftaph* (p. 246), and *honorificabilitudinitatibus* (p. 201), and *inverecund* (p. 366), and *hypsospadia* (p. 465), and *selenographical* (p. 654), and *tetragammation* (p. 676), but also to plod through countless passages which, even after several readings, appear to make no sense whatever.

Here are some words which we have picked at random from the book:

| | PAGE | | PAGE |
|---|---|---|---|
| whelks | 30 | mavrone | 191 |
| cataletic | 37 | greydauburn | 193 |
| strandentwining | 38 | hierophantic | 209 |
| houyhnhnm | 40 | bosthoon | 231 |
| froeken | 43 | tympanum | 245 |
| hismy | 50 | henev | 246 |
| quadrireme | 137 | demisemiquaver | 276 |
| fellaheen | 138 | videlicet | 281 |
| crubeen | 140 | cruiskeen | 283 |
| parallax | 159 | pralaya | 289 |
| cygnets | 180 | loodheramaun | 293 |
| entelechy | 182 | oxter | 308 |
| umbrel | 184 | sinhedrim | 309 |
| yogibogeybox | 184 | topiary | 665 |
| nookshotten | 185 | hebdomadary | 676 |
| apocrypha | 188 | epicene | 684 |

These are not egregious examples; there are thousands of others as difficult in the book. Furthermore, there is constant recurrence of such incomprehensible paragraphs as the following:

> Ineluctable modality of the visible: at least that if no more, thought through my eyes. Signatures of all things I am here to read, seaspawn and seawrack, the nearing tide, that rusty boot. Snotgreen, bluesilver, rust: colored signs. Limits of the diaphane. But he adds: in bodies. Then he was aware of them, sure. Go easy. Bald he was and a millionaire, maestro di color che sanno. Limit of the diaphane in. Why in? Diaphane, adiaphane. If you can put your five fingers through it, it is a gate, if not a door. Shut your eyes and see. (p. 37)

Here is another paragraph:

> That it was not a heaventree, not a heavengrot, not a heavenbeast, not
> a heavenman. That it was a Utopia, there being no known method from
> the known to the unknown; an infinity, renderable equally finite by the
> suppositious probable apposition of one or more bodies equally of the
> same and of different magnitudes: a mobility of illusory forms immobi-
> lised in space, remobilised in air: a past which possibly had ceased to exist
> as a present before its spectators had entered actual present existence. (p.
> 654)

There is no reason to multiply illustrations. If one opens *Ulysses* at random
almost anywhere, one will confront passages meaningless on the surface, and
decipherable only after concentrated study. The book is a treasure-trove, to be
sure; but its riches are so well hid in grottoes of recondite learning, of classical
allusions, of literary and scientific profundities, that the average seeker—
blindly groping about in the surrounding maze—soon tires of the venture
and turns back.

6. There is no need in this memorandum to analyze the stream-of-
consciousness method which Joyce brought to such a high degree of
perfection in *Ulysses*. It will suffice to say that the nature of this method in
itself is such as would discourage and repel rather than attract the average
reader.[40] The latter is interested in action, not in cerebration.

## B. EXTRINSIC CIRCUMSTANCES

Certain collateral facts have a definite bearing on the possible obscenity of
a book, and should be given due weight. (U.S. v. Smith, 45 Fed. 476, 477)
Among these are the author's literary reputation, the opinions of critics, the
attitude of librarians, the acceptance of the book in representative libraries
and institutions of learning, and the mode of distribution.

> Rosen v. U.S., 161 U.S. 29;
> Peabody Book Shop v. U.S., United States Customs Court, Second
> Division, Protest 298623-G-5556, *et seq.*;
> Halsey v. N.Y. Society, 234 N.Y. 1;
> People v. McBride, *et al.* (not reported);
> People v. Muller, 96 N.Y. 408, 413;
> St. Hubert Guild v. Quinn, 64 Misc. 336;
> In re Worthington Co., 30 N.Y. Supp. 361, 362.

In United States v. Mary Ware Dennett, 39 Fed. (2d) 564, this Court said:

> Even the Court in Regina v. Hicklin, L.R. 3. Q.B. at page 367, which
> laid down a more strict rule than the New York Court of Appeals, was
> inclined to adopt in People v. Eastman, 188 N.Y. 478, said that *"the
> circumstances of the publication" may determine whether the statute has
> been violated.* (Italics ours.)

1. There is conclusive evidence that Joyce is a supreme literary artist (See Appendices.) It has been said of him that his virtuosity in the manipulation of words has never been surpassed; that when it comes to psychology or realism, beside him "Balzac is beggared and Zola bankrupted"; that in *Ulysses* he evidences "a genius of the very highest order, strictly comparable to Goethe's or Dostoevsky's"; that in power of thought he has no peer but Pascal; that he is the only man in English letters worthy of a place beside Shakespeare.

2. When *Ulysses* first appeared in 1922, there were many literary commentators that were staggered and confused by its magnitude and complexities. Today there is scarcely a critic of note who has not paid tribute to the book. One wonders whether there has ever been a work that has called forth such spirited defense as is evidenced in Appendices 2, 4 and 9.

3. About a year ago, the claimant herein circulated a questionnaire on *Ulysses* among hundreds of leading librarians throughout the country. The librarians were requested to voice their opinion of the book freely. With scarcely a dissenting voice they conceded its greatness (Appendix 4.)

4. *Ulysses* has been translated into French, German, Spanish and Japanese (Appendix 7.)

5. It goes without saying that pornography finds no place on the shelves of reputable libraries. Many of the librarians answering the questionnaire above referred to, stated that they had copies of *Ulysses*. The catalogues of outstanding libraries reveal the following: the Library of Congress has the English original and the French translation; the Bibliothèque Nationale at Paris has the English original (the catalogue we consulted was not up to date; the French translation is most likely also available by now); the Widener Library at Harvard University has two English copies; the general catalogue of the New York Public Library at 42nd St. and Fifth Avenue, New York City, lists more than thirty items—books, pamphlets, magazine articles—dealing with James Joyce and/or *Ulysses*.

6. It would be absurd to assume that an obscene work would appear as assigned reading in our leading institutions of learning. Yet no course dealing with twentieth century English letters, given at any of our colleges or universities, fails to include Joyce and *Ulysses*. For instance, the book has been on the reading list at Harvard in connection with English 26, given in 1932 by T.S. Eliot, the distinguished poet (then occupying the Charles Eliot Morton Chair of Poetry), and three years ago by I.A. Richards, Professor at Cambridge and Peking. During his course Professor Richards said:

> *Ulysses* is one of the most heart-shaking of books. It was written, as someone has stated, to put the fear of God into man.[41]

7. Pornography bears the stigma of stealth and secrecy. Printed smut is produced anonymously, is distributed through subterranean channels and is

sold at back doors or behind counters.[42] The claimant's reputation, the high character of its list (Appendix 8), are persuasive indication that in issuing *Ulysses* the claimant has sought to add another classic to its roster.

## POINT VII

*Ulysses* must be judged as a whole, and its general purpose and effect determined. On that basis it must be cleared.

A book is to be judged in its entirety, not by isolated fragments. The judicial test is to be applied to the *whole* book, and not to excerpts which may be singled out.

> Konda v. United States, 166 Fed. 91, 92;
> Clark v. U.S., 211 Fed. 916, 922;
> United States v. Dennett, 39 Fed. (2d) 564, 569;
> Peabody Book Shop v. United States, U.S. Customs Court, Second Division, Court of Baltimore, Protests #298623-G-5556 *et seq.* (unreported);
> Halsey v. New York Society, 234 N.Y. 1, 4;
> St. Hubert Guild v. Quinn, 64 Misc. 336, 339.

The *Peabody* case, *supra*, was quite similar to the proceeding herein, except that it arose in the Customs Court under the Tariff Act of 1922. The Collector of Customs at the Port of Baltimore sought to exclude from the United States *Daphnis and Chloe* by Longus, *Satyrs and Sunlight*, but Hugh McCrea and *The London Aphrodite*. The Court ruled that these works should be admitted and said:

> . . . a careful reading of the works satisfies us that they are not obscene and are not of the class of publications which Congress ordained should not be allowed to enter into this Country. There are passages in the books in question which, published separately and alone, would be considered indecent and their distribution or importation prohibited but a literary work cannot be called obscene, if, here and there may be found some expression which is obscene. If a book can be condemned because of the existence of occasional indecent language, Shakespeare's work would be prohibited. *Books must be considered in their entirety and if they have literary merit and are clearly not published with an object to parade obscenity and attract readers with debased minds, they are not of the class which Congress intended to exclude* . . . While it is true that there are a few passages in the books which might be considered obscene if published alone, the whole work is not obscene and *we must judge each book as a whole.* (Italics ours.)

In *Halsey v. New York Society for the Suppression of Vice, supra,*[43] the Court said, at page 4:

No work may be judged from a selection of such paragraphs alone. Printed by themselves they might, as a matter of law, come within the prohibitions of the statute. So might a similar selection from Aristophanes or Chaucer or Boccaccio or even from the Bible. The book, however, must be considered broadly as a whole.

To the same effect, *St. Hubert Guild* v. *Quinn, supra.*

*Ulysses* should not and cannot be judged on the basis of isolated passages. Granting that it contains occasional episodes of doubtful taste, the fact remains that obscenity is not a question of words nor of specific instances, nor even of whole chapters. To justify the condemnation of *Ulysses* it must be deemed to violate the law as a whole. This it does not do, for such portions of it as may conceivably be challenged are a negligible fraction of the whole.

## CONCLUSION

1. It is true that *Ulysses* employs a few Anglo-Saxon words to denote certain human organs and functions. However, this does not render it obscene. Such words recently appeared in Ernst and Seagle's *To the Pure,* Hemingway's *Death in the Afternoon, Lawrence of Arabia* and other books, all of which have been accepted by the community.[44]

2. *Ulysses* is the story of a single day in the life and thought of a man. Though the element of sex is present, it is relegated to a position of relative unimportance. As a matter of actual content it represents an insignificant segment of the book. It might be said to occupy less relative prominence in *Ulysses* than it would in the actual life of the average individual.

3. *Ulysses* is essentially a novel of the mind, not of actual physical occurrences. It is doubtful if people are influenced by what they read. Assuming that they are, we are constrained to admit that they are more likely to be influenced by narratives of what other people *do* than by what other people *think*. By far the greater portion of *Ulysses* deals with the vagaries of consciousness, not with the actual doings of people.

4. The notion of pornography is wholly inconsistent with an artist's serious effort to mirror and perpetuate truth in literature. Says Herbert S. Gorman:

> . . . pornography is as abhorrent to the writer as didacticism
> . . . . Truth in itself is not pornographic; it is made so by the unevenly
> developed consciousness of the observer.[45]

5. It has been said by some that in *Ulysses*, Joyce depicts the human consciousness as a stream more muddied that it actually is. Edmund Wilson has answered this:

> . . . I cannot agree that Mr. Joyce has represented the human mind as more disintegrated or more debased than it actually is . . . one sees the

gross ill-drained body of humanity itself touched divinely by cloudly visions of its creative splendours yet profoundly shaken and bound by its laboring flesh. . . .

6. Although *Ulysses* is a modern classic it need not be proved to be such in order to win vindication in this proceeding. Whether we regard it, to use the words of Shane Leslie, as "an abandonment of form and a mad Shelleyan effort to extend the known confines of the English language" or as an assault on human intelligence; whether we concede that its "chapters are monuments to the power and glory of the written word" or contend that they are the fruit of an "extraordinary and monstrous" undertaking; whether we look upon Joyce as the peer of Shakespeare and Flaubert and Voltaire or as an amazing prestidigitator of language—we cannot deny the importance of the book and the author. Such importance alone is sufficient to confer immunity.

7. It may be that in *Ulysses* Joyce has seen fit to cast light into some of the murky chambers of the human mind. It is only by such exposure that we can hope to banish darkness and taint. Joyce's penetration and courage deserve praise, not condemnation. What Macaulay wrote in his essay on Milton applies with equal force to Joyce:

> There is no more hazardous enterprise than that of bearing the torch of truth into those dark and infected recesses in which no light has ever shone. But it was the choice and pleasure of Milton to picture the noisome vapours and to brave the terrible explosion, while, in general, he left to others the credit of expounding and defending the popular parts of his religious and political creed. He took his own stand upon this which the great body of his countrymen reprobated as criminal.

8. "*Ulysses*", says Paul Jordan Smith, "can have no universal appeal; its reading is too formidable a task for that; but as a writer's source book, it is an inexhaustible mine of strange treasures, a veritable encyclopedia of the human soul, and a song of ecstasy. But it does bear a universal message—a weird cry from the very depths of Dublin to the rim of the world—the cry of tortured conscience, 'agenbite of inwit.' "[46]

To bar it from our shores, to brand it obscene, to compel our libraries and universities to sweep it from their shelves, is to assure for ourselves the lasting derision of generations to come.

9. To many of our literary critics, it was incredible that back in 1933 *Ulysses* should have been placed on trial for its life. After its complete exoneration by Judge Woolsey, the government's appeal has drawn caustic editorial comment.[47]

10. If the appellant prevails, *Ulysses* will be relegated to the class of smutty French postcards and outright pornography such as *Willie's First Night, Only a Boy*, and the like. The result will be no different than if we were to place Dante's *Inferno* in the same category with *Fanny Hill*. We do not say

that an adverse decision will kill the book; it has too much vitality for that. But instead of being legitimately circulated, it will be placed at the mercy of bootleggers.[48]

11. When, more than seventy years ago, a charge of criminal obscenity was brought against several of Shelley's noblest works, his counsel, T.N. Talfourd, delivered an eloquent plea in his defense on June 23, 1841. The case (The Queen v. Moxon, 2 Mod. St. Tr. 356) is referred to in St. Hubert Guild v. Quinn, 64 Misc. 336, by Seabury J, at page 339. Talfourd adjured the court in its justice to reject the charge as "an unexampled attempt to degrade and destroy the law under the pretence of asserting it"; and to "have the courage and the virtue to recognize the distinction between a man who publishes works which are infidel or impure, *because* they are infidel or impure, and publishes them in a form and at a price which indicate the desire that they should work out mischief, and one who publishes works in which evil of the same kind might be found, but who publishes them because, in spite of that imperfection, they are on the whole for the edification and delight of mankind; between one who tenders the mischief for approbation and one who exposes it for example."

## POINT VIII

The decree below should be affirmed.

Dated, New York, May 1, 1934.

Respectfully submitted,

GREENBAUM, WOLFF & ERNST,
Attorneys for Claimant-Appellee,
285 Madison Avenue,
Borough of Manhattan,
New York City.

Of Counsel:
MORRIS L. ERNST,
ALEXANDER LINDEY.

## Note Concerning Appendices

We ask the Court to take judicial notice of the information set forth in the following appendices. It is proper for the Court to do so even though the material is not part of the evidence.

In the Halsey case (234 N.Y. 1, 4, 5, 6), the Court of Appeals quoted estimates (not in the record) of critics concerning the book involved, to show "the manner in which it affects different minds." Among the critics and publications quoted were Sainte-Beuve, Henry James, Arthur Symons, James Breck Perkins, *The Nation* (Nov. 2, 1893), the *Atlantic Monthly* (June 1868), Professor Benjamin W. Wells and three encyclopedias. In the *Frankie and Johnnie* case (258 N.Y. 451, 452), the Court of Appeals referred to Dr. Sigmund Spaeth's mention of the folk-song in his work *Read 'em and Weep*. This work was *not* before the Court as evidence. Mr. Justice Brandeis of the Supreme Court has in many of his opinions availed himself of information not in the record, as in the famous *Oklahoma Ice* Case, New State Ice Co. v. Liebmann, 285 U.S. 262, 280-311 (dissenting opinion).

In the following cases the Court went beyond the record and referred to outside material, the nature of which is indicated:

> Mugler v. Kansas, 123 U.S. 623, 662 (Statistics);
> Jacobson v. Massachusetts, 197 U.S. 11 (Encyclopedias);
> People v. Lochner, 177 N.Y. 145 (Encyclopedias, etc.);
> Smith v. Command, 231 Mich. 409 (Scientific writings);
> State v. Feilen, 70 Wash. 65 (Scientific writings);
> See also: Wigmore on Evidence, 2nd Ed. 1923. Section 2555 (d); "The Consideration of Facts in Due Process Cases", *Columbia Law Review*, Volume XXX, No. 3 at page 371.[49]

---

## APPENDIX 1

### Editorial Comment on Judge Woolsey's Decision

Practically every newspaper and periodical in the United States commented favorably on Judge Woolsey's decision. A few typical editorials, culled at random, are given below. For additional newspaper praise, see Appendix 2.

Editorial, *New York Herald-Tribune*
December 8, 1933

### The "Repeal of Squeamishness"

"*Ulysses* may, therefore, be admitted into the United States." The opinion wherewith Judge Woolsey sustains this historic decision is studded with important contributions to the tangled and unsatisfactory law of literary suppression. It is true that the effect may be limited, for the customs law, as Judge Woolsey points out, required him to decide only whether *Ulysses* was "obscene" and not whether it might fit any others in the "spectrum of condemnatory adjectives" commonly used by similar statutes. To take some examples of these spectra, the Criminal Code bars from the mails not only obscene books but those which are "lewd or lascivious" or "filthy" or of "an indecent character." New York law widens this list, so far as publications are concerned, by the addition of "disgusting," and in respect to theatrical productions bars those which are "immoral or impure" as well as those fitting the other categories. James Joyce's celebrated (and singularly unreadable) literary monument, cleared after a decade of the charge of obscenity, may thus still fall into some other part of the far-flung and lamentably loose-woven nets spread by the legislators for the protection of our morals. Yet if Judge Woolsey has shed light upon the definition of "obscenity" alone, his sane conclusions are bound to have an effect upon the interpretations of the other mysteries involved in the application of these laws.

Judge Woolsey clearly declares the principle that the book must be considered "in its entirety." He rejects that narrow scrutiny of selected passages upon which censors have so often relied (to the vulgar edification of courts and jurors) and refuses to be swayed by a "dirty" word if the general character of the work demonstrates that in purpose and probable effect it is not pornographic. To the distinguished company of the "reasonable man" and the "man learned in the art"—fictitious personages who have long been pillars of other branches of legal interpretation—he adds the "person with average sex instincts" as the testing standard by which the general effect of a book is to be determined. And finally, in applying that test, he introduces canons of intelligent literary criticism. "If Joyce did not attempt to be honest in developing the technique which he has adopted in *Ulysses* the result would be psychologically misleading" and "artistically inexcusable." This alone is not enough to free any consequence of an honest technique from the charge of obscenity; it is, however, only sensible to extend the legal purview to such considerations in passing upon the question of general purpose and effect.

The public has learned illegally to take its *Ulysses* or leave it through the last ten years or so, and it is scarcely to be expected that the sudden stamp of legality will lead to any greater abuses of Irish literature than have developed with Irish whisky. In view, moreover, of the great burden of personal judgment which the principles of the Woolsey opinion would still impose upon the individual jurist, Mr. Morris Ernst may be too quick in proclaiming that "squeamishness in literature" has been repealed as completely as prohibition. Yet that the opinion does represent a substantial victory for proportion, common sense and legal flexibility in the difficult areas of literary censorship, few will doubt.

Editorial, *New York World-Telegram*
December 8, 1933

## *Ulysses*

The eminently intelligent, scholarly and likewise courageous Federal Judge John M. Woolsey has lighted another lamp of literary freedom.

"If one does not wish to associate with such folks as Joyce describes that is one's own choice," Judge Woolsey said in admitting the heretofore proscribed novel *Ulysses* to the United States for publication.

In a civilization which hopes to be adult and to grow that is an indispensable license for the writer. There must be other ways than the policeman's club and the fine collector's warrant to stay the blush from the maiden's cheek when she deliberately pries into books not intended for her.

But this is not the full test of Judge Woolsey's dictum. He does not uphold salaciousness, pornography and other salty or obscene writings when such are cooked up and vended as a commercialized "come on" unconnected with genuine literary intentions.

Judge Woolsey, who found the book to be "brilliant" and at the same time "dull" and "a rather strong draught to ask some sensitive, though normal, persons to take," held it also to be "a sincere and serious attempt to devise a new literary method for the observation and description of mankind."

Half the value of the notable opinion lies in this judicious definition. Judge Woolsey does not sail in and make the sky the limit for unbridled writing. It must be serious and sincere in intent and execution. That is the test, and an eminently just and necessary one.

No limit is put on the frankness of writing done for experts in medicine, biology, physiology and other intimate sciences. Non-professional members of the general public can have as legitimate an interest in explorations into frank domains such as that treated in *Ulysses*.

Judge Woolsey's opinion is an emancipation of the knowledge-seeking laymen in fields too long closed with the sign "Verboten."

Editorial, *New York Herald-Tribune*
December 16, 1933

### Beyond *Ulysses*

The first complaint against Judge Woolsey's decision in the *Ulysses* case appears in *The Nation*, and I suspect it comes from the cadenced pen of Joseph Wood Krutch. After praising most of the decision, *The Nation*, and I agree with it, wishes that Judge Woolsey might have added something like this:

> Only a legal fiction makes it necessary to pretend that the real question at issue is whether or not *Ulysses* is likely to "stir the sex impulses." At least half the recognized diversions of civilized mankind are intended to do that to a greater or less extent, and society recognizes the process as

not only permissible but necessary to its welfare. Only hypocrisy could insist that the law makes any pretense of interfering with such discussions, for if it did, then it would be necessary not only to proceed against almost every love story but to raid the very dances sponsored by the Young Women's Christian Association. The real question is whether or not Joyce's rare use of four Anglo-Saxon monosyllables constitutes a threat to society sufficiently great to engage the attention of the law. Since the prominence of these same four words in the epigraphy of the public school outhouse makes them familiar to every literate person long before he is acquainted with the meaning of most of the other words in *Ulysses*, I Hold that the police and the courts have more important business to attend to.

Editorial Excerpt, *New York Evening Post*
March 15, 1934

It so happens that Judge Woolsey's decision is one of the most civilized opinions to be handed down from our bench in a good many years.

Editorial, *Publisher's Weekly*
April 14, 1934

### Statesmanship in Advertising

The case of *Ulysses* will be long remembered in trade history. Here was a book by an author of established international repute who was obliged, by the thrust of censorship, first to publish in Paris with the imprint of a bookstore established there by an American girl, a book of so individual a type that it created new trends in writing and provided for the future a mirror of the confusions of the 1920's.

With this background it finally comes to the American market (the English market is soon to be tested) after an ably-handled court test and an illuminating and competent judicial decision by a Federal judge.

To our mind, the handling of this publishing problem by Random House has been not only exceedingly competent but continuously dignified. There have been no specious arguments in the publicity and no cheap attempts to take advantage of the type of discussion which could so easily develop.

At one point the publishers deserve special praise as the double-page advertisement of the book in the *Saturday Review of Literature* of March has been recognized by publishers and public alike as real statesmanship in advertising. This advertisement (for which a credit line might have been carried for Aaron Sussman of the Spier and Sussman agency) gave an amazingly effective picture of what this great book really is. It was an inspired effort to give the book a real chance with those who were getting acquainted with it rather than to let them approach the reading as if this were a book only of forbidden passages.

It is to be hoped that the appeal taken to Judge Woolsey's decision will not mar this successful and creditable piece of publishing.

## APPENDIX 2

### Excerpts From Critical Reviews of *Ulysses*

#### A. RECENT REVIEWS
(Published after Judge Woolsey's decision)

Boston, Mass. *Transcript*, January 26, 1934:

Today it is an established classic.

Lloyd Morris,
*Brooklyn Daily Eagle*, Sunday Book Review, January 21, 1934:

Like *Don Quixote*, again, it has set forth a parable of human life and human destiny so completely responsive to the inarticulate temper of its day that future generations may find in it the quintessence of an epoch.

Gilbert Seldes,
*New York Journal*, January 27, 1934:

*Ulysses* is one of the most significant and beautiful works of our time.

*Newark Evening News*, January 25, 1934:

As for the book itself it remains a masterpiece, with its extraordinary mingling of lovely poetry and nauseating filth, with its magnificent architectural layout and its rich dialogue, its psychological insight and its literary variety and ingenuity.

Chicago, Ill. *Herald-Examiner*, February 10, 1934:

It is timeless, as it will be, probably, deathless.

Portland, Me. *Express*, February 10, 1934:

. . . the art which Joyce employs in portraying these characters gives the book the distinction of being as great a revelation as any in our language.

Joseph Henry Jackson,
San Francisco, Cal. *Chronicle*, January 26, 1934:

. . . but as a writer's source book it is an inexhaustible mine of strange treasures, a veritable encyclopedia of the human soul, and a song of ecstasy.

Wilson Leary,
Miami, Florida, *News*, February 18, 1934:

It is a strange book, an irritating book, a humorous book, a sad book, and, above all, a great book.

*Kansas City Star*, February 10, 1934:

It is doubtful if anyone prior to Joyce has recorded with such fidelity and accuracy the private train of thought.

Chicago, Ill. *News*, January 31, 1934:

But first of all it is a pure joy in the matter of its poetry, its characterization and description.

Galveston, Texas *News*, January 28, 1934:

*Ulysses* is much more than an ordinary novel: It is a super-novel, dealing with the inner as well as the outer lives of men and women.

*Honolulu Star Bulletin*, January 24, 1934:

. . . it is a coherent and human story, sounding the profound depths of our pitiful souls.

*Denver Rocky Mountain News*, February 4, 1934:

After all these years it may be said now that *Ulysses* is a great book because it tells a superb and compelling story in an English language which perhaps no writer ever has equalled for power, richness and beauty.

Los Angeles, Cal. *Times*, February 11, 1934:

It is one of the unique books of the world; a novel that defies classification . . .

*Cincinnati Times Star*, February, 1934:

If any judgment on contemporary letters is safe, it is that *Ulysses* along with Mann's *The Magic Mountain* and the great gallery of Proust, will comprise the great triumvirate of novels in the first quarter of the century.

Jacksonville, Fla. *Times-Union*, January 28, 1934:

A more moral book was never written.

Salt Lake City, *Utah Tribune*, February 25, 1934:

The book's emergence into the full light of day may broaden its influence and bring added vision to persons whose life experience is made richer through reading.

James T. Farrell,
*Scribner's*, February, 1934:

. . . Proust gave to literature the picture of a dying class; Joyce recreated a world.

*New Outlook*, March, 1934:

Nothing need be said about it, except that of all the literature produced in our time, it seems the surest of a place with the best of English writing—of writing in English, that it towers so high it has already cast its shadow on the important writing done since it appeared.

*New Yorker*, January 27, 1934:

James Joyce's *Ulysses* stands among the dozen or so greatest literary works of all time. Like most books of magnificent stature, it is a whole literature in itself.

William Troy,
*The Nation*, February 14, 1934:

For out of his pride and contempt and ambition, Joyce has given us a work which leaves us, at the end, with a still passionate faith and trust in the reality which even societies must keep in mind if they are to survive.

*Time*, January 29, 1934:

But a growing body of modern critical opinion on both sides of the Atlantic has already acclaimed *Ulysses* as a work of genius and a modern classic.

## B. EARLIER REVIEWS
### (Published prior to Judge Woolsey's decision)

Edmund Wilson,
*The New Republic*, December 18, 1929, p. 90:

One of the most important features of *Ulysses* is its interest, as an investigation into the nature of human consciousness and behavior. Its importance from the point of view of psychology has never, it seems to me, been properly appreciated, though its influence on other books and, in consequence, upon our ideas about ourselves, has already been profound. Joyce has attempted to set down as comprehensively, and to render as accurately as it is possible in words to do, what our participation in life is like—or rather, what it seems to us like, as from moment to moment we live. In order to make his record complete, he has been obliged to disregard a number of conventions of literature and taste which, especially in English-speaking countries, have in modern times been pretty strictly observed, even by the writers who have aimed to be most scrupulously truthful. Joyce, in *Ulysses*, has studied the trivial, the base, the dirty elements of our lives with the relentlessness of a modern psychologist; and he has also, what the modern naturalist has seldom been poet enough for, done justice to all those elements in our lives which we have been in the habit of describing by such names as love, nobility, beauty and truth.

Rebecca West,
*The Bookman*, September 1928, pp. 20, 23:

I do most solemnly maintain that Leopold Bloom is one of the greatest creations of all time: that in him something true is said about man. Nothing happens to him at the end of *Ulysses*. Nothing is suggested in the course of the book which would reconcile him to the nobility of life. Simply he stands before us, convincing us that man wishes to fall back from humanity into the earth, and that in that wish is power, as the facade of Notre Dame stands above us, convincing us that man wishes to rise from humanity into the sky, and that in that wish is power. . . . I claim that the interweaving rhythms of Leopold Bloom and Stephen Dedalus and Marion Bloom make beauty, beauty of the sort whose recognition is an experience as real as the most intense personal experiences we can have, which gives a sense of reassurance, of exultant confidence in the universe, which no personal experience can give.

Edwin Muir,
*The Nation*, October 14, 1925, p. 423:

*Ulysses* gives one a lively notion of how difficult it is for a great work of art to be born and after inconceivable hazards to come to completion in our day; but it shows also, what is still more important, that this achievement is not impossible.

Shane Leslie,
*The Quarterly Review*, Vol. 238, October 1922:

Mr. James Joyce has put the best years of his life into its pages, toiling during the world's toil and refusing to collapse with the collapse of civilization. . . . In the matter of psychology or realism Balzac is beggared and Zola is bankrupted.

Dr. Joseph Collins,
The *New York Times Book Review*, May 28, 1922, p. 6:

An egocentric genius, whose chief diversion and keenest pleasure is self-analysis and whose lifelong important occupation has been keeping a notebook in which has been recorded incident encountered and speech heard with photographic accuracy and Boswellian fidelity. Moreover, he is determined to tell it in a new way . . . in parodies of classic prose and current slang, in perversions of sacred literature, in carefully metered prose with studied incoherence, in symbols so occult and mystic that only the initiated and profoundly versed can understand—in short, by means of every trick and illusion that a master artificer, or even magician, can play with the English language. . . . It will immortalise its author with the same certainty that Gargantua and Pantagruel immortalised Rabelais, and *The Brothers Karamazov* Dostoyevsky . . . comes nearer to being the perfect revelation of a personality than any book in existence . . . I have learned more psychology and psychiatry from it than I did in ten years at the Neurological Institute.

Arnold Bennett,
*The* (American) *Bookman*, Vol. LV, August 1922, p. 570:

James Joyce is a very astonishing phenomenon in letters. He is sometimes dazzlingly original. If he does not see life whole he sees it piercingly. His ingenuity is marvellous. He has wit. He has a prodigious humor. He is afraid of naught. And had heaven in its wisdom thought fit not to deprive him of that basic sagacity and that moral self-dominion which alone enable an artist to assemble and control and fully utilize his powers, he would have stood a chance of being one of the greatest novelists that ever lived. The best portions of the novel (unfortunately they constitute only a fraction of the whole) are superb. I single out the long orgiastic scene, and the long unspoken monologue of Mrs. Bloom which closes the book. The former will easily bear comparison with Rabelais at his fantastical finest; it leaves Petronius out of sight. It has plenary inspiration. It is the richest stuff, handled with a virtuosity to match the quality of the material. The latter (forty difficult pages, some twenty-five thousand words without any punctuation at all) might in its utterly convincing realism be an actual document, the magical record of inmost thoughts thought by a woman that existed. Talk about understanding "feminine psychology" . . . I have never read anything to surpass it, and I doubt if I have ever read anything to equal it. My blame may have seemed extravagant, and my praise may seem extravagant, but that is how I feel about James Joyce. The book is not pornographic. . . .

## APPENDIX 3

### Map of the United States Showing the Location of Libraries
### That Have Expressed a Desire to Circulate *Ulysses*

Possibly the most illuminating feature of the hundreds of laudatory comments concerning *Ulysses* which have been furnished by librarians (and some of which are set forth in Appendix 4) is that such comments have come in from all quarters of the country. The Court's attention is directed to the enclosed map of the United States. The dots indicate the cities in which city or university librarians have stated that they either have copies of *Ulysses* or would place the book on their shelves if it were made available. The purpose of the map is to show that *Ulysses* has won nation-wide recognition and acclaim, and that it is not being championed by radical or ultrasophisticated literary cliques located in large metropolitan centres.

---

## APPENDIX 4

### The Comments of Librarians

About a year ago Random House, Inc., the claimant herein, circulated a questionnaire on *Ulysses* among several hundred of the leading librarians throughout the United States. This was done in order to ascertain the attitude of librarians throughout the country toward the book. They were requested to voice their opinions freely. With scarcely a dissenting voice they conceded its greatness. A few of their characteristic comments, culled at random from hundreds, appear below. The claimant herein will be glad to place at the disposal of the Court the original answers to the questionnaires, if the Court so desire.

LOUIS SHORES, Professor of Library Science, Fisk University, Nashville, Tennessee: "I protest against the assininity which bars a work in which I was unable to discover anything as objectionable as the insulting mediocrity in talkies, tabloids and terrible novels. Its significance in literary history is of the first importance. It is an essential text we feel handicapped at not being able to supply to our professors of comparative literature. No study of literary development in the 20th century can mean anything without *Ulysses*."

SUSIE L. HOWARD, Head of Circulation Department, Carnegie Library of Atlanta, Georgia: "The most original and characteristic book of this period. The book could do no one any harm and should be available to all those seriously interested in literature.

ETHEL McVEETY, North Dakota Agricultural College, Fargo, N.D.: "*Ulysses* deserves unrestricted circulation as a contribution to literature. Compelling and provocative."

WARD EDWARDS, State Teachers College Library, Warrensburg, Missouri: "Certainly no other 20th century book has exerted so great an influence."

FRED A. BESTOW, Free Public Library, New Brunswick, N.J.: "Important as a new type; should be in every library."

WILLIAM P. LEWIS, Pennsylvania State College Library, State College, Pennsylvania: "An American publication would be of value because it forms the basis of many of the tendencies in recent English and American Literature."

WINIFRED E. SKINNER, Pasadena Junior College, Pasadena, California: "A book which cannot be ignored. Definite place in the historical development of the psychological novel."

MARY E. HOYT, Colorado School of Mines, Golden, Colorado: "Very influential, monumental work, one of the greatest of the century."

LUISE F. KAMPF, Coburn Library, Colorado College, Colorado Springs, Colorado: "The most important of the stream-of-consciousness novels."

MERRITT H. MOORE, faculty, University of Chicago, Chicago, Illinois: "It is a valuable portrayal of the mind at work beyond the constraining limits of rules or contexts."

L.T. IBBOTSON, University of Maine, Orono, Maine: "Inestimable literary influence."

A.B. METCALF, Wellesley College Library, Wellesley, Massachusetts: "As the first English novel to use the stream-of-consciousness method, it has had a very considerable influence."

GILBERT H. DOANE, Librarian in chief, University of Nebraska Library, Lincoln, Nebraska: "The book should be in all libraries of a scholarly nature, because of its literary historical importance."

HELEN A. STRATLEY, Binghamton Public Library, Binghamton, New York: "Think it a stupendous piece of work; of use to authors."

ELIZABETH M. RICHARDS, Flora Stone Mather College Library, Cleveland, Ohio: "It is of sufficient importance to be needed wherever courses are given in contemporary literature."

ANNE C. KEATING, Ohio University Library, Athens, Ohio: "Every college library should have a copy of this volume as representative of a trend in literature."

ALBERTA CAILLE, Carnegie Free Public Library, Sioux Falls, South Dakota: "Outstanding in its literary and psychological contribution."

BLANCHE PRICHARD McCRUM, Washington and Lee University Library, Lexington, Virginia: "Regardless of its ethical purport or its literary significance, I think a book so much discussed should be available to students of the new literary movement."

J.S. IBBOTSON, Colby College Library, Waterville, Maine: "It is honest, therefore psychologically interesting."

ANNIE L. CRAIG, Denison University Library, Granville, Ohio: "Apparently a stupendous piece of work; worthy of serious study."

J.F. MARRON, Jacksonville Public Library, Jacksonville, Florida: "The book is one of the monuments of modern art. Of the greatest importance both to the cultured reader and all students of the age. It has been nothing short of a crime that the book has been lost to American readers for so many years."

CATHERINE BEAL, South Branch, Omaha Public Library, Omaha, Nebraska: "I think its influence has been tremendous; a book of such importance as *Ulysses* should be available to adults."

EVELYN M. BARRETT, Silas Bronson Library, Waterbury, Connecticut: "I think that every library of any size should have those books which show the trend of modern literature."

M.E. McCLAIN, University of Oregon Library, Eugene, Oregon: "It will always be of significance as literary history."

ELIZABETH SIGULTEARY, Santa Clara Free Library, San Jose, California: "One of the greatest contributions to modern literature."

W.M. SMITH, University of Wisconsin, Madison, Wisconsin: "It is a work of literary significance. In our opinion the American edition of *Ulysses* ought to be available for University and other scholarly libraries."

MRS. RUTH E. DELZELL: Free Public Library, Amarillo, Texas: "It is a masterpiece."

## APPENDIX 5

### List of Books Dealing with James Joyce and/or *Ulysses*.

*James Joyce—His First Forty Years*
 by Herbert S. Gorman
 Heubsch, New York, 1925

*The Key to the Ulysses of James Joyce*
 by Paul Jordan Smith
 Covici-Friede, New York

*James Joyce and the Making of Ulysses*
 by Frank Budgen
 Harrison Smith and Robert Haas, New York, 1933

*The Impuritans*
 by Harvey Wickham
 Dial Press, New York, 1929

*Axel's Castle*
 by Edmund Wilson
 Scribner's, New York, 1931

*Men Seen*
 by Paul Rosenfeld
 Dial Press, New York, 1925

*James Joyce and the Plain Reader*
 by Charles Duff
 D. Harmsworth, London, 1932

*The Dance of Life*
 by Havelock Ellis
 pp. 175-177

*Pavanes and Divisions*
 by Ezra Pound
 A chapter

*Joyce Intimo Spogliato in Piazza*
 by Alessandro Francini-Brund

*Literary Studies and Reviews*
 by Richard Aldington
 New York, 1924, pp. 192-207

*James Joyce und Sein Ulysses*
 by E.R. Curtius
 Zurich: Verl. d. Neuen Schweizer
 Rundschau, pp. 70

*Bardes d'Irlande*
 by Suzanne Tery
 1924

## APPENDIX 6

### List of Magazine Articles Dealing with James Joyce and/or *Ulysses*

"The Strange Case of James Joyce"
  by Rebecca West
  *Bookman*, 1928—Volume 68, pages 9-23

"Mr. James Joyce and the Modern Stage"
  by Ezra Pound
  *Drama* (Chicago), 1916—Vol. 6, pages 122-132

"James Joyce and the New Word"
  by Harold J. Salemson
  *Modern Quarterly* (Baltimore), 1929—Vol. 5, pages 294-312

"Some Contemporaries—James Joyce"
  by Peter Munro Jack
  *Indianapolis*, 1929—Vol. 1, pages 24-27, 102-108

"James Joyce"
  by Michael J. Lennon
  *Catholic World* (New York), 1931—Vol. 132, pages 641-652

"Technik und Thematik von James Joyce"
  by Ernst Robert Curtius
  *Neue Schweizer Rundschau* (Zurich), 1929—Jahrg. 22, Heft. 1, pages
    47-68

"Concerning James Joyce's *Ulysses*"
  by Arnold Bennett
  *Bookman*, 1922—Vol. 55, pages 567-570

"James Joyce's *Ulysses*"
  by Bernhard Fehr
  *Englische Studien* (Leipsig), 1925—Bd. 60, pages 180-205

"Zum *Ulysses* von James Joyce"
  by Giedion-Welcker, Carola
  *Neue Schweizer Rundschau* (Zurich), 1928—Jahrg. VI, pages 18-32

"An Irish Ulysses—The Hades Episode"
  by Gilbert Stuart
  *Fortnightly Review* (New York), 1929—N.S. Vol. 126, pages 45-58

"*Ulysses* and the Handling of Indecencies"
  by Ford Madox Hueffer
  English Review (London), 1922—Vol. 35, pages 538-548

"James Joyce"
  by Edmund Wilson
  *The New Republic*, December 18, 1929

"The *Ulysses* of James Joyce"
   by Valéry Larbaud
   *Criterion* (London), 1922—Vol. 1, October, pages 94-103
"*Ulysses*"
   by Shane Leslie
   *Quarterly Review* (New York), 1922—Vol. 238, pages 219-234
"The Meaning of *Ulysses*"
   by Edwin Muir
   *Calendar of Modern Letters* (London), 1925—Vol. 1, pages 347-355
"James Joyce et Pecuchet"
   by Ezra Pound
   *Mercure de France* (Paris), 1922—Annee 33, Tome 156, pages 307-320
"The Influence of Mr. James Joyce"
   by Richard Aldington
   *English Review* (London), 1921—Vol. 32, pages 333-341
"James Joyce in Trieste"
   by Silvio Benio
   *Bookman*, 1930—Vol. 72, pages 375-380
"L'Oeuvre de James Joyce"
   by Louis Cazamian
   *Revue Anglo-Americaine* (Paris), 1924—Annee 2, pages 97-113
"Homer of Our Time"
   by I. Goll
   *Living Age*, August 15, 1927, pages 316-320, 333
"Novel from James to Joyce"
   by J.W. Beach
   *Nation*, June 10, 1931—pages 132, 634-6
"Growth of a Titan"
   *Saturday Review*, August 2, 1930, pages 7, 17-19
"Portrait of James Joyce"
   by Padraic Colum
   *Dublin Magazine* (Dublin), 1932—N.S., Vol. 7, April-June, pages 40-
      48
"A Sidelight on James Joyce"
   by Louis Golding
   *Nineteenth Century* (London), 1933—Vol. 113, pages 391-497
"Farthest North: A Study of James Joyce"
   by Elliott Paul
   *Bookman* (Camden), 1932—Vol. 75, pages 156-163

"James Joyce's Jugendbildnis"
by E. Birkenfeld
*Orphid*, 1926, III, 63-6

"The Lyrics of James Joyce"
by Morton D. Zabel
*Poetry*, July 1930, XXXVI, 206-13

"The Position of Joyce"
by Cyril Cassou
*Life and Letters*, April 1911, 273-90

"James Joyce"
by E.R. Curtius
*Die Literatur*, XXXI, 121-8

"Anna Livia Plurabelle" (A review)
by G. Heard
*Week End Review*, June 1, 1930, 492-3

"La Traduction Allemande de L'*Ulysse* de James Joyce"
by H. Buriot-Darailes
*Revue Litteraire Comp.* X, pp. 772-4, October 1930

"Mr. Joyce and Shakespeare"
by B.J. Morse
*English Studio*, 65, No. 3; 367-81 (1931)

"Position of Joyce"
by Cyril Connoly
*Life and Letters*, April 1929, pages 273-90

"Joyce et Homere: Les 'Rochers Errants' "
by Stuart Gilbert
*Revue de Geneve*, March 1930, pages 274-87

"James Joyce"
by R.H. Pender
*Deutsche Rundschau*, 203: 285-6 (July 1925)

"New Writers"
by J.L. Edel
*Canadian Forum*, 10: 329-30, July 1930

"James Joyce: Poem"
by M.N. O'Brien
*Canadian Forum*, 12: 294, May 1932

"Gyring and Gimblyng: Or Lewis Carroll in Paris"
*Saturday Review of Literature*, 3: 777 (April 30, 1927)

"Advent in America of a New Irish Realist"
*Current Opinion*, 62: 275 (April 1917)

"Over the Top With the New Novelists"
  *Current Opinion*, 66: 387-8 (July 1917)

"Scrutinies", Vol. 1, by various authors.
  Contains an essay on Joyce

"On Hearing James Joyce"
  by A.T. Curringhame
  *The Modern Scot*, Vol. II, No. 3, October 1931

"Introduction to *Dubliners*"
  by Padraic Colum
  Modern Library Edition

"Gens de Dublin" (Translation of *Dubliners*)
  by Valéry Larbaud

"Obscenity and Censorship"
  by Ben Ray Redman
  *Scribner's*, 1934—Vol. XCV, No. 5, pages 341-344

----

## APPENDIX 7

### Data Concerning Translations of *Ulysses* into Other Languages

*Ulysses* has been translated into French and German—stupendous tasks, when one realizes the length of the book and its linguistic idiosyncrasies. To say that only a work of exceptional merit could have prompted such herculean enterprises is to state a truism which will bear no denial. The German translation was made by the distinguished scholar, Georg Goyert, and was published by Rhein-Verlag-Basel, a reputable publishing firm, with offices at Zurich, Berlin, Leipzig and Strassburg. The French translation was made by two eminent men of letters, Auguste Morel and Stuart Gilbert, and was published by Adrienne Mounier.

The *Encyclopedia Universal Illustrada* (1932) mentions a Spanish translation by Demaso Alonso; and says that the book has been translated into nearly all languages. We have recently heard of two rival translations, both unauthorized, in Japan.

----

## APPENDIX 8

### Data Concerning the Claimant and Its Publications

Random House, Inc. was organized several years ago for the purpose of printing and distributing in America books of significant content and typographical distinction. Most of the Random House publications have been printed by the Pynson Printers, one of the finest printers in America.

In the years 1927, 1928 and 1929, Random House published numerous notable books. The first was an edition of *Candide*, with illustrations by Rockwell Kent, which *The New York Times* declared to be the most beautiful book ever produced in America. Other expensive editions were Hawthorne's *The Scarlet Letter*, Emily Brontë's *Wuthering Heights*, Robert Louis Stevenson's *Dr. Jekyll and Mr. Hyde*, the collected poems of Robert Frost, *Beowulf*, and Mark Twain's *Adventures of Tom Sawyer*. The most elaborate book produced was an edition of four hundred copies of Walt Whitman's *Leaves of Grass*. It sold for $100 a copy.

In addition to publishing books under its own imprint, Random House has acted as exclusive American distributor for three of the outstanding presses in the world, to wit, The Nonesuch Press, and the Golden Cockerel Press of England, and the Cranach Presse of Germany.

The current list of Random House includes the following:

| Title | Author |
|---|---|
| *Troilus and Cressida* | Chaucer |
| *Play and Poems* | W.S. Gilbert |
| *Complete Works* | Coleridge |
| *Romance of Leonardo da Vinci* | Merejkowski |
| *Wuthering Heights* | Emily Brontë |
| *Poetry and Selected Prose* | John Donne |
| *Prose and Poetry* | William Blake |
| *Selected Essays* | William Hazlitt |
| *Moby Dick* (Rockwell Kent) | Herman Melville |
| *Candide* (Rockwell Kent) | Voltaire |

## APPENDIX 9

### Testimonials Concerning *Ulysses* Furnished by Distinguished Persons in Various Walks of Life

The following are excerpts from letters addressed to Random House, Inc.:

W.A. NEILSON, President, Smith College, Northampton, Mass.
May 18, 1932:

> I am not a great admirer of *Ulysses*, but that fact does not make me any the less willing to protest against the regulations which prevent its sale in some parts of the United States. It seems to me preposterous to attempt to prevent the intelligent public from getting access to a book of such international importance, and you are at liberty to use my name as one of those protesting.

HENRY S. CANBY, Critic, Editor, *The Saturday Review of Literature*,
April 19, 1932:

> I was one of the first Americans, I think, who read *Ulysses* and I think now, as I thought then, that the book has some very bad passages and some magnificent ones and that as a whole it is a work of great literary importance. That it has great influence and has become a monument of international literature is, of course, known to everyone. I do not regard its occasional indecencies as a bar to publication and I believe that those who like myself are interested in literature should most certainly have free access to it and should be allowed to purchase it in this country. I cannot conceive of morals being damaged by a work of this kind which is much too erudite and too psychological to attract the prurient seeker after erotica. In fact the only qualification I should make would be that it ought not to be published as erotica or advertised as such, and I am sure your firm is not likely to do this. In short, here is one of the books of the last twenty years which however so we may doubt its absolute excellence and permanence in literature is certainly a milestone in literary history.

CARL VAN DOREN, Critic, Editor-in-Chief, The Literary Guild of America,
May 10, 1932:

> I am delighted to hear that Random House has acquired the American rights to *Ulysses* and I look forward to its early publication in this country without further annoyance from certain authorities who seem to me to have been misguided in their attitude to this great book. It is, I am convinced, a very great book, certainly one of the half dozen greatest novels in the English language and certainly a book that must rank with the most important books ever produced in English in any of the forms of literature. I see no better reason for restricting its

circulation than for restricting the circulation of Chaucer, Shakespeare, Swift, Byron, or the *New English Dictionary*. Every word in *Ulysses* which has been objected to appears, I believe, in one or more of these unquestioned classics. Moreover, the book as a whole can have nothing argued against it except that it is unprecedentedly truthful. This does not seem to me a valid objection to the circulation of any book.

ROBERT MORSS LOVETT, Professor in the Department of English, University of Chicago:

> Many contemporary critics if asked to name the most significant novel of the day would without hesitation choose *Ulysses*, by James Joyce. It is significant in two senses: significant as revealing current tendencies in artistic expression, in thought, and in attitude toward life; and significant in its influence on the novel as a form of art. The very qualities which give it value as a social document are those which have roused protest against it, for it represents the attempt to fuse the warring elements of experience, and such an attempt is bound to have issued in ugliness as well as in beauty. Yet this effort to weld the facts of science and the dreams of man into some workable unity is the most urgent demand upon the thinking person faced with the social and moral upheaval due to the effects of war, of modern research, and of present social conditions. Leopold Bloom, who has been called "the most complete character in fiction" includes all the attributes of humanity—its loneliness, its fatuity, its bewilderment, its ugliness, its wistfulness, its aspiration. He inspires both scorn and sympathy; indeed, it is as difficult to react simply to the characters of *Ulysses* as to the book itself, and the book comprises the flux, the confusion, the relativity of human life. This complexity, this mingling of dross with gold and of obscurity with clarity, is responsible for the partial comprehension which has caused the type of person who Bowdlerizes Shakespeare and the Bible to urge suppression of Joyce's work. It is also responsible for the high value of *Ulysses*, both as a literary achievement and as a social document.

JOHN ERSKINE, Author, Professor at Columbia University, Head of Juilliard Foundation,
May 11, 1932:

> I can't for the life of me see the sense of prohibiting the sale of the book if anybody wants to buy it. There are plenty of dirty and coarse passages in it as there are in many books of a still more certain fame, but I know nothing in it which could be subversive of morals. I am not conscious of any damage to myself from having read it.

ELLIS W. MEYERS, Executive Secretary, American Booksellers Association, May 12, 1932:

It does not seem as though it is necessary to present a brief for James Joyce, except to point out that in his novel *Ulysses*, he has probably done more for literature than we of this generation are aware. To suppress this work, to withhold it from free circulation among intelligent people, is to commit a crime against letters.

JOHN COWPER POWYS, Author:

There are very few books that by sheer force of genius mount up during an author's lifetime to an unassailable and classical position. Such however has been the fate of *Ulysses*. . . . From the viewpoint of defending this epoch-making book from hasty, ill-considered, and illiterate charges of an offence against public morals, it cannot be stated too often that where the work is naturalistic and out-spoken, it is so in the interest of the general aesthetic effect, and in no sense out of any morbid intention of erotic provocation.

This is proved to intelligenct readers by the complete absence of any sort of insidious seductiveness. Those who are offended by its frankness must also be offended by the frankness of many other world-writers, such as Aristophanes, Petronius, Rabelais, Swift, Cervantes. Fastidious and thin-skinned readers may be shocked and startled; but, unlike so many voluptuous modern books, *Ulysses*, while imaginatively realistic, is never flippant or perverse.

WILLIAM ROSE BENÉT, Poet, Contributing Editor to *The Saturday Review of Literature*, May 7, 1932:

I think that *Ulysses* is unquestionably one of the great books of the century. It is already a classic. Its publication in this country is as legitimate as the publication of such classics as Fielding's *Tom Jones*, the works of Rabelais, and other classics. It, also, is a work of genius. In its own way it is as penetrating a study of the human comedy as Balzac ever made. It should be considered in this category. As a social document it is most important. There should be no ban against it.

JOHN FARRAR, of the publishing house of Farrar & Rinehart, May 17, 1932:

Any novel of such really tremendous consequence—a novel which stands not only in the first line of literary acclaim but in the first rank of influence on the writing and thought of a period and which has been so important to the development of psychology in literature—that has been treated in the manner *Ulysses* has by the courts, certainly deserves defense on the part of anyone of sensitiveness and intelligence.

MALCOLM COWLEY, Editor, *The New Republic*,
May 6, 1932:

> James Joyce's position in literature is almost as important as that of Einstein in science. Preventing American authors from reading him is about as stupid as it would be to place an embargo on the theory of relativity.

LOUIS UNTERMEYER, Poet, Critic, Anthologist,
May 11, 1932:

> To say that *Ulysses* is a great work of art would scarcely be a "personal" opinion; it would merely be adding platitude to an axiom. Apart from its literary value, however—and I find it hard to separate the literary from the social aspect—it is a document of these times so revealing, so significant, that it can no more be ignored than the daily depression. What Freud is to modern psychology, or Einstein to our revised notions of time and space, *Ulysses* is to the novel. Joyce has given new dimensions not only to a literary form but to consciousness. . . . I don't say that everyone will enjoy the volume—I am certain that not everyone will understand it, and those that fail to comprehend it will be loudest in their condemnation. But I do know that one who reads it without prejudice can never quite forget it. And I am equally certain that it is one of the monuments—grotesque and forbidding, if you will, but certainly classical—of our age.

ROBERT BRIFFAULT, Anthropologist, Author of numerous scientific works,
May 20, 1932:

> Whatever may be one's literary predilections or judgment, *Ulysses* is, by almost universal consent, the one fastidiously finished monument of English literature which the present century has produced. One result of the ban has been, not to give advertisement to a work which needs none, but to draw the attention of persons of imperfect culture, to whom the work is neither addressed nor is intelligible, to the two or three lines in its 735 pages where Anglo-Saxon words are used for which synonyms are employed in the translation of the Bible. That base and insulting treatment of an English classic as a pornographic book, while it is without any effect on their morals, discourages them from the close study of a difficult masterpiece which might otherwise raise their minds above the vulgarian level of ignorance and deficient taste at which official action does its best to keep them.

THEODORE DREISER, Author,
May 13, 1932:

> *Ulysses* is, of course, a highly intellectual work. To read it is to spend a day inside a seeking and profoundly observant human mind, to learn

its mysterious wanderings and secret paths. And because it is what it is, some things enter into which are not generally recorded. But, and for precisely that reason, these things add to its value as an amazing, if not unique, social and literary document.

JOHN DOS PASSOS, Author:

To ban *Ulysses* is as absurd as it would be to ban *The Canterbury Tales* or the Book of Genesis. Banned or not, it will remain a great piece of English prose; sooner or later even customs officers will have to regard it as such.

---

## APPENDIX 10

**Photostatic Copy of R.H. Macy & Company Advertisement of March 20, 1932, *New York Times Book Review***

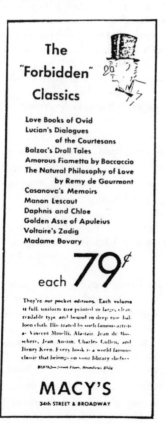

# *Notes*

1. U.S. v. Mary Ware Dennett, 39 Fed. (2d) 564; Youngs, etc. v. Lee etc., 45 Fed. (2d) 103; U.S. v. *Married Love*, 48 Fed. (2d) 821; U.S. v. *Contraception*, 51 Fed. (2d) 525; People v. Wendling, 258 N.Y. 451.

2. On December 8, 1933, the *New York Herald-Tribune* made the following editorial comment: "The opinion wherewith Judge Woolsey sustains this historic decision is studded with important contributions to the tangled and unsatisfactory law of literary suppression . . . that the opinion does represent a substantial victory for proportion, common sense and legal flexibility in the difficult areas of literary censorship, few will doubt."

3. In *James Joyce, His First Forty Years*, Herbert S. Gorman, eminent critic, says that this book "speedily assumed its proper position as the most important experiment in the English-written novel since the influence of *Madame Bovary* had slipped across the Channel. It was the key to a great door which swung open and revealed an entire new world for the novel." (pp. 99-100)

4. It is this austerity that has prompted McGreevy to say of Joyce that "he writes about human beings as the most enlightened and humane of father confessors might, if it were permitted, write about his penitents." (*Transition*, 1932, p. 254)

5. On January 25, 1934, Lewis Gannett wrote in the *New York Herald-Tribune*: " . . . his influence is apparent in virtually every serious novel published today. No man in our generation, unless it be Proust, has so profoundly influenced other writers; and that is enough to say of any man."

6. *Homage to James Joyce*, Stuart Gilbert; *Transition*, 1932.

7. *The Strange Case of James Joyce*, Rebecca West; *The Bookman*, September, 1928.

8. *Men Seen*, Paul Rosenfeld, Dial Press, 1925; pp. 32, 35, and 42.

9. Herbert S. Gorman estimates that *Ulysses* is as long as seven ordinary novels. (*James Joyce, His First Forty Years*, p. 121)

10. Idem, pp. 121, 122, and 123.

11. Mention should be made of Donald Henderson Clarke's *Female*, against which two obscenity proceedings were instituted recently. Magistrate Van Amringe dismissed one complaint in Manhattan; on the other, there was a conviction in Special Sessions in Queens. An appeal is pending.

12. It should be noted that the statute is directed only against an *obscene* book. The word *immoral* is not used therein in connection with printed matter.

13. A detailed discussion of the evolution of the rule laid down in *Regina* v. *Hicklin* appears in this brief.

14. Tyomies Pub. Co. v. United States, 211 Fed. 385; United States v. Kennerley, 209 Fed. 119; Konda v. United States, 166 Fed. 91; Knowles v. United States, 170 Fed. 409; Clarke v. United States, 38 Fed. 500, 502, 503; Griffin v. United States, 248 Fed. 6, 8, 9.

15. We direct the Court's attention to Appendices 1 and 2. Magon v. United States, 248 U.S. 201.

16. Judge Woolsey defined pornography to mean something "written for the purpose of exploiting obscenity" (fol. 72).

17. Ernst and Seagle, *To the Pure*, p. 253.

18. Schroeder, *Free Press Anthology*, p. 257.

19. See Lewis S. Gannett's reviews of Ford Maddox Ford's *Return to Yesterday*, *New York Herald-Tribune*, January 15, 1932.

20. Mark Twain's *Autobiography*, Vol. 2, p. 335.

21. Horace M. Kallen, *Indecency and the Seven Arts*, p. 17.

22. Thompson, *Philosophy of Fiction*, p. 191; see also Bowerman, *Censorship and Other Papers*, p. 32.

23. Mordell, *Notorious Literary Attacks*, pp. 122–37.

24. Halsey v. N.Y. Society, 234 N.Y. 1.

25. Ernst and Seagle, *To the Pure*, p. 43.

26. Dr. Spaeth was referred to, apparently as an authority, by the Court of Appeals in People v. Wendling, 258 N.Y. 451, 452.

27. See Appendix 10.

28. See Stuart Gilbert's scholarly analysis of "indecency" in *Ulysses: James Joyce's Ulysses*, pp. 19–22.

29. See Appendices 1, 2, 3, 4 and 9.

30. See *ante*, p. 9. The statute, insofar as books are concerned, restricts itself to the word *obscene*; it does not use the word *immoral* to apply to printed matter. Hence it is not necessary for the Court to inquire into the *morality* of *Ulysses*; the sole question is, is it obscene as a matter of law?

31. Since the *Swearingen* decision, there has been a long line of cases holding that the material charged must be "calculated to incite to immorality relating to sexual impurity." U.S. Journal Co., Inc., 197 Fed. 415; U.S. v. Klauder, 240 Fed. 501; U.S. v. Durant, 46 Fed. 753; U.S. v. Moore, 104 Fed. 78; U.S. v. Reinheimer, 233 Fed. 545; U.S. v. Clarke, 38 Fed. 732; Dysart v. U.S., 4 Fed. (2) 765.

32. In this connection two kinds of abnormal persons may be considered: the morally weak and the prudishly supersensitive.

33. As to the former, even if this Court were convinced that *Ulysses* might conceivably harm the fatuous and the impressionable, the susceptible and the morally weak, the Court would not be justified in passing adversely on it. Our literature is not to be judged by the standards of morons. Said the Appellate Division of the Supreme Court, First Department in People v. Philip Pesky (230 App. Div. 200): "These matters must be judged by normal people and not by the abnormal. Conditions would be deplorable if abnormal people were permitted to regulate such matters."

As to the prudery-ridden, it does not matter if their sensibilities are offended. As the Court of Appeals pointed out in the *Wendling* case (p. 454) a work "may be repulsive to puritanical ideal of propriety"; it "may be offensive to the more liberal minded as lacking in taste and refinement"; it "may be gross and its characters wanting in moral sense"; it may "depict women who carry on a vicious trade"—yet it cannot be deemed obscene unless it comes within the narrow definition laid down by the courts, that of arousing lustful and lecherous desires.

In exonerating *God's Little Acre*, Magistrate Greenspan wrote in part:

> This is not a book where vice and lewdness are treated as virtues, or which would tend to incite lustful desires in the normal mind. *There is no way of anticipating its effect upon a disordered or diseased mind, and if the courts were to exclude books from sale merely because they might incite lust in disordered minds, our entire literature would very likely be reduced to a relatively small number of uninteresting and barren books.* The greater part of the classics would certainly be excluded.

34. The article was reprinted in the *New York Law Journal*, Editorial Page, April 27, 1929.

35. See Appendix 8.

36. Lewis Gannett said in the *New York Herald-Tribune*, January 25, 1934: "Young hunters for

the pornographic will have to work hard to locate, or to comprehend, Joyce's sexual passages; and they will find them discouragingly intellectual when they are not dully matter-of-fact. Which is not to say that *Ulysses* will not shock most readers who have the energy to plow through it. Nothing so distastefully honest has before appeared in legal print."

37. The Court will note that in effect the *Jurgen* motion was quite similar to the cross-motions before the Court below.

38. *James Joyce's Ulysses*, pp. 27–28.

39. Idem, p. 160, *et seq*.

40. Joyce himself has referred to *Ulysses* as a "chaffering allincluding most farraginous chronicle." *James Joyce's Ulysses*, Stuart Gilbert, p. 42.

41. " . . . what is the stream of consciousness method? The solitary thoughts of characters in novels have been overheard by god-like authors and yet we do not apply the phrase 'stream of consciousness' to these mappings of thought. The difference is in the word 'stream.' This new method is an attempt through the application of the author's psychological astuteness and intuition and profound knowledge of his character's mind, its depths, its subconscious impulses, inhibitions, and buried urges, to set down the undisturbed flow of thought—not always conscious, perhaps, to the thinker—that pours through the restless mind, a stream that is diverted constantly by a thousand and one extraneous objects, word-connotations, stifled emotions, from the consistent and built-up delineations of thought-processes to be found in the older novelists. (Herbert Gorman: *James Joyce: His First Forty Years*, p. viii)

Men before James Joyce have been aware of the parasitic and independent nature of our upper-story lodger, yet the Irish poet can fairly pretend to being his artistic discoverer and portrayer of his form. The protagonist of his vast novel is no creature of flesh. The hero of the *Odyssey* may have been an individual. But the being whose wanderings are set forth in the modern tragi-comic parallel is not other than 'mind in the making' perceived through types of the floating dislocated intellect of our time. . . . He has placed the interior soliloquy of the human being on a plane and a parity with his exterior 'action' and boldly mixed the two. . . . He has represented mind's play, the manner of drunken existence led by him, with a queer gusto at once sour and Rabelaisian, with pity, tenderness and Irish mischief, and upon an heroic scale and with heroic richness of illustration. And none of Joyce's coevals, neither Miss Stein nor Miss Richardson nor Ernest Hemingway, has made it an object of contemplation with a relentlessness and bravery in any way comparable to his. Quite as the painted slides of glass in medical museums give in finest segments the physical aspects of the brain, so does his method render all the strata of mind in their manifold interpenetrations. We are shown the mind we reveal to each other; and the mind full of fears and fantasies, monkey-like preoccupations and ignoble interests which we try to reveal to no one and to keep utterly to ourselves; and through representations of the dreamlike and hallucinatory states in which the activities of the brain assume a definite corporeality, the mind which seeks to conceal itself and its fixations and traumas and outlawed impulses from ourselves, too. We are shown its motion, its rattling activity, broken rhythms, starts, attitudes and relationships, and made to observe it under the influence of bodily states, colored and given form and direction. . . . (Paul Rosenfeld, *Men Seen*, pp. 24–26)

42. Distribution is one of the determinants of obscenity.
> U.S. v. Harmon, 45 Fed. 414;
> U.S. v. Wroblenski, 118 Fed. 495;
> U.S. v. Grimm, 50 Fed. 528;
> Grimm v. United States, 156 U.S. 604;
> Lynch v. U.S., 285 Fed. 162;
> *Stephen's Digest of Criminal Law*, 7th Edition (1926) Article 247;
> U.S. v. Clarke, 38 Fed. 732;
> U.S. v. Smith, 45 Fed. 476, 477;
> U.S. v. Chesman, 19 Fed. 497;
> Burton v. U.S., 142 Fed. 57;
> U.S. v. Dennett, 39 Fed. (2nd) 564;
> People v. Muller, 96 N.Y. 408;

Halsey v. New York Society, 234 N.Y. 1;

People v. Boni & Liveright, Inc., Magistrate Oberwager, September 27, 1922;

In re Worthington Co., 30 N.Y. Supp. 361.

43. This case sustained a judgment against Mr. Sumner's society for malicious prosecution growing out of the attempted suppression of *Mademoiselle de Maupin.*

44. Emerson, the staid New Englander, philosopher and transcendentalist, lamented that our language lacked earthiness and forthrightness. He said:

> What a pity that we cannot curse and swear in good society! Cannot the stinging dialect of the sailors be domesticated? It is the best rhetoric and for a hundred occasions those forbidden words are the only good ones . . . This profane swearing and barroom wit has salt and fire . . . One who wishes to refresh himself by contact with the bone and sinew of society must avoid what is called the respectable portion of his city and neighborhood. (*New York Herald-Tribune*, April 1, 1932)

45. *James Joyce: His First Forty Years*, page 93.

46. *The Key to the Ulysses of James Joyce*, page 89.

47. On May 12, 1932, Lewis S. Gannett, literary editor of the *New York Herald-Tribune*, wrote in that paper:

> It is almost ludicrous to think that such a book still has to fear the hurdles of the obscenity law; if ever there was a serious, earnest book, it is *Ulysses*. Already it has acquired the corpselike color of a 'classic.' It is discussed for its effect on other writers. It seems, like Anthony Comstock, to be a curious phenomenon of a remote past.

48. Before the Woolsey decision, it said that 30,000 copies (largely pirated editions from which the nearly-blind Joyce derived no benefit) were sold by clandestine methods here and abroad. *Time* Magazine, December 18, 1933.

On March 11, 1934, the New York *Times* published an interview with Judge Woolsey, in the course of which he said: "There is a pleasant story about a woman who tried to put a stop to the sale of liquor in Cambridge University. She felt that the students should not be permitted to drink, and wrote to Sir Walter Raleigh, a professor of poetry in the university, suggesting that a ban should be placed upon it. In a charming reply Sir Walter Raleigh said, 'Young gentlemen who come up to Cambridge come, not to learn how to obey, but to learn how to choose.' There is the secret of the whole thing. Censorship cannot prevent the circulation of forbidden books. The only prophylactic against books that should not be circulated is to set up, by the development of educated taste in the individual, an inhospitality to books which are unworthy of the marketplace. The same method must be employed in other things. In this country we do not have to go far for a clinical illustration of the effect of censorship. The experience of the country with prohibition tells the story. Education, not law, must solve problems of taste and choice."

49. There are two methods of presenting pertinent facts to the Court. One is the introduction of evidence; the other is the presentation, in a brief, of relevant material of which the Court may take judicial notice of its own accord. The latter method was first used on an extensive scale by Mr. Justice Brandeis in his celebrated brief in support of the Oregon statute limiting the hours of labor for women. Resort to extrinsic sources of information is all the more important in cases which involve the circulation of *ideas*; and if relevant general data are not furnished to the Court, the Court is subjected to the inconveniences of seeking out and collating the facts.

[Doc. 261]

*New York Herald-Tribune*
May 3, 1934
Random House Files Reply in *Ulysses* Case

---

**Changing Standards Pleaded in Answer to Appeal From Woolsey Decision**

---

**Obscenity Charge Denied**

---

**Book Called 'Classic, To Be Judged as a Whole'**

---

The answering brief to the government's appeal from Judge John M. Woolsey's decision in Federal Court holding that James Joyce's *Ulysses* is not obscene or immoral and should be surrendered to the importer, was pled yesterday with the United States Circuit Court of Appeals by Morris L. Ernst and Alexander Lindey, of counsel for Random House, Inc., owners of the imported copy of the book which was impounded by customs authorities.

*Ulysses,* which has been a *cause célèbre* in literary circles for more than a decade, has become perhaps the most controverted prose work of this generation. It has evoked international critical acclaim and, according to the brief, Judge Woolsey's decision of last December 6 "has met with overwhelming public approval as has rarely been accorded in recent years to a judicial disposition."

It is the contention of the claimant-appellee that the book must be judged in the light of present day standards. "The standards of yesterday, the abhorrence of any mention of certain biological functions, excessive prudery, the sex taboo, are as definitely dead today, " the attorneys wrote, "as the horse-drawn carriage and the donkey engines on the Elevated. We have developed sturdier tastes, and grown wiser in the process."

It is further alleged that *Ulysses* does not violate the obscenity statute, "viewed against our contemporary background." Also, the attorneys hold, because Judge Woolsey intimated the book is a classic it cannot be judged to be obscene, in that the words *classic* and *obscene* "represent polar extremes." They further contend that the book must be judged as a whole, and not on the "basis of isolated passages."

### Forward March of Courts Urged

"There is a peculiar timeliness about this appeal," the brief states. "Coming as it does, in logical sequence after the *Dennett* case, the *Youngs* case, the

*Married Love* case, the *Contraception* case, the *Wendling* case, *Ulysses* calls for an affirmance of its vindication as a fitting climax to the salutary forward march of our courts."

The attorneys state that if *Ulysses* is not legally circulated, it will result in the book being illegally distributed through bootleg channels.

Giving an outline biography of the author of the volumnious work, which Joyce himself characterizes as a "chaffering all-including most farraginous chronicle," the brief asserts that he was "hailed ten years ago by the untutored and the misguided as a juggler of words, today even his harshest critics concede his greatness. It is monstrous to suppose that a man of Joyce's stature would or could produce a work of obscenity."

Citing a quantity of recent cases involving books at one time considered questionable for distribution, the brief calls attention to the fact that "in recent years there has not been a single instance where a book generally acclaimed by the press and literary critics was ultimately condemned by the courts, even though prosecuted at the outset for obscenity."

### Judgment by the Present Pleaded

In the opinion of the claimant-appellee, the test of obscenity is a living standard, and the book must be judged by the mores of the day.

"Evidence of our current mores are everywhere around us. Our tabloids carry stories of passion and lust, of crime and perversion, told with a degree of graphic vividness and frankness unheard of a generation ago.

"Every man, woman and child in the community has easy access to the complete details of suicides, of sash-weight murders, of torch murders, of marital infidelities, of boudoir intimacies, kidnapings and abnormalities. For the press of today a spade is spade. No longer are such squeamish phrases as 'statutory offense' resorted to. Such outspokenness would have horrified us in 1900. Today it is accepted as a matter of course.

"Nor have the movies contented themselves with stripping away prudish coverings. They have in recent years given us a collection of sex films too numerous to mention, culminating in Mae West's frank and unashamed *She Done Him Wrong*."

Other present day notions of propriety as depicted on the stage, in songs, in letters and in the graphic and plastic arts are outlined in some detail in the brief, all treating of the variableness of moral concepts.

Appended to the brief are transcripts from editorials in the daily press, mostly lauding Judge Woolsey's decision, reviews of the book in question clipped from newspapers and magazines the country over, and testimonials concerning *Ulysses* "furnished by distinguished persons in various walks of life."

A date for the hearing has not been set.

[Doc. 262]

---

*New York World-Telegram*
May 3, 1934

**Publishers File *Ulysses* Reply**

---

**Answer to U.S. Appeal Warns Book Will Be Bootlegged if Ruled Obscene**

---

The reply of the publishers of James Joyce's *Ulysses* to the government's appeal seeking a reversal of Federal Judge John M. Woolsey's decision holding the book was not obscene, was on file today in the United States Circuit Court of Appeals.

"The standards of yesterday, the abhorrence of any mention of certain biological functions, excessive prudery, the sex taboo, are as definitely dead today as the horsedrawn carriage and the donkey engines on the Elevated," the reply says. It was filed by Morris L. Ernst and Alexander Lindey, counsel for Random House, Inc., the publishers.

The book will be bootlegged anyhow, if the higher court reverses the decision and bans *Ulysses* now, the brief asserts.

The book, which Joyce, the author, once described as "a chaffering all-including, most farraginous chronicle," cannot be obscene because it is a classic and was so characterized by Judge Woolsey, the appellee declares.

No date has yet been set for the hearing.

---

[Doc. 263]

*New York World-Telegram*
May 12, 1934

---

***Ulysses* Called Too Subtle to Corrupt "Unsubtle Mind"**

---

James Joyce's *Ulysses* could not possibly corrupt a person of unsubtle mind, because such a person could not understand it, Morris Ernst and Alexander Lindey, counsel, held today in asking the Circuit Court of Appeals to uphold the decision of Judge John M. Woolsey exonerating the book of obscenity.

In substantiation they offer a list of thirty-two words, "picked at random from the book," which constitute a kind of Joyce word game. Here they are:

| | |
|---|---|
| whelks | mavrone |
| cataletic | greydauburn |
| strandentwining | hierophantic |
| houynhnm | bosthoon |
| froeken | tympanum |
| hismy | henev |
| quadrireme | demisemiquaver |
| fellaheen | videlicet |
| crubeen | cruiskeen |
| parallax | pralaya |
| cygnets | loodheramaun |
| entelechy | oxter |
| umbrel | sinhedrim |
| yogibogeybox | topiary |
| nookshotten | hebdomadary |
| aprocrypha | epicene |

These, say the attorneys, "are not egregious examples." They might have cited such truly exceptional words as contransmagnificandjewbangtantiality (page 38) or weggebobbles (page 158).

In exonerating James Branch Cabell's *Jurgen* in 1923, the brief recites, General Sessions Judge Nott, said in part:

> In fact, it is doubtful the book could be read or understood at all by more than a very limited number of readers.

"Beside it (*Ulysses*)," the attorneys declare, " *Jurgen* is a child's primer." "The unabridged lists eighteen of the thirty-two words, that is, if "cataletic" is intended to be "catalectic"—wanting a letter.

---

[Doc. 264]

*New York World-Telegram*
May 16, 1934

**Ulysses, "Unchaste and Lustful," No Lunchtime Story for 3 Judges**

---

Blushing, stammering, rocking nervously on his heels, United States Attorney Martin Conboy today read to the United States Circuit Court of Appeals twenty-five passages which he considered obscene in James Joyce's *Ulysses*.

Each of the three Justices on the bench held a yellow pencil in his hand and had a copy of the disputed book open before him on the bench. They all looked solemn.

Mr. Conboy was appealing the decision last December of Federal Judge John M. Woosley which held *Ulysses* not obscene. Since then, 35,000 copies have been sold, said Saxe Commins, representative of Random House, the publishers.

The passages Mr. Conboy read contained, he said, words which he characterized as "unchaste and lustful."

The Justices were Martin T. Manton, Learned Hand and Augustus Hand, and they followed the text carefully while Mr. Conboy read it aloud.

"Are you going to read the whole book?" Justice Learned Hand interrupted.

"Well, I'll give you a generous sampling," said Mr. Conboy earnestly.

He defined obscenity as "that which suggests lustful ideas or is offensive to decency or delicacy" and cited an English review which called *Ulysses* the "most infamous and obscene book in ancient or modern literature."

Lunch adjournment interrupted Mr. Conboy in the middle of a sentence. The sentence was: "It would seem that the passages I have cited would prove this book to be—"

The Justices stood up and filed out.

---

**[Doc. 265]**

*New York Daily News*
May 17, 1934

---

### Is Conboy's Face Red as He Reads *Ulysses* in Court

Three solemn, elderly gentlemen sat staring selfconsciously at copies of James Joyce's *Ulysses* in the United States Circuit Court of Appeals yesterday while a fourth, flushed and determined, read passages to prove the book was obscene.

The three solemn gentlemen were Judges Martin T. Manton, presiding; Learned Hand and Augustus N. Hand, and the elocutionist was United States Attorney Martin Conboy, who was appealing the decision last December of Federal Judge John M. Woolsey, which held *Ulysses* not obscene.

### Calls It Filthy, Offensive

"This book," said Conboy, "is filthy, offensive to modesty, subversive of decency, therefore it complies with all the definitions of obscenity which I have read."

"You do not believe that the Court should read it?" inquired Judge Learned Hand.

"I will read a generous sampling from this product of the gutter," answered Conboy, reddening.

Which he proceeded to do until lunch adjournment interrupted him.

### Adjournment Ends Blushes

When they came back, Conboy read for forty minutes more. Then Judge Manton again interrupted his blushing to announce another adjournment until today, when Conboy will go on reading.

After he finishes, Morris L. Ernst and Alexander Lindey, attorneys for Random House, publishers of the book, will be heard.

---

[Doc. 266]

*New York Herald-Tribune*
May 17, 1934

### Conboy Opens U.S. Appeal to Bar *Ulysses*

---

**One Woman Quits Court, Another Stays to Hear Selected Passages of Book**

---

**Held 'Product of Gutter'**

---

**Prosecutor Cites Review That Stressed Obscenity**

---

While one woman left the courtroom but another stuck it out to the end, Martin Conboy, United States Attorney, yesterday read into the record portions of James Joyce's *Ulysses*, to prove to three justices of the United States Court of Appeals that it is "a filthy, obscene book" and subject to confiscation by the Customs.

Mr. Conboy was prosecuting the government's appeal in the case of *United States* vs. *Ulysses* before Judges Martin T. Manton, Learned Hand and Augustus N. Hand in the Federal Building. Previously Judge John M. Woolsey had ruled in United States District Court that, while the book was "a rather strong draught," it was "a serious attempt to devise a new literary method for the observation and description of mankind," and should be admitted. Random House, Inc., which has issued an American edition with

Judge Woolsey's opinion as a foreword, is opposing the appeal, with Morris L. Ernst as chief counsel.

### Selected Passages Read

Selected passages, with particular reference to the stream-of-thought soliloquizing of Mrs. Molly Bloom at the end of a hard day, running upward of fifty pages, were read off by Mr. Conboy, who could not keep a shocked note from creeping into his voice.

Judge Manton, who presided, kept his face in a copy of the book, making no comment save to ask occasionally what the page was. Judge Learned Hand essayed a mild bit of humor at the beginning of the session, but subsided afterward.

"The government's case is that this is an obscene book." Mr. Conboy had said, "The only exhibit is the book itself."

"Do you believe the court should read it?" asked Judge Learned Hand with a smile.

"No," replied Mr. Conboy gravely. "I will read a generous sampling from this product of the gutter. I do not believe it will be necessary for your honors to read the entire book."

### Reads Critic's Opinion

After reading various definitions of what *obscene* means from standard lexicons and having found that they were all in substantial agreement that it meant "offensive to modesty, chastity, delicacy, purity and decency," Mr. Conboy proceeded to show that the publishers of the book had admitted that it was all of these things. He read from a blurb on the jacket a criticism by one James Douglas, writing in *The Sunday Express*, of London. He cautioned the judges to remember that this criticism was adopted by the publishers and used by them for advertising purposes. "It shows, at least," he said, "that the character of the book is realized by those who sell it."

Mr. Douglas' critique went as follows:

"I say deliberately that it is the most infamously obscene book in ancient or in modern literature. The obscenity of Rabelais is innocent compared with its leprous and scabrous horrors. All the secret sewers of vice are canalized in its flood of unimaginable thoughts, images and pornographic words. And its unclean lunacies are larded with appalling and revolting blasphemies directed against the Christian religion and against the name of Christ.

"The book is the Bible of beings who are outcasts in this and every other civilized country. It is also adopted by the Freudians as the supreme glory of their dirty and degraded cult."

### Sketches Novel to Court

Then Mr. Conboy sketched briefly the outline of the novel, saying that it had nothing to do with that Ulysses who was the hero of the *Odyssey* but rather "a setting forth of what purports to take place in one day in the life of a Hungarian Jew in Dublin, together with his thoughts and ruminations and those of his wife."

"All vices and all licentious thoughts are set forth without restraint and without attempt to palliate or minimize their offensiveness," he told the court. "Sexual practices, normal and abnormal, are dealt with, as is the use of contraceptives. A large part of the book is taken up with minute descriptions of performances and conversations in a brothel, where the supposed hero spends a lot of time."

Mr. Conboy then began to read his selected passages. He had not read more than ten minutes when a woman in the rear of the room arose and left. There was one other woman, besides an unusually large number of male spectators. The other woman stayed until the last, but left quickly after the forty-minute session was over.

Mr. Conboy will continue this morning, with Mr. Ernst yet to be heard from.

After the session, Mr. Ernst said that he would ask the judges to read the book in its entirety before coming to their decision, as it was manifestly unfair to take selected passages out of the context as a whole and come to a conclusion, through them, about the whole book.

---

[Doc. 267]

*New York World-Telegram*
May 17, 1934

### *Ulysses* Unspeakable Filth, Conboy Tells Appeals Court

---

### Begins with Blasphemy and Ends in Obscenity, U.S. Attorney Declares, but Ernst Defends Joyce as "Author of Majestic Genius"— Lone Woman in Court

---

Ulysses, the wily mythical wanderer whose honeyed line beguiled the witch Circe as she schemed to turn him into a hog, would have felt his cheek mantle with shame if he could have heard United States Attorney Martin Conboy's comment on his modern prototype, the hero of James Joyce's book, before the United States Circuit Court of Appeals today.

Homer's Ulysses played around the Mediterranean while his faithful Penelope knitted at home. Joyce's Ulysses was just as wayward a fellow and no fit companion for the fireside, Mr. Conboy assured the Court, made up of Judges Learned Hand, Augustus N. Hand and Martin T. Manton.

### Appeals from Decision

Concluding his argument begun yesterday against the admission of Joyce's *Ulysses* into this country, Mr. Conboy said the volume "begins with blasphemy, runs the whole gamut of sexual perversion and ends in inexpressible filth and obscenity."

The government is appealing from a decision of Federal Judge John M. Woolsey, who decreed some time ago that after a careful perusal of *Ulysses* he saw no reason why it was not entitled to a place on American library shelves.

Today the pretty lady in the brown ensemble, who took such a keen interest in yesterday's proceedings, refusing to be routed by the bandying of some of the wickedest words in the language, was again in her seat in the courtroom. She was the only one of her sex who ventured to listen to the arguments. A second young woman retired in confusion when the connotations of Joyce's paragraphs were commented on in Anglo-Saxon by the contending attorneys.

Morris L. Ernst, counsel for Random House, Joyce's New York publishers, called Joyce an author "of majestic genius" and said that "the real protagonist for this book is the human mind."

### Action in Skull

"The arena of the action of *Ulysses*," Mr. Ernst told the Court, "is not a Dublin brothel but the human skull."

"We can't bind the masses by the rules that actuated the saints," he said. "The government was unfair in citing only excerpts from this book. It is necessary to consider it as a whole. The definition of obscenity remains the same, but the standards of the times change. No great work of fiction has survived unless it has provided some sexual stimulation. If you blush at them the blush minimizes their corrupting influence. The fact that they shock you shows you are disgusted with them."

Justice Learned Hand interrupted to say:

"You can imagine writings that are rude without being lustful. They would be merely disgusting. Is that your point?"

"That is right, Your Honor," Mr. Ernst replied.

The Court reserved decision.

---

[Doc. 268]

*New York Daily News*
May 18, 1934

### Conboy Recites From *Ulysses* And Girl Flees

*Two little girlies*
*Went to court for fun;*
*The lawyers read Ulysses—*
*Then there was one.*

The Federal court, usually a place of utmost decorum, took on the atmosphere of a gathering of Greenwich Village intellectuals yesterday when United States Attorney Martin Conboy began reading passages from James Joyce's novel *Ulysses*, sale of which he is seeking to have banned as indecent.

Two girls were in the audience when Conboy filled the room with some pretty husky Anglo-Saxon verbiage. One of the young women gasped and dashed for the door, her cheeks flaming. The other, a determined young lady in a smart brown ensemble, stood her ground and remained throughout the reading.

### Appeals Federal Ruling

Conboy, appealing a Federal Court ruling that *Ulysses* was not obscene, appeared before the United States Circuit Court of Appeals yesterday armed with a copy of the book. Despite the objections of defense counsel Morris Ernst that paragraphs had nothing to do with the intent of the author and that the court could not rule out a work merely because of nasty allusions, Conboy insisted on reading various passages.

"We can't bind the masses by rules that actuated the saints," said Ernst. "No great work of fiction has survived unless it provided some sexual stimulation."

### Insists It's Obscene

"This is an obscene book," protested Conboy. "It begins with blasphemy, runs the whole gamut of sexual perversion, and ends in inexpressible filth and obscenity."

The court reserved decision.

[Doc. 269]

*New York Herald-Tribune*
May 18, 1934

*Ulysses* Fate Up to Court as Arguments End

---

**Conboy Reads Florid Excerpts, Ernst Declares Writer 'Majestic Genius'**

---

**University Use Is Cited**

---

**U.S. Circuit Tribunal to Rule on Federal Appeal**

---

Three justices of the United States Circuit Court of Appeals reserved decision yesterday as to whether James Joyce's *Ulysses* is an obscene book, as charged by Martin Conboy, United States Attorney, who is prosecuting the government's appeal from the decision of Federal Judge John M. Woolsey admitting the book for sale in this country.

The justices listened gravely to Mr. Conboy as he concluded reading the more florid passages of the book and waved a damning finger at it, crying, "It is obscene, obscene." Then for an hour they heard Morris L. Ernst, appearing for Random House, Inc., which has issued an American edition, praise the book as "a great work of fiction" and its author as a "majestic genius."

After Judge Martin T. Manton, who presided, and Judges Learned Hand and Augustus N. Hand had left the bench, lawyers who had packed the courtroom stood in little groups discussing the arguments. A woman in brown, the only one in the courtroom, pulled a gray fox furpiece snugly about her throat, slipped her Robin Hood hat lower on her face and hurried from the building, stopping to speak to no one.

### Joyce Described as Genius

"Every university library in the country has a copy of this book," began Mr. Ernst after Mr. Conboy in his shocked voice had concluded, "and those few that have not want one. James Joyce is a majestic genius."

The lawyer belittled the government evidence of an English critic who had written a "blurb" for a jacket of the book in which it was described as "an infamously obscene book," and said that while fifty or more famous critics had commended the work, the government had produced only one who had been shocked.

"The real arena of action in *Ulysses* is not a Dublin brothel," Mr. Ernst said, "but rather a human skull. English 26 at Harvard would not be a real

English course without *Ulysses*. You cannot take excerpts from this book and know it. You must take the entire book.

"*Casanova's Homecoming, The Well of Loneliness* and *God's Little Acre* were subjected to the same attack as this book, but the courts decided they were not corrupt. No great work of fiction that has survived is without sexual stimulation. We cannot bind the masses to the rule of the saints. Not only in sophisticated New York but in the small towns of the South and the Middle West, *Ulysses* is sought in every library."

### Standards Found Changing

Mr. Ernst said that although the definition of obscenity had remained the same, the standards of the time have changed toward greater liberty. In the last seventeen years, the lawyer said, there had been no upholding under appeal of the conviction of any dealer who had dealt in any book or books openly published under the name of the author.

"There are two questions pertinent to the issues in this case," Mr. Ernst said. "The first is, has the book been accepted and dealt in openly or has it been dealt in under the counter? The answer is that is has been dealt in openly. The other question is that of the intent of the author. As to that I do not think there can be any serious derogatory comment. This book was written to present a study of the human mind, and emotions in certain phases, and it has not been hawked about in a coarse, grasping sense.

"Those shouting loudest for censorship are the big business fellows who tell dirty stories in Pullman cars. If you blush, it minimizes the corruption and acts as a repellent."

Judge Learned Hand asked Mr. Ernst if he was not trying to make the point that writings might be lewd without being lustful or that they might be disgusting. Mr. Ernst answered in the affirmative.

"If reasonable men differ on *Ulysses*," the lawyer concluded, "then, according to the precedent of our law, the decision of Judge Woolsey must stand."

Judge Woolsey had ruled when the government first sought to confiscate copies of *Ulysses* shipped into this country that while the book was "a rather strong draught," it was "a serious attempt to devise a new literary method for the observation and description of mankind" and should be admitted.

———————

[Doc. 270]

UNITED STATES DISTRICT
COURT OF APPEALS FOR
THE SECOND CIRCUIT

UNITED STATES OF AMERICA,

Libellant-Appellant,

—against—

BY JAMES JOYCE,
RANDOM HOUSE, INC.,

Claimant-Appellee.

OPINION

Before: MANTON, L. HAND and AUGUSTUS N. HAND, Circuit Judges.

Appeal from United States District Court for the Southern District of New York.

From a decree granting the motion of the claimant-appellee to dismiss the libel filed by the United States of America praying for the forfeiture of *Ulysses*, written by James Joyce, on the ground that it was an "obscene book" within the meaning of Section 305(a) of the Tariff Act of 1930, the libellant appeals. Affirmed.

Martin Conboy, United States Attorney, for Libellant-Appellant; Martin Conboy, Francis H. Horan and John F. Davidson, Counsel.

Greenbaum, Wolff & Ernst, Attorneys for Claimant-Appellee; Morris L. Ernst and Alexander Lindey, Counsel.

AUGUSTUS N. HAND, Circuit Judge:

This appeal raises sharply the question of the proper interpretation of Section 305(a) of the Tariff Act of 1930. That section provides that: "all persons are prohibited from importing into the United States from any foreign country . . . any obscene book, pamphlet, paper, writing, advertisement, circular, print, picture, drawing, or other representation, figure or image on or of paper or other material. . .", and directs that upon the appearance of any such book or matter at any customs office, the collector shall seize it and inform the District Attorney, who shall institute proceedings for forfeiture. In accordance with the statute the collector seized *Ulysses*, a book written by James Joyce, and the United States filed a libel for forfeiture. The claimant Random House, Inc., the publisher of the American edition, intervened in the cause and filed its answer denying that the book was obscene and was subject to confiscation and praying that it be admitted into the United States. The case came on for trial before Woolsey, J., who found that the book, taken as a whole, "did not tend to excite sexual impulses or lustful thoughts but that its net effect . . . was only that of a somewhat tragic and very powerful commentary on the inner lives of men and women." He accordingly granted a decree adjudging that the book was "not of the character the entry of which is prohibited under the provision of Section 305 of the Tariff Act of 1930 . . . and . . . dismissing the libel," from which this appeal has been taken.

James Joyce, the author of *Ulysses*, may be regarded as a pioneer among those writers who have adopted the so-called stream of consciousness method of presentation, which has attracted considerable attention in academic and literary circles. In this field *Ulysses* is rated as a book of considerable power by persons whose opinions are entitled to weight. Indeed it has become a sort of contemporary classic, dealing with a new subject matter. It attempts to depict the thoughts and lay bare the souls of a number of people, some of them intellectuals, and some social outcasts, and nothing more with a literalism that leaves nothing unsaid. Certain of its passages are of beauty and undoubted distinction, while others are of a vulgarity that is extreme and the book as a whole has a realism characteristic of the present age. It is supposed to portray the thoughts of the principal characters during a period of about eighteen hours.

We may discount the laudation of *Ulysses* by some of its admirers and reject the view that it will permanently stand among the great works of literature, but it is fair to say that it is a sincere portrayal with skilful artistry of the "streams of consciousness" of its characters. Though the depiction happily is not of the "stream of consciousness" of all men and perhaps of only those of a morbid type, it seems to be sincere, truthful, relevant to the subject, and executed with real art. Joyce, in the words of *Paradise Lost* has dealt with "things unattempted yet in prose or rime"—with things that very likely might better have remained "unattempted", but his books shows originality and is a work of symmetry and excellent craftsmanship of a sort. The question before us is whether such a book of artistic merit and scientific insight should be regarded as *obscene* within Section 305(a) of the Tariff Act.

That numerous long passages in *Ulysses* contain matter that is obscene under any fair definition of the word cannot be gainsaid, yet they are relevant to the purpose of depicting the thoughts of the characters and are introduced to give meaning to the whole, rather than to promote lust or portray filth for its own sake. The net effect even of portions most open to attack, such as the closing monologue of the wife of Leopold Bloom, is pitiful and tragic, rather than lustful. The book depicts the souls of men and women that are by turns bewildered and keenly apprehensive, sordid and aspiring, ugly and beautiful, hateful and loving. In the end one feels, more than anything else, pity and sorry for the confusion, misery and degradation of humanity. Page after page of the book is, or seems to be, incomprehensible. But many passages show the trained hand of an artist, who can at one moment adapt to perfection the style of an ancient chronicler, and at another become a veritable personification of Thomas Carlyle. In numerous places there are found originality, beauty and distinction. The book as a whole is not pornographic, and while in not a few spots it is coarse, blasphemous and obscene, it does not, in our opinion, tend to promote lust. The erotic passages are submerged in the book as a whole and have little resultant effect. If these are to make the book subject to confiscation, by the same test *Venus and Adonis, Hamlet, Romeo and Juliet*, and the story told in the Eighth Book of the *Odyssey* by the bard Demodocus of how Ares and Aphrodite were entrapped in a net spread by the outraged Hephaestus, amid the laughter of the immortal gods, as well as many other classics, would have to be suppressed. Indeed, it may be questioned whether the obscene passages in *Romeo and Juliet* were as necessary to the development of the play as those in the monologue of Mrs. Bloom are to the depiction of the latter's tortured soul.

It is unnecessary to add illustrations to show that, in the administration of statutes aimed at the suppression of immoral books, standard works of literature have not been barred merely because they contained *some* obscene passages and that confiscation for such a reason would destroy much that is precious in order to benefit a few.

It is settled, at least so far as this court is concerned, that works of physiology, medicine, science, and sex instruction are not within the statute, though to some extent and among some persons they may tend to promote lustful thoughts. United States v. Bennett, 39 Fed. (2d) 564. We think the same immunity should apply to literature as to science where the presentation, when viewed objectively, is sincere and the erotic matter is not introduced to promote lust and does not furnish the dominant note of the publication. The question in each case is whether a publication taken as a whole has a libidinous effect. The book before us has such portentous length, is written with such evident truthfulness in its depiction of certain types of humanity, and is too little erotic in its result that it does not fall within the forbidden class.

In Halsey v. N.Y. Society, 234 N.Y. I, the New York Court of Appeals dealt with *Mademoiselle de Maupin*, by Theophile Gautier, for the sale of which the plaintiff had been prosecuted under a New York statute forbidding the sale of obscene books, upon the complaint of the defendant. After acquittal, the plaintiff sued for malicious prosecution, and a jury rendered a verdict in his favor. The Court of Appeals refused to disturb the judgment because the book had become a recognized French classic and its merits on the whole outweighed its objectionable qualities, though, as Judge Andrews said, it contained many paragraphs which "taken by themselves" were "undoubtedly vulgar and indecent." In referring to the obscene passages, he remarked that: "No work may be judged from a selection of such paragraphs alone. Printed by themselves they might, as a matter of law, come within the prohibition of the statute. So might a similar selection from Aristophanes or Chaucer or Boccaccio or even from the Bible. The book, however, must be considered broadly as a whole." We think Judge Andrews was clearly right and that the effect of the book as a whole is the test.

In the New York Supreme Court, Judge Morgan J. O'Brien declined to prohibit a receiver from selling *Arabian Nights*, Rabelais, Ovid's *Art of Love*, the *Decameron* of Boccaccio, the *Heptameron* of Queen Margaret of Navarre, or the *Confessions of Rousseau*. He remarked that a rule which would exclude them would bar "a very large proportion of the works of fiction of the most famous writers of the English language." In re Worthington Co., 30 N.Y. Supp. 361. The main difference between many standard works and *Ulysses* is its far more abundant use of coarse and colloquial words and presentation of dirty scenes, rather than in any excess of prurient suggestion. We do not think that *Ulysses* taken as a whole tends to promote lust and its criticised passages do this no more than scores of standard books that are constantly bought and sold. Indeed a book of physiology in the hands of adolescents may be more objectionable on this ground than almost anything else.

But it is argued that United States v. Bennett, Fed. Cas. No. 14,571, stands in the way of what has been said, and it certainly does. There a court, consisting of Blatchford, C.J., and Benedict and Choate, D. JJ., held that the offending paragraphs in a book could be taken from their context and the book judged by them alone, and that the test of obscenity was whether the tendency of these passages in themselves was "to deprave the minds of those open to such influences and into whose hands a publication of this character might come." The opinion was founded upon a dictum of Cockburn, C.J., in Regina v. Hicklin, L.R., 3 Q.B. 360, where half of a book written to attack the alleged practices of the confession was obscene and contained, as Mellor, J., said: "a great deal . . . which there cannot be any necessity for in any legitimate argument on the confessional . . . ." It is said that in Rosen v. United States, 161 U.S. 29, the Supreme Court cited and sanctioned *Regina* v. *Hicklin*, and *United States* v. *Bennett*. The subject matter of *Rosen* v. *United States* was, however, a pictorial representation of "females in different attitudes of indecency." The figures were partially covered "with lamp black that could be easily erased by a piece of broad." (p. 31) The pictures were evidently obscene and plainly came within the statute prohibiting their transportation. The citation of *Regina* v. *Hicklin* and *United States* v. *Bennett* was in support of a ruling that allegations in the indictment as to an obscene publication need only be made with sufficient particularity to inform the accused of the nature of the charge against him. No approval of other features involved in the two decisions was expressed, nor were such features referred to. Dunlop v. United States, 165 U.S. 489, also seems to be relied on by the government, but the publication there was admittedly obscene and the decision in no way sanctioned the rulings in *United States* v. *Bennett* which we first mentioned. The rigorous doctrines laid down in that case are inconsistent with our own decision in United States v. Bennett, 39 Fed. (2d) 564, as well as with Konda v. United States, 166 Fed. 91, 92; Clark v. United States, 211 Fed. 916, 922; Halsey v. N.Y. Society, 234 N.Y. 1, 4 and St. Hubert Guild v. Quinn, 64 Misc. 336, 339, and in our opinion, do not represent the law. They would exclude much of the great works of literature and involve an impracticability that cannot be imputed to Congress and would in the case of many books containing obscene passages inevitably require the court that uttered them to restrict their applicability.

It is true that the motive of an author to promote good morals is not the test of whether a book is obscene and it may also be true that the applicability of the statute does not depend on the persons to whom a publication is likely to be distributed. The importation of obscene books is prohibited generally and no provision is made permitting such importation because of the character of those to whom they are sold. While any construction of the statute that will fit all cases is difficult, we believe that the proper test of whether a given book is obscene is its dominant effect. In applying this test, relevancy of the objectionable parts to the theme, the established reputation of the work in the estimation of approved critics, if the book is modern, and the verdict of the past if it is ancient, are persuasive pieces of evidence, for works of art are not likely to sustain a high position with no better warrant for their existence than their obscene content.

It may be that *Ulysses* will not last as a substantial contribution to literature and it is certainly easy to believe that in spite of the opinion of Joyce's laudators, the immortals will still reign, but the same thing may be said of current works of art and music and of many other serious efforts of the mind. Art certainly cannot advance under compulsion to traditional forms and nothing in such a field is more stifling to progress than limitation of the right to experiment with a new technique. The foolish judgments of Lord Eldon about one hundred years ago, prescribing the words of Byron, Shelley and Southey, are a warning to all who have to determine the limits of the field within which authors may exercise themselves. We think that *Ulysses* is a book of originality and sincerity of treatment and that it has not the effect of promoting lust. Accordingly it does not fall within the statute, even though it justly may offend many.

Decree affirmed.

(Judge Manton dissents with opinion)

[Doc. 271]

## UNITED STATES CIRCUIT COURT OF APPEALS
## FOR THE SECOND CIRCUIT

UNITED STATES OF AMERICA,

> Appellant,

—against—

ONE BOOK ENTITLED *ULYSSES*
BY JAMES JOYCE, RANDOM HOUSE, INC.,

> Appellee.

MANTON, Circuit Judge (dissenting):

I dissent. This libel, filed against the book *Ulysses*, prays for a decree of forfeiture and it is based upon the claim that the book's entry into the United States is prohibited by Sec. 305 of the Tariff Act of 1930, 19 U.S.C.A. 1305 (a). On motion of appellee, the court below entered an order dismissing the libel and the Collector of Customs was ordered to release the book. The motion was considered on the pleadings and a stipulation entered into by the parties.

The sole question presented is whether or not the book is obscene within Sec. 305 (a) which provides:

> All persons are prohibited from importing into the United States from any foreign country . . . any obscene book, pamphlet, paper, writing, advertisement, circular print, picture, drawing, or other representation, figure or image on or of paper or other material. . . .
>
> Upon the appearance of any such book or matter at any customs office, the same shall be seized and held by the collector to await the judgment of the district court as hereinafter provided. . . . Upon the seizure of such book or matter the collector shall transmit information thereof to the district attorney of the district in which is situated the office at which such seizure has taken place, who shall institute proceedings in the district court for the forfeiture, confiscation, and destruction of the book or matter seized. . . .
>
> In any such proceeding any party in interest may upon demand have the facts at issue determined by a jury and any party may have an appeal or the right of review as in the case of ordinary actions or suits.

The parties agreed as to the facts in the stipulation. There is no conflicting evidence; the decision to be made is dependent entirely upon the reading matter found on the objectionable pages of the book (pages 173, 213, 214, 359, 361, 423-424, 434, 467, 488, 498, 500, 509, 522, 526, 528, 551, 719, 724-727, 731, 738-739, 745-746, 754-756, 761-762, 765, Random House Edition). The book itself was the only evidence offered.

In a suit of this kind upon stipulation, the ultimate finding based solely on stipulated facts is reviewable on appeal to determine whether the facts support the find. Lumbermen's Trust co. v. Town of Ryegate, 61 Fed. 2d, 14 (C.C.A. 9); Order of United Commercial Travelers of America v. Shane, 64 Fed. 2d, 55 (C.C.A. 8). Moreover, the procedure in this suit *in rem* conforms to that obtaining in suits in admiralty (Coffey v. United States, 117 U.S. 233) where the appellate courts may review the facts. The Africa Maru, 54 Fed. 2d, 265 (C.C.A. 2); The Perry Setzer, 299 Fed. 586 (C.C.A. 2).

Who can doubt the obscenity of this book after a reading of the pages referred to, which are too indecent to add as a footnote to this opinion? Its characterization as obscene should be quite unanimous by all who read it.

In the year 1868 in Regina v. Hicklin, L.R., 3 Q.B. 359, at 369, Cockburn C.J. stated that:

> the test of obscenity is this, whether the tendency of the matter charged as obscenity is to deprave and corrupt those whose minds are open to such immoral influences, and into whose hands a publication of this sort may fall.

In 1879 in United States v. Bennett (Fed. Cases No. 14,571) Judge Blatchford, later a justice of the Supreme Court, in this Circuit, sitting with Judges Choate and Benedict, approved the rule of the *Hicklin* case and held a charge to a jury proper which embodied the test of that case. The *Bennett* case clearly holds the test of obscenity, within the meaning of the statute, is "whether the tendency of the matter is to deprave and corrupt the morals of those whose minds are open to such influence and into whose hands a publication of this sort may fall." The court held that the object of the use of the obscene words was not a subject for consideration.

Judge Blatchford's decision met with approval in United States v. Rosen, 151 U.S. 29. The court had under consideration an indictment charging the accused with depositing obscene literature in the mails. There, instructions to the jury requested that conviction could not be had, although the defendant may have had knowledge or notice of the contents of the letter, "unless he knew or believed that such paper could be properly or justly characterized as obscene, lewd and lascivious." The court said the statute was not to be so interpreted.

> The inquiry under the statute is whether the paper charged to have been obscene, lewd and lascivious was in fact of that character, and if it was of that character and was deposited in the mail by one who knew or had notice at the time of its contents, the offense is complete, although the defendent himself did not regard the paper as one that the statute forbade to be carried in the mails. Congress did not intend that the question as to the character of the paper should depend upon the opinion or belief of the person who, with knowledge or notice of its contents, assumed the responsibility of putting it in the mails of the United States.

The evils that Congress sought to remedy could continue and increase in volume if the belief of the accused as to what was obscene, lewd and lascivious were recognized as the test of determining whether the statute has been violated. Everyone who uses the mails of the United States for carrying papers or publications must take notice of what, in this enlightened age, is meant by decency, purity and chastity in social life and what must be deemed obscene, lewd and lascivious.

Further the Supreme Court approved the test of the *Hicklin* case. On page 43 the court states:

That was what the court did when it charged the jury that "the test of obscenity is whether the tendency of the matter is to deprave and corrupt the morals of those whose minds are open to such influence and into whose hands a publication of this sort may fall." "Would it", the court said, "suggest or convey lewd thoughts and lascivious thoughts to the young and inexperienced?" In view of the character of the paper, as an inspection of it will instantly disclose, the test prescribed for the jury was quite as liberal as the defendant had any right to demand.

Again the Supreme Court, in Dunlop v. United States (165 U.S. 486), reviewed a charge in a criminal case upon the subject of obscene publications as follows:

Now, what is (are) obscene, lascivious, lewd or indecent publications is largely a question of your own conscience and your own opinion; but it must come—before it can be said of such literature or publication—it must come up to this point: that it must be calculated with the ordinary reader to deprave him, deprave his morals, or lead to impure purposes. . . . It is your duty to ascertain in the first place if they are calculated to deprave the morals; if they are calculated to lower that standard which we regard as essential to civilization; if they are calculated to excite those feelings which, in their larger field, are all right, but which transcending the limits of that proper field, play most of the mischief in the world.

In approving the charge, the court said:

The alleged obscene and indecent matter consisted of advertisements by women, soliciting or offering inducements for the visits of men, usually "refined gentlemen", to their rooms, sometimes under the disguise of "Baths" and "Massage", and oftener for the mere purpose of acquaintance. It was in this connection that the court charged the jury that, if the publications were such as were calculated to deprave the morals, they were within the statute. There could have been no possible misapprehension on their part as to what was meant. There was no question as to depraving the morals in any other direction than that of impure, sexual relations. The words were used by the court in their ordinary signification and were made more definite by the context; and by the character of the publications which have been put in evidence. The court left to the jury to say whether it was within the statute, and whether persons of ordinary intelligence would have any difficulty in divining the intention of the advertiser.

Thus the court sustained a charge having a test as to whether or not the publications depraved the morals of the ordinary reader or tended to lower the standards of civilization. The tendency of the matter to deprave and corrupt the morals of those whose minds are open to such influence and into whose hands the publication of this sort may fall, has become the test thoroughly entrenched in the Federal Courts. United States v. Bebout, 28 Fed. 522 (D.C.); United States v. Wightman, 29 Fed. 636; United States v. Clarke, 38 Fed. 732; United States v. Smith, 45 Fed. 476; Burton v. United States, 142 Fed. 57 (C.C.A. 8); United States v. Dennett, 38 Fed. 2d, 564 (C.C.A. 2). What is the probable effect on the sense of decency of society, extending to the family made up of men, women, young boys and girls, was said to be the test in United States v. Harmon, 45 Fed. 414.

*Ulysses* is a work of fiction. It may not be compared with books involving medical subjects or description of certain physical or biological facts. It is written for alleged amusement of the reader only. The characters described in the thoughts of the author may in some instances be true, but, be it truthful or otherwise, a book that is obscene is not rendered less so by the statement of truthful fact. *Burton* v. *United States, supra*. It cannot be said that the test above has been rejected by United States v. Dennett, 39 Fed. 3, 564, nor can that case be taken to mean that the book is to be judged as a whole. If anything, the case clearly recognizes that the book may be obscene because portions thereof are so, for pains are taken to justify and show not to be obscene, portions to which objection is made. The gist of the holding is that a book is not to be declared obscene if it is "an accurate exposition of the relevant facts of the sex side of life in decent language and in manifestly serious and disinterested spirit." A work of obvious benefit to the community was never intended to be within the purview of the statute. No matter what may be said on the side of letters, the effect on the community can and must be the sole determining factor. "Laws of this character are made for society in the aggregate, and not in particular. So while there may be individuals and societies of men and women of peculiar notions or idiosyncrasies whose moral sense would neither be depraved nor offended . . . yet the exceptional sensibility or want of sensibility of such cannot be allowed as a standard." *United States* v. *Harmon, supra*.

In United States v. Kennerly, 209 Fed. 119, the *Bennett* case was followed despite the dictum objecting to a test which protected the "salacious" few. By the very argument used, to destroy a test which protects those most easily influenced, we can discard a test which would protect only the interests of the other comparatively small groups of society. If we disregard the protection of the morals of the susceptible, are we to consider merely the benefits and pleasures derived from letters by those who pose as the more highly developed and intelligent? To do so would show an utter disregard for the standards of decency of the community as a whole and an utter disregard for the effect of a book upon the average, less sophisticated member of society— not to mention the adolescent. The court cannot indulge any instinct it may have to foster letters. The statute is designed to protect society at large—of that there can be no dispute—notwithstanding the deprivation of benefits to a few, a work must be condemned if it has a depraving influence.

And are we to refuse to enforce the statute Congress has enacted because of the argument that "obscenity is only the superstition of the day—the modern counterpart of ancient witchcraft." Are we to be persuaded by the statement, set forth in the brief, made by the judge below in an interview with the press, that "Education, not law, must solve the problems of taste and choice (of books)" when the statute is clear and our duty plain?"

The prevailing opinion states that classics would be excluded if the application of the statute here argued for prevailed. But the statute provides as to classics that they may be introduced into the commerce of the United States provided "that the Secretary of the Treasury . . . in his discretion, admit the so-called classics or books of recognized and established literary or scientific merit, but may, in his discretion, admit such classics or books only when imported for non-commercial purposes." The right to admission under this proviso was not sought nor is it justified by reason thereof in the prevailing opinion.

Congress passed this statute against obscenity for the protection of the great mass of our people—the unusual literator can, or thinks he can, protect himself. The people do not exist for the sake of literature; to give the author fame, the publisher wealth, and the book a market. On the contrary, literature exists for the sake of the people; to refresh the weary, to console the sad, to hearten the dull and downcast, to increase man's interest in the world, his joy of living and his sympathy in all sorts and conditions of men. Art for art's sake is heartless and soon grows artless; art for the public market is not art at all, but commerce; art for the people's service is a noble, vital and permanent element of human life.

The public is content with the standard of salability; the prigs with the standard of precosity. The people need and deserve a moral standard; it should be a point of honor with men of letters to maintain it. Masterpieces have never been produced by man given to obscenity or lustful thoughts— men who have no Master. Reverence for good work is the foundation of literary character. A refusal to imitate obscenity or to load a book with it, is an author's professional chastity.

Good work in literature has its permanent mark—it is like all good work, noble and lasting. It requires a human aim—to cheer, console, purify or ennoble the life of people. Without this aim, literature has never sent an

462

arrow close to the mark. It is by good work only that men of letters can justify their right to a place in the world.

Under the authoritative decisions and considering the substance involved in this appeal, it is my opinion that the decree should be reversed.

---

[Doc. 272]

*New York Evening Post*
August 7th, 1934
**_Ulysses_ Pure; Customs "Goofy"**

---

### The Nice Little Tome Isn't Even Obscene, U.S. Circuit Court Rules

---

*Ulysses* wins. It's neither lewd, immoral nor obscene. Customs men who held otherwise were goofy or something.

So ruled the United States Circuit Court of Appeals today, with one of the three judges dissenting.

The ruling was pleasing to both James Joyce, the author of *Ulysses*, and to Random House, Inc., to which concern a copy of the book imported from Europe must be turned over by the customs without further let or hindrance.

#### Judge Is Pleased
It was pleasing to Federal District Judge John M. Woolsey, too, for the verdict was on appeal from a Woolsey finding of December 6, 1933, that though *Ulysses* perhaps was "somewhat emetic" to some readers, it nowhere tended to be an aphrodisiac.

The book, story of the thoughts and doings of Dublin folk on a certain June day of 1904, had been bootlegged throughout the United States for years prior to the court test.

Judge Woolsey spoke of modern frankness in discussions of sex and such. He spoke of *Ulysses* as an "amazing tour de force"; spoke of "the screen of consciousness with its ever-shifting kaleidoscopic impressions," of "plastic palimpsest," of "penumbral zone residua of past impressions" and a lot of other things.

He summed up by calling *Ulysses* a "sincere and honest book."

Said the Circuit Court of Appeals today, in an opinion written by Judge Augustus N. Hand and concurred in by Judge Learned Hand, with Presiding Judge Martin T. Manton disagreeing:

"Art certainly cannot advance under compulsion to the traditional forms, and nothing in such a field is more stifling to progress than limitation of the right to experiment with a new technique."

Judge Manton, dissenting, retorted that characterization of *Ulysses* as obscene "should be quite unanimous."

---

[Doc. 273]

*New York World-Telegram*
August 7th, 1934

### *Ulysses* Wins In U.S. Appeal On 2 To 1 Vote

---

### Circuit Court Rules Joyce Book Is Not Immoral—Can't Restrict Art

---

### Woolsey Ruling Upheld

---

### Judges Declare Conboy Failed to Prove Work Had Effect of 'Promoting' Lust

---

James Joyce's *Ulysses* was given a relatively clean bill of health today by the United States Circuit Court of Appeals, which voted two to one to sustain the decision of Federal Judge John M. Woolsey that the book was not lewd, immoral or obscene.

The prevailing opinion was written by Judge Augustus N. Hand and concurred in by Judge Learned Hand. Presiding Judge Martin T. Manton filed a dissenting opinion.

In Judge Woolsey's ruling of last December, in which Random House was given permission to import the book and to publish it here, he said that "it is monstrous to suppose that a man of Joyce's stature would or could produce a work of obscenity."

#### Don't Go That Far

The Judges today were hardly ready to go that far, but they held that District Attorney Martin Conboy, who pressed the appeal, had not proved the book had the effect of "promoting lust."

The prevailing opinion read, in part:

"It may be that *Ulysses* will not last as a substantial contribution to literature, and it is certainly easy to believe that in spite of the opinion of Joyce's laudators the immortals will still reign; but the same may be said of the current works of art and music and many other serious efforts of the mind."

### Right to Experiment

"Art certainly cannot advance under compulsion to the traditional forms, and nothing in such a field is more stifling to progress than limitation of the right to experiment with a new technique. The foolish judgments of Lord Eldon about 100 years ago proscribing the works of Byron, Shelley and Southey are a warning to all who have to determine the limits of the field within which authors may exercise themselves.

"We think that *Ulysses* is a book of originality and sincerity of treatment and that it has not the effect of promoting lust. Accordingly it does not fall within the statute even though it justly may offend many."

Judge Manton in his opinion cited many authorities and set forth the numbers of many pages of the book.

"Who can doubt," he proceeded, "the obscenity of this book after a reading of the pages referred to, which are too indecent to add as a footnote to this opinion. Its characterization as obscene should be quite unanimous.

"*Ulysses* is a work of fiction. It may not be compared with books involving medical subjects or description of certain physical or biological facts. It was written for alleged amusement of the reader. The characters described in the thoughts of the author may in some instances be true, but, be it truthful or otherwise, a book that is obscene is not rendered less so by the statement of a truthful fact.

"If we disregard the protection of the morals of the susceptible, are we to consider merely the benefits and pleasures derived from letters by those who pose as the more highly developed and intelligent? To do so would show an utter disregard for the standards of decency of the community as a whole and an utter disregard for the effect of the book upon the average less sophisticated member of society, not to mention the adolescent."

Morris L. Ernst and Alexander Lindey represented the defendants.

---

[Doc. 274]

*New York American*
August 8, 1934
### *Ulysses* Wins 2d Court Fight

---

James Joyce's controversial book, *Ulysses,* was accepted as proper for American readers by a two to one vote of the U.S. Circuit Court of Appeals yesterday.

In upholding Federal Judge Woolsey in his ruling that the book was not lewd, immoral or obscene, the higher court ordered that a seized volume be admitted to the port and turned over to Random House, Inc.

That, at least, was the majority ruling, but it had bitter dissent from Presiding Judge Manton.

[Doc. 275]

New York Herald-Tribune<br>
August 8, 1934<br>
Higher Court Holds Ulysses Is Not Obscene

---

Joyce Novel Wins Approval of Judges A.N. Hand and Learned Hand on Appeal

---

Woolsey Verdict Upheld

---

Manton Dissents From U.S. Circuit Court's Finding

---

Judges Augustus Noble Hand and Learned Hand, of the United States Circuit Court of Appeals, decided yesterday that James Joyce's *Ulysses*, taken on the whole of its 768 pages, was not obscene, thereby sustaining the ruling of Judge John M. Woolsey in District Court that importation of the book into the United States was permissible. Presiding Judge Martin T. Manton filed a dissenting opinion.

The majority opinion, written by Judge Augustus Noble Hand and concurred in by his cousin, held *Ulysses* to be a work of originality and sincerity of treatment, and without "the effect of promoting lust," thus making it admissible to the United States "even though it justly may offend many." Random House, Inc., publishers, first brought the case to a test by importing a copy of the work, which was promptly seized by customs authorities and impounded under section 305(a) of the Tariff Act.

### Conboy May Appeal Again

Martin Conboy, United States Attorney, who argued the government's case before the Circuit Court of Appeals in May, mainly by reading aloud the more robust passages in the book and branding each one in turn as obscene, had not decided yesterday whether to make a recommendation to the Solicitor General that a petition of certiorari be filed with the United States Supreme Court in a final effort to obtain a reversal. When pressed for a statement, Mr. Conboy merely said he had read the opinions and "might" carry the case further.

"James Joyce," the prevailing opinion said, "may be regarded as a pioneer among those writers who have adopted the so-called stream of consciousness method of presentation which has attracted considerable attention in academic and literary circles. In this field *Ulysses* is rated as a book of considerable power by persons whose opinions are entitled to weight. It has become a sort of contemporary classic dealing with new subject matter.

"It attempts to depict the thoughts and lay bare the souls of a number of people, some of them intellectuals, some social outcasts and nothing more, with a literalism that leaves nothing unsaid.

"Certain passages are of beauty and of undoubted distinction, while others are of a vulgarity that is extreme, and the book as a whole has a realism characteristic of the present age."

### "Sincere, Truthful and Real Art"

It was the feeling of Judges Hand that Joyce's depiction of character is "sincere and truthful and executed with real art." They felt that the author dealt with "things that very likely might better have remained unattempted," but that his book was "a work of symmetry and excellent craftmanship of a sort."

. . .

*Ulysses* contains many long passages that are obscene, but they are relevant to the author's purpose of depicting the thoughts of his characters and are introduced to give meaning to the whole, "rather than promote lust or portray filth for its own sake." The net effect of certain sections most open to attack, Judge Hand said, citing the famous soliloquey of the character Mrs. Bloom as an example, "is pitiful and tragic, rather than lustful."

"The book depicts the souls of men and women by turns bewildered and keenly apprehensive, sordid and aspiring, ugly and beautiful, hateful and loving," the opinion said. "In the end, one feels pity and sorrow for the confusion, misery and degradation of humanity."

It was conceded that page after page of the book was incomprehensible, but "many passsages show the trained hand of an artist who can at one moment adapt to perfection the style of an ancient chronicler and at another become the veritable personification of Thomas Carlyle."

The book was not pornographic as a whole, the court held, "although in not a few spots is it coarse, blasphemous and obscene." However, the erotic passages were submerged in the complete book, the court ruled.

### How About *Hamlet* Then?

"If those are to make the book subject to confiscation," Judge Hand remarked , "by the same test *Venus and Adonis, Hamlet, Romeo and Juliet,* and the story in the eighth book of *The Odyssey,* of the entrapment of Ares and Aphrodite in a net spread by the outraged Hephaestus, amid the laughter of the immortal gods, as well as many other classics, would have to be suppressed."

Doubting the ultimate durability of *Ulysses,* the opinion further set forth that "it may be the book will not last as a substantial contribution to literature and it is certainly easy to believe that in spite of the opinion of Joyce's laudators, the immortals will still reign; but the same may be said of the current works of art and music and of many other serious efforts of the mind."

"Art certainly cannot advance under compulsion to the traditional forms," it said, "and nothing in such a field is more stifling to progress than limitation of the right to experiment with a new technique. The foolish judgments of Lord Eldon about 100 years ago proscribing the works of Byron, Shelley and Southey are a warning to all who have to determine the limits of the field within which authors may exercise themselves."

## Manton Insists It's Obscene

In his dissenting opinion Judge Manton said he could find no conflicting evidence and cited several authorities in support of his contention that *Ulysses* was obscene. He included in his opinion the numbers of pages on which the allegedly lewd passages might be found as pointed out by Mr. Conboy in his argument.

"Who can doubt the obscenity of this book after reading the pages referred to, which are too indecent to add as a footnote to this opinion?" the jurist wrote. "Its characterization as obscene should be quite unanimous."

Because *Ulysses* is a work of fiction, Judge Manton said, it may not be compared with books involving medical subjects or describing certain physical or biological facts. He maintained it was written for the alleged amusement of the reader only.

"The characters described in the thoughts of the author may in some instances be true," he said, "but, be it truthful or otherwise, a book that is obscene is not rendered less so by a statement of truthful fact.

"If we disregard the protection of the morals of the susceptible are we to consider merely the benefits and pleasures derived from letters by those who pose as more highly developed and intelligent? The court cannot indulge any instinct it may have to foster letters."

## Defines Purpose of Literature

"The people do not exist for the sake of prevailing literature, or to give the author fame, the publisher wealth, and the book a market. On the contrary, literature exists for the sake of the people; to refresh the weary, console the sad, hearten the dull and downcast, to increase man's interest in the world, his joy of living and his sympathy in all sorts and conditions of men.

"Art for art's sake is heartless and soon grows artless; art for the public market is not art at all, but commerce; art for the people's service is noble, vital and a permanent element of human life. The people need and deserve a moral standard and it should be a point of honor among men of letters to maintain it.

"A refusal to imitate obscenity or to load a book with it is an author's professional chastity."

Morris L. Ernst and Alexander Lindey argued the case for Random House, Inc., and Mr. Conboy was aided by Francis H. Horan and John F. Davidson, Assistant United States Attorneys. To be valid, a recommendation to the Solicitor General must be made within ninety days from the entry of the Appellate Court's order.

[Doc. 276]

*New York Times*
August 8, 1934
*Ulysses* Is Upheld By Appeals Court

---

**Book Declared Neither Lewd Nor Obscene in Decision Backing Judge Woolsey**

---

**Defends Freedom Of Art**

---

**The Majority Opinion Warns of Acts That Stifle Progress— Judge Manton Dissents**

---

By a vote of two to one the United States Court of Appeals yesterday upheld Federal Judge John M. Woolsey in his opinion that *Ulysses*, by James Joyce, was not lewd, immoral or, as charged by Martin Conboy, United States Attorney, obscene.

The court held, as a result, that a volume seized by customs authorities when an attempt was made to import it by Random House, Inc., should be admitted to this port and turned over to the corporation.

Judges of the higher court who wrote the opinion were Judges Learned Hand and Augustus N. Hand. Judge Martin T. Manton dissented.

"It may be that *Ulysses* will not last as a substantial contribution to literature." Judge Learned Hand wrote, "and it is certainly easy to believe that in spite of Joyce's laudators immortals will still reign. But the same may be said of the current works of art and music and many other serious efforts of the mind.

"Art certainly cannot advance under compulsion to the traditional forms, and nothing in such a field is more stifling to progress than limitation of the right to experiment with a new technique.

"The foolish judgments of Lord Eldon about 100 years ago proscribing the works of Byron, Shelley and Southey are a warning to all who have to determine the limits of a field within which authors may limit themselves.

"We think that *Ulysses* is a book of originality and sincerity of treatment and that it has not the effect of promoting lust. Accordingly, it does not fall within the statute, even though it may justly offend many."

Judge Manton in a dissenting opinion wrote:

"Who can doubt the obscenity of this book after a reading of the pages referred to, which are too indecent to add as a footnote to this account. Its characterization as obscene should be quite unanimous.

"If we disregard the protection of the morals of the susceptible, are we merely to consider the benefits and pleasure derived from letters by those who pose as the more highly developed and intelligent?

"To do so would show an utter disregard for the standards of decency of the community as a whole and an utter disregard for the effect of the book upon the average less sophisticated member of society, not to mention the adolescent."

---

[Doc. 277]

At a Stated Term of the United States Circuit Court of Appeals, in and for the Second Circuit, held at the Court Rooms in the Post Office Building in the City of New York, on the 14th day of August one thousand nine hundred and thirty-four.

UNITED STATES CIRCUIT COURT
OF APPEALS SECOND CIRCUIT

Present:
Hon. Martin T. Manton,
Hon. Learned Hand,
Hon. August N. Hand,
    Circuit Judges.

UNITED STATES,

                    Libellant-Appellant,

            vs.

ONE BOOK ENTITLED *ULYSSES*,
BY JAMES JOYCE,
RANDOM HOUSE, INC.,

                    Claimant-Appellee.

Appeal from the District Court of the United States for the Southern District of New York.

This cause came on to be heard on the transcript of record from the District Court of the United States for the Southern District of New York, and was argued by counsel,

ON CONSIDERATION WHEREOF, it is now hereby ordered, adjudged, and decreed that the decree of said District Court be and it hereby is affirmed.

It is further ordered that a Mandate issue to the said District Court in accordance with this decree.

Wm. Parkin<br>Clerk

---

[Doc. 278]

UNITED STATES CIRCUIT COURT
OF APPEALS FOR THE SECOND CIRCUIT

UNITED STATES OF AMERICA,

Libellant-Appellant,

—against—

ONE BOOK ENTITLED *ULYSSES*
BY JAMES JOYCE,
RANDOM HOUSE, INC.,

Claimant-Appellee.

STATE OF NEW YORK
COUNTY OF NEW YORK      SS.:
SOUTHERN DISTRICT OF NEW YORK

EARLE N. BISHOPP, being duly sworn, deposes and says that he is an Assistant United States Attorney for the Southern District of New York, and that he is familiar with the facts in the above entitled case.

That this appeal was argued before this Court and an opinion was handed down on August 7, 1934, affirming the District Court; that thereafter the Attorney General at Washington was advised of the affirmance and a copy of the opinion rendered by the Court was forwarded.

That in view of the affirmance the Attorney General of the United States must be afforded an opportunity to determine whether a petition for a writ of certiorari to the Supreme Court of the United States should be filed.

That the attorneys for the claimant-appellee have declined to consent to a stipulation staying the issuance of the mandate of this Court; that the attorneys for the claimant-appellee have this day been advised of this application.

WHEREFORE, it is respectfully prayed that an order be entered staying the issuance of the mandate of this Court for a period of sixty days from the date of this order, pending the application for a writ of certiorari to the Supreme Court of the United States; that no previous application for the relief herein prayed for has heretofore been made.

Sworn to before me this
22nd day of August, 1934.

EARLE N. BISHOPP

---

[Doc. 279]

> At a Stated Term of the United States Circuit Court of Appeals for the Second Circuit, held in the U.S. Courthouse & Old Post Office Building, in the City of New York, Borough of Manhattan, this 23rd day of August, 1934.

PRESENT:

HONORABLE MARTIN T. MANTON
U.S.C.J.

UNITED STATES OF AMERICA,

Libellant-Appellant,

—against—

ONE BOOK ENTITLED *ULYSSES*,
BY JAMES JOYCE,
RANDOM HOUSE, INC.,

Claimant-Appellee.

Upon reading and filing the annexed affidavit of Earle N. Bishopp, Assistant United States Attorney, duly verified this 22nd day of August, 1934, and upon all the proceedings and pleadings heretofore had herein, it is, on motion of Martin Conboy, United States Attorney for the Southern District of New York, attorney for Libellent-Appellent herein,

ORDERED that the issuance of the mandate in the above entitled case be and the same hereby is stayed for a period of sixty days from the date of this order, and it is

FURTHER ORDERED that if a petition for a writ of certiorari be filed in the Supreme Court of the United States within said period, that the issuance of the mandate of this Court herein be stayed until the disposition of said petition.

MARTIN T. MANTON
U. S. C. J.

[Doc. 280]

*New York Herald-Tribune*
October 13, 1934

## Columbia Gets *Ulysses* Copy Freed by Trial

### Impounded Volume, Subject of Rulings in 2 Federal Tribunals, Gift to Library

### Ceremony Is Proposed

### Publishers Assure Preservation on Harkness Shelves

The copy of James Joyce's *Ulysses* impounded by customs agents when Random House, Inc., publishers, tried to import it to this country to force a test case as to its obscenity, and which for the last two years has languished in the hands of the government while the fight it started was being waged through two courts, will be returned to the publishers and eventually find a home at Columbia University, it was learned yesterday.

Bennett Cerf, president of Random House and The Modern Library, explained that as soon as it became apparent that the case would not have to be carried to the United States Supreme Court, his firm had requested that the original volume be returned. Yesterday, he said, word was received from James J. Hoey, Collector of Internal Revenue for the 2d District, New York, that the book was being forwarded to the Custom House and would be available whenever the firm cared to call for it.

Mr. Cerf, feeling that the volume had become somewhat of a national institution, decided that it should be given to Columbia as soon as the new Harkness Library is opened on the campus. At that time, he said, it will be presented to some university official after dedicatory remarks.

Doubt that the university would accept the book, either because of its contents or its reputation, was set aside by Roger Howson, librarian of the university.

"Certainly we will accept it," Mr. Howson said. "It has not yet been formally offered to us, but I have heard about it and I see no reason why we should refuse. However, I think it is a little early to talk of any dedication or ceremony."

The book was impounded early in 1933, and in August action was started in Federal Court by George Z. Medalie, then United States Attorney. Judge John M. Woolsey read the book for nearly four months, and on December 6 handed down a decision admitting the work for publication in the United States.

Mr. Medalie expressed himself as content with the decision, but Martin Conboy succeeded him as United States Attorney before the expiration of the three-month period during which an appeal may be filed, and carried the case to the United States Circuit Court of Appeals, where *Ulysses* won again. No further appeal has been taken.

---

**[Doc. 281]**

October 24, 1934.

Mr. P. Sheehy,
Customs Bureau,
New York Post Office,
31st St. & 8th Ave.,
New York, N.Y.

Sir:

Reference is made to a mail package containing a copy of the book *Ulysses* by James Joyce, consigned to Random House, Inc., 20 East 57th St., New York, N.Y. which was detained on or about May 5, 1932.

In view of advice received from the United States Attorney that there will be no appeal taken from the decision of the Circuit Court, which has confirmed Judge Woolsey's decision that the book is not obscene under the provisions of Section 305 (a) of the Tariff Act of 1930, the book in question should be released to the consignee.

Respectfully,
Assistant Collector

cc to:
Greenbaum, Wolff & Ernst
285 Madison Ave., N.Y.C.
att. Alexander Lindey

474

**[Doc. 282]**

October 25, 1934.

Mr. Bennett Cerf,
c/o Random House,
20 East 57th Street,
New York City.

Dear Bennett: Re: *Ulysses*

I have been trying to reach you for at least a week.

For some time now we have been fussing around with the office of the U.S. Attorney and with the Collector of Customs to secure the release of the libeled copy of *Ulysses*. As is usual, the buck has been passed around royally. The U.S. Attorney's office has been claiming right along that he has returned the copy to the Collector; the Collector has contended that he has not received the copy. By dint of considerable sleuthing we finally discovered that the book was sent to the "Collector", but believe it or not it was sent to the wrong Collector. It should have gone to the Collector of Customs. It went to the Collector of Internal Revenue. You can laugh, but this is how a bureaucracy operates.

I have before me a letter dated October 24, 1934, from the Assistant Collector of Customs to the effect that the book will be delivered to you by direct mail.

Will you please advise me as soon as you receive it. If nothing happens within the next few days let me know so that I can get on the Collector's trail again.

Cordially yours,

AL:BBO

[Doc. 283]

Random House
20 E. 57
New York

November 1, 1934.

Mr. Alexander Lindey,
c/o Greenbaum, Wolff & Ernst,
285 Madison Avenue
New York City.

Dear Lindey:

The famous of copy of *Ulysses* has just been received. It is torn practically to tatters, but we will try to patch it up sufficiently to make it worth a presentation to the Columbia Library. I will keep you posted on that business.

Cordially,
Bennett A. Cerf

---

[Doc. 284]

November 2, 1934.

Bennett A. Cerf, Esq.,
c/o Random House,
20 East 57th Street,
New York City.

Dear Bennett:                          Re: *Ulysses*

Eureka! But don't think that the famous copy just found its way to you under its own momentum. I have been after the United States Attorney's office, the Collector of Internal Revenue, the Collector of Customs and the solicitors to the Collector of Customs for weeks.

You ought to be able to get swell publicity on the presentation to the Columbia Library. What with your success in playing up Saroyan, I don't suppose you need any hints on this.

Anyhow, the famous case of *United States* v. *Ulysses* is finally, definitely and conclusively closed. And I may say, happily.

Sincerely,

AL:JF

[Doc. 285]

> At a Stated Term of the United States Circuit Court of Appeals for the Second Circuit, held in the United States Court House, Old Post Office Building, in the Borough of Manhattan, City of New York, on the 26th day of November, 1934.

PRESENT:
  HON. MARTIN T. MANTON
    U.S.C.J.

UNITED STATES OF AMERICA,

  Libellant-Appellant,

—against—

ONE BOOK ENTITLED *ULYSSES*,
BY JAMES JOYCE,
RANDOM HOUSE, INC.,

  Claimant-Appellee.

The above named appellant having procured an order of this court on the 23rd day of August, 1934, staying the issuance of the mandate herein for a period of sixty days from the date of the order and further ordering that if a petition for writ of certiorari be filed by the appellant in the Supreme Court of the United States within said period, the issuance of the mandate of this court herein be stayed until the disposition of said petition, and the period of the stay being expired and no petition for such writ for certiorari having been filed, it is on motion of Greenbaum, Wolff & Ernst, attorneys for the appellee

ORDERED that a mandate issue to the District Court of the United States for the Southern District of New York in accordance with the decree of this court dated August 14, 1934.

MARTIN T. MANTON
U. S. C. J.

I hereby consent to the entry of the foregoing order.

MARTIN CONBOY
U.S. Attorney, Attorney for United States.

[Doc. 286]

UNITED STATES OF AMERICA, SS.:

The President of the United States of America:

> To the Honorable Judges of the District Court of the United States for the Southern District of New York.

GREETING:

WHEREAS, lately in the United States District Court of the United States for the Southern District of New York, before you or some of you, in a cause between United States of America, and One Book called *Ulysses*, Random House, etc., a decree was entered in the office of the Clerk of said Court in the words and figures following, to wit:

Issue having been joined by the service and filing of the claimant's answer herein on December 19, 1932; and a stipulation having been entered into between the parties on May 15, 1933, which provided, among other things, that trial by jury be waived, and that the parties cross-move for decrees in their favor; and the libellant having moved this Court by notice of motion dated May 15, 1933, for a decree of forfeiture and destruction; and the claimant having cross-moved this Court by notice of motion dated May 17, 1933, for a decree dismissing the libel herein; and the aforesaid motions having duly come on to be heard before Hon. John M. Woolsey, one of the Judges of this Court, on November 25, 1933,

NOW, on reading and filing the libel dated December 9, 1932, the claim verified December 16, 1932, the answer verified December 19, 1932, the above-mentioned stipulation dated May 15, 1933, the libellant's notice of motion dated May 15, 1933, and the claimant's notice of motion dated May 17, 1933; and Samuel C. Coleman, Esq., and Nicholas Atlas, Esq., Assistant United States Attorneys, appearing for the libellant in support of the motion for a decree of forfeiture and destruction in support of the motion for a decree of forfeiture and destruction and in opposition to the motion to dismiss the libel; and Morris L. Ernst and Alexander Lindey, Esqs., of Greenbaum, Wolff & Ernst, attorneys for the claimant herein, appearing for the claimant in support of the motion to dismiss the libel and in opposition to the motion for a decree of forfeiture and destruction; and the Court having handed down its opinion dated December 6, 1933,

NOW, on motion of Greenbaum, Wolff & Ernst, attorneys for the claimant, it is

ORDERED AND ADJUDGED that the book entitled *Ulysses* is not of the character the entry of which is prohibited under the provisions of Section 305 of the Tariff Act of 1930, and Title 19, United States Code, Section 1305, and should not be excluded from entry to the United States of America under the provisions thereof; and it is further

ORDERED AND ADJUDGED that the motion for a decree dismissing the libel herein is granted without costs, and the libel is dismissed; and it is further

ORDERED AND ADJUDGED that the motion for a decree of forfeiture and destruction is denied; and it is further

ORDERED AND ADJUDGED that the book entitled *Ulysses*, heretofore seized by the Collector of Customs of the United States at the Port and Collection District of New York, be released to the claimant herein.

Dated, New York, N.Y., December 15, 1933.

WOOLSEY,
United States District Judge.

as by the inspection of the transcript of the record of the said Court, which was brought into the United States Circuit Court of Appeals for the Second Circuit, by virtue of an appeal, agreeably to the act of Congress, in such case made and provided, fully and at large appears

AND WHEREAS, in the present term of October, in the year of our Lord one thousand nine hundred and thirty-three, the said cause came on to be heard before the said United States Circuit Court of Appeals for the Second Circuit, on the said transcript of record, and was argued by counsel: On Consideration Whereof, IT IS HEREBY

ORDERED, ADJUDGED AND DECREED that the decree of said District Court be and it hereby is affirmed.

YOU, THEREFORE, are hereby commanded that such further proceeding be had in said cause, in accordance with the decision of this Court as according to right and justice and the laws of the United States, ought to be had, the said appeal notwithstanding.

WITNESS, the Honorable CHARLES EVANS HUGHES, Chief Justice of the United States, the 26th day of November, in the year of our Lord one thousand nine hundred and thirty-four.

WILLIAM PARKIN
Clerk of the United States Circuit
Court of Appeals for the Second Circuit

---

[Doc. 287]

At a Stated Term of the District Court of the United States, held in and for the Southern District of New York, at the Courthouse thereof, Old Post Office Building, in the Borough of Manhattan, City of New York, on the 9th day of January, 1935.

PRESENT:

HON. JOHN C. KNOX
U. S. D. J.

UNITED STATES OF AMERICA,

Libellant,

—against—

ONE BOOK ENTITLED *ULYSSES*,
BY JAMES JOYCE,
RANDOM HOUSE, INC.,

Claimant

A. 110-59

The above named libellant having appealed to the United States Circuit Court of Appeals, for the Second Circuit, from a decree of this Court, entered in this action on the 18th day of December, 1933, in the office of the Clerk of this Court, and the United States Circuit Court of Appeals, Second Circuit, having heard said appeal, and having ordered and adjudged that the decree so appealed from be affirmed, and the mandate remitted from that Court having been filed,

NOW, on motion of GREENBAUM, WOLFF & ERNST, attorneys for the claimant, it is

ORDERED that the said decree of the United States Circuit Court of Appeals, for the Second Circuit, be and the same is hereby made the decree of this Court, and it is further

ORDERED and ADJUDGED that the decree of this Court, heretofore entered herein on the 16th day of December, 1933, be and the same hereby remains and continues to be the decree of this Court.

JOHN C. KNOX
U. S. D. J.

I Hereby Consent to the
Entry of the Foregoing Order.

_____MARTIN CONBOY_____
United States Attorney, Attorney
for United States.

[Doc. 288]

May 2, 1935.

Mr. Bennett A. Cerf,
20 East 57th Street,
New York City.

Dear Bennett:

Somebody told me that you finally went through with the suggestion I made of donating the original copy of *Ulysses* to Columbia. Let me have the facts, if it is true, because I would like to have my file complete as to the history of a fairly amusing case.

Yours sincerely,

[Morris Ernst]

---

[Doc. 289]

May 21, 1935.

Dr. Hellmut Lehmann-Haupt,
Columbia University,
The Library,
New York City.

Dear Dr. Lehmann-Haupt:

Various accounts of the *Ulysses* case have appeared in newspapers and magazines, but I think I can give you all the facts that you want most succinctly in this letter.

The reason that we chose to fight our case against the government through the expedient of importing a copy and having it seized by the Customs was for the purpose of economy. Had the government refused entry of the volume and had its claim been sustained by the courts, we would have been out only the cost of this single copy plus, of course, the advance that we had paid Mr. Joyce and legal fees. The other alternative was to set up the book in America and publish it and then wait for our tilt with the government. This, of course, would have been a very expensive way of doing things.

Once we had decided to import a copy and have it seized, it became essential that the book actually be apprehended and not shipped through in one way or another. We therefore were forced to the somewhat ludicrous procedure of having our own agent at the steamer to make sure that our property was seized by the Government. The copy itself was a rather special one since inside its blue paper cover (Columbia blue, by the way) were pasted critical essays on the book by leading authors and critics of both England and France. Only by having these reviews pasted inside the copy were we able to quote from them when the case actually came before the court.

In due course Judge Woolsey tried the *Ulysses* case with the results that you know. It was only in the courtroom that we got a second look at our copy of *Ulysses*. The impeccable copy that we had imported was already in the tattered, dog-eared condition in which you now find it. Obviously, everybody in the Customs department spent some time on this erudite volume. The District Attorney had also gone to the trouble of marking with a heavy cross every line of the book that he considered pornographic. This marking will undoubtedly be of great help to Columbia students who, I hope, will have a chance to examine this volume in the years to come.

I hope that this is the story that you wanted. I too enjoyed meeting you and Mrs. Lehmann-Haupt. I hope that I will see you both soon again.

Cordially yours,

Bennett A. Cerf
Random House

---

**[Doc. 290]**
[Ernst acknowledged receipt of the inscribed *Ulysses* on October 18, 1937. The date of this letter must be September or October of that year.—ED.]

7, Rue Edmond Valentin,
Paris VII$^E$.

Dear Mr. Ernst:

By a post boat a few days ago I sent you a copy of the (still highly-priced) trade [?] edition of *Ulysses* with a few words inscribed which are a very meager return for the great service you have done to me and it. The reason I did not send you a copy before is that, until I had the pleasure of meeting Mrs. Ernst and yourself here and of talking with you, I had no idea that you were "my" lawyer, that is, enlisted almost voluntarily and from conviction for the general and particular causes you sustained so brilliantly: Evidently I was in error; and I hasten to repair my *bévue*.

Thank you for the copy of the book about the censorship law. I shall send this on to my London lawyer when I have read it.

Please tell Mrs. Ernst I have ordered her book through Brentano's here and if she has not already succeeded in getting a copy of Charlotte Yonge's book in the U.S. I believe I can find one for her over here.

With kindest regards to you both from us.

Sincerely yours,

James Joyce

---